Flowers:
Creative Design

a revision of FLOWERS: Geometric Form

" 'TIS better to give a flower
        than a jewel.
Thou canst not help but weigh the price of the jewel
        to value the gift;
but a flower brings true sentiment
        shorn of all but love."

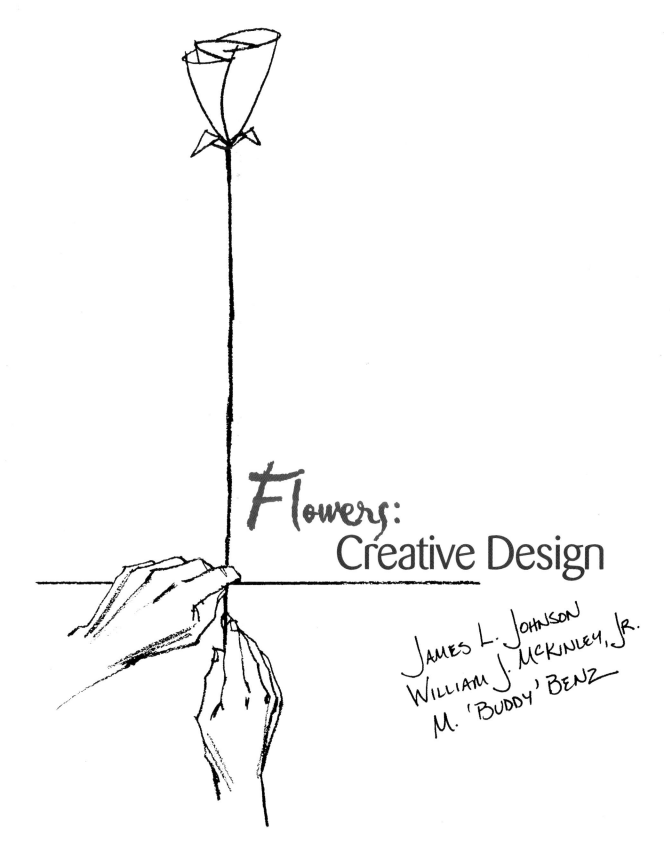

Flowers:
Creative Design

James L. Johnson
William J. McKinley, Jr.
M. 'Buddy' Benz

Copyright © 2001 by

San Jacinto Publishing Co.

4354 TAMU, College Station, Texas 77843–4354

International Standard Book Number 1-58544-171-6
CIP Data are available from the Library of Congress

Distributed by Texas A&M University Press, www.tamu.edu/upress

First Printing — July 1952   First Edition FLOWERS: THEIR CREATIVE DESIGNS

Second Printing — February 1953

Third Printing — March 1958

Fourth Printing — June 1962   Second Edition – Revised FLOWERS: CREATIVE DESIGNS

Fifth Printing — September 1966   Third Edition FLOWERS: GEOMETRIC FORM
        (Complete revision of text and photographs of FLOWERS: THEIR CREATIVE DESIGNS)

Sixth Printing — September 1968

Seventh Printing — January 1970

Eighth Printing — October 1973   Fourth Edition Revised – in color

Ninth Printing — May 1980   Fifth Edition Revised – in color

Tenth Printing — January 1986   Sixth Edition Revised – in color

Eleventh Printing — July 2001   Seventh Edition Revised – in color, FLOWERS: CREATIVE DESIGN
        (Complete revision of text and photographs of FLOWERS: GEOMETRIC FORM)

Photography, original
M. "BUDDY" BENZ
BESSIE HINTON–EIDSON
Benz School of Floral Design, Houston, Texas

Photography, Sixth Revision
LAURA CICARELLA

Photography, Seventh Revision
MICHAEL KLEIN
JAMES LYLE

Design and Producion, Seventh Revision
IMAGINATION ii, D.H. WARR, F. MATA, Abilene, Texas

Manufactured in Singapore by Tien Wah Press

Preface:

In 1952 M. "Buddy" Benz set out to give his readers a book that would examine basic floral design concepts and mechanics. His book became a "bible" for designers wishing to make their floral establishments better places to buy flowers. He standardized floral terminology and shared proven techniques that could be used in remote areas as well as those places with every convenience at hand. Mr. Benz was the first commercial floral artist to teach the value of style and artistic expression consistent with history and culture. As a result, much of what he wrote is still useful.

Buddy wrote, *"Among the creations of God none are more beautiful than flowers. Close companions to the soul of man, they speak for man, expressing his deepest emotion, and the most vital relationships – love, hope, faith and gratitude – as no other material things can express them.*

Since art is the spiritual expression common only to man; those working with flowers assume a challenge to display them in such a manner that their natural beauty will be shown to the best possible advantage. In floral art this challenge exists whether the designer is arranging flowers for his own pleasure or meeting the challenges of his career."

FLOWERS: Creative Design is the culmination of a life span of research and development on one subject – floral design – as applied to American tradition. This book tells not *what* to do – it shows *how* and *why* beauty and stability are important. Efficiency is also important, but quality is never sacrificed for convenience. Techniques are used that produce the very best results.

Nature teaches us that flowers have their own life cycle — that their seeds will germinate, mature and blossom; that their petals and leaves will drop and new ones will grow in their place. The evolution of this book follows the cycle of nature, as does the floral industry. With this new edition many petals and leaves have been dropped — and replaced with new ones. Even the title has changed — back to a variation of the original.

Acknowledgments:

Help and guidance have come from many wonderful people, such as **Bill McKinley** who wrote the chapters on *Care and Handling of Cut Flowers and Foliage, Color Alternatives, and Preserving Flowers and Foliage*. He was a source of inspiration throughout the entire revision. My friend **Pat Hermés** led the way in motivation and the vital but thankless role of proofreading. The lovely wedding cakes were created with the unique artistry of **Catherine Godfrey**. The mechanics of getting the printed word on the page were salvaged on an "almost" daily basis by **Dustin Long**, my friend and expert computer teacher.

Special thanks to **Dan Harwell** for generously allowing me to borrow from his book *Searching for Design*, and to the American Institute of Floral Designers for quoting freely from their *Book of Floral Terminology*.

I wish I could say more than "Thanks!" to **Michael Klein** and **James Lyle**, who used the magic of their cameras and their wits to transfer the fleeting beauty of fresh flowers into the lasting beauty of the printed page. Speaking of fresh flowers, the beautiful and unique orchids were grown and provided by **Dan** and **Eddie Ruth Chadbourne**.

One of the most challenging aspects of revising a book is figuring out how to put the information and photographs from across the years together in a cohesive, yet fresh manner, and for this Herculean effort I thank **Debra Warr**, artist and designer of books. Another challenge was finding a local church that would allow us to bring in all the paraphernalia to photograph the wedding ceremony settings, and for this, I appreciate **St. Thomas Episcopal Church**, College Station, Texas, more than they can ever know. **Vicki McPherson** and **Monie Smith** were instrumental in assisting with the ceremony decorations and photography, thank you both.

Creative design talent and pure inspiration have been contributed to this book by some of my former students and best friends. **Wayne Becker, David Schmalz, David Simpson, Melanie Tipton, Courtney Painter, Ashlye McCormick, Henry Flowers, Bill Knox** and **Robert Buchhorn** have carried the "Benz genius" to new heights in their designs. Finally, I want to express my undying appreciation to **Ann Boney**, my administrative assistant and friend who simply facilitated every aspect of this project. Friends indeed, all of these people were always there with knowledge, honesty, creativity, encouragement and daring – making me stretch. I hope this book will help you stretch your talents in the same ways these people have inspired me.

Jim Johnson

Flowers: Creative Design
Table of Contents

Part 1 – ELEMENTS AND PRINCIPLES OF DESIGN

Part 2 – DESIGN STYLES

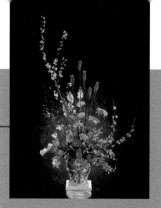

Part 3 – DESIGN COMPONENTS

Part 4 – SPECIAL EVENT DESIGNS - Weddings and Parties

Part 5 – PERSONAL FLOWER DESIGNS

Phoenix — A style of design in which tall materials burst out from the center of a rounded mass, is based on the mythological bird that lived in the Egyptian desert for 500 years and then consumed itself by fire, later to rise renewed from its ashes. This design of unsurpassed beauty created by David Schmalz, represents the renewal of floral design expressed in this new version, *Flowers: Creative Design*, of the former edition, *Flowers: Geometric Form*

Flowers:
Creative Design

Part 1
Elements and Principles of Design

Chapter 1 INTRODUCTION

Elements and principles of design might well be called "Tools of Design." These concepts are not arbitrary; they are constant. They are the tools of all the arts, and no artist can vary them until he has mastered them. A careful study and understanding of these elements and principles of design enable one to express his or her personality in floral art. It is through this mastery that distinction and individuality are created and reflected in design. Distinction is that extra note of quality, taste, and originality for which all persons strive.

The principles of design are fascinating as a theoretical study. When actively combined with the joys of flower arranging, they are among the most rewarding of all human endeavors. Flowers placed in a vase without any particular design are satisfying for the simple reason that flowers, in themselves, are satisfying. These same flowers arranged according to certain basic principles of design become a work of art (Plate 1). The placing of a single rose in a simple bud vase shows the impression of beauty and a desire to intensify it. Flower arranging in its complex forms is even more challenging and more rewarding. Flowers alone among the creations of God are able to express one's deepest feelings; as a result, floral art is in a category apart from other arts. The principles of floral art are, nonetheless, comparable to those of the other arts - painting, for example. A floral design is nothing more than a picture painted with living plant materials and a few accessories. The artist's materials are pigments, brushes, canvas, and frame. The artist is interested in completing a unit within a frame that interprets his or her impressions of the subject. When you design with flowers, you likewise make a picture, and an interpretation, but there are differences. We work with perishable materials and our "picture" is not framed. We must consider in our plan the ultimate placement and surroundings of our design.

Plate 1
Uncommon Beauty – A floral design is simply a picture painted with living plant materials and a few accessories. There are no actual blossoms in this picture, but the onions and mushrooms that take their place are grouped at the focal area and create unity by repeating the color, texture and form of the container.

In previous editions of this book the elements and principles of design were considered as one and the same in an effort to simplify design theory. However in recent years, floral design in general has acquired new layers of stimuli from related arts and foreign cultures. It follows then, that floral artists and even their customers have benefited from greater exposure and increased understanding of the arts. This book will now separate the elements from the principles and discuss each one individually.

When these concepts have been diligently mastered and creatively applied, they impart to an arrangement the precious ATTRIBUTES of EXCELLENCE - distinction, individuality, and originality.

DISTINCTION is that quality of unique charm, taste, and originality - "that clear decision" - which sets a design apart and for which all persons strive to achieve. It is that superior or worthy quality, gained through skillful use of materials, which amplifies intrinsic characteristics, thus attracting immediate attention and bringing special honor.

INDIVIDUALITY is the expression of a designer's personality. It is that quality which is immediately recognizable in style, color selection, and sensitive appreciation of materials, which combine to make a design "personal."

ORIGINALITY is the reflection of creative thinking, imagination, vision, and interpretation; it incorporates both distinction and individuality. This quality of excellence is often achieved with an unexpected use of material and usually adds excitement to the design.

In developing a floral picture there are two terms that one must understand and whose importance must be realized. These terms, composition and suitability are closely related. **Composition** *is the grouping of the various parts to make the design* (Plate 2). All components must be so related that the eye sees them as a cohesive unit, flowing smoothly together. **Suitability** *is the state of being appropriate to the circumstances and/or the location.* In a corsage, the flowers and ribbon must not only be coordinated with each other but also with the personality of the wearer, her dress, and the occasion for wearing it. Choosing a bowl of flowers for a specific room offers similar problems of composition; the flowers should be coordinated with the furnishings of the room, textures of its curtains, and colors of its walls. Discordant materials and unrelated accessories should be omitted. If objects do not add materially to an idea being expressed, they should be ruthlessly discarded regardless of their intrinsic value. Each component should contribute its full value to the completed whole. An arrangement of flowers in a container may fulfill all the requirements of good design; how-

Plate 2
Fruit and Flowers – Apples and plums provide a transition between the pristine lilies and the rustic basket creating visual and emotional harmony in this composition of diverse components.

ever, should it not be compatible with its setting or blend with the decor of the room, it will be unsatisfactory, because unity will be lost. Its purpose as a decorative piece will be thwarted. In a different situation a flower arrangement may have to exhibit the colors of a club or an organization, in which case it may not match the room. Its purpose is to simply represent the organization on a particular occasion.

Only personal preference as to "good taste" - which means the right design, the right time, the right place, and the right purpose - can answer this question of suitable composition. For festive occasions, one may decorate with designs not compatible with the interior of the home, e. g., Christmas, Halloween, special parties, etc. The design gives the theme of the affair, but in designing a decorative piece for the home, one must unify the composition to complete the room decor. However, when entering a design in flower show competition, one must follow the rules of the schedule.

Composition need not be restricted to definite periods or any one category. It gains distinction by its originality in selection of materials and their skillful blending.

Chapter 2 ELEMENTS OF DESIGN

Design is everywhere in the universe, but it is hidden from us until we become aware of it. There is design in the largest things we know and in the smallest…in the shapes of coastlines along continents washed by ocean waves, and in a grain of sand…in deep gorges cut by rushing rivers and in a drop of water. There is design in reaching branches shaped by growth through countless ages. There is design in fleeting shadows that change with the moving sun and shift with every breeze. Each leaf has its place in the pattern it helps to make. Every flower adds a colorful note to its place in the garden.

The elements of design are basic visual qualities — line, form, space, texture, pattern, color and size that are intrinsic to the design's components themselves. They are the most basic "tools" of the designer. These visual qualities are vital to the organization of a design.

Line

Line is the visual path the eye follows to produce motion. The element of line is one of the most important in any design. This essential has inherent qualities that appeal to our reason and senses. It may be severe and masculine, exhibiting strength and vitality, or it may be whimsical or feminine, expressing gentleness and delicacy.

Plate 3 (circa 1986)
Horizontal Hogarth – A top view of this horizontal Hogarth curve shows exquisite progression of tightly furled calla lilies from the tips toward the open center blossom. White freesia accents the focal area and galax foliage repeats the horizontal line of the flat cystal plate.

Its use provides the skeletal pattern and satisfies aesthetic taste. Line is produced by the use of linear materials (stems, branches, or line flowers), or it is developed by the placement of round, mass forms in sequence, creating a feeling of direction (Plate 4). The height and character of line depends to a great degree on the growing habits of the plant. The development of line may give balance, create rhythm, convey swift motion, or reflect repose, reverence, and other emotional qualities. The mood or theme of a design may be expressed with line. Motion is created in sculpture and other art forms primarily by this element.

Line is never static; it offers a dynamic quality implying movement, giving a feeling of growth and life to the design. To maintain movement, line continuity must never be broken. A restless quality and nervous feeling will be imparted by a design if line confusion exists. Cross-hatching of stems or misplacement of them so they do not emanate from their logical point of origin causes a nervous reaction, breaks the rhythm, and the design appears to fall apart. In Figure 1A, the composition lacks unity because no line pattern is developed. The undetermined direction of lines here causes confusion. In Figure 1B, correction of line divergence is made.

Plate 4
Emerging Line – In this design line is produced by the use of a variety of materials: linear foliage (cattail), branches (ligustrum and ming), and singular irises placed in a sequence creating a feeling of direction.

The understanding of line, and its emotional qualities, enables one to make a compatible selection of flowers, foliage, and container to express a desired idea or mental picture. One lets the lines of architecture, the furnishings of a room and the location of the arrangement govern the line pattern of the design.

Today, the expression of line, like our change in design concepts, assumes new meaning of great importance. The powerful, almost primitive, parabolic arc is most expressive. This line appears to defy the force of gravity. Its dynamic flow may start with a long, forceful curve that seems almost straight, and end with an abrupt tense arc that appears to enclose space. The parabolic curve is a line of force, grace, and rhythmical balance.

Figure 1A
Cross hatching of stems causes confusion.

Figure 1B
Corrected line defines focal point—rhythm is created.

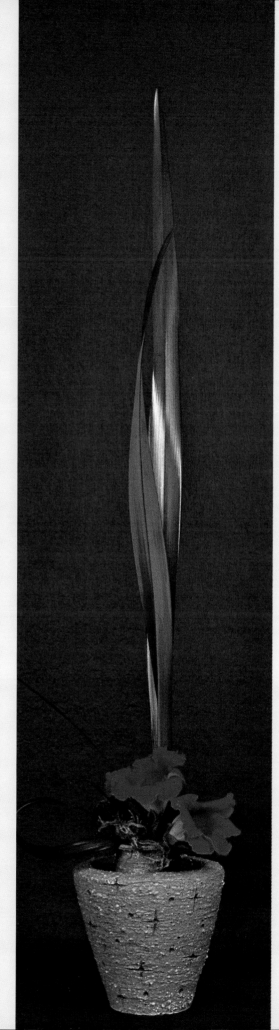

A simple straight line draws the eye along to a point at either end thus producing motion. If placed in a vertical position it becomes an exclamation point and produces a feeling of stability in the composition. The line that moves in a complete circle expresses unity and security. A diagonal line may be powerful and dramatic while several lines spreading from a center point suggest a burst of vitality. Erratic lines like those found in a bolt of lightening or in a curly willow branch exhibit the greatest motion of all. All of these lines demand attention. The eye cannot look away; it cannot be satisfied until every twist and turn has been explored.

Plate 5 (circa 1986)
Exclamation Point!
The dark toned flax leaves create the strong vertical line that terminates with red gloxinia blossoms.

Plate 6 (circa 1986)
Contemporary Line
Fresh bamboo reinforces the bold line of the container while the apple blossom and liatris create a delicate feeling. The three diagonal stems add interest to the otherwise serene design. Nerine lilies and white azalea afford the eye a place of rest.

Form

Form is defined as the shape or contour of the individual components in a composition. In floral design, the materials, like machinery parts, have definite shapes. They fit together with the same precision as does a good mechanical assembly. It is the combination of forms that gives interest, imparts vitality, and prevents monotony. "Variety is the spice of life." The integrating of forms, one with another, produces the floral picture. Each shape plays a specific role. The recognition of these shapes will enable one to solve many design problems and prevent others from arising. One type may be used alone in an arrangement, or any two or more forms may be combined. The flowers remain individual and are recognized by their own characteristics even though they may be grouped together. The plan that is followed in making a design exactly right for a particular use depends upon the element of form. Where the plan is perfect the result is perfect — in size, in weight, in strength and in coloring. In nature, both the broccoflower and the ginger blossoms (Plate 7) are good examples of this. Each of these materials is perfect for its use in nature and each can be taken by a designer to fit a purpose in a design. See Flower and Foliage Forms, page 112.

The element, form, can be expressed in another way. *It is the overall three-dimensional configuration or shape of a design or composition.* Designs in the shape of geometric forms such as ovals, triangles and fans are easy to comprehend as forms, while compositions identified as vegetative, formalinear and parallel would be considered configurations. The overall shape of the design must be in harmony with the architecture of its surroundings to be effective.

Space

Space is the element of design that we think of as referring to the open areas around the individual components in a composition. However, in floral design this must include total designed space, which is the entire area occupied by the composition itself. It follows then, that the total designed space can be divided into two categories: positive space and negative space. *Positive space is the area occupied by materials and negative space is the part of the composition NOT occupied by materials.* Negative space is open space.

Plate 7
Classic Formalinear – This design style, formalinear, is named after its forms and lines. The great variety of forms imparts tremendous vitality to this composition.

Plate 8 (circa 1986)
Pairs Repeated – The lines of this design are arranged in pairs; the lines of the white allium are repeated by the two gerberas and those of the curly willow are echoed by the flax. As these lines lead the eye into the focal point, perfect balance is achieved. Note how the eggplant repeats the form and texture of the vase.

In Plate 9 the curly willow defines the negative space around the irises and calls attention to them, thus emphasizing their importance in the composition. If we focus our attention on the individual open iris blossom or willow branch, we can see that each petal and twig positively occupies that space. Therefore this is known as positive space. Conversely, each unoccupied area between each petal and twig is known as negative space. This understanding of space will help the designer achieve any desired effect in the placement of material. The spaces within a design must be planned and organized so as to produce the desired result.

Texture And Pattern

Texture is relative; *it refers to physical surface qualities of plant materials (smoothness, glossiness, roughness, etc.), or the composition of the arrangement and size of leaves, twigs, or branches on main stems.* Leaf and stem patterns of plants affect texture. Slender elm twigs have a lacy texture when compared to the stubby branches of sturdy oaks. Ferns have a more delicate texture than huckleberry or salal (lemon) foliage. Earthenware has a rather coarse, rough texture even though it may be smooth to the touch; fine china, however, is delicate. In clothing material the texture is determined by the type of weave and the thread. The texture in floral design is embodied in the qualities affecting the sense of sight and touch, along with associated values.

In design, the texture of each part of a composition must be so related that it blends pleasingly with its neighbor, or it may be in strong contrast, causing one part to complement the other. Often, bold or strong contrasts

Plate 9
Soaring in Space – The curly willow defines the negative space around the irises and calls attention to them, thus emphasizing their importance in the composition. (See Plates 7, 33, 37.)

Plate 10
Vegetative Tapestry – The coarse texture of the woven cattail ribbon is in bold contrast to the smooth grapes but the leathery limes provide a perfect transition between the two.

in texture add interest as seen in the interesting combination of textures in the decorative arrangement in Plate 10. The strong and coarse texture of the woven cattail ribbon is in bold contrast to the smooth grapes, however, the leathery surfaced limes become transitional and tie the extremes of coarse and smooth textures together. The texture of some flowers (e.g. roses, lilies, and orchids) is relative, and will harmonize beautifully with various textures, from soft and smooth to coarse and rough.

When texture is enlarged it is called *pattern*. For example the herringbone weave of a woolen fabric would be expressed as texture. The same orderly and measured arrangement of units marked by separations in a basket or brick floor would be known as pattern. Physical surface qualities are relative. For instance: the soft and delicate leaf arrangement of asparagus ming would be thought of as texture while the long needles of a ponderosa pine would be perceived as pattern.

Both texture and pattern are to be seen in Plate 10. Notice how each artichoke scale exhibits its own specific texture, but when the artichoke is perceived in its entirety, the combination of scales becomes pattern. And finally, the vase itself is a good example of how coloration gives the impression of texture to a smooth surface. Speaking of color, strong contrasts in texture will prevent a monochromatic color scheme from being monotonous.

Texture vs. Pattern
Texture, though visual, is truly perceived by the sense of touch. When texture is enlarged it becomes pattern, and is less likely to be perceived by touch.

Plate 11 (circa 1986)
Exotic Potpourri – The contemporary ceramic container holds an interesting collection of colors and textures. White alliums create strong clear horizontal lines that are counterbalanced by rustic protea and dried kelp. Heather, ming, galax and fungi provide interesting transition at the focal point of the design.

Color

INTRODUCTION

Color is the visual response of the eye to various reflected wavelengths and pigments. Color gives a design energy and "personality". Aside from personal preferences, the "language of color" is universal. Color has the same psychological effect on the natives of the Yangtze Valley as on the natives of Kankakee, Illinois. Color strongly influences emotion. One color creates an atmosphere of warmth, another produces a cooling quality; others may add dignity or informality.

The psychological effect of color is generally the same for all people; however, preference, impact, and meanings vary with individuals. People react differently to the same color, but generally speaking a person's reaction to color is influenced first by his nervous response and, secondly, by his educational training (en-

Plate 12
Living Color! – The traditional color chart has been "straightened out" and designed with fresh materials. It is easy to see that the warm colors come forward while the cool colors recede. Different values (tints, tones, and shades) of hues are included.

vironment). Considering the first, color is seen as the result of a stimulus (light) reacting on the retina of the eye. This response is transmitted to the brain, which registers the stimulus - thus color is seen. Each individual will naturally react according to his personality. This personal response gives individuality and originality to a design. The second cause of color preference is traceable to the intensity of the sun in one's homeland. A person's homeland governs his youthful training and education. The term "education" in this instance includes childhood training, and encompasses the regional color preferences of the area in which the individual's formative years are spent, as well as referring to his schooling. Education is knowledge gained from everyday associations with one's fellow man - experience. A person from the tropics generally has a liking for brilliant colors, a taste for highly spiced foods, and usually possesses a strong personality and quick temper. Nature repeats this brilliancy in the plumage of the birds, in the vibrant colors of flowers, and in the luxuriant plant growth. People coming from the cooler climates where the sun is less intense prefer subdued colors. They have to be educated to the appreciation of intense, rich colors and spicy foods. Color hues have developed symbolic meanings in various countries, and tradition and symbolism are reflected in color connotations (flags, emblems). White stands for purity in the United States, while in China it means mourning. In this country, black is the color of mourning. The native Indians of Guatemala use the petals of orange flowers when praying for the souls in purgatory and white petals for the souls in heaven.

Historical periods had color schemes. The Victorian era used jewel tones, rich reds and purples with trims of gold. American provincials used warm, gay colors. The contemporary trend is toward contrasts of almost pure chroma.

An understanding of the function of color and a mastery of its use increases the versatility of any person and strengthens his ability to create the desired atmosphere and effect. Through use of almost any color, desired impressions can be easily produced. To illustrate this truth consider the merrily chatting dinner guests who walked into a Chicago hotel's dining room and took their places at the table. As they did, the lighting underwent a subtle change. Within a few minutes some of the guests were violently ill, others mildly sick, and all were without appetite for the exceptionally fine food that had been prepared for them. The celery on the table had turned a gaudy pink, the steaks a whitish gray, the tall glasses of milk were a blood red, and the salads were a sickly blue. What had been fresh green peas one moment were black, over-sized caviar the next. The side dishes of peanuts were a weird crimson.

It was not a demonstration of magic, but an interesting experiment to determine the influence of light and color on human senses. Instead of the usual dining room lights, the host had illuminated the room by especially-designed filter lamps which cut out all colors of the spectrum except green and red. The host, a lighting engineer, thought his guests would have their stomachs turned - his experiment was a success. After restoring normal lighting he told them that it was a demonstration of the effect of light and color not only on the sense of sight but upon the related senses of taste, touch, and smell. Color, he reminded his guests, could excite and stimulate a person acutely.

The result of this color experiment demonstrates the value of color as a potential tool to trigger human reactions and desires. Often, color dislikes are caused by association with an early childhood experience. Blondes who were forced to wear blue during their childhood usually have a dislike for the color. Few people realize the great psychological impact of color on our health and happiness.

There are no ugly colors. It is improper use or placement of color that makes a color objectionable. The associative and psychological aspects of color influence a person's choice and appreciation of color harmony. Contemporary use of color eliminates such fixations by placing importance on the sensuous impact of color. Personality traits greatly influence color preferences.

Color gives life and personality to designs. Harmonious colors produce designs that satisfy even though they lack structural quality. Conversely, if arrangements are perfect in form but poor in color selection, the results may be unpleasant. Design can exist without color and be aesthetically beautiful, but color in flower arrangements cannot be art without design.

Color is just as important to a work of art as the work's structural pattern (design) or shape. Design (the skeletal pattern of a piece of art) pleases the sense of physical balance and proportion, while color satisfies the esthetic inclination - senses of sight, taste, touch, and smell. As illustrated in photography, a black and white picture shows the skeletal pattern only, stripped of the influence of color. The beauty lies in the relationship of its parts which takes into account only balance, proportion and pattern. The addition of color adds personality to these photographs. This quality is stimulated by the addition of the enormous influence of color. A composition out of balance and proportion, but striking in color combination, will be satisfying; however, the same arrangement in black and white will reveal the poor design. It is the color combination that makes the composition acceptable.

It is not necessary to understand color theory or the scientific facts concerning color to make beautiful floral arrangements, just as it is not necessary to understand the theory of the internal combustion engine to drive a car. It is imperative, however, to know and understand human reaction to color and how to employ such reaction skillfully.

Plate 13 (circa 1966) Color Triad — An advancing red, a receding blue, and a cheerful yellow to brighten, are the primary color tools used in this design.

Color Chart And Spectrum

The center colors (red, yellow, and blue) are the Primary colors from which all others are made. They are the building blocks for the entire color pigment system. Nature has provided red which is advancing, exciting, and warm; blue which is receding, cool, and quieting; and yellow which is brilliant and cheerful. An advancing red, a receding blue, and a cheerful yellow to brighten, are the primary color tools used in Plate 13.

The mixture of any two Primary colors produces a secondary color: orange, green, or violet :

> orange - yellow and red
> green - blue and yellow
> violet - red and blue

The proportion of the primary color in a mixture is important. In orange, if there is a greater amount of yellow than red, yellow-orange is produced. If a greater amount of red is used, the result will be a red-orange. The same is true with other color mixtures. More yellow in green makes a yellow-green, and more blue makes a blue-green; more red in violet makes a red-violet, and more blue makes a blue-violet. The six tertiary colors are formed by mixing a secondary color with one of its primary parents. These make up the third "generation" of colors.

The primary and secondary colors compose the color spectrum. They are the colors seen when light is refracted through a prism and subdivided into its seven component parts or when sunlight passes through the moisture in the air to form a rainbow.

All colors as seen by the eye are composed of light waves of varying wave-lengths, each wave-length producing its characteristic color. When light contacts an object, some of the wave-lengths are reflected back to the eye, and others are absorbed. Reflected wavelengths are the ones that enable us to see colors. An object appears red only because the red wavelengths are reflected to the eye and all other wavelengths are absorbed. If a red object were to be illuminated by a green light, it would appear black, since all wave lengths (in this case only green) are absorbed and none can be reflected.

By placing colors of the spectrum in their proper sequence in a straight line, the degree of warmth and coolness of each color may be illustrated graphically. In the color blocks (Plate 15) of the same size we see that the warm colors advance and seem larger, while the cool colors recede and appear smaller.

Red, which is first in the sequence, looks like blood or fire and is, therefore, a warm color. The excitement caused by fire or blood causes the heart to beat faster and naturally warms a person. Yellow, third in the sequence, is the color of the sun. It, too, is warm and brilliant. Orange, a mixture of two warm hues, red and yellow, is also warm. Blue, fifth in the spectrum, is a cool, receding color. It supplies a mental image of deep water and a cool limitless sky. If blue is mixed with yellow, cool green results. It is comparatively cool because of its blue parent. Violet, a mixture of red and blue, may be either warm or cool, depending on whether the warm red or cool blue predominates.

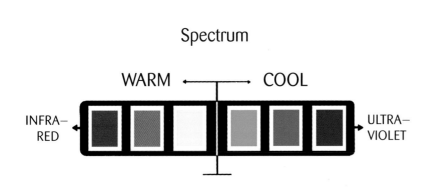

Spectrum

WARM ← → COOL

INFRA–RED   ULTRA–VIOLET

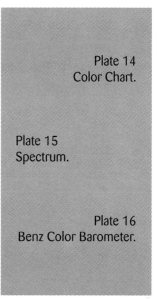

Plate 14
Color Chart.

Plate 15
Spectrum.

Plate 16
Benz Color Barometer.

Color Chart

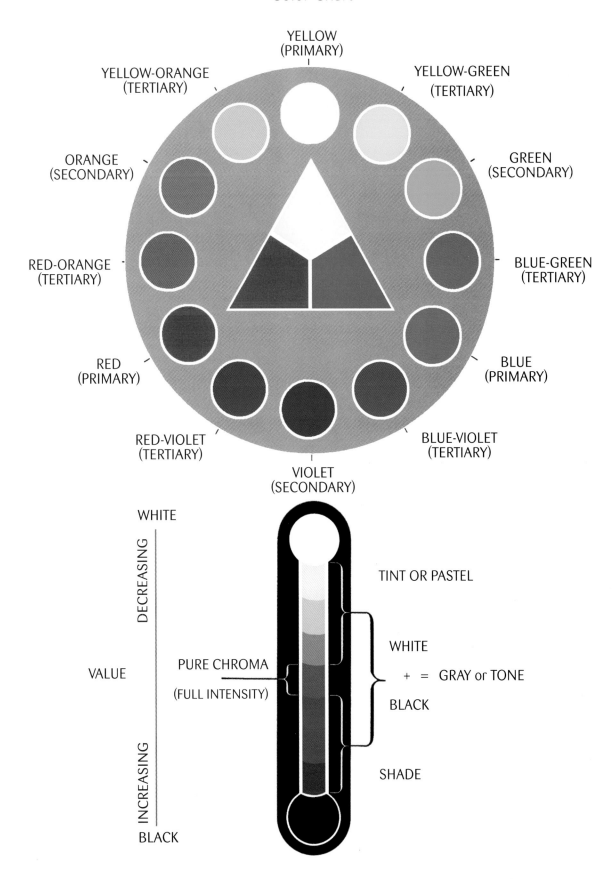

YELLOW
(PRIMARY)

YELLOW-ORANGE
(TERTIARY)

YELLOW-GREEN
(TERTIARY)

ORANGE
(SECONDARY)

GREEN
(SECONDARY)

RED-ORANGE
(TERTIARY)

BLUE-GREEN
(TERTIARY)

RED
(PRIMARY)

BLUE
(PRIMARY)

RED-VIOLET
(TERTIARY)

BLUE-VIOLET
(TERTIARY)

VIOLET
(SECONDARY)

WHITE

DECREASING

VALUE

INCREASING

BLACK

TINT OR PASTEL

PURE CHROMA

(FULL INTENSITY)

WHITE

+ = GRAY or TONE

BLACK

SHADE

Neutral Colors

Pure black, white, or gray are rarely found in the plant kingdom, although they can be easily produced artificially by combining pigments. The combination of black and white gives gray. Gray is also produced when the three primary colors are mixed together. This fact is important to remember, for a garish combination can be subdued when using the complement of a color - a gray impression is the result when seen by the eye. The result of mixing a color with its complement is a muted color.

Although black and white do not appear in the spectrum, they are available in pigments and are very useful. Neither pure white nor black flowers appear in nature. "White" flowers have a pink, green, yellow or blue cast. "Black" flowers are of dark hues of red, purple (violet), or brown, closely resembling black.

Black and white are used to change the value or tonal quality of a color. White lessens color value, making it lighter. Black increases color value, making hues darker and adding depth. Mixing a hue with either alters the tonal value of a color.

White, black, and gray are useful. A white background blends colors and harmonizes hues. This is because the highly reflective quality of white provides more competition for the visual impact of the color displayed against it. Pastels harmonize well because of the large quantity of white they contain. To blend two colors that appear to "fight" one mixes the two in the mind's eye. White mixed with this resulting color gives the pastel. This pastel will blend the two colors and supply the "go-between" or transition that is needed.

Light colored objects exhibit greater reflective quality and thus are cooler than dark objects. Black, since it absorbs more light rays, increases the brilliancy of red, blue, yellow, orange and green, but tends to eliminate violet due to its intrinsic shadowy quality. Shadow box displays and the inside of florists' refrigerators are often painted black so that light will be absorbed thus eliminating any reflective competition for the flowers. This black background makes flowers stand out and look brighter.

Definition Of Terms

The following terms and definitions present the background necessary before color harmony can be clearly understood and used to advantage in all art forms.

COLOR HARMONY - the various usable or pleasing combinations of colors (hues).

HUE - a particular color. Red, yellow, and green are hues, regardless of the quantity of black or white they may contain.

CHROMA - pure hue, undiluted with white, black or gray. Very little pure chroma is found in nature. Plant materials have mixtures of other hues in their composition. Although some flowers appear to have pure chroma, it is the translucent quality, cell moisture, chlorophyll, and type of illumination that vary their true colors.

VALUE - term used to designate the lightness or darkness of a hue. The addition of neutral pigments changes the value of a color. White lessens the value, making a hue lighter; black increases the value, making the hue darker (heavier). The values of red, for example, range from light pink to dark maroon.

TINT - any color to which white has been added, e.g., red plus white becomes pink, etc. Also known as pastels.

SHADE - a color to which black has been added, e.g., maroon is red with black added.

TONE - a color grayed by its complement or the addition of gray. Tones do not become lighter or darker, they simply have less brilliance.

Review these terms collectively and study Plate 12. Color is called a "hue." A hue in its pure, brilliant form is a pure chroma. When chroma is weakened with white, it becomes a tint or pastel. When chroma is strengthened with black, it gains in value and is called a shade. A color (hue) with a gray cast is a tone. It is readily understood from these definitions why black and white are considered neutral and used to vary the value of colors. They change the tonal quality of colors, but not their chroma or position on the spectrum or color wheel.

Color Properties

Scientists report that each hue, has a different focal length; hence, some colors (the warm ones) seem to advance, while others (the cool ones) recede. Another phenomenon in color harmony is created by the eye's automatically noting the complement of a color just registered. This is called "after-image." The eye sees colors in pairs. If the eye is looking at a strong red object, the after-image will be the complementary color, green. Complementary combinations are the least tiring and most pleasing. Radiant, luminous effects are produced by the juxtaposition of complementary colors. In theatrical stage settings the colored lights used produce shadows complementary to the main colors. In a monochromatic combination, the eye is led smoothly through a gradation of tints and shades of one hue, and the eye has a minimum of adjustments to make. This situation will become monotonous unless the material has strong character (See Plates 10, 17). In an analogous scheme, the gradation is smooth because of the use of one primary hue's influence on the combination. Dominance of a strong color is important in this combination.

Advancing colors (red) or strong intensity (pure chroma) colors may become trying when used profusely. As accent colors they are excellent. For gala occasions strong color is needed to create excitement, provided the affair is for a short time and not to be lived with for days. (Compare Plates 2 and 18.)

In color harmony, texture plays an important part - it varies color perception. The smooth, shiny surface of an anthurium is quite different from the velvety appearance of a rose or the quality of a carnation, even though each flower may be of the same hue and value. Grayed colors often have a subtle appearance, while colors that have black added may have a rich appearance. Browns often imply a rustic feeling that tends toward a coarse texture, resulting in a masculine quality. The same material in pale pink or light blue gives a delicate, feminine feeling. (Plates 1, 2, 7, 8, 10, 17)

When one is working with color harmony, if there is doubt about the true color of a flower or object, it should be placed next to the pure chroma which predominates in the flower or near the strongest color of the materials to be used with the flower. The comparison will give the true color perception. If a red rose is placed near true red, it will be obvious whether the rose tends toward blue or yellow. The red rose in its natural setting in the garden will be bright; however, placed in a room decorated in red it will lose its brilliancy and fade into the background.

Emotional Response

With the various terms and characteristics used to describe colors firmly in mind, one considers the emotional response to color. Color cannot be generalized even though the language of color (response) is universal and most people of a given race react similarly. In the United States color has double meanings - either positive or negative.

YELLOW, when positive, is cheerful and has the power, like sunshine, to dispel gloom. Those who have spent the winters in the cold gray North know the thrill of the first yellow crocus and the daffodils in bloom. Nature uses this hue to announce spring. A word of warning - too much yellow becomes blinding; it repeats and builds up brilliance. A shade should be used to subdue its intensity. Its negative meaning is cowardice or weakness.

RED, used positively, is a stimulating, exciting color. It has vitality and warmth. Red is aggressive and attacks. This, also, is a color to be used with caution. When decorating a long room that one wishes to foreshorten, he should use red at the far end. Nature has toned down most natural reds so that they do not have full intensity. Reds used for Valentine or Mother's Day to express love have a blue cast; while reds used for Christmas are cardinal in that they lean toward yellow. Christmas red is exciting, joyful, and produces a festive mood. Red used negatively denotes anger, danger, and disgrace.

Positive BLUE is a pleasing color; it is quiet, cool, and retiring. Blue has the quality of dignity and formality and is almost universal in its appeal. Blue is most attractive when seen by natural lighting; with artificial illumination it takes on a gray-purplish cast. Its receding quality suggests depth. When decorating a room, blue can be used to increase its size rather than to foreshorten it. Negative blue connotes depression, melancholy, timidity, and fright.

ORANGE is not as bright as yellow or so aggressive as red, but used positively it is warm and has strong decorative value. Shadowy places such as hallways respond well to orange, or it may be used to advantage deep within an arrangement. Tints of orange — peach and beige — may be used lavishly. Such tints are flattering to most skin tones. Orange has a negative, ghost-like connotation, since it is well established with black and is used at Halloween. It is associated with the souls in purgatory. It often means caution and grief.

GREEN is nature's favorite. It has both the cheerfulness of yellow and the coolness of blue. It counteracts the effects of heat and the brightness of sun. It is restful and is used in the abatement of excitement (the opposite of red). Green is the color of safety and the olive branch of peace. Negative green, however, means non-ripe, nausea, envy, and poison.

VIOLET is a shadowy color, and may be either warm or cool, depending upon the percentage of red and blue in its makeup. The darker violets are solemn, dignified, and regal. The lighter tints are feminine. It is the only "shade" used at Easter time; all other colors used at this time are pastels. It denotes the royalty of Christ

Plate 17
Monochromatic Color Harmony – Different values of one hue make up this harmony. Color gradations must be used with care, with the strongest value or striking form placed at the center of interest. Contrasting textures prevent monotony.

Plate 18
Analogous Color Harmony – The bloodline of the primary parent (red) is easy to see in the "aunts, uncles and cousins" pictured in this design. Quite a hot-blooded family! Analogous color schemes require a visible transition from one hue to the other for the sequence to be readily apparent. Notice in the picture on the title page that yellow and yellow green are missing from that "family" portrait and though beautiful, the transition from yellow orange to green is lacking.

and the solemnity of the Easter service. Violet can be used only when there is strong natural light available, near windows or with bright backgrounds. Negatively, it means melancholy and aged.

With the basic characteristics of color in mind, and a working knowledge of the terms used to describe them, "Creative Design" takes on new significance.

Color Harmony

A MONOCHROMATIC color scheme is composed entirely of one hue (mono meaning one and chromatic meaning color). The hue remains constant but its value changes up or down the scale - tints, shades, and tones of one hue are used. One value must predominate for interest. A design will become monotonous unless the materials have strong character in form and texture. Color gradations must be used with care, with the strongest value or striking form placed at the center of interest. An arrangement of mauve carnations and mauve roses would be harmonious in color, yet greater interest is gained by changing to pale mauve stock and the contrasting form of the fuji chrysanthemums. The deeper values of mauve in the waxflower, candle and ribbon streamers create additional interest (Plate 17).

ANALOGOUS harmony is achieved through the use of three or more hues in sequence on the chart. An analogous scheme attains its harmony by having the colors related to each other by a common primary color parent. The parent color (primary red, blue, or yellow) predominates over the other hues. Analogous harmony produces a mood or seasonal effect — as yellow, orange, and brown suggest the colors of fall.

The analogous color sequence in Plate 18, gains distinction by its use of vibrant hues. Red, the primary color, in the anthuriums carries the eye to the red-violet dendrobium orchids. The strong color of the anthuriums attracts attention and prevents monotony. Darker green ti leaves with their reddish accent provide a transition to the giant allium blossoms which are a tint of violet. Analogous color schemes require a visible transition from one hue to the other for the sequence to be

readily apparent.

COMPLEMENTARY colors are opposites on the color wheel. They are unrelated opposites on the color chart. Red and green are complementary — as are blue and orange and yellow with violet. Complementary colors are used to attract attention and create interest.

Dramatic emphasis can be gained through the combination of intense values of chroma. In such cases, one color intensifies the other. The complementary combination is vibrant and expresses life and growth. Generally, for everyday use, the most effective complementary harmonies are achieved by using a greater percentage of cool colors over warm colors. Plate 19 illustrates this by showing a bold corsage combining a greater amount of cool blue and green with a lesser amount of warm orange. The natural complementary color harmony found in the Bird of Paradise blossom is dramatized by the addition of the intense blue delphinium florets.

SPLIT COMPLEMENTARY color schemes are similar to complementary combinations, although the two colors to either side of the actual complement color are selected. For example, using yellow as the main color, violet is its complement. The split complementary color harmony would be red-violet and blue-violet which are located opposite yellow on the color wheel.

TRIAD is another interesting color scheme commonly used. It is the combination of three hues equally spaced on the color chart. If the triangle on the chart (Plate 14) is revolved, its three points will always indicate a triadic color harmony. A unique parallel floor design with horizontal stem placements is enhanced by an unexpected triadic color harmony of secondary colors - orange, green and violet (Plate 20).

TETRAD, another color harmony, is one that involves any four colors equally spaced on the color wheel. An example would be orange, yellow-green, blue and red-violet.

A POLYCHROMATIC color harmony is

Plate 19
Opposites Attract! – The natural complementary color harmony found in the Bird of Paradise blossom is dramatized by the addition of the intense blue delphinium florets.

Plate 20
Triadic Color Tower – A unique parallel floor design with horizontal stem placements is enhanced by an unexpected triadic color harmony of secondary colors - orange, green and violet.

made up of many different hues - poly meaning many and chromatic meaning color (Plate 21). This common way to mix colors may be determined by any given situation. For example colors are selected to match a room, a fabric, a theme or a person's mood.

ACHROMATIC color harmony is made up of neutral colors. There are no colors from the color wheel involved. Various combinations of black, white and /or gray are used to create this harmony. Spray paints are often used to change the natural colors of plant parts to black, white, silver or pewter, and these in combination with man-made materials (plastic, fabric, glass, metal, etc.) are used to create interesting compositions.

Plate 21
Garden Mix – This polychromatic color harmony is made up of many different hues - poly meaning many and chromatic meaning color.

Color Recipe
– Percentage Scale

Color balance is as important in traditional design as is the balancing of ingredients in making a cake. Too much of one element will spoil the whole. Call this correct color proportion a "recipe" or "percentage scale." Learning color value will aid one greatly in achieving variety and creating color rhythm. A few color-balance principles also help.

Balance: Use the strong chroma-vivid or darker values in the focal area, and the weaker (pastels) to the outside.

Proportion: The more dominant the color, the less it is used. As with spices in cooking - a little will aid greatly - too much will spoil the dish.

Interest: Dominance and transition will be gained by the percentages, and rhythm will be created by the variation in amounts.

The following percentages will be an invaluable guide to use in achieving color balance, to add variety and interest to an arrangement, and create color rhythm:

50-75 % of a tint
10-15% of strong chroma (intensity)
15-25 % of a shade (or dark tone)

The basket design of garden flowers in Plate 21 follows this recipe. Tints (50-75%) are represented by liatris, scabiosa, daisies, miniature carnations and bits of pale foliage. Strong chromas (10-15%) are found in the freesia, ranunculus and calendulas. The basket, its handle of woven curly willow and the snapdragons contribute the remaining 15-25% (shades) of the total recipe. The application of these percentages is not a hardbound rule, but the recipe is a guideline for using colors successfully.

Apply the percentages suggested to the selection of flowers for a corsage to complement a dress. If the dress is primarily a tint, the flowers could furnish the shade or intense color, with the ribbon completing the alternate color in the percentage chart.

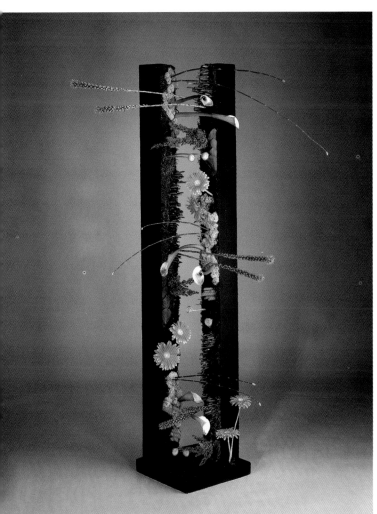

GENERAL SUGGESTIONS

1. Tints tend to harmonize in most combinations. Since the original hue has been lessened in value by the addition of white, tints may be used lavishly.

2. Shades are darker and are heavy in visual weight. They are used to increase the depth and richness of color combinations.

3. To subdue the intensity of a pigment, use its complement. This combination has a neutralizing effect.

4. Tones, hues to which gray has been added, may be considered either light or dark and may be used where subtle coloring is called for.

5. Group colors, letting one flow into the other to produce rhythm in color harmony. Do not spot color around, as such a practice produces a salt and pepper effect. Have a definite pattern for each color.

6. Choose intense, vivid colors for focal areas. The colors here must be stronger or in greater contrast than elsewhere in the design.

7. When combining colors, change the value of each color to avoid monotony. Only one hue should dominate.

8. Use intense colors for dramatic combinations. They express activity and are appropriate for joyous occasions.

9. To create a dainty, feminine arrangement, use a combination of tints.

10. Red, yellow and orange and many of their derivatives, show up normally under artificial light because of their advancing qualities. They will be enhanced by incandescent light and flattened by fluorescent light.

11. Remember that blues, violets and greens become less intense under artificial incandescent light. Blue may become purplish-gray; green will exhibit a yellowish cast and violet will look pinkish. On the other hand the cool colors will be fresher looking and more lively under artificial fluorescent light.

12. Because of the advancing quality of warm colors, their size appears larger than the same quantity of a cool, receding color.

13. Warm, advancing colors accent an arrangement and are seen first by the viewer.

14. Cool colors supply depth and create a third-dimensional feeling in an arrangement.

15. Darker colors appear heavier and generally should be used lower. But if the heavy color appears in the smaller, finer-textured flower, and the lighter color in the larger mass forms, then color placement will be reversed.

Plate 22
Diving for Treasure – Size is the most important issue in this underwater design. Since curved glass magnifies objects underwater, it is vital to select blossoms of a size that won't look too large. Then, of course, the wood, flowers and foliages must be in proportion to the vase and the underwater flowers. After positioning the wood on the vase, a plastic wrapped block of wet foam was secured into a crevice in the wood, then flowers were added.

Size

Size is a measurement of the amount of space something occupies such as a design or a component of a design. It is the dimension of line, form and space. Size is what distinguishes between our perception of texture and pattern. Size is a key word used in describing both the primary principle of proportion and the seondary principle of scale.

In floral design size is one of the controlling factors in the selection of container, plant material, accessories and mechanical aids. It relates also, to price, perceived value and satisfaction as experienced by the customer. In fact the concept of size is present in everything we do — from start to finish (Plate 22).

Chapter 3   PRINCIPLES OF DESIGN

The Principles of Design are fundamental guidelines that help a designer achieve excellence in a composition. They are expressed visually through the use of the elements of design. The principles of design govern the organization of materials in accordance with the Laws of Nature. Often they will reinforce one another.

The principles of design are organized into two categories: primary principles and secondary principles. The primary principles of design are strong enough to stand on their own as tools to enhance and interpret the elements of design. The secondary principles may supplement the primary principles by being more specific in their contribution to the excellence of a design.

The Primary Principles of Design are Proportion; Balance; Dominance; Rhythm; Contrast; Harmony; Unity.

The Secondary Principles of Design are Scale; Focal Area/ Focal Point; Repetition; Accent; Depth; Transition; Opposition; Tension; Variation.

Proportion (primary principle):

Compares the relationship of the units of a composition to each other in size, quantity and degree of emphasis within the composition. It is the relationship of one part to another or of one part to the whole design.

"Proportion is the one principle which has a close relationship to all of the elements and principles of design. Proportion is the mathematical ratio or the quantitative comparison of form or material used in one part of a design to those of another part. It is the mathematical fiber that ties the entire composition or design together to make it work and become a creation of beauty. It is interesting to note that if these proportions are close to Fibonacci's 3-5-8, or Phi, they are usually more aesthetically pleasing to the human eye." *

Plate 23
Uncommon Beauty – Complex relationships often appear in simple designs such as this one, when thoughtful application of principles of design is applied. Contrast of textures provides interest – similar colors and forms unify. Contrast of lines and forms excite – concentration of visual weight at the center stabilizes. All of this "play" back and forth takes place within the golden proportion thus giving an overall feeling of beauty and comfort.

From the Japanese, American flower arrangers have learned that proportion will be pleasing if materials are approximately $1^1/_2$ times the height of the container if it is tall, or $1^1/_2$ times its width if it is low. A "low" container is one whose width exceeds its height. A "tall" container is higher than it is wide. This $1^1/_2$:1 ratio has proven invaluable and has been established through constant use and experimentation over hundreds of years in all types of art, and therefore may be used with safety. This Japanese idea of proportion is almost identical to the Golden Proportion that we know from Leonardo Fibonacci the Greek mathematician and Phidias, the Greek sculptor, designer and architect of the Parthenon, a building which is described as having perfect proportions. The following explanation of the Golden Proportion is taken from the book, *Searching For Design* by Dan Harwell:

In 1202, at the age of 27, Leonardo Fibonacci wrote: "Someone placed a pair of rabbits in a certain place enclosed on all sides by a wall to find out how many pairs will be born in the course of a year. It being assumed that every month a pair of rabbits produce another pair and that rabbits begin to bear young two months after their birth."

When he counted the rabbits at the end of each month, he came up with the following number sequence: 1+1=2, 2+1=3, 3+2=5, 5+3=8, 8+5=13, 13+8=21, ...or, 1, 2, 3, 5, 8, 13, 21, 34, 55, 89, 144, 233, 377, 610, 987, 1597, 2584, ...

Each number in the Fibonacci sequence is the sum of the previous two numbers and the ratio between each when dividing the smaller into the larger is equal to 1.6180339.... (1.618 is almost the same as 1.5 or $1^1/_2$ the height of the

*Searching For Design, by D. Harwell

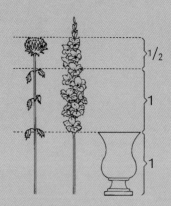

Figure 2A
Correct proportion –
measuring vertical
container; tallest stem $1\frac{1}{2}$
times height of container
plus the depth.

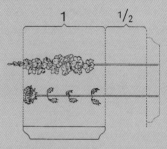

Figure 2B
Correct proportion –
measuring horizontal
container; $1\frac{1}{2}$ times the
width of container plus the
depth.

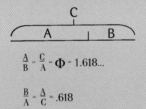

$$\frac{A}{B} = \frac{C}{A} = \Phi = 1.618...$$

$$\frac{B}{A} = \frac{A}{C} = .618$$

Figure 2C
The golden section – formed
when any line segment is
divided in such a way that
the ratio of the smaller
segment (B) to the larger
segment (A) is equal to the
ratio of the larger segment
(A) to the whole (C).

container as previously mentioned). An easy way to remember this proportional guideline of container to flowers is to say that the container should be approximately $1/3$ of the total and the flowers approximately $2/3$ of the total composition.

This ratio between each number is called phi, Φ (from the first letter of the name of the Greek sculptor, Phidias). These Fibonacci numbers and the ratio of Phi are found throughout nature in both plants and animals and are the foundation for our understanding and appreciation of what looks "right" to us in a composition (Plates 23, 24). This concept is known as the Golden Proportion.

The Golden Proportion is also referred to as the golden ratio, golden section, golden rectangle, and golden spiral, or simply the golden cut or golden mean. Definitions of these terms are as follows:

Fibonacci — A shortened version of Leonardo Pisana's nickname, Filius Bonacci. He was a brilliant mathematician who lived in the 1200's and rediscovered the logarithmic number sequence which bears his name (Fibonacci): 1,1,2,3,5,8,13, 21,34,55,89,144… Each succeeding number has a ratio of 1.618… (Φ) and plays an important role in the morphology of life and growth, especially in the human body and botany.

Golden Section — The point which divides a line segment into two unequal parts that have a ratio of 1.618… larger to smaller, or .618… smaller to larger respectively. This same relationship occurs between the whole and the larger section of the line segment.

Golden Ratio — The ratio which has a value of 1.618… or its reciprocal .618. This ratio is found between each Fibonacci number, the dimension of the "Golden Rectangle", and the dimension of the "Golden Spiral". It is called phi, (Φ).

Golden Rectangle — A rectangle that has the ratio of 1:1.618… between its height and width.

Golden Spiral — The spiral formed when tracing corresponding points of the golden rectangle as it descends harmoniously.

Phi — The name given to the ratio of 1:1.618…, after the Greek sculptor, Phidaes. He was the architect of the Parthenon and sculptor of many of the ancient Greek statues. All of his works were rich with the ratio of phi, (Φ).

It has already been said that the elements and principles of design are guidelines — not arbitrary rules. Therefore, since this book is written for the artist, a certain amount of liberty is taken to use these terms interchangeably without going into all the rigors and discipline needed for mathematical proof. The artist will accomplish beauty if phi is applied to the elements and principles because it has visual validation.

Plate 24
Unexpected Simplicity — The intrinsic qualities of each component in this design offer contrast and interest while the background provides depth and unity. The sequential placement of colors in space — white/white (base to flower), brown/brown (vase to bark-covered stem), green/green (bear grass to nandina foliage), orange/red (persimmon to berry) provide contrast, unity and visual direction.

The numbers 3-5-8 (phi) have been pulled out of the Fibonacci series for use only as a tool of communication. These numbers simply designate comparative values. They should apply to line (length, width, height), form (the size of small forms in relation to larger ones), and space (quantity of open or negative space compared to closed or positive space). In addition, 3-5-8 can apply to volumes or amounts of colors, textures and patterns in comparison to each other. This is a simple way to analyze a design to guarantee that it is interesting and pleasing to the eye.

In Plate 24 the golden section can be seen by mentally drawing a vertical line from the top of the nandina to the bottom of the base and dividing it at the rim of the container. The lower portion (container) represents $3/8$ of the total height while the top portion represents $5/8$ of the total. The entire composition from top to bottom is, of course, $8/8$ of the total. This is close enough to our standard "1 $1/2$ times the container" to be considered one and the same. The same thought may be applied to the width of the composition by considering the width of the container with base to be $3/8$ of the total; container plus bear grass, $5/8$; total width at the top, $8/8$.

Plate 23 illustrates the Golden Proportion or phi in different ways — through volumes of color and texture. The scaley texture and claret color of the onions occupies the designated value of "3" of the composition whereas the smooth texture and deep copper color of the container take up the value of "5" of the total. The frilly green of the sea oats and foliage approximate a value of "8" in relation to the others. Designs are generally more satisfying when this ratio of phi is applied.

Scale (secondary principle):

The relative ratio of the size of a composition to its surroundings. The scale of an arrangement is governed by the furnishings of the room in which the flowers are to be placed. A heavy oak dining table in a room with paneled walls needs an arrangement of strength and mass. Fragile materials in such a setting would be lost. A room decorated in classic French style such as Rococo, with a delicate décor of flowing lines and soft pastel colors is complemented by an arrangement of similar floral materials. In a contemporary home that is open, well-lighted, and functional, design must be tailored to the demands of the time and the location.

To determine the scale of an arrangement for a dining room table, there are two important factors to consider: first, the number of guests, and second, where the dinner is to be given. When arranging for a home, one considers the size of the dining room, the table, and the number of guests to be seated, all of which will determine the size of the arrangement. The greater the number of guests, the longer the design can be. The height of the arrangement should not exceed approximately 14 inches at its highest point, measured from the table level (not counting the length of the buds when using line flowers or unopened buds of mass and form flowers). This height assures clear vision so guests will not have to play "peek-a-boo" when talking with others across the table. The manner of serving, whether family style or formal plates, will determine the number of dishes on the table and may limit the spread of the arrangement. An alternative presentation for a seated dinner in

a room with high ceilings would be to place the arrangement atop a tall thin pedestal allowing conversation to flow easily below. For speakers' tables, buffets, standing teas, and other formal affairs, the arrangements may be as tall as the proportions of the room will permit.

A country club or nightclub table arrangement is governed by the same taste used in a home arrangement, but chair spacing in these places is an important consideration. Nightclubs seat people very close together and at small tables, 24- to 30 inches wide. These tables are also placed as close to each other as guest circulation will allow. Here flower arrangements must be low and compact to allow for conversation and for freedom of movement.

In a country club or exclusive town club, larger tables and wider spacing allow expansion of a design.

Balance (primary principle):

Balance is a state of equilibrium and is achieved when the components of a design are so composed that they give a feeling of stability and security. In fact, a synonym of balance is stability. It is achieved in two ways :

1. Symmetrical - formal, with perfect symmetry, man-made equilateral (Plate 25).

2. Asymmetrical - informal, without perfect symmetry, natural (Plate 26, 27).

Plate 25
Symmetrical Balance – Formal balance is achieved by the placement of the two horizontal gladiolas, as if they were a mirror image of each other. The central column of flowers is directly over the center of the container. The slight variation in placing the pussy willow and the lilies avoids monotony without interfering with the perfect symmetry.

Plate 26
Graceful Equilibrium – All stems enter the ceramic block at the central axis of the design but different lengths of ligustrum and the slightly offset lily create a feeling of visual asymmetrical balance and stability.

Symmetrical Balance is *formal, man-made, and characterized by perfect symmetry.* It is associated with a soldier standing at attention or with identical pairs of objects. Generally, objects on one side are matched with those on the other. An arrangement for a dining room table has formal balance when its high point is over the center of the container and it flows out equally to either side. In wedding decorations, the center axis may be the aisle of the church, terminating at the altar and dividing the whole picture. Formal gardens in landscape architecture are completed on this symmetrical basis. The center of interest is the dominating feature and is centered.

In Plate 25, the classical white ceramic urn holds the symmetrical design for a formal occasion. This is an excellent illustration of structural, man–made balance. The Greek period in history greatly influenced the use of symmetrical balance in art and architecture. Strong vertical and horizontal lines from this time period are illustrated in both the container and the design.

Asymmetrical Balance *is natural, informal, and it is not a mirror image of both sides of a plane, axis or point* (Plate 26). An accomplished ballet dancer may be motionless on points, but the weight is so distributed that a feeling of equilibrium is produced; grace and beauty result. The Leaning Tower of Pisa is balanced by weight in relation to the center of gravity, but it does not have visual balance; therefore, a disturbed feeling is experienced by the viewer. An arrangement so constructed gives the viewer an uneasy feeling. The subconscious mind is disturbed by faulty balance. In asymmetrical balance, a high vertical line appears on one side and is counterbalanced on the other by a low horizontal line (Plate 27). Good balance can be achieved without perfect symmetry. Equilibrium is produced by the careful distribution of quantities on either side of the central axis. One generally has a high-left side in the pattern that is counterbalanced by the placement of blossoms low in the opposite direction. The eye is carried along a graceful, sweeping curve from the high point to the low side.

Plate 4, is an excellent example of informal balance in pattern and interplay of materials. Line flows downward from the cattail leaf through the iris and into the black ligustrum berries. This line is counterbalanced with a sizable branch of ming foliage.

Plate 27
Asymmetrical Beauty – Equilibrium is produced by the careful distribution of quantities on either side of the central axis. One generally has a high-left side in the pattern that is counterbalanced by the placement of blossoms low in the opposite direction. The eye is carried along a graceful, sweeping curve from the high point to the low side. The feeling of stability is enhanced by the extension of Scotch broom for height and the dominant gerberas at the focal point.

Mechanical *or structural balance is gained by the proper placement of main stems forming design or pattern.* These materials establish the skeletal pattern of the desired composition. This may be referred to as "skeleton".

Visual Balance *is gained by the selection of correct sizes of materials, and the use of color, texture, etc.* (Plate 7, 9, cover). The eye unconsciously considers these related elements. A pound of feathers and a pound of lead have equal weight and balance (mechanical); however, they do not have visual balance. Compared by size, they are out of proportion. The floral design in Plate 28 is a useful study in visual balance. The downward angle of the camera increases the size of the wood and reduces the impact of the vase thus creating a considerable lack of visual balance between these two components. However the heavy concentration and bright coloring of the sunflowers and roses produces enough impact to counterbalance the wood. The individual flower composition - its petal arrangement - produces visual balance. A composite flower with many

Plate 28
Forward Thrust – The heavy concentration and bright coloring of the sunflowers and roses produces enough impact to counterbalance the wood and establish visual balance. Note that the two foremost sunflowers have no petals thus reducing their impact.

petals sturdily set on the stem will have greater weight than a similar flower with delicate petals gracefully attached to the stem. For example: the Fuji chrysanthemums in Plate 17 have much less visual weight than the sunflowers in Plate 28.

Another excellent way of obtaining visual weight is to reflex the outer petals of the flower. A tulip, peony, or rose gains weight and importance by this treatment. In Plate 30 the roses at the focal area in this Hogarth curve design have been reflexed to gain visual weight and prominence. In some instances an accessory may be used to gain visual balance. There is an example of this in Plate 23.

The onion at the base of the container counterbalances the extension of sea oats. Though relatively small, it gains visual weight through its color, form and texture. To continue the study of balance, a look at Plate 29 shows how asymmetrical balance can be exhibited by specific placement of individual related objects. In this composition light, shadow and space play very important roles. A slight change in the position of each stem, blossom or bud would change the balance in this design.

Dominance

(primary principle):

The visual organization of a design that emphasizes one or more aspects. Dominance is synonymous with authority. It is the leading character in the play of materials within the arrangement, and in placement of the arrangement in its setting. Individual materials may also exhibit dominance due to their intrinsic characteristics: line, form, texture or color, (Plate 29). Dominance may be the development of a center of interest in conventional designs (Plate 27) or it may be the development of a theme or mood in an interpretive design. Abstract designs may have line, color, texture or space as the dominant factor. Vegetative designs may have a dominant theme as the primary influence over the composition, (Plates 46–50). In a parallel design something as simple as stem placement may be strong enough to prevent conflict among the various materials used. In Plate 20 the black metal parallel columns so dominates the surroundings that the center of interest is on this unusual container. Lines of the design are suggested and controlled by the metal artwork. The material is sympathetic and blends so perfectly with the container that it is hard to picture one without the other. Unity in line, texture, and design, in both container and floral arrangement, is so compatible that dominance is achieved.

Dominance prevents conflict. It subordinates lesser units to the main idea. It is natural for the materials in an arrangement to have a starting point which is the logical place of dominance, the point to which the eye is first attracted. This center of interest is vital to geometric patterns, but in other design styles it becomes less important because the theme or mood is often the focus itself.

Plate 29
Dance of the Freesias —
Asymmetrical balance can be exhibited by specific placement of individual related objects. In this composition light, shadow and space play very important roles. A slight change in the position of each stem, blossom or bud would change the balance in this design.

Focal Area/Focal Point (secondary principle):

Area(s) of greatest visual impact or weight; center(s) of interest which naturally attracts the eye. In traditional Western flower arrangement the focus is the point of origin or convergence to which the eye is drawn because of the perspective in geometrical pattern (Plate 27). Sometimes it is a defined "bull's-eye" where a single design component is emphasized by its characteristics and by the arrangement of supporting material so that they converge. This spot may dominate the composition. Even though the stems of the flowers do not always reach this point, their lines, if continued, would converge at this terminus (radiating lines). By the careful placing of the materials in relation to the focal point one is able to produce stability in a design.

Floral art, in the years preceding the free form movement generally emphasized the concept of focus. Other design tenets emphasized this focus or focal point by leading the eye into it through development of line or transition of materials and colors. As Western flower arrangement developed, it became necessary to establish guidelines for the understanding of this principle. The strongest color or the most fully developed blossom was used at this well-defined focal point, or "bull's-eye" (Plate 8).

In a corsage or a wedding bouquet the focal point is purposely man–made and is just as important as in arrangements. In Figure 3 the focal point is that point where the stems are tied together. Should a ribbon bow be used, it would be tied at this point. Handles of wedding bouquets extend from focal points, their centers of gravity. In wedding ceremony decorations the focal point is the terminus of the central axis, the altar, where the bride and groom take their vows. Thus in geometrical pattern, the focus is clearly defined. The main axis of a design runs through this focus, and the balance is governed by the division of materials. The more fully developed blossoms, the greatest weight, and the most vivid tonal values are placed to give importance to the focus, which must be at a logical point governed by the design. In symmetrical design (formal) the focal point is centered; in asymmetrical design (informal) it is placed toward the high side of the arrangement. Cross-hatching of stems confuses focal point development. Compare plates 17, 23, 24, 25, 27.

Accent (secondary principle):

Detail added to a design to enhance interest and emphasize other stronger elements. Accents may be botanical or non-botanical and are frequently associated with the focal area or theme of a design. Plate 1 illustrates accent through the addition of white mushrooms and Plate 17 demonstrates accent by incorporating

Figure 3
Focal point – wedding bouquet showing lines converging to the center.

mauve colored ribbons into the design. In both instances the accent is adding interest to, and drawing attention to the focal area.

Emphasis (secondary principle):

An area in a composition that is given importance to make it stand out. Emphasis may assist with the development of the elements and principles of design. In Plate 17, emphasis is exhibited by the addition of the bare stock stems. This aids in the establishment of balance (symmetrical) and enhances contrast through color. Plate 1 illustrates emphasis with the addition of the twisted, curved kiwi vine to assist with visual balance and increase the importance of the horizontal line. The inclusion of the philodendron leaf gives strength to the focal area. In Plate 32 the framing technique of the palm inflorescence serves to emphasize the giant allium blooms.

Rhythm (primary principle):

Visual movement throughout a design, usually achieved by means of repetition or gradation. Rhythm is that all-important element that encompasses each of the other principles in measured relationship, the governing force of harmony, that binding force which produces pleasure and satisfaction. It is a quality we strive to achieve in all designing, for it gives life and feeling to our arrangements. Rhythm is the apparent flow of line from the visual center of gravity or focal area (Plate 30); the repetition of materials giving force and movement without monotony (Plate 31); the sequence of color harmony, and the graduation of the materials (Plate 28). Proper transition gives aesthetic value, creating a quality of excellence.

As in music, rhythm is the flow of melody, the development of a theme, the feeling of motion. The "beat" of rhythm can be expressed musically as soft, delicate and flowing or it can be lively, staccato, even thunderous. Often modern music sounds strange and discordant; its

Plate 30
Classical Melody – Rhythm is the apparent flow of line from the visual center of gravity or focal area. This "flow" is accomplished by moving from open roses to snapdragons to astillbe. Even the ribbon streamers contribute to the rhythm of this design.

Plate 31
The Beat Goes On – Circling callas, evenly spaced create forceful movement. The contrasting textures of plumosus and curly willow along with the circular reflections in the plate prevent monotony.

melody is hard to follow, but when we become familiar with the melody and the mood the composer is trying to convey, we then appreciate the work. So it is with flower arrangement - new, daring combinations or exotic designs are startling, but with familiarity they take on a new interest. In creating rhythm, line is important and its careful use imparts vitality, life, and movement. Rhythmic motion is achieved in a design by the use of line to produce the proper perspective; it must arrive at a logical, determined location, as shown in the discussion on Line (Figure 1B). The interrupted flow causes the design to fall apart — rhythm is broken (Figure 1A). Compare the rhythm in Plates 7, 8, 9, 11, 18, 20, 27, 29, 31, 32.

Depth (secondary principle):

Placement of materials at different levels in and around an arrangement. Depth creates the third dimension, visual and physical (actual). In an arrangement depth can be the distance from front to back (frontispiece) as well as the distance from the surface to the interior (Plate 12). Depth can be achieved by having a material "jump out" of the design (Plate 24) and by the use of light and shadow (Plates 11, 18). As illustrated in Plate 21, the vegetative style of design naturally expresses depth by simply placing stems as they grow in a garden.

Repetition (secondary principle):

The repeating of like elements within a composition; i.e., line, form, space, color, texture, pattern or size. In a floral design the organization of materials accordingly will prevent two potential problems — monotony and hodge-podge. (See Plates 18, 20, 24, 27, 31).

Transition (secondary principle):

The easy visual movement that comes from gradual degrees of change in line, form, color space, pattern and size; i.e., small to large; light to dark; closed to open; smooth to rough. Transitions of these kinds are excellent ways of developing harmony and creating unity in designs. (See Plates 11, 28, 30).

Harmony (primary principle):

The aesthetic quality created through the pleasing interaction of a combination of components in a composition. This relationship exists when the various units of a composition do not conflict but form a concordant whole. Good composition will not rescue an arrangement whose parts are not in harmony. Harmony in music is achieved when all instruments are playing the same melody or variations of it, but when the orchestra is tuning up there is no harmony even though each instrument can be heard.

Harmony is an interesting concept because it relates to intangibles such as theme and mood just as it relates to tangibles such as forms and colors. Plate 32 expresses harmony in many ways. There is visual distinction of form and color in all of the materials including the container. Everything is unique which in itself is a "harmonizer" for the various shapes and colors in this composition. Boldness and clarity are found throughout; nothing is lost in the shuffle. One gets the feeling that all of the "instruments" in this design are playing the same tune. In this composition the other elements and principles bring everything together, thus creating the impression of completeness. It is this quality of being one in spirit, mood, theme and purpose, which completes the whole. Harmony is created. However, a work may represent all the principles and elements carefully executed, but still fail in the final result because of its placement in the environment.

Harmony is often difficult to understand because it is an abstract term that varies with personal taste. Fast social and scientific advances are changing one's concepts of harmonious units. Tradition is rapidly being broken. One person's perception of harmony may be in total contradiction to another's due to his personal experience, attitude and emotional response. In dealing with intangibles, appreciation and personal preferences often are the deciding factors.

Unity (primary principle):

A oneness of purpose, thought, style and spirit. The organization of components into a harmonious whole resulting in a cohesive relationship of all parts is unity. Unity is a blend of components. A composition of compelling units is "easy on the eyes". There are no rough edges, no irritants of any kind. All elements

Plate 32
Tropical Concert – This floral symphony appears to have each "instrument" residing in its own section, and all sections appear to be playing the same tune. Harmony is an interesting concept because it relates to intangibles such as theme and mood just as it relates to tangible forms, colors and textures.

and principles come together in perfect unity in Plate 30. In comparing this design to a symphony, it looks as if all the instruments are playing the same chord thus creating a beautiful blend.

It is important to understand the difference between unity and harmony. Unity is expressed more clearly as the relationship between the individual components of the composition, i.e. color, texture, shape; whereas harmony is expressed in the overall relationship between all of the components, the theme, the mood and the final effect of the design. Compare Plates 30 and 32.

Contrast (primary principle):

The difference between objects when they are placed next to each other. A good use of contrast provides excitement and prevents boredom. Contrast can be shown between different lines, forms, colors, textures, sizes and patterns. Proper use of contrast can prevent hodge-podge. There is so much in the way of contrast available to the floral artist that great skill is required in the selection of materials. If a design is intended to be quiet, the amount of contrast should be small but nevertheless present, for without some contrast it would be dull. The other extreme, a dramatic even shocking design would call for the strongest possible contrasts. Contrasts in form, line and color can be quite dramatic. Textural contrasts are easy to achieve but are often overlooked. For instance placing larkspur next to stock would be a poor decision as both flowers would compete for attention but "cancel each other out" due to a lack of contrast. Textures are floral personalities that must show their full value in each design. In a musical composition contrast is provided by the crash of cymbals, by the trumpet solo, or by the flutes flying above the French horns. Plate 19 through color, texture and form produces beautiful contrast that thrills the eye. Line, balance and accent play their roles to perfection in this dramatic corsage.

If we look again at Plate 32 we can enjoy the great contrast in color, form, texture and line of the alliums, anthuriums and birds of paradise, and the palm inflorescence. This plate is a good summary of the principles of harmony, unity and contrast as each principle is beautifully represented. Unity is seen particularly with the similar lines of the pedestal, copper vessel and birds of paradise. Contrast is found in different colors, forms and textures, and harmony is especially felt in how each flower form and color supports the overall exotic theme of the design. Successful designs usually find these three principles in good relationship to each other.

Variation (secondary principle):

Basic similarity but with minor differences. Interest is produced by variation. The more variation a composition has the more interesting it is. Interest may be created not only by variety of line, form, color and size but also by a variety of unequal contrasts or differences among these elements; i.e. large, medium or small intervals in placement. In other words unequal intervals (spacing) create interest through variation whereas equal spacing can be monotonous and less interesting. (See Plates 29, 30, 31, 32).

Opposition (secondary principle):

Total contrast that brings about contradiction in a design. Opposition is particularly exciting when applied to color (Plate 19) and to the direction of line. In Plate 32 notice how the composition is built on contrasting line directions; i.e. the dendrobium orchids flow gracefully to the right while the inverted birds of paradise shoot outward and upward to the left. One side of the design is relaxing and the other expresses energy. This kind of opposition creates interest in the design. Similar opposition is expressed between the forceful upward direction of the alliums and the relaxed path of the palm inflorescence. The bending palm returns the eye back into the composition.

(Plate 29)

(Plate 30)

(Plate 31)

(Plate 32)

Tension (secondary principle):

A dynamic aesthetic quality expressing action or the force of energy within or upon a design component by the skillful use of contrast. To achieve tension in a design is to convey the beauty of opposition or contradiction. In Plate 28 tension can actually be felt because of the contrast of color, texture and visual balance between the sunflowers, roses and weathered wood. This composition is somewhat like a tree that grows outward from a cliff. The balance "feels" precarious and yet the curve of the wood brings the eye back into the "safety" of the focal area. As in nature, tension can produce feelings of unease and ecstasy at the same time! The complexity of this subject can also be seen in Plate 29. Can you see and feel the primary principle of contrast and the secondary principles of variation, opposition and tension in the composition? Even though the three jars of freesia make up a unified whole there is contrast in color and line direction. Spacing gives variation and the right hand freesia is in opposition to the other two, and this expresses tension.

GENERAL SUGGESTIONS

To summarize Part I, a composition, Plate 33, has been designed that will serve to illustrate all of the elements and principles of design:

1. Line — strong vertical lines are established by the placement of linear materials (kiwi vine and foxtail foliage.
2. Form — is expressed by the strong intrinsic qualities of each of the materials, anthurium, ficus and foxtail foliages, montbretia, kiwi and protea.
3. Space — Each prominent form is affirmed by the open space that surrounds it. The variation of spaces provides interest.
4. Texture — contrasting surface qualities from smooth to fuzzy enhance the overall visual appeal.
5. Pattern — the separation of the florets in the yellow montbretia creates pattern.
6. Color — vibrant colors speak of the tropics and give personality to this design. They are used

according to the golden proportion: yellow = 3; related reds (container, proteas, kiwi) = 5; greens = 8, thus preventing monotony.

7. Size — The inherent size of the individual protea blossoms and the container govern the size of everything else.

8. Proportion — Large open spaces and heavy base objects allow the tallest materials that are light in visual weight, to extend beyond the normal 1 $1/2$: 1 ratio of design to container. Phi is expressed with the total height being divided thus: container = 3; top protea = 5; total height = 8. Another way to see phi in this design: container = 3; design width = 5; total height = 8.

9. Balance — Visual balance is achieved by the asymmetrical placement of the materials into the composition, one at a time.

10. Dominance — individual forms dominate this design.

11. Focal area/Focal point — all lines converge at the base of the lower protea that is heavy and bold in color and form.

12. Accent — the small yellow-green protea below the montbretia blossoms provides a detail of added interest.

13. Emphasis — the group of eucalyptus at the container rim assists with the development of the focal area and with the creation of depth.

14. Rhythm — repetition of lines, forms, colors and textures create a strong visual movement throughout the design.

15. Depth — the terraced Fuji chrysanthemums draw the eye deep into the design helping to create the third dimension.

16. Transition — is evident in the upward progression from the chrysanthemums to the Queen protea and on. In addition, negative spaces gradually increase in size from the bottom of the design to the top.

17. Harmony — the components of this composition, though diverse, are not in conflict; they form a pleasing concordant whole.

18. Unity — the cohesive relationship between the individual components is due to their analogous color harmony and their tropical origin.

19. Contrast — excitement is provided by the differences between the many objects in the composition.

20. Opposition — opposing line directions produce interest: anthurium to ficus and montbretia florets turning down to the vertical foliages and proteas.

21. Tension — the unexpected force of movement of the kiwi vine through the montbretia blossoms suggests opposing forces of energy.

22. Variation — textural diversity among all of the materials in this design give examples of both subtle and strong contrast.

Plate 33
Floral Symphony – This composition of floral "instruments" grouped by kind, is playing its melody loud and clear. It is a summary of the principles of design. Not a single note is missing!

Plate 34
East Meets West — Various characteristics of American floral design are descended from both the Orient and the Occident. This composition is rooted in the style of the Flemish paintings; the concept of grouping like materials is from modern Europe; the extending forsythia branches reflect the heaven and earth lines of Japanese design; the vase is Chinese; the pedestal classical Greece; the overall design is thoroughly American.

Part 2

Design Styles

Chapter 4   INTRODUCTION

The appreciation of flowers by all races of people has caused them to use flowers in their daily living and in their religious and ceremonial festivities. In the Western world blossoms are used as the main portions of floral designs, whereas, in the Orient, as exemplified by the Japanese schools, designers use plant materials to show appreciation of the growing plant and its environment. The blossoms in an Oriental design are often secondary; more stress is placed on the rhythmic lines formed by the plant materials. Contemporary floral designers are combining the good points of both Western and Oriental approaches, molding them to fit modern homes and surroundings.

Oriental artists apply the principles of design to represent nature. Their use of material is highly restricted and is suggestive of the seasons. Each twig, stone, and flower - even the water in the container - plays a vital part in Oriental design.

In the Western world many countries have contributed their cultural personalities to the floral arts. In the typical floral design today, the classifications are based on periods of history or on countries whose flower arrangements have definite characteristics. A new concept has evolved from the floral work of the past. Contemporary trends and pure form, using basic principles of art, are forging into prominence. Freedom of expression currently evolving in floral art is indicative of the contemporary changes in other art forms such as painting, sculpture, and architecture. This modern trend is toward less conformity to fashion and tradition, toward simplification of materials and of presentation, and toward the yielding to international influences. Art changes, along with scientific advances, are producing a totally new culture. In any transition, much that is extreme and bizarre always appears, but inevitably there emerge from the experimental stages excellent examples of stable new art forms.

Until the introduction of *Free Form – Interpretive Design** floral patterns were derived from geometrical forms perfected by the Greeks in their development of architecture before the time of Christ. Grecian design principles were applied to all art - sculpture, painting, building design, etc. In America, floral designers depended heavily on mathematical configurations established by the Greeks. The circle and its segments, the triangle, the rectangle, and conic sections, were often employed as design vehicles. These geo-

metrical floral patterns are the principal contribution started by the great American Garden Club movement. Its theory was perfected in *Flowers: Geometric Form* by M. Benz, the book that precedes this one.

The seven primary categories of design styles that are discussed in this book are: Ikebana, Vegetative, Geometric, Formalinear, Parallel, Interpretive and Abstract. Various characteristics of these styles are descended from both the Orient (East) and the Occident (West). In the United States we have, more than in any other country, a mixture of cultural heritages, and this gives us an appreciation for diversity in floral design.

Design assumes a new, clear meaning. True creative ability finds a new path for expression without being encumbered by rules and limitations. Designing techniques are compatible with present-day thinking, interior decor, architecture, and education.

Design is the harmonious arrangement and balance of all elements and principles for the development of a single idea or theme. A design must not only have unity of composition, but it must also be compatible with its setting in order to create a concordant whole; the surroundings, as well as the single unit, are seen; the inter-relatedness of the parts seen by the eye, plus what the subconscious mind perceives. The psychological effects of materials – their associational value in addition to personal preference - influence our understanding of design. One will say an arrangement lacks design, when actually it is one's own lack of appreciation, knowledge, or cultural background that is influencing a poor decision.

The word *design* is somewhat elusive and vague to many people who are starting in a new field of endeavor. They may see the "blueprint" on paper, but to develop the actual design with fresh materials they cannot. We who wish to construct attractive flower arrangements can gain much by following the architect's example. It is helpful though not necessary that we sketch our ideas on paper,

Flowers: Free Form – Interpretive Design, by M. Benz.

but we should - we must - have a definite picture in mind before we start to work. We must have a mental plan for the result we are trying to achieve. The construction of our mental picture depends first and foremost upon stem placement, of which there are four basic classifications: radial, parallel, abstract and integrated.

Radial - having materials arranged like rays coming from a common center; spokes of a wheel; a peacocks tail. This is sometimes referred to as "growth point". Plate 35.

Parallel - Two or more lines that have the same direction and with continuous equal space in between them; railroad tracks; picket fence; organ pipes. Plate 36. This can be another type of "growth point – as in a row of corn.

Abstract - Non-realistic placement of stems with no relation to a growth point or a water source. The stem placement is done solely to give form to direction or mood, and create a new visual image in space, i.e., a blossom or leaf suspended in a design with its head down and stem up. Plate 37.

Integrated - This is a combination of two or more of the above - listed stem placements and is frequently used in current design styles. Plate 38.

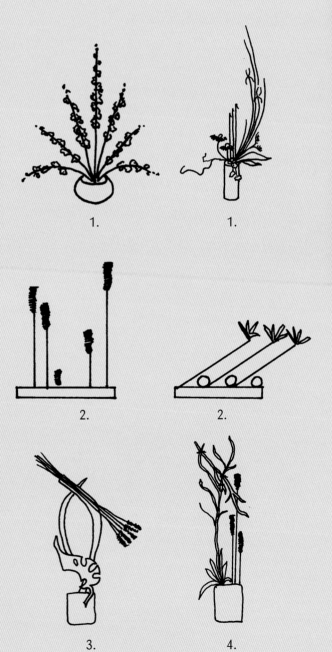

Plate 37
Abstract Placement—
Non-realistic positions.

Figure 4
Stem Placements:
1. Radial
2. Parallel
3. Abstract
4. Integrated

Plate 38
Integrated Placement –
Radial and parallel stem placements are both used in this design.

Plate 39
Family Reunion – All of the fresh materials in this decorative composition: broccoli, Brussels sprouts, cabbage, cauliflower, kale and stock belong to the same botanical family, Cruciferae. Don't they look happy together?

The skeleton of our bodies actually establishes our shape. Whether we are thin or muscular our outer contours conform to that supporting structure. It is the same in floral design — the outer contours conform to the basic skeleton, which is established with the first few stem placements. Clothing for the human body, like floral fillers, accents and accessories serve to embellish the basic structure.

In most design styles a composition can range from being very elaborate (decorative) to being excessively simple (graphic). Decorative designs are filled with masses of materials and elaborate details with little space allowed (Plate 39). These ornamental designs are very

complex; the hand of man over nature is seen in making these designs. This concept is a product of Western cultures and is very popular in current consumer magazines. (Plates 52, cover). Graphic designs are in complete contrast as they are constructed to look very clean, clear and often abstract. These designs sometimes have an object-like appearance. Form and space are the key elements with color and texture next. The human eye's normal demand for space is not considered. Graphic designs are descendents of early Ikebana and the more recent abstract movement in Europe and America. (Plate 40).

Plate 40
Vivid Impression – The shape of this simple form is suggested by the container. This design could be labeled graphic for its simple, clean and intense shape or it could be called volumetric for its solid mass. In either view the individual blossoms though beautiful and luxurious, are secondary to the overall impression.

Chapter 5 IKEBANA

The development of Ikebana actually began in China, which has rightly been called the "Mother of Gardens". Love of natural beauty and her magnificent scenery gave the Chinese their deep appreciation for flowers and art.

Chinese floral art is suggestive rather than representative. It follows the dictates of nature. The Chinese did not develop schools or masters. Due to the genial, gracious temperament of the Chinese, arrangements were bountiful and lush with material being placed with careless abandon. This can be seen in their prints, screens and paintings. Several arrangements were often used in combination, expressing love for the art.

In the East, Chinese culture first made use of plant materials to augment and stimulate daily living and religious ceremonies. Buddhist monasteries became the centers of this culture, for the monks were free of having to earn a living. They had time to develop the use of flowers into an art form. The elements and mysteries of nature that surrounded them were expressed in floral symbols. Native materials at hand were used to represent concepts that were beyond understanding. The Buddhist fostered symbolism. This fact is revealed in an old legend that is the answer to many queries as to the origin and use of flowers. The story goes that Buddha was preaching on Mount Ko-zan. There appeared the heavenly King Diabon who offered Buddha a golden lotus blossom and asked him to preach the law. Buddha took the flower, held it in his hand but remained silent. His meditation was not understood by anyone in the assembly but by Kasho, one of his devoted followers, who smiled. The Blessed One said to him, "I have received the wonderful thought of Nirvana, the right law that I shall now give to you." This is called the doctrine of transmuted thought. Flowers then became an important symbol of faith.

Japan

Japan (586 – present time). The Japanese are the only group of people dedicated to floral art. Their's is a "way of life," a means by which they practice self-control and humility. This art tells a continuous history which dates from the 6th century. With the introduction of Buddhism, and because of the philosophy of the Japanese people toward harmony with nature, they accepted the Chinese teachings without question. Due to their love of nature, a persistence to carry on the ideas of their ancestors, and reverence for their masters they have maintained floral art in its original form. Many modifications have appeared, but the basic principles remain.

The Japanese symbolize features of their beautiful island scenery, of mountains, rivers, rocks, etc., in floral art. Their basic designs emphasize simplicity and asymmetrical balance with dynamic linear form. They follow the dictates of the growing plant. Blossoms and color are secondary; the arrangements feature the natural growth of plants, thereby presenting the importance of their identity. Classical Japanese design requires that stems originate at one point and remain as one unit for four inches (nemoto) to exemplify growth. This nemoto expresses strength in the arrangement comparable to the trunk of a tree. The function of floral art suggests, but does not emphasize flowers. Often a leaf is torn to simulate insect or storm damage, (Plate 42). In their flower arrangements, the principle part of the design inclines toward the place of honor and the guest; it is prominent and shows detail. The secondary portion indicates the host and is smaller. It supports the main subject and maintains proper balance in spacing. The third portion is an attribute adding interest and tri-dimension.

The Japanese religions (Shintoism and Buddhism) do not recognize a heaven as we know it in Christianity; thus, the terminology of the three main lines of Japanese design – heaven, man and earth – is not correct; how-

ever, common usage has established their permanence. The three terms began with Josiah Condor, an English missionary, reading a paper before the London Asiatic Society, and repeating them in his book "Flowers and the Flower Art of Japan." Later an American missionary, Mary Averill, again repeated these names in her book, "Flower Art of Japan," written in 1910, thus establishing the heaven, man, earth concept in our literature. She also indicated a proportion of $1\frac{1}{2}$ times the container, which was a great aid to Americans in understanding approximate measurements of Oriental design.

The Japanese use visual proportions and balance, eliminating measuring. The character of the growing plant suggests height and proportion. They do not have rules as we know them, except in the modern schools.

Ikebana is a familiar word in Japan and freely interpreted means the art of flower arranging. Its literal translation, "living flowers," probably originates from the Buddhist yearning to prolong or preserve all life. The word *hana*, the English equivalent of which is "flower," includes stems, branches, reeds, grasses, foliage, blossoms, in addition to natural elements, e.g., snow, rocks, water, etc. The love of line in all Oriental art rather than mass or color is perhaps the most salient feature, and is more apparent in their flower arrangements, differentiating their floral art from other countries. They prefer a linear, commonplace gnarled branch, carefully placed to exhibit its graceful flowing line, rather than a group of lovely massed, brightly colored blossoms. When a flower is used, it presents the growing aspects of the plant. To better understand the Orientals and their high esteem for floral art, study their attitude and philosophy. The Japanese blends himself with nature — his is a philosophy of interpreting nature. The American tends to conquer nature and make it subservient to his desire.

Japan was a closed country, living an isolated, artful existence, until the 20th century when Occidental invasion industrialized the nation. This changed the Japanese business attitudes, but not attitudes toward floral art.

The story is told of a simple farmer in Japan who specialized in chrysanthemums. His were famous throughout the land for their perfection. The Emperor heard of the farmer's fine blossoms and expressed the desire to see them. The farmer and his small family worked many long hours in the fields preparing for the visit. When the Emperor arrived there stood only one perfect blossom. The field of blooming plants had been destroyed. The Emperor knelt before this lone blossom for many hours to enjoy its beauty. We in America would pride ourselves on the number of blossoms and the expanse of the field.

Symbolism in floral art illustrates many different spiritual attributes. These aspects permeated daily living and symbolism grew to be a significant part of floral art. Their arrangements are an idealism of nature, bringing into harmony the life and growth of plant and man. Not only are the arrangements to depict the growth of plants, but the season, surroundings, and conditions under which they grow.

For example:

Plate 42
Classical Ikenobo Aspidistra—The original concept of Ikebana is exemplified in this design. The three segments (heaven, man and earth) shin — spiritual truth, soe — harmonizer, and tai — material substance, form the asymmetrical characteristic of classical Japanese design. Two of the leaves retain insect holes as a reminder that the life cycle of the plant depends upon the insect for pollination.

The materials	Bamboo	- stern quality that bends but does not yield
	Plum (apricot)	- courage that blossoms in the Winter while snow is on the ground
	Aspidistra	- purity which unfolds in solitude
	Chrysanthemum	- nobility which possesses wisdom
The stage	The future	- buds, suggesting future growth
	The present	- half-opened flowers or perfect foliage
	The past	- mature flowers, pods or dried leaves
Type arrangement	Spring	- vital growth, vigorous curves
	Summer	- full and spreading, open arrangement
	Autumn	- sparse and thin arrangement
	Winter	- dormant and bare

Figure 5
The front view of a classical Ikenobo design showing the nemoto as one stem.

Closely allied to the symbolism of Ikebana is the association of certain flowers with tradition, literature, and custom. Every holiday has a special flower or foliage:

New Years - pine, white chrysanthemums, nandina
Doll Festival - cherry and peach blossoms
Boys' Festival - iris blossoms

Nanten - the Japanese word for nandina (*N.domestica*) has significant meaning at New Years. "Nan" is the term for difficulty and misfortune; "ten" means turning from. In floral art nandina signifies the turning from misfortunes of the old year to the happy future of the new year.

To present an insight to the importance and symbolic meaning in Japanese floral design, this illustration will clarify to the Occidental their interpretation. An American writer once visited a provincial Japanese home to familiarize himself with the interior, their mode of living, and to gain an insight to the general "atmosphere." While sipping tea with his hostess, he became aware of the severity of the interior, noting the only decoration in the room was in the alcove, that being the tokonoma. This decoration consisted of three branches of shrub hanging from a small fish basket that was suspended from a post in the alcove. As a backdrop for the flower arrangement, a long, narrow scroll with lines suggestive of flowing water was used. The branches were bare of leaves and flowers; only a few buds showing touches of color were apparent. The guest, being acquainted with Japanese etiquette, complemented his hostess on her arrangement. Later, the memory of its sparseness returned many times to the writer's mind. After becoming familiar with Japanese flower arrangements and symbolism, he realized that, though the whole composition was bare and the family he had visited was living in moderate circumstances, the subtlety contrived in this arrangement foretold the family's salute to on-

coming Spring. The kakemono (scroll) suggested the melting snows and flowing streams. The bud-bearing branches of plum tree were suggestive of early Spring bursting into bloom while snow was still on the ground.

The *Ikenobo* or classical school preserves the tradition of the original concept of *Ikebana*, which began in the 6th century. The *Ikenobo* school developed three segments, *Shin* (spiritual truth), *Soe* (harmonizer), and *Tai* (material substance). These segments are known to the Western designer as heaven, man, and earth. In Western eyes, the groups form an asymmetrical triangle. The first is an upright group, heaven ($1^1/_2$ to 3 times the container); the second, and intermediate group, man (approximately $2/_3$ length of heaven) leaning away from the upright; and the third is lower, earth (about $1/_2$ - $1/_3$ of man), on the opposite side and also leaning forward. Notice how closely these proportions conform to the *golden proportion* (3-5-8). The various modern schools have their own measurements for each division.

In Plate 42, Classical Ikenobo Aspidistra, Japanese orchid foliage is arranged in the classical style of the *Ikenobo* school. The container, an antique ogencho, is placed on a kwadai, which is proper for the display of the arrangement. This photograph shows the side view in order that the placement of the stems forming the nemoto càn be clearly seen. The front view would appear to have one stem. The tallest line (Shin) originates in the center of the container, gracefully curves upward, ending directly over the point of origin. The addition of a leaf to either side are attributes, adding interest, strength, and rhythmically descending to the man line (Soe). A leaf is torn to indicate ravages of nature. The eye then follows smoothly into the third group (Tai) in which there are graceful accentuated curves, symbolic of earth rhythms.

During the 15th century the ruling military leaders practiced the arts. They felt the need of a religion that would be simple for camp life. They found this in the *Zen* sect of Buddhism. The attainment of Zen is aimed at the harmony of man and nature. It was during this period that the tea ceremony, *Cha-No-Yu*, was perfected. Simplicity and naturalism marked a deviation from the staid formal life and affected the arts. The tokonoma or alcove was also developed during this period, in the main room of the home. It became popular for even the most humble dwelling to have a recessed wall portion or tokonoma - the place of honor for a cherished possession, a kakemono (scroll), or a flower arrangement. No more than three decorative objects are placed in this alcove at one time, each carefully selected and placed to achieve maximum harmony. This created a new direction in flower arranging. Cha-bana or tea-flower and *Nageire* "thrown- in" designs emerged (Plate43). This form was more in keeping with the simple life and humble dwellings. The tokonoma became a place of study and meditation. The kakemono was hung in this alcove complementing the flower arrangement. It was generally a poem or painting depicting the season and constituted a favorite gift to the bride.

In Plate 43, Summer *San-ju-giri*, a san-ju-giri (three level bamboo container) is selected for the *Nageire* arrangement to express informality, simplicity, and naturalism showing change from the formal *Ikenobo* school. The plant material is representative of the three regions: Flowering quince expresses upright growth on the hillsides; the gracefully flowing descending branches of the jasmine suggest plants overhanging the rock cliffs; the center flower, onion, is from the meadowland, and the callas placed in the lower section are indicative of the lake region. The three segments, Shin, Soe, Tai, are maintained. Note the flow of line originating in the callas, directing the eye upward into the flowering quince, then down into the natural placement of the jasmine branch, which completes the circulation. The base, *shiki-ita*, is made of a segment of a tree. The Oriental visualizes the three regions represented in the container and the plant materials which may recall many happy experiences of late Spring.

With the introduction of the Western flora, which generally had short stems, a new form of *Ikebana* developed. This was the third great deviation from the formal style of the *Ikenobo* school. Unshin Ohara recognized its value and developed a freer design form called *Moribana* style (piled-up flowers). He maintained the three segments, but placed them in a low-type container, a suipan or sunabachi, which permitted greater abundance of flowers and foliage than the more severe predecessors. He divided the three main groupings in their placement in the container. Naturalness of growth prevailed. This school was handed down to his son, Koun Ohara, in 1916 and to the grandson, Houn, in 1938.

In Plate 44, Mountain Stream, the sunabachi conjures much mysticism and symbolism for the development of this floral picture.

Plate 43
Summer San-ju-giri –
This Nageire expresses informality, simplicity and naturalism. A three level bamboo container is selected to portray the three regions of plant growth. Flowering quince and jasmine depict growth on the hillside, onion is from the meadowland, and callas placed in the lower section are indicative of the Japanese lake regions.

Plate 45
Transition —
Last years seed pods
unwilling to give up,
represent the transition
from winter into spring as
the new growth of these
sweet gum branches (shin
and soe) comes forth. Late
spring is depicted by the
low grouping (tai) of Reiger
begonia. Note how well the
color and texture of the
branches complement the
carved stone bowl.

Plate 44
Mountain Stream —
A Moribana arrangement is
developed in the sunibachi.
Large rocks represent the
mountains from which rise
plant materials. Wisteria
branches (shin and soe) are
reinforced with hollyhock
foliage. The radiating veins in
the hollyhock leaves repeat
the pattern of the wisteria
inflorescence. Low growing
iris and miniature roses are
grouped separately. The
space between the two
groups is suggestive of the
mountain stream, called, in
Japan, "a place for the fish to
swim through."

Large rocks represent the mountains from which rise the plant materials. The wisteria blossoms (Shin and Soe), give strength by their firm placement and restricted curves. The attributes, hollyhock foliage, are placed to form a strong nemoto. The solid plane of the hollyhock leaf adds weight to this main line, repeats the formation of the rocks, and its veining complements the radiating line of its companions. The "Tai" grouping has been arranged separately, allowing space between the main grouping which is suggestive of the mountain stream, and as the Japanese say, "a place for the fish to swim through." The low grouping of iris and miniature roses, with their foliage was selected to represent "Tai".

It was Buddy Benz' great fortune to be a guest in the home of Houn Ohara-san, one of the great floral masters of Japan, whose grandfather initiated this third great change in *Ikebana*. Upon arriving Mr. Benz was ushered into the main room of his lovely home. It was bare except for a table and pillows in the center of the room. In the tokonoma was a flower arrangement in his honor. Custom required him to sit before the alcove quietly before speaking and admire the work done to welcome him. While he was doing so, the Master entered. No word was spoken until he had time to meditate on the flower arrangement. After due time Mr. Benz turned and the host greeted him. Then it was appropriate for him to express his joy and appreciation. This ceremony is strictly observed with visiting friends and those visiting in their country — seldom is an Occidental so honored in a Japanese home. They are usually taken out to be entertained and not invited into the private home.

Many schools sprang up to teach the Westerner the art of Japanese floral design. Each Japanese Master has his/her own conception of arranging and their own set of rules and measurements. Within each school there is much variation from the classical art form. Today, as in America, there is a tremendous urge for freedom, a strong force for the mod-

ern or abstract. The floral masters of Japan are involved in Free Form - Interpretive (Free Style), and even Abstract designs. Many of these contemporary works of floral art are somewhat puzzling to the untrained eye, but they are considered masterpieces. New art forms are developing in floral art just as they did in painting and sculpture some years ago in Europe. We owe a great debt to Oriental design for our employment of line and proportion. (Plate 45)

Chapter 6   VEGETATIVE DESIGN

Vegetative designs copy nature. This design philosophy is in opposition to geometric design where the hand of man controls the flowers by placing them into triangle shaped compositions, etc. The vegetative design philosophy allows nature to control the hand. Man imitates nature.

Vegetative design is a naturalistic design style in which flowers and plant materials are placed the way they grow. A purist would combine materials that would be found together in nature with emphasis placed on climatic, seasonal, geographical or topographical compatibility. Heights of materials would correspond as they do in nature. Plate 46 illustrates an overgrown garden with cultivated plants fighting for their existence along with "weeds." The sunflowers, yarrow and marigolds are positioned at heights realistic to one another. Weeds are represented by the low-growing rosemary, solidaster and dill, and by the brown sour dock, a noxious weed. The color and texture of the dock ties the composition to the rusted iron pot, which represents the sustaining earth. Plate 47 reveals greater refinement in the designer's intent by using more control in the artistic placement of similar materials. The cattail leaves are allowed to soar while the small sunflowers are kept low. Looped blades of grass provide accent.

The upper story of Queen Anne's Lace

Plate 46
Overgrown Garden – This naturalistic vegetative composition is a bit on the wild side. There is a great feeling of nature, a cacophony of textures and the satisfaction of having a complete contrast with our hi-tech lifestyle.

and the under story of pink ranunculus in Plate 48 offer a naturalistic but more decorative expression of nature. The fresh mushrooms growing on the mossy floor under this thicket of flowering plants provide an accent that emphasizes the vegetative style of design.

In developing vegetative "gardens" several stems of one variety are inserted into the same growth point to create a natural looking plant. Accents such as insects or birds and accessories like rocks, weathered wood or broken pottery must be placed, also, as they would normally be found in the garden. Vegetative designs may express various ecological systems such as mountains, prairies, marshlands and seashores. There is much opportunity for creativity as we can see in Plate 49, a vegetative composition that interprets a desert area that runs down to a seashore. Shells, mosses and succulent plants represent various features of the land and flora in the unique ecosystem of such a place. Pussy willow forms a dramatic vertical line representing the strong contrast between desert and sea, yet creating unity with color and texture.

In Plate 50 we see how vegetative design can be adapted to a frequent request in the flower shop: decorating a podium. This garden has been constructed in three 18" utility trays, each holding two blocks of wet foam. The use of three individual units facilitates delivery and installation. Notice how the principles of balance and scale have been developed to draw attention to the speaker. This concept is useful in providing garden themes for special event and wedding decorations. The imitation of nature began with the Japanese hundreds of years ago. It then became popular in Holland and Germany during the 1970's and 80's when ecological concerns rose to the forefront. Now vegetative design is firmly established in America. This design style is in perfect harmony with our cultural concerns for home, garden and environment.

Plate 47
Stylized Garden – This garden has been quite refined by the artist's hand as seen in the placement of cattail and grass foliages.

Plate 48
Decorative Garden – This vegetative design is filled with masses of flowers showing little interest in space.

Plate 49
Interpretive Garden – This composition allows succulents and seashells to speak of an unusual ecosystem.

Plate 50
Commercial Garden – This setting shows just how useful the vegetative style can be in special event work.

Chapter 7   GEOMETRIC DESIGN

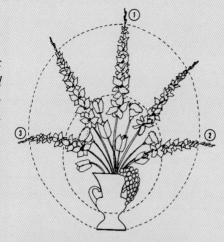

A geometric design is *a composition with a definite geometric shape composed of line, mass, or line-mass concepts, with radial stem placements.* Recognizable patterns include various circular and triangular shapes, Hogarth curves and crescents, and linear shapes that include vertical, diagonal and horizontal axes. Current geometric designs have evolved from the many Occidental historical periods. Floral art forms in the West have always leaned toward the bouquet type in flower arranging. They are prone to let the individual develop his/her own talent. Europeans did not have the leisure time to devote to hobbies or avocations. They are not "club joiners" as we are in America, therefore, their floral arrangements and design did not develop pattern or a set of rules and regulations. The European art form has been characterized by quantity of flowers and massed designs. The trend was toward specimen blossoms rather than planned arrangements. Selected blossoms were grouped to illustrate horticultural advances rather than to create design or to express an idea. (Plate 52)

Prior to 1900, flower arranging in America was not the distinct art that it is considered today. Horticultural specimens were still preferred. They were widely used for medicinal purposes and various social occasions. Flowers did not attain the great symbolism that early Egyptians, Grecians or Orientals attributed to them. In 1914, Liberty Hyde Bailey's "Standard Cyclopedia of Horticulture" lists some of the principles of design. Later the garden clubs began to include classes for artistic arrangements in flower shows held mainly for horticultural interest. After World War I this art gained much impetus from the Garden Club movement. These clubs made great strides in improving a community's natural beauty. Numerous articles and books on the subject began to appear. Geometric design in floral art became established.

In Geometric design the basic skeletal structure can be established by the placement of the first three main lines. The development of the pattern is dependent on this foundation. In approximately 90% of the times when an arrangement is "not right," the fault will be with these first three stems. Number one stem (or blossom) sets the height, number two stem gives the width in one direction and is often horizontal, and the number three stem establishes overall size and/or width in the opposite direction. Number 3 stem may be equal in length to number two stem, as in the symmetrical triangle and oval patterns, or shorter, for asymmetrical designs. These three stems setting the height, width and shape, also establish the size of the design.

Figure 6
Circular — oval, round; focal point centrally located.

Plate 51
Oval Tapestry — The hand of man brings the blossoms under his strict control to form an oval.

Plate 52 ▶
Fifteenth Century-Dutch — The hand of man "listens" to the flowers and let's them express themselves naturally.

Circular Patterns
Oval, Round

The full circular pattern is like a spot. It catches the eye and holds the viewer within the orbit. It leaves little to the imagination compared to other geometrical patterns which lead the eye along graceful, flowing lines. The circular arrangement is excellent to use at the terminus of an axis, e.g., an altar in a church, or at the end of a room, etc. It has the quality of holding the viewer's attention to its location, which makes it a dominant feature. Containers that lend themselves to this design are usually urn-shaped or they are similar classical types, Figure 6.

In Plate 51, *Oval Tapestry*, the arrangement illustrates an oval- mass design. Its shape is established by the line flowers (snapdragons). To create interest within the oval pattern heather is "interwoven" throughout to simulate a texture like the faux finish of a hand-painted egg. This gives an interesting combination of texture (heather) and pattern (snapdragons). By contrast, Plate 52, *Fifteenth Century-Dutch*, is much less structured. Balance is achieved by grouping the colors and flowers in various areas of the mass. A contemporary interpretation is given this traditional composition with the graceful reaching branches of pistache, ligustrum, eleagnus and pyracantha. These lines and groupings subtly draw the eye through the composition and into its interior depths where the pomegranates reside. Texture, pattern and color work together

to produce a harmonious effect, especially against the richly colored background. This composition is a contemporary interpretation of the Flemish paintings from the 1500's.

The round bouquet is a popular contemporary design because in commercial floristry every recipient can find an appropriate place to display it. The round bouquet exhibits symmetrical balance and radial stem placement. It can show obvious structure, great depth and be suffused with open space as in Plate 53. Conversely, a round design may be chock full of a mixture of kinds and colors and include accents such as the spires of heather that we see in Plate 54.

Plate 54►
Deluxe Round – A luxurious combination of types, colors and textures fill this bouquet.

Plate 53
Open Round – Space surrounds each blossom giving a more clean and lean look.

In designing a round bouquet whether it looks formal and structured or informal and naturalistic, it is begun with a skeleton. In Plate 55A, a top view shows the number one flower to be in the center. This flower is vertically straight and establishes both the central axis and the height of the design. Three flowers, numbered two, three and four, are equally spaced around the number one blossom. The last three skeleton flowers, numbered five, six and seven, are equally spaced between the second, third and fourth blossoms, but on a lower level touching or near the rim of the container. This spacing technique assures even dispersion of visual weight throughout the design. This can be seen in Plate 55B along with the addition of filler flowers (daisy spray mums) (Plate 56A) and foliage (leatherleaf fern). Notice that the filler materials all radiate up and out from the center of the design. A feeling of both visual depth and uniformity should be present at this stage. The accent ribbon has been added to bring visual movement into this design in lieu of the presence of any line materials. The last material to be inserted is the most delicate – gypsophelia (Plate 56B). It must appear to float like a delicate mist uniformly throughout the design. If gypsophelia is too crowded or too unevenly placed, its unique characteristic of delicacy is lost. The most delicate materials should be the last ones to go into a design as they can be easily broken by later trying to reach through them with ribbons or foliage.

A prevalent design style for arranging a dozen long stemmed roses is the round bouquet in a tall vase. Plate 57 shows such a design. The mechanics to hold this arrangement in place consist of a grid of waterproof adhesive tape over the mouth of the vase (Figure 26, page 132). This method works best when some of the foliage is placed first, followed by the outer perimeter of roses. This order of insertion allows several stems to interlock with each other before the tallest roses are placed in the center. Excellent stability is gained without the use of floral foam. The blossoms themselves, should be evenly dispersed throughout the design, and the vase should appear to occupy approximately one third of the total height. The graceful clasping of stems in clean, clear preservative solution is part of the beauty of arranging flowers in a transparent vase.

Plates 55 A & B
"School Figures" — Establish the skeleton and cover mechanics.

A   B

Plate 57
Old Reliable – Decorative foliage gives this "daily dozen" greater "looks-value".

Plates 56 A & B
"School Figures" – Add volume and dress it up.

A   B

Radiating Lines - Fan Shaped

In Plate 58 stocks form the framework of the design. Each is equal in length and is placed in the urn to simulate a half-circle or fan. Pink carnations alternate as a mass and add color contrast. Line flowers as a rule develop this type of pattern to the utmost; their lines suggest the radiating lines of the sun or the ribs of a fan (Figure 7). As in the oval and round, three main lines set the radiating pattern, and the remaining lines fall within the skeleton and are similar in length. Practically any round or oval design in a formal urn may be made into a fan by changing the container to a low bowl as would be used on a mantel. The finished arrangement will be very similar. The ribs of a fan never alternate with two kinds of line flowers. Colors are never alternated, since a manufactured appearance would be produced.

Radiating Lines- Crescent Design

A portion of a circle may be used effectively in floral design. In circular patterns continuous, smooth curved line becomes a vital element; it creates motion which is essential. For a dramatic, clear, concise design the plant material should have strong characteristics and bare stems Plate 59. The stems have almost as much value as the flowers because they contribute the element that is most important - line, thus delineating design. Callas, gingers, tritomas, anthuriums, etc., lend themselves beautifully for this purpose. The lines radiate from a point on the circumference of the circle forming a crescent or semi-circle. The design becomes a magnetic spot holding the eye within the circular boundary, Figure 8. The No. 1 blossom is best placed directly over the center of gravity; this point is determined by the placement of the foam. No. 2 blossom will be shorter, having the same curve as No. 1 but it flows in the opposite direction completing the circular motion. Additional blossoms conform to these lines. Line flowers or those with pointed corollas, e.g., callas and anthuriums must direct the eye with their points. When using an accessory with this circular pattern its lines must conform to, or contrast with, the curves of the design. Should a figurine be used within the design, its lines either repeat those of the flowers Plate 59, or in the case of a candle, stand in contrast. The vertical axis running through the center of gravity will pass through the center of the figurine (or candle).

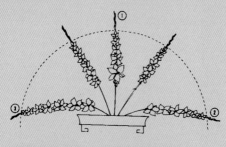

Figure 7
Circular – radiating lines, fan shaped; focal point centrally located.

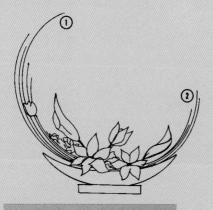

Figure 8
Circular – cresent; focal on circumference of circle.

Plate 58 (circa 1966)
Radiating lines – Fan –
Stock blossoms radiate like
the ribs of a fan, establishing
the half circular pattern.
Carnations and iris are used
alternately and repeat the
design.

◄ Plate 59 (circa 1966)
Crescent Callas
The semi-circular design is
created by the lines of No. 1
and No. 2 blossoms. The
lines in the accessory curve
with No. 1 blossom when it
is used within the
arrangement.

Plate 60
Vivid Impression – This
graphic/volumetric design
forms a crescent, resulting
from the flexibility of our
principles of design.

In Plate 60, the shape of the Murano glass container has
been interpreted with an extravagant crescent of roses. It appears
that the circular segment of the roses is "opening" to be in harmony
with the lines of the vase. In this design the container truly forms
a visual foundation from which the design rises.

"S" Curve - Hogarth Curve

The adage "Curved is the line of beauty - straight is the line of duty," has more truth than poetry. No artist created greater beauty than did William Hogarth (1697-1764) with his curving lines. His name has been so much associated with the "S" that any curved line immediately has this connotation. In the lower corner of the painting Hogarth did of himself and his dog, Trump, he drew on a palette a serpentine curve with the words, "The Line of Beauty." To establish and justify his concept of "fluctuating ideas of taste," he documented his ideas in a treatise called "Analogy of Beauty" in 1753. The lazy "S" (Hogarth curve) has had a great influence on design in America. Flowing grace, gentleness, softness, style, and fashion are but a few attributes of this type of arrangement.   The development of the "S" curve pattern has many variations. The line may be continuous and developed with the same blossoms; (Figure 9, Plate 64) or it may be a suggested line developed with various floral materials (Plate 62), each repeating the line of the preceding one and flowing into the next; or the pattern may be one of suggestion where the floral material is seen at one end and reappears in the opposite direction Plate 61. When the ends of the "S" are continued, double circles are formed. The upper segment of the circle is designed generally larger to create better visual balance. This upper curve of the Hogarth always has to defy the force of gravity, therefore the use of wire or other mechanics must be employed. With this in mind, pre-planning this design and its delivery is a must. Pre-wired permanent materials work very well in this design concept. Plate 63, Classical Melody, shows a "reverse curve" interpretation of the traditional Hogarth curve in which the ribbon streamers complete the lower segment of the design.

Figure 9
"S" or Hogarrth curve.

Plate 61 (circa 1966)
Patio Lantern
Flame roses establish the line from which gladioli with Scotch broom form the Hogarth curve.

Plate 62 (circa 1986)
Blue Hogarth
Scotch broom forms the top of the "S" curve, while curly willow completes the bottom of the curve. Blue iris flows from the upper lines into the focal point of vibrant cineraria.

Plate 63
Classical Melody.

Plate 64 (circa 1986)
Horizontal Hogarth

Triangular Designs

The second geometrical category of shapes is the triangle, which is either symmetrical (formal) or asymmetrical (informal) according to the degree of the angles. The patterns derived from this figure are very interesting and pleasing, and it was one of the leading designs of American flower arrangement from the 1950's through the 70's This design yields greater beauty with fewer flowers than the oval or round forms. It stimulates the imagination and carries the eye through its various parts, or it may point to another object of importance.   Triangular pattern may be used as a line, a mass, or combination of line-mass arrangement. The most frequently used is that of line-mass.

Symmetrical Triangle

The symmetrical triangle is formal and man-made. It has perfect symmetry, having the elements of one side similar to those of the other and equally distributed about the central axis. The No. 1 blossom establishes the height of the arrangement (apex of the triangle) and is centered toward the back of the container. The No. 2 and No. 3 blossoms are equal in length and extend out to either side, establishing the width. They lie horizontally over the edge of the container, completing the other two points of the triangle. Additional material falls within the three points of the triangle (Figure

Plate 65
Radial Placement –
Symmetrical Triangle.

Figure 10
Symmetrical triangle –
formal.

10 and Plate 65). This additional material may form a graceful, sweeping curve within these boundaries, or it may adhere closely to the three main stems forming a severe, stylized, contemporary design. Should flowers or foliage cross the imaginary boundary lines connecting the points, the result would be to make the design bulge thus approaching a fan arrangement.

When combining several types of flower forms, one may use line flowers to establish the pattern outline (skeleton), and mass flowers within the framework as in Plate 65.

Arrangements for dinner tables should not exceed fourteen inches in height unless the dinner is very formal. The fourteen inch height allows easy conversation between dinner guests without their having to play hide and seek. The symmetrical triangle is a common skeletal pattern used in a low orientation for table centerpieces. The number one flower is cut short to comply with the scale of the environment.

In determining the size of an arrangement to be made for a table, one should ask the customer the number of guests to be seated and where the dinner is to be held. This information will give an indication of the size and type of arrangement needed. In fine country clubs and town clubs, more space is allotted for guests (generally two feet or more) than in night clubs where tables are narrow and people are seated much closer together (sometimes as close as sixteen to eighteen inches per person). If the arrangement is for the dining table in a home, the size can easily be judged according to the number of guests.

The construction of a basic table centerpiece is shown in Plates 66A, B, C, D, E. In Plate 66A note that before the flowers are inserted, the wet foam has been cut to fit into a watertight plastic liner and secured with adhesive tape. The foam extends approximately 3/4 inch above the basket rim allowing for horizontal stem insertions. The number one stem (stock) is centered vertically in the foam and does not exceed fourteen inches in height. The number two and three stems extend horizontally to establish the length of the centerpiece which depends upon the size of the table and number of guests and serving dishes that will be present. Plate 66B shows that symmetrical balance is achieved from the top view as well as both sides. In Plate 66C foliage is added to cover the foam and to fill in some of the open space. Next come the roses (mass flowers) which will add more volume to the design as they continue to open (Plate 66D). The finished centerpiece (Plate 66E), includes Monte Casino filler flowers adding a third texture and at the same time softening the outline. Notice how the stark shape of the skeleton has now been fully integrated into the composition. That is as it should be in traditional design.

Symmetrical Cone Triangle

The cone or conical design is similar in shape to the pyramids, although it may be round in form. To be dramatic, the arrangement must be tall. This pattern was first used in the Near Eastern culture, especially during the Byzantine period. The Turkish turban is suggestive of this particular design. It may be developed by using foliage closely applied to a conical foundation with ornaments of clustered fruit or a garland of fruits and flowers spiraling from its base to the apex. In formal urns, this pattern may be developed beautifully using solid masses of blossoms or foliage for design on a newel post; the design works well in a pair of arrangements on either end of a mantel. Floral development in this manner is dramatic, and reflects a taste for classical forms (Plates 67, 68, 69). Figure 11, illustrates the importance of height in designing a cone with long stemmed flowers.

Plate 67 (circa 1966)
French Influence —
This elegant Louis XIV, antique pink marble urn, with gold accents, a gift by Napoleon to one of his generals, is designed in a formal cone. This is an example of what is currently known as Volumetric design.

Figure 11
Symmetrical triangle — vertical, cone or pyramidal.

Plate 68 (circa 1986)
Spring Pyramid
The conical arrangement is
developed to reproduce the
lines of the container.
Clusters of lily–of–the–
valley, heather, and lilac
with accents of Rex begonia
leaves create a flowery
modern "Christmas" tree.

Plate 69 (circa 1966)
Topiary Tree
Garlands of fruit and
flowers, tied with red velvet
ribbon, spiral up the cone–
shaped tree of sheared
boxwood.

Asymmetrical Triangle

The asymmetrical triangle lacks the restriction of perfect symmetry and is therefore less formal and more interesting. Its asymmetry stimulates the imagination more than other geometrical patterns. It may show great vigor and vitality with extended lines. Perfect visual balance may be achieved by proper placement of the first three stems (Figure 12A). Fewer materials may be used to achieve greater results with an asymmetrical triangle.

There are two additional triangular floral patterns derived from the asymmetrical triangle. The first is the right angle design whose tall main line is perpendicular to the base (Figure 12B). The second is "scalene"; its central axis is at an oblique angle to the base, thus causing unequal sides and angles (Figure 12C).

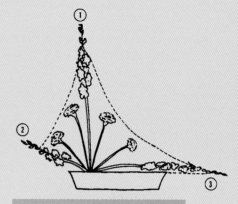

Figure 12A
Asymmetrical triangle – right angle; No. 2 stem is placed outside of right angle.

Asymmetrical Triangle- Right Angle

The focal point generally is developed toward the high side of the arrangement in an oblong or rectangular container. When one uses a pin holder or wet foam, it is secured toward the high side of the container. The extra portion of container exposed on the low side of the arrangement helps counterbalance height and gives good visual balance.

Notice in Plate 70A and Figure 12A the number one flower is inserted off-center toward the high side of the design, and at the same time toward the back of the block of foam. This placement allows more depth from front to back in the finished design. The number two flower is angled at 45 degrees between the vertical and horizontal planes of numbers one and three. Number three extends outward a bit more than number two thus allowing the low side of the design to counter balance the high side. In Plate 71 the remaining snapdragons and roses are positioned inside the imaginary boundary lines that could be drawn from the number one flower to both numbers two and three. If these boundaries are crossed this triangle will lose its distinctive shape and take on aspects of a circular design. The addition of lilies add volume and visual weight in the focal area, and the two flax leaves increase the feeling of vigor and emphasize both height and asymmetrical balance. You will notice in this basic design that all materials including the foliage, follow the lines of the three skeleton flowers. This stem placement technique clarifies the pattern and helps train the novice designer's eye to see balance and proportion in a design.

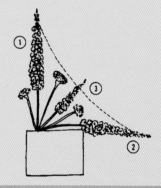

Figure 12B
Asymmetrical triangle – right angle; No. 3 stem is placed inside of right angle.

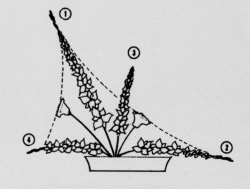

Figure 12C
Asymmetrical triangle – scalene; No. 3 blossom is placed either within the angle or to the outside.

A

B

C

Plate 70 A, B, C
"School Figures" – As
before, the skeletal pattern
is established, the
mechanics covered,
volume is added, and the
design is finished with
details.

Plate 71 Traditional
Asymmetrical Triangle.

In Plate 72 one snapdragon has been shifted slightly to allow room for the additional flax leaf, which is necessary to counter balance the visual weight of the pink carnations. It often happens that a designer is "one flower short" for a design's required visual balance. In this design the swirling pink ribbon flows to the left to make up for the missing carnation. This works because the ribbon is the same color as the carnations. Another variation of the asymmetrical triangle is shown in Plate 73. Squeezing the entire garden into a triangular shape is not easy! The outline of this triangle is softened a bit to harmonize with the container, but the stone base emphasizes the triangular concept by adding definition to the design. Plate 74 expresses the opposite extreme: asymmetrical balance which combines

Plate 72
Half and Half — Traditional asymmetrical
triangle, non-traditional division of color.

Plate 73
Decorative Asymmetrical Triangle —
Polychromatic abundance.

Plate 74
Open View – Simple drama is created with four foliages. Galax leaves cover the pvc pipe column and are also fashioned into a rosette at the focal point of the design. Ample space allows the diverse personalities of the palm, button fern and spider plant to "shine".

Plate 75 (circa 1966)
Right Angle – The No. 3 stem is kept short.

(Figure 12B)

Plate 76 (circa 1966)
Stylized Right Angle – The No. 3 stem is even shorter in this design.

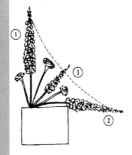

the minimalism of early Ikebana with the Western taste for ornamentation.

In Plate 75, Figure 12B, another right angle design is developed; however, the No. 3 stem is between the No. 1 and No. 2 lines. In this case the main stem (No. 1) appears to be a continuation of the side of the container; both are straight. The main stem does lean slightly to the rear giving depth but as viewed from the front, it is parallel to the lines of the container. In the hands of experienced designers, the asymmetrical triangle lends itself to many variations. In Plate 76, a severe, stylized right angle has been made by greatly shortening the position of the No. 3 flower stem. Bells of Ireland followed by tulips develop the vertical (No. 1) and horizontal (No. 2) lines. The remaining blossoms fall within the design. In each of these asymmetrical illustrations, the development of the vertical line has been placed to the high side of the design. In Plates

77 and 78, liberty is taken; the vertical stem has been centered in both containers. The No. 2 stems have been lowered below the horizontal level creating a more obtuse angle and thus approaching the scalene design. To maintain equilibrium, the flowers and foliage have been carefully placed to either side of the central axis, thereby equally distributing weight and gaining visual balance.

A pair of asymmetrical designs may be used to frame an object such as a painting or a mirror above a mantel (Plate 79), or a cross on a church altar. It can be seen that intimacy is created by the framing technique of positioning the lower extensions toward the center. The two arrangements produce formal balance in the composition as a whole. The frame has been delineated by the floral pattern definitely outlining its corners and holding the eye within this area. Together, the two asymmetrical arrangements give perfect symmetry. It is interesting to use them in pairs, thus giving formal balance. When decorating for formal dinner parties or receptions, a candelabrum or statuette may be used in the center of the table and flanked with an arrangement to either side or to either end of the table.

In Plate 80, twelve roses have been arranged to show full looks-value. The pattern is the same as shown in Plate 71 except that when line flowers form the pattern, one line flower is equivalent to 2, 3, or even 4 mass flowers. The remaining mass flowers are positioned within the skeleton, in such a way that no two round forms are on exactly the same horizontal plane. In addition, the larger more open roses are placed in the center to strengthen the focal area. In this design the irises with their receding color serve as filler between the roses and they create depth in the design. This design technique allows less expensive short stemmed flowers to be combined with more expensive long stemmed ones.

Plate 77   (circa 1986)
Queen Protea
An asymmetrical triangle has been produced with flax, ti and salal foliage. The protea provides a focal point while the heather emphasizes the vertical line of flax.

Plate 78   (circa 1986)
Asymmetrical Paradox
The vertical exclamation
point of liatris combines with
a crescent of anemones to
form this asymmetrical
triangle. The variegated ti
leaves add weight to the left
point.

Plate 79 (circa 1966)
Parenthesis — A matching
pair of asymmetrical
triangles frame an object and
create perfect symmetry
overall.

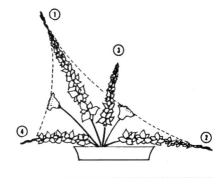

(Figure 12C)
Asymmetrical triangle – scalene; No. 3 blossom is placed either within the angle or toward the front.

Plate 80 (circa 1966)
Roses and Iris
Blue iris adds contrast in color and form to pink roses with an accent of lycopodium.

Plate 81 (circa 1986)
Cabbage Rose
A purple cabbage that has been deeply cut six ways and submerged in water for 5 hours, allowing it to expand into the shape of a giant rose, makes a dramatic focal point. Liatris and tulips establish the scalene lines.

Asymmetrical Triangle - Scalene

The other asymmetrical pattern derived from the triangle is called the *scalene*, named from the triangle whose angles are unequal. The axis is not perpendicular to the base, but is on the oblique beginning with the high side, terminating at the frog and indicating the direction of the lower side. The scalene lends itself beautifully to the placement of natural branching materials from spring blossoms to autumn berries. The informal reach, extension and flow combine beautifully with driftwood, cornucopias, baskets, sea shells and vines. In Figure 12C, we see a typical scalene line skeleton- the basic triangle appears to lean. This particular design carries the eye and leaves much to the imagination, giving the appearance of having a greater quantity of flowers than is actually used. Its pleasing, sweeping motion stems from the absence of stiff right angles in the lines forming the skeleton.

The No. 1 blossom or line is placed off center to the high side, and leans backwards. Depth is gained by this placement. No. 2 stem is shorter and more fully developed; it gives weight. It is placed over the edge of the container in a horizontal position, uniting the container with the arrangement. The No. 3 branch or flower extends downward over the rim of the container and its length is based on the visual counterbalance needed for the number 1 and 2 stems. The No.4 material must draw the eye into the focal area. It must be kept low but at the same time it functions as a way to create depth, Plate 81. The scalene design lends itself beautifully to driftwood designs and Thanksgiving and harvest arrangements of flowers, fruits and vegetables, and berry branches.

Vertical

From the discussion of line, Chapter 2, we learn the various effects this element has on our senses. Patterns in floral design derived from the use of line have emotional appeal. The vertical line is associated with perfect equilibrium, or a soldier at attention. Severe vertical arrangements act like exclamation points! They are dramatic and demand attention (Plates 82, 83, and 84). When linear flowers or foliage are not used to create the vertical pattern, this design may be developed by the placement of mass or form flowers in sequence in either a straight or curved line.

Plate 83
Jet Propulsion – This interpretive vertical not only demands attention, it holds the eye with its interesting basing details.

◄Plate 82
Vertical Odyssey – The straight gladiola spikes repeat the lines of the container perfectly, but the height necessary to create the golden proportion was added with the chinaberry branch, which also frames the two precious flowers and repeats the gold color on the container.

Plate 84 (circa 1986.)
Oriental Extreme
The undulating curly willow draws the eye down to a timid focal flower. The antique bronze usabata legs reflect the character of the curly willow.

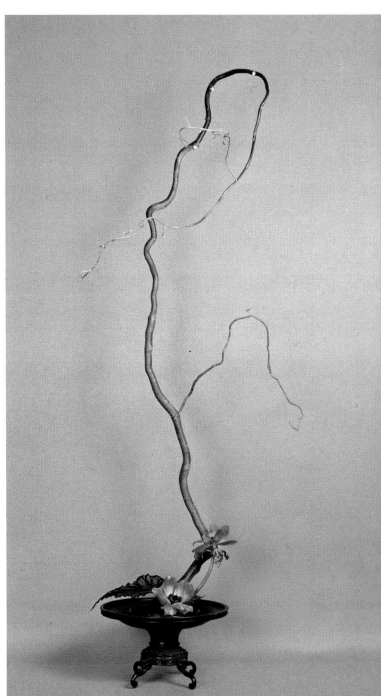

Plate 85
Rose Plateau — The clear
plane of rose heads at the
top of this design is
dramatic. It looks sharp,
yet there are some softer
features at the base. This
vertical design is a very
forceful presentation of
roses.

It is possible to design a dozen roses in a vertical pattern (Plate 85). A block of wet foam allowing enough room for a reservoir of water has been anchored into a watertight plastic liner inside the basket. Twelve roses of identical stem length have been inserted into the wet foam to create a distinctive contemporary composition. An interesting piece of weathered wood bisects the vertical line creating a transition from container to flowers. The serpentine ribbon treatment repeats the horizontal lines of the rose heads, the wood and the basket edges, producing unity. The color of the ribbon accent harmonizes the foliage and the wood with the blossoms.

Horizontal

Horizontal arrangements are interesting as an occasional variation from the usual patterns. The height-to-width-to-length relationships should fall into the 3-5-8 ratio. If the vertical line is too high the dominance of the lateral extensions will be spoiled. These designs may be used on dining room and coffee tables, on mantels under mirrors and paintings, or on occasional tables where lamps cast their glow over the blossoms (Plate 86). In designing for narrow tables, as in banquet halls where space is limited and conversation is the dominant feature, horizontal designs are most effective. The length of a design is set by the flower's extension to either side from the focal point, and symmetrical or asymmetrical balance is acceptable. At the center of interest, the materials used are either in clusters, groups or in single mass. Either will add the necessary weight at the focal point (Plate 1).

The container will largely regulate the development of a horizontal design. A cornucopia used for a Thanksgiving table is an excellent example. This container suggests a bountiful harvest overflowing onto the board. Fruit and flowers will follow the line of this container in a smooth easy manner. The larger material should be used nearest the mouth of the container, with the small fruit or line material repeating the point of the cornucopia at the end of the arrangement. Conch shells also lend themselves to this design, as do shallow bowls whose sides flow outward.

Family heirlooms made of silver and crystal are exquisite when designed with a horizontal pattern (Plate 88). In Plate 87 the weight and volume of the weathered wood "basket" governs the free-form extensions of beech foliage and berried branches. The open roses grouped over the contrasting moss draws the eye into the focal area of this decorative design of natural materials.

Plate 86 (circa 1966)
Audubon Print
The horizontal lines in the arrangement and color of the flowers accent the charm that Audubon captured in this American flamingo.

Plate 87
Woodland Tapestry – The weight and volume of the weathered wood "basket" governs the free-form extension of beech foliage and berried branches. Strands of gold bullion and a few "shooting" twigs add a touch of the unexpected.

To summarize this chapter on geometric design the *first* step in arranging flowers is to develop a mental picture of the shape of the piece that is to be made. The *second* step is to establish this shape with the skeleton flowers; these flowers may be of any type. The *third* step is the addition of secondary flowers and foliage within the established pattern.

Additional blossoms, irrespective of their type, or accessories, are placed within this framework and form the body of the design. Filler flowers are added last, especially if they are very delicate; they contribute to the depth of the design and eliminate voids. These are usually inexpensive and are never used where they will hide the main flowers. Placing filler flowers too high or too far forward causes them either to cover or to subdue the main blossoms.

In connection with designs that we have been discussing, we only mentioned the skeleton *flowers* - those establishing the actual framework. This framework may also be made with *foliages* that have specific charac-ter, or with accessory material, such as driftwood. When fo-liage is being added to an arrangement where flowers set the pattern, keep in mind that the foliage takes the *same* skeleton shape established by these flow-ers. Foliages must be handled carefully; beautiful arrangements are often destroyed by foliage, which chokes or dominates the design. There must be space between flowers and fo-liage. Too often, inexperienced persons will try to cover mistakes in their work by filling the void with a ribbon bow or continuing to add flowers or foliage, when the error really lies in the skeleton of the design. It is a very expensive and poor habit to cram a container with foliage and then try to create the desired effect with flowers.

Plate 88 (circa 1966)
Galax–Roses
The French ornate silver bowl holds bunches of fresh white grapes and galax–roses with accent lines of ivy.

GENERAL SUGGESTIONS:

1. Have a mental picture of the design before trying to arrange - this will save hours of time and damage to the flowers and foam.
2. In poor designing, when it just does not "look right" - the fault is generally with the placement of one of the first three stems-the skeleton or foundation. Always stand back from your design and scrutinize it for correct balance and proportion before continuing on.
3. Crowding detracts; let each flower retain its individuality except when clustering. *Abstract and Interpretive design*: flowers may be massed for color, texture, or form.
4. In traditional design multiple centers of interest are confusing. There should be only one, and it should be where the lines converge. Do not have a "bull's-eye" development at this point. *Abstract and Interpretive design*: need not have the well-defined center of interest that is desirable in geometric patterns.
5. In geometrical design the container either blends with or is subordinate to the arrangement. *Abstract and Interpretive design*: the container may be the featured point of interest, with flowers only an enhancement.
6. Geometric Design: the top margin of the container is broken by allowing foliage or flowers to flow over the edge to add unity. *Abstract and Interpretive design*: the margin of the receptacle may be completely visible.
7. Attain balance without perfect symmetry, thus preventing rigid formality, when a feeling of naturalness is desired.
8. Strong lines, heavy colors or open blossoms used low give stability and balance.
9. Alternating flowers or colors will give a "salt and pepper" appearance and this will lessen the impact on, and confuse the eye.
10. Combinations of colors and materials may be unexpected and in strong contrast, but they must follow some logical reasoning.
11. Take advantage of the natural curves and lines in flowers, foliage and branches. Such awareness adds grace and beauty; creativity is expressed. Distinction is gained.
12. Keep form flowers prominent and well spaced. Generally, only one or a few of this type should be used in an arrangement. Do not crowd them.
13. Arrangements for round tables should have three points horizontally. Two will bisect, dividing the table in half. Four points will form an "X," which is poor design.
14. When using a few flowers in a design, group them smartly to achieve a greater impact on the eye.
15. Do not use a transparent container for a design when using stems that decay in water.
16. Mechanics (foam) in traditional design must be hidden, but in contemporary work mechanics like metallic wire and raffia etc., may be exposed as part of the design.
17. Flower arrangements for exhibition or competition purposes, must comply with the rules of the organization, even though a designers creative ability may be somewhat restricted.
18. Eliminate from stems, foliage that deteriorates under water as this will invite bacteria to grow and clog the stems, preventing water uptake.
19. Ribbons have a rightful place in arrangements for festive occasions, but they are no substitute for flowers. When a bow is used it should be placed skillfully into the flowers at the focal point or used as an accent. Wired ribbons are best used in interesting serpentine effects with the ends turned upward as if floating on air.
20. Hospital arrangements must be cheerful and pleasant. Do not send flowers that shed quickly (e.g., larkspur); they create undue work for the hospital staff. Flowers with strong odors become objectionable quickly in small hospital rooms. The more upright designs generally fit better into hospital rooms since space is usually limited. Be informed of hospital regulations.
21. Fresh fruit and vegetables may be anchored into designs by piercing them with one or more wood picks. It is always best to use types that will not deteriorate quickly.

Bunches of grapes may be threaded with medium gauge wire that is twisted around the stem leaving both ends of wire as long as possible. Both the wood picks and long wires should be inserted at a sharp downward angle deep into the foam for security.

22. Use plastic liners in silver, fine china, antiques and objects d'art. Do not risk damaging any container with adhesive tape, clay, glue, wire or any other mechanical aids.

Chapter 8   FORMALINEAR DESIGN

The term Formalinear (Formal-linear; Formal Linear) came to the United States from Holland and Germany in the 1980's. The closest word to Formalinear in our own vocabulary was "High Style", and everyone had a different idea of what that meant. Formalinear has a specific definition: *it is an asymmetrically balanced design of interesting materials, each of which is few in number and usually grouped, that emphasizes forms and lines.* Generous use of space accentuates the individual flowers, leaves, stem angles, colors and textures. Radial stem placement is typical. High style was a catch-all word that included almost any modern design that had strong lines, forms and colors. Because of the uncertainty of how to define high style, formalinear quickly became integrated into our vocabulary (Plates 7 and 9). Check the following criteria against these plates for a clear understanding of this design style:

(Plate 7)
Classic Formalinear

1. Reduce the amount of materials to a minimum. Too many lines confuses the eye and too many colors and forms creates hodge-podge.
2. Don't use too many quantities or types of material.
3. Foliage is just as important as flowers and plays the same role.
4. Asymmetrical balance is typical.
5. Radial stem placement is typical.
6. Pay close attention to the natural expression (visual appearance, attitude) of the materials so they can be used to their best advantage.
7. Consider the amount of space required by each component to showcase it.
8. Strong color contrasts can increase the impact of both the individual components and the entire design.
9. Formalinear may have vegetative characteristics, but forms and lines must dominate.
10. Similar surface textures are not placed next to each other.
11. Strong forms usually have long stems allowing them to extend to the outer limits of the design, but they may also be cut short to create a dramatic focal point.
12. Formalinear designs must be displayed in front of plain or muted backgrounds that won't compete for attention.

(Plate 9)
Soaring in Space

In summary, successful formalinear designs are built on contrast and its constituents: variation, opposition and tension. Harmony and unity definitely play secondary roles in this style of design.

Chapter 9
PARALLEL DESIGN

Parallelism is a relatively new design theory in which all stem placements run in the same direction. In nature this concept is familiar to us in fields of corn and wheat. We also see bamboo, equisetum and many water-loving plants growing in this manner. Plate 36 presents a simple but compelling image of calla lilies designed according to this concept. Obviously, this is an excellent format in which to present a single kind of material. A more specific definition of parallel design *affirms that it is a concept in which the individual stems or groups of stems are placed in the same direction, and are always the same distance apart from end to end*. There are no major components that have radiating lines; however at the base there may be various basing materials radiating outward.

Parallel design offers opportunities for extreme simplicity as in Plate 89. In this design negative space has almost as much value as the flowers; it gives relief from competition and allows the flowers to dominate as they "grow" upward from the rectangular-shaped container, showing the influence of the Oriental moribana style. The harmony of container, background, color, texture and flowers is so blended that the mood and theme become one. Simplicity is the key-

(Plate 36)
Parallel Placement – These graceful "organ pipes" make an arresting monofloral presentation. The fresh mushrooms at the base create a transition between the austere calla lilies and the ornate container without interfering with either personality.

note. Unity in this illustration, shows how the smaller right-hand grouping of flowers, aided by the open space, has almost equal importance with its neighbor to the left.

Often the growth of the plant material suggests the pattern. It is important to see these possibilities and take advantage of their shapes. In Plate 90, a fascinating composition of allium and iris form this graphic design. The angular growth of the allium (garlic) stem suggests a parallel formation. This design reveals how the unusually shaped garlic stem turns radial stem placement into a parallel design!

Plate 91 combines two design styles: vegetative and parallel. It is properly called a vegetative parallel design because the overall concept is parallel, especially since the individual roses and gerberas are parallel to each other. However the two major groupings of pink larkspur and cattail leaves each emerge from a "growth point" (vegetative) in addition to being parallel to each other. As we have shown, parallel designs offer opportunities for variation, another being illustrated in Plate 92. This is a decorative parallel design, so named because the stems are placed like organ pipes into a classical container leaving no room for space. This design clearly combines the historic preference for mass into a parallel concept. There is a clear example of Phi, the 3-5-8 proportion in the use of texture: linear equisetum = 3; frilly delphinium = 5; and the smoother surfaces of vase and roses = 8. Even the volumes of color express Phi: blue-violet = 3; white = 5; and the total amount of green foliage = 8.

Simple parallel designs are shown in this chapter, but sometimes there is a need to create a larger, more complex series of parallel designs that become components in a more extensive presentation. This would be known as a parallel system.

Plate 89 (circa 1986)
Parallel Lines —The distinct parallel lines of liatris and lilac establish the rectangular pattern of this stylized contemporary design.

Plate 90 (circa 1958)
Graphic Parallel —This is a dramatic example of why it is so important to let the plant material tell the designer what to do. We may never again see a garlic stem shaped like this one!

Plate 91
Integrated Placement —
This is a vegetative parallel
design that combines both
radial and parallel stem
placements. The effect of
parallelism dominates.

Plate 92
Decorative Parallel — The
complete omission of
space in this design makes
it look very heavy, very
ornamental. It could also
be called a massed parallel
design.

GENERAL SUGGESTIONS

1. The majority of materials (individuals or groups) must be placed parallel to each other.
2. The dominate parallel lines may be vertical, horizontal or diagonal.
3. The composition must clearly express a type of balance: symmetrical or asymmetrical.
4. There may be many like materials, many different materials, or there can be few materials.
5. Parallel designs may be classified as vegetative, decorative, graphic or simply parallel.
6. Spaces between individual components or groupings are very important and must be properly achieved.
7. The color, form and textural relationships between the materials must correctly illustrate the intent of the entire design.
8. Proportion and directional movement of lines are important.
9. Purposely crossed lines can increase the effect. These may be connecting lines that unite one area to another.
10. Basing materials and effects may add interest, but they must not dominate the design. See the mushrooms in Plate 89.

Chapter 10   FREE FORM –
INTERPRETIVE DESIGN

In 1960 Buddy Benz wrote, "Floral art today has reached a milestone marking its maturity. This art stands at the threshold of the greatest advancement of its history through the introduction of a new trend — *Free Form—Interpretive Design*. The principles that guided floral art in the past, through their continued usage, became set rules. These rules were necessary for growth and expansion, to teach the novice, and to point the way. Moreover, they set a standard of excellence by which to judge artistic quality."

In the forty years since Mr. Benz recorded those words, there have been rapid advances in the social sciences, industrial environment, and manner of living and thinking. Society has become matured. With this maturity comes the ability to accept, to understand, and to use in daily living, unbridled freedom of thought and expression. This freedom has been responsible for great developments in floral art. It is today's mode of living, concept of distance, time, and space that affect current floral design. This new concept of floral design is influenced by space: form cutting its own design in atmosphere. Traveling was once held to earth's surface; the airplane released man. Then came travel by jet that released distance. Having passed supersonic speed, and then into space by missile — man is ready to grasp the universe.

American floral designers have been open to influences from other societies, particularly those of Europe and the Orient. A new vocabulary that describes both the beauty and function of form and the newest design techniques, must be understood to appreciate the extent of floral art.

Free–form design is *a style of creative design inspired by unconventional ideas, styles and patterns yet adhering to the elements and principles of design.* There is no geometric pattern in free form design. The second term, Interpretive, is defined as *the organization of design elements to suggest a given theme, idea, occasion, mood or atmosphere.* The two terms used together imply a freedom of expression with a particular design goal in mind.

In the category of free form–interpretive design styles, there are two groups: *realistic* and *non-realistic.*

FIRST — *Realistic* interpretive design follows the dictates of nature and tradition, though free of geometric pattern and its rules of organization. This is most pleasing for one is accustomed to its design. The deviation from accepted form has not been too great. One feels at ease with this design and readily understands the meaning of the theme. Like many contemporary works of art, these designs are appreciated for what they are: color, texture, pattern

and interesting use of space. The arrangement has beauty and is appreciated not only for design of functional form and suitability of purpose, but for the intrinsic value of the materials themselves. The beautiful curve of a branch, flower, or cabbage leaf for that matter, is complete within itself, or it may be combined with other features if desired.

In Plate 93, an elegant interpretation of "Mr. McGregor's Cabbage Patch", the intrinsic value of the materials lies in the colors and textures of individual members of a family — the Cruciferae family. Yes, stock is a member of the cabbage family! The leaf pattern on the container is a reflection of the cabbage leaf focalized just above it, accentuating the theme.

The flowing composition in Plate 94 showcases the natural characteristics of each of its components by releasing the lines and forms from the restriction of geometric pattern. This freedom, which is typical of so many interpretive designs gives rise to the term

Free–Form — Interpretive Design which was coined by Buddy Benz. In Plate 94 notice how the asymmetry of spilling foliage, concentration of pavéd roses, the plush moss, and the rich brilliance of the gold buillon interpret the "harvest– holding cornucopia" in a unique and unexpected manner.

Floral materials are being appreciated today the same as cherished objects of art. The great architect, Frank Lloyd Wright, blended functional form and natural surroundings with such harmony that natural transition from one material to the other added emphasis to each. Free–form designing also recognizes the built–in values of form, texture, color, etc., and blends all units into a harmonious whole. Simplification in presentation is one of the keynotes. In Plate 95, the definite shapes of the chinaberry and gladiolas are the objects of importance. Their strong lines create beauty and pattern as they ascend into space. See Plate 108 for an excellent example of *Realistic* interpretive design.

SECOND – *Non–realistic* interpretive design is the unusual use of materials producing form that is striking and bizarre with no illusion to reality; approaching the abstract. Objects in this category are used to produce effect. Flowers give color, texture or form – not considering the blossoms in their natural state as such. True creative ability finds expression in emotion and inspiration. The term "abstract" is used in this writing to explain the use of materials in an unnatural manner but not to the point of being grotesque.

Plates 96 and 97 offer two more variations of interpreting a container. In both examples we, again, see forms instead of flowers. The yellow–orange marigolds have been clustered to produce one very bold textured form. A single contrasting material in each design adds interest, emphasis, accent, or tension – depending on how you see it. Careful study and knowledge of materials, with thorough training in basic elements and principles, and logical planning, are requirements for creating successful works of interpretive design.

Plate 94
Woodland Tapestry – One expects to find treasures when walking in the woods: moss, mushrooms, a perfect leaf. This experience is interpreted with roses, gold bullion and berries.

Plate 95   (circa 1970)
Vertical Odyssey – Each material expresses it's own personality.

Plate 96
Mushroom – This non-realistic expression of flowers leads one to see a floral object, not flowers. This design could be called volumetric.

Plate 97
Mushroom with Green Cap – A fanciful title for a fanciful design! What do you see?

In contemporary work a structural purity is found, with a clear definition of form and bold frankness of expression. This freedom of design is made possible by the acceptance of the allied arts giving impetus to floral design, e.g., music, dance, painting and architecture may inspire the floral artist. In Plate 98, we see a "living sculpture", not a bouquet. The important but small circular opening in the black ceramic container is emphasized by the placement of many solid circular forms above it. The golden crespedias are seen as colored forms, not flowers. A single lavender liatris offers both contrast and unity – contrast of color, unity in its repetition of the strong vertical lines of the container.

Plate 98
Positive/Negative, Ying/Yang – In this non-realistic free-form interpretive sculpture, the flowers are secondary to the container. The round hole in the container (negative space) echoes the round crespedias (positive space).

Plate 99
Poised Bird – A birds' head appears to be emerging from its wings in accordance with the principles of Cubism, which are illustrated by the flattening and superimposing of planes, and the polyhedral fragmentation of volumes.

Chapter 11   ABSTRACT DESIGN

Understanding the word "abstract" should not be difficult for we have been experiencing the act of "abstracting" every day of our lives – since we were children. Remember, as a child, looking at the clouds moving across the sky – and seeing elephants; seeing the face of a monster in an old gnarled tree trunk?

Abstract: To take from, e.g., materials removed from nature and use in an unexpected form to emphasize a point; copper tubing removed from the plumber's shelf and placed in a glass vase to create a serpentine line embracing anthurium blossoms.

Abstract: *Non–realistic use of natural or man–made materials solely as elements of pure line, form, color, texture, in space, to create new images. Abstract design gives form to vision by expressing emotion through an intellectual process.* The degree to which abstractions evolve depends upon the imagination of the *viewer* as well as the artist, for the eye can only see what the mind understands. Imagination is the result of an individual's keen insight, experience, education and skill. The function of an artist is to help one see (understand) the work created – not to convince or change opinion; to open broader vistas, giving new meaning to the familiar; to increase one's awareness and appreciation of order (beauty) in the mundane.

Abstract design has evolved through a series of progressive steps of traditional designs as outlined in the following:

Classic — established standard of excellence; timeless; work of enduring worth as influenced by ancient Greece or Rome;

Romantic — is visionary, strongly emotional, passionate, dominated by beauty;

Realistic — is a faithful reproduction of nature, photographic, objective, with one point perspective; seeing the world as it is – everyday themes;

Geometric — reflects perfect order; definite mathematical and geometric design; was developed from geometric patterns (circles, triangles, cones, etc.);

Free Form – Interpretive Design — is pure design, which evolves its own concept, independent of preconceived patterns; intrinsic value expressed in aesthetic beauty; expressive, with unlimited imagination;

Abstract — is visionary, intuitive, reflecting the essence of purity in line, form, color, and texture in space – expressing rhythm and emotion through an intellectual process.

Beauty is abstract – spiritual. It cannot be defined. Beauty is that illusive aesthetic quality that gives pleasure to the senses or pleasurably exalts the mind or spirit; a quality of loveliness that varies with one's taste. It is relative, functional in form, and it approaches the ultimate in perfection. Beauty is truly in the eyes of the beholder.

Style is transitory, the expression of a time or period; the outgrowth of preference, motif, fashion, and materials; a distinctive, characteristic mode of presentation.

In creating an abstract design, the floral artist must take natural forms and use them to develop his design free of the natural growing habits of plant life. He may start with objective material, the symbol of whose form remains fixed to past remembrances, and reshape it, or mass it, for form, color, and texture, in a non–realistic manner to achieve results. Or, he may choose material that is familiar, or even exotic and strange, and though it is used with great imagination, the recognized form remains.

Since this art is no longer hampered by set rules, abstract arrangements can be approached with an open mind. Thus, true creative ability finds expression in the unfolding of ideas.

Plate 100
Double Talk – Are these two arguing, gossiping or sharing a secret?

Plate 101
Spider in Her Web – This is strictly "non-realistic use of natural and man-made materials" The succulent is made of leather!

(Plate 2)
Fruit and Flowers.

Part 3
Design Components

Chapter 12   CONTAINERS

Today's mode of living has completely changed ideas of the word "container." Traditionally, the container was a utilitarian receptacle for holding something (either liquids, grains, fruit or flowers), or an object of art (Wedgwood, Dresden, or Sevrés porcelain). Interior trends and new concepts of design have opened unlimited

(Plate 17)
Monochromatic Color Harmony.

(Plate 25)
Symmetrical Balance.

(Plate 27)
Asymmetrical Beauty.

vistas in the search for so-called "containers". There is freedom of choice and unrestricted scope as to what constitutes a container. The traditional and utilitarian type are familiar; they are seen everywhere. But the use of the unusual, free form, even unique containers that cause excitement is what contemporary styles demand.

The container is an integral part of any flower arrangement. It is the starting point or foundation on which the three-dimensional picture is built. What kind of a container is just right? What constitutes *"Suitability"?* It is a big word in floral art and covers a multitude of conditions. The suitability of a container contributes to the proper mental attitudes necessary to accomplish the final results. Whether for the home, church, or other display, the container must be studied for suitability. Visualize the container in use before choosing one. A really "good" container is one that is a pleasure to use; it fits well into its surroundings and lends itself to various types of designs. Practical value is vital; price is not always a criterion.

Traditional or conventional design never allows a container to dominate a composition (Plates 2, 17, 25, 27). The flowers, the container, and the decor of the room must complement each other. Containers must not "steal the show" in conventional designing, but may be the featured part in contemporary design (Plates 20, 24, 101 and 102). A simple, tailored-to-fit, unadorned container may often be

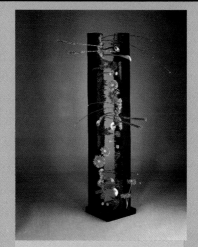

(Plate 20)
Triadic Color Tower.

(Plate 24)
Unexpected Simplicity.

Plate 102   (circa 1986)
Henry the Clam –
An underwater environment
is called for by the abstract,
hand–built ceramic
container. Directional
movement is expressed by
the placement of finger
sponges, foliage, and
hand–crafted tropical fish
– to impart the feeling of
ocean currents.

more effective than the ornate, highly decorative pieces (Plates 32, 68 and 103). Containers with good, simple design, curved or straight line, and of muted color, will be the most popular ones. Undesirable containers are those that either present a problem of balance or create a second center of interest. Similarly, the container that has a large mouth opening and decreases in size toward the bottom with no additional base is also undesirable. This type will appear top-heavy when the flowers are placed in it and will create an uneasy feeling. Visual balance as well as mechanical balance is lost.

In *Free Form-Interpretive Design,* it may be the container that is featured. In such cases all materials are subordinated to accent the intrinsic value of this object.

A container can create atmosphere through association and thus complete harmony to unify the composition. A classic urn

(Plate 32)
Tropical Concert.

Plate 103   (circa 1986)
Diagonal Rhythm – The rustic crock blends with the dried composition, which exhibits rhythmic lines and asymmetrical balance.

(Plate 68) (circa 1986) Spring Pyramid – The containers in plates 103 and 68 are made of heavy ironstone. The floral materials in both designs have been brought downward over the rims to reduce the visual impact and create better visual proportion.

is immediately associated with the Empire period, or the French or Italian Renaissance. Iron kettles, bean pots, and other culinary utensils are reminiscent of the Early American period and often imply casual living. A pumpkin container establishes a fall idea for Thanksgiving or Halloween. Half of a fresh watermelon used as a "bowl" with flowers arranged in it will be suitable for a patio party. Free form vases or bowls that are angular and strong in color or texture are associated with contemporary design. Thus, the mood and emotional response to a design may be established by featuring a container. The associative value of the container has great significance in floral designing.

The *Weight* of the container, either actual weight (e. g., pottery, brass, iron, or bronze) or the apparent visual weight (e. g., dark colors and heavy texture) affects the proportion of the arrangement to the size of the container. Pottery gives the appearance of having more weight than fine china. Pewter, iron, and bronze are heavier in actual weight than pottery or crystal of the same shape. Also the color of a container will change its apparent visual weight, e. g., a dark receptacle equal in size and shape to a light colored one will appear heavier.

In a heavy container of either pottery, metal, or earthenware, one can exceed the standard proportion of $1^1/_2 :1$ or the Golden Proportion. Good judgment guides in this case. The fine quality of bone china or clear crystal will hold a design within the limits of the accepted proportions of $1^1/_2 :1$. This concept is so close to the Golden Proportion (1.68:1) that they are considered to be one and the same. Refer to Proportion in Chapter 3 for a complete explanation.

The *Lines* of the container may often dictate the lines of the arrangement, thus determining the floral composition. Unity is apparent in such instances. By following these lines suggested by the container, logical movement and rhythm are created; the arrangement comes alive. When a water pitcher is used as a container, one visualizes the flow of liquid over the lip. This curved line establishes the line of the flower arrangement. The flowers should follow the direction indicated by the lip, thus completing the mental picture, which the mind's eye formulates on seeing this type of receptacle.

Color plays an important part in container selection. It must either blend or contrast with the floral material or with the decor of the room. When the color of the container blends with the main flowers, it will tend to fade into the background harmoniously; or if there is a contrast, the color will enhance the design.

Clear crystal containers are fascinating to use and are a challenge to the designer. Unusual design effects can be displayed, presenting dramatic conversation arrangements. During the Victorian era, glass domes were popular for dried flower arrangements. A somewhat similar effect is obtained today when one is designing within clear crystal containers. There are a great number of clear glass containers available, e.g., cylinders, ginger jars, bubble bowls, rectangular blocks, etc.

Novelty containers or ones with decorative motifs are always popular when the occasion demands, e.g., hearts for Valentine's Day, bride and groom for weddings, animals for circus parties. Interest and enthusiasm are as high with adults as with children. Novelties can be used to set the theme for an occasion. In planning a flower arrangement, each detail must be coordinated and harmonious with flowers and setting. The idea expressed in containers must be suitable. Plate 104 shows a loaf of French bread used as the container and accented with spaghetti to set the theme for a bistro party. In Plate 105 the soft-sculpture cradle, which holds a waterproof liner makes a charming novelty container for celebrating the birth of a new baby. When planning a festive occasion, select one of the units for a dominant feature and subordinate all other details. Study the characteristics of the chosen

Plate 104 (circa 1986) French Bread – Red carnations and spaghetti are arranged in a small cup that is placed into the loaf of French bread. All is tied with a bandanna and ready to celebrate a spaghetti dinner.

container, the meaning it portrays, its design features, and then use the flowers and foliage to emphasize these characteristics. The feature has value of its own, and this feature must be clearly visible when the design is completed. When flowers cover the novelty, its value is lost; the flowers and novelty must be a single unit.

Plate 105 (circa 1986)
Drifting Cradle –
The soft–sculptured cradle looks as if it is wafting along to the gentle tug of the balloons. The cradle, balloons, ribbons and flowers are in perfect alignment with the imaginary breeze.

Accessories

Accessories are accent objects, or items sometimes necessary for the completion of a harmonious composition. Driftwood, orbs, medallions, dried materials, mirrors, fruit, etc. are included in this category. They add interest to designs and help to "set the stage" or theme. A note of authenticity is given the composition by their use (Plate 102). Any accessory should stimulate the imagination. It should tell a story, set the mood, or complete the idea. It must be an integral part and harmonize in all aspects. An accessory may often supply a needed element, e.g., add weight for balance, add accent line, or give necessary color, etc. Use restraint in the choice of accessory materials; if they do not contribute full value, leave them out. Avoid stereotyped, monotonous use of figurines; dullness is imparted when they are over-used; originality is destroyed.

For those accessories that have definite lines and motion, it is important that these lines follow the pattern set by the flowers. They must either flow with the motion in the arrangement or carry the eye back into the design. Should a round mirror or tray be used, the main lines follow the edges, suggesting circular motion. The accessory should feel "at home" in its place. Dry land objects should not be used in water nor should aquatic types be combined with cacti.

Accessories should be firmly and securely attached to the design or be obviously independent. Depressions in the floral foam in combination with a wooden pick fence surrounding the accessory base or a more permanent attachment with pan glue and wooden picks may be used. Protect the bases of water-sensitive accessories from the moisture of floral foam with polyfoil, plastic bags or cellophane wrap prior to use.

(Plate 108)   (circa 1970)
Accessory.

(Plate 24)
Unexpected Simplicity.

Bases

Bases add importance to an arrangement. A base produces the same effect of completion in the composition as a frame contributes to a painting, a pedestal to a sculptured piece, or a floor covering to a room. Careful selection will enhance the design and give dignity where only a common place feeling existed until the base was added. The base or pedestal may be considered a part of the container, as in Plates 13 and 24.

When weight is needed, it can be gained by the use of bases. They may be small Oriental tables, pedestals of classical designs, mirrored plaques, discs of various types, bamboo mats, segments of tree trunks, or whatever the occasion dictates. A container that may have all the prerequisites for a design but is too light in visual weight can be made satisfying by the addition of a base.

Chapter 13
FLOWER AND FOLIAGE FORMS

Flower Forms

In all styles, shapes, and classifications of floral design, each flower has a definite shape. They should fit together with the same precision as does a good mechanical assembly. It is the combination of these forms that gives interest, imparts vitality, and prevents monotony. The recognition of these shapes will enable one to solve many design problems and prevent others from arising.

The four major groups of flower types are *line, mass, form, and filler.*

Figure 13
Line flowers – gladiolus, stock, cattail

Line flowers, Figure 13, are generally erect, tall spikes of blossoms with florets blooming along the stem. They give a feeling of length and definitely create linear pattern. This type of flower establishes pattern, sets proportion, and is the framework or skeleton on which the design is built. When measuring *line* flowers with the container, the buds beyond the half-opened blossoms on the upper portion of the stem are not counted in the pattern. Other flower types, when combined with *line* flowers are used lower, within the framework set by the line types. Gladiolus, larkspur, stock, delphinium, snapdragon, and cattail are examples of *line* flowers.

Figure 14
Mass flowers —rose, carnation, chrysanthemum

Mass flowers, Figure 14, are single stems with one solid head. They are usually placed toward the focal point within the framework of linear materials, adding volume to the design. When they are used alone in an arrangement, the buds or smaller ones are placed to the outer edges and farther apart. As the focal point is approached, larger *mass* flowers are placed closer together to add weight for stability. Vary the depths and heights of *mass* flowers so that each one reveals its individual shape, giving a feeling of depth to an arrangement. The chrysanthemum, dahlia, peony, rose, carnation, and aster are a few examples of *mass* flowers.

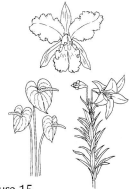

Figure 15
Form flowers – orchid, anthurium, lily

Form flowers, Figure 15, have distinctive shapes, a fact from which this group derives its name. Their intrinsic value lies in their characteristic forms. It is imperative that space be left between them if they are to remain individuals. They are sufficient unto themselves; other shapes may detract from them. *Form* flowers are frequently used in the focal area due to their strong individuality and distinctiveness. They are superior for this position. Some of them, such as bird-of-paradise, anthurium, and calla, have strong outlines and can be used as silhouette blossoms on the outer edges of an arrangement. Generally, they are more beautiful when used alone.

Filler flowers, Figure 16, may be either multi-branched or feathery and are used to "fill in" arrangements. They follow the pattern set by the main blossoms, but having less importance, are used in the background and low in the arrangement. They add emphasis to the main blossoms. The *branched fillers* are generally flowers having many stems with small mass-type heads; micro-mini spray chrysanthemums, spray asters, and feverfew are included in this group. The *feathery fillers,* gypsophila, caspia, or seafoam statice, are used like branched fillers but give a misty, delicate appearance to an arrangement. Other filler flowers are alstroemeria, miniature carnations, spray roses and regular spray mums.

In review of traditional design, it can be said that line flowers are used *"out,"* establishing the pattern; mass flowers are used *"toward"* the focal area within this framework; form flowers *"at"* the focal point: filler types used *"behind"* these main blossoms (Figure 17). Again, it can be said that any one group or combination of groups may be used in an arrangement. From studying several examples it is obvious how each of the four forms *(line, mass, form* and *filler)* plays its part in the design.

Abstract and Interpretive Design styles are not dictated to by the characteristic shapes of the four groups; the floral material is used for its intrinsic value, color, texture, etc., to meet the demands of the artist. Liberties are taken with blossoms and foliage to produce "abstract" effects and to express ideas. Flowers may lose their identity.

Foliage Forms

Foliage is appreciated today for its intrinsic value and interesting characteristics. Floral designers realize its great importance in design. Until recent years foliage was considered just an "extra," a secondary item of little importance that might be added. But today foliage components are gaining as much prominence as the flowers themselves. The scope of floral designing has been increased in recent years by the introduction of new plants, improved practices in handling, and availability. Architects and interior designers place much emphasis on the decorative value of green plants, thereby encouraging the use of interesting foliage in arrangements, and even all–foliage designs.

In summary then, it should be remembered that many foliages except the filler types have almost as much value as the flowers themselves. In fact, foliages of strong character and definite line may be used to set the pattern of a design (Plate 8).

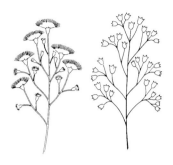

Figure 16
Filler flowers – spray aster, baby's breath, (bunch flowers)

Figure 17
Four types of flowers in combination – line flowers establishing "skeleton"; mass flowers used "toward" focal point; form flowers "at" focal point; filler flowers "behind" main blossoms

(Plate 8) (circa 1986)
Pairs Repeated – Four types of flowers and foliage are used in this composition: Curly willow and the column of ti leaves serve as line material, the tulips are mass flowers, the eggplant, allium and gerbera serve as form material, and the heather is filler. It is interesting to note that ti leaves alone are mass forms, but here they are fashioned into a line.

One lovely bridesmaid's bouquet is made of assorted foliages (Plate 106). The focal area is distinguished by a "rose" made of galax leaves. In Plate 107, the beautiful green ti leaves are looped and marshaled into a dramatic asymmetrical living sculpture. In Plates 5, 62, 77, and 108, foliage establishes the pattern; flowers and accessories do enhance the composition and may be changed without interfering with the design.

Plate 106 (circa 1966)
Foliage Potpourri — A crescent arrangement of foliages — galax rosettes are outlined with caladium and acuba leaves with sprays of tradescantia and variegated ivy.

Plate 107 (circa 1970)
Foliage Sculpture — Foliage of strong character is designed in a bold, asymmetrical pattern for a contemporary effect.

(Plate 5)
Exclamation Point!

(Plate 62)
Blue Hogarth.

(Plate 77)
Queen Protea.

In Plate 108, the entire echeveria plant is used at the focal point. The story of floral composition is built around this plant. The flowers are secondary; foliage is featured.

Foliage, like flowers, may be classified according to shape. First, *Linear* foliage adds strength and vitality, enhances line, imparts dignity, and adds soft curves. Some types are sword-like, e.g., bear grass, New Zealand flax, horsetail *(Equisetum)* and sanseveria (Figure 18), or they may branch freely but still give a linear effect lycopodium, scotch broom, tall myrtle and English ivy (Figure 19).

Plate 108 (circa 1970)
The Focal Point –
A strong focal point is established by the lines of the foliage and the anthuriums directing the eye to the echeveria rosette. The lines of the bamboo mat (base) and the carved wooden figure (accessory) direct the eye towards the focal area. All components in this design work together to create unity.

Figure 18
Sansevieria

Figure 19
Ivy – No. 1, English No. 2, Devil's ivy or philodendron

A second group of foliage is noted for its *Mass,* which, like mass flowers gives volume and adds weight to a composition. Magnolia, galax, aspidistra, and anthurium foliage are examples. Their broad surfaces form excellent backgrounds for blossoms. Wide and narrow leaf Chamadorea (Figures 20 and 21) when overlapped across the back of a design give the effect of mass foliages.

A third type of foliage is used for its *Form.* Its value is in its distinctive shape or brilliant coloring. Philodendron, strelitzia, spiral eucalyptus and caladium are examples (Figures 22, 23, 24).

The fourth group is of the *Filler* type. Some of the most popular are huckleberry, plumosus, leatherleaf, pittosporum, boxwood and lemon leaf or salal (Figure 25). Similar to filler flowers, this foliage is used primarily for background and to "fill in" the arrangement. It does not have enough character or importance to establish the pattern but is useful in blending units together.

The combination of flowers with their own foliage can rarely be improved upon. Such combinations give a natural look. When this is not feasible, select foliage which complements the flower in line, texture, color, etc. The strong forms of callas, anthurium, strelitzia, etc., require foliage of similar character. Delicate flowers, such as sweet peas, are arranged best with adiantum or other delicate foliages.

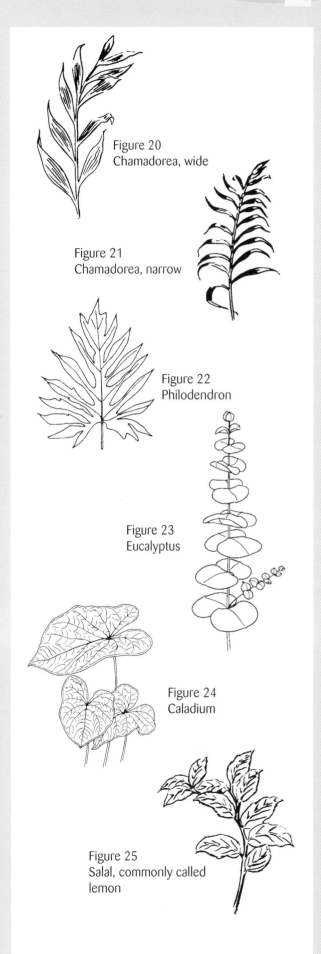

Figure 20
Chamadorea, wide

Figure 21
Chamadorea, narrow

Figure 22
Philodendron

Figure 23
Eucalyptus

Figure 24
Caladium

Figure 25
Salal, commonly called lemon

Chapter 14
CARE AND HANDLING OF CUT FLOWERS AND FOLIAGE

Good habits formed in the care and handling of cut flowers will pay big dividends in longer flower life. Whether flowers are purchased locally or transported great distances, the basic rules of flower care must be observed. Flowers represent a big investment in time and skill to bring them to their full beauty. Unless flowers serve their purpose and live the normal period of expectancy in an arrangement, all effort is lost.

Cut flowers and foliage, even though separated from the parent plant, are living, actively metabolizing plant parts. These parts undergo the same basic aging process as the entire plant - only more quickly. However, the rate of deterioration can be manipulated by supplying the cut flower with its basic needs. The first and foremost need of a cut flower is **water**. Second is **food**. In addition, certain damaging factors such as exposure to ethylene gas, microbial attack, and rough handling must be avoided.

From a practical point of view, a controlled rate of opening is needed as well as maintenance of good color. All of these factors must be considered by everyone who handles the product. This includes growers, wholesalers, and retailers. In order to be competitive in the marketplace, our product must be desirable to the consumer. Our flowers must have plenty of life left in them for the customer to enjoy!

Factors Affecting Quality

There are several factors which play a part in keeping the quality of cut flowers at a high level: 1. production; 2. transpiration; 3. floral food; 4. temperature; 5. humidity; 6. ethylene; and 7. microbial activity. While at first some of these factors seem more important than others, they are all so interrelated that it is difficult to determine which would be the most important.

Production

The grower plays a very important part in determining the post-harvest lasting qualities of cut flowers. The National Floriculture Conference on Commodity Handling says that it has been estimated that 70% of the post-harvest characteristics are pre-determined at harvest. In other words, the ultimate vase life of flowers may be determined by the plant's specific genetic qualities, growth environment and management practices. This estimation, even if high, should make us want to become aware of the practices and procedures that growers are using to produce cut flowers. Even if you provide optimum conditions for your flowers, it will not do much good if they are received from the grower in a state of poor condition.

Genetic

The genetic make-up of a flower can determine its lasting ability. The rose is one flower with which much work has been done to determine and produce only cultivars that have the longest vase life. This has been done out of necessity because of their popularity and their inherent short vase life. New varieties of roses typically have a vase life of 7-14 days compared to the older varieties' 3-5 days. Growers and geneticists are continuing their research on roses and many other cut flower crops to improve vase life through genetic manipulation.

Environmental

The environmental factors of greatest importance are spacing, light intensity, and temperature. The spacing of plants is important because, if spaced too closely, the amount of carbohydrates stored will be reduced. The amount of carbohydrates stored is the result of photosynthesis, and with plants closer together, the lower foliage receives less direct sunlight reducing the area that is able to efficiently photosynthesize. Low light levels also may cause substandard flower production; flowers would be fewer and of lower quality. Conversely, excessive light intensities may cause short "clubby" flowers with poor color. Finally, the growing temperature has an effect on vase life. Roses have an increased vase life if grown at 70 degrees F rather than at 60, or 80 degrees F. Not only does it affect the vase life of roses, but also flower pigmentation. There tends to be less intensity of color at higher temperatures.

Management

The grower's management practices, which have the most significant effect on the lasting quality of cut flowers, are the application of fertilizer and stage of harvest. While the plant needs the proper fertilizer to produce a flower of high quality, over fertilization can be detrimental. For example, too much nitrogen applied to chrysanthemums will decrease bloom size and shorten vase life, and increased potassium causes abnormally thick stems. Harvesting flowers too soon has as detrimental an effect on the keeping quality of cut flowers as harvesting too late. Flowers cut prior to their preferred harvest stage will have difficulty opening and maturing properly. It is likely that the tight buds will never open. These extremely tight buds are known as "bullheads" in roses. Also, cutting flowers past their prime harvest stage can greatly reduce vase life due to shipping damage of petals, inability to recover after dry shipping, and dehydration simply because the flowers are too mature.

Transpiration

Upon receiving the cut flowers, it is imperative to provide water immediately. The flowers should take up as much water as they are losing. The natural loss of water in plants and flowers is called **transpiration**. This occurs through small openings in the leaves and petals called stomata. Many flowers are lost through wilt or dehydration because moisture is transpired out of the flower quicker than it is taken in through the stem. A high level of moisture in the petals (turgidity) is necessary for the flowers to develop from a bud into a mature blossom. Transpiration is also the key physiological process by which the transport of post-harvest chemicals is facilitated. Replenishing water lost through transpiration establishes a continuously moving column of water inside the flower. This column of water carries the post-harvest chemicals throughout the flower so that they can serve their intended function; provide energy, restrict bacteria growth, etc. (see floral food section).

Floral Food

Once water balance has been established with a solution of water that is of reasonable quality, the next thing to establish is an energy source for the flower. Adding a commercial floral food to the water provides this energy source; sugar (usually dextrose). The sugar extends the vase life of flowers by replacing the natural sugars and carbohydrates that are used up by the flower, through bud opening, flower maturation, and general plant maintenance.

It is always important to provide the floral food, but now many growers are making a once-over harvest, rather than harvesting by hand and judging each flower as to its stage of maturity. Consequently, many tight buds are being cut and shipped. A sugar is needed as a source of carbohydrates for a bud to mature and fully open. (see floral food section for details).

Temperature

Another factor in determining vase life is temperature. A decreased storage temperature results in decreased respiration and transpiration, which in turn delays maturity, thereby resulting in a longer vase life. Respiration is actually the use of food (sugar) to release energy, produce growth, and maintain plant functions.

It has been found that cut roses, at a temperature of 60 degrees F, respire three times as fast as those at a temperature of 40 degrees F. The rate of respiration is six times faster at 77 degrees F than it is at 40 degrees. In other words, one day at 77 degrees is equivalent to six days at 40 degrees!

As can be seen, the refrigeration temperature plays an important role in determining vase life. However, not all flowers have the same optimum storage temperature. Because of these differences in temperature requirements, it would be ideal to have three coolers, one with a temperature of 34-36 degrees for roses, gardenias, and carnations, a second with a temperature of 38-42 degrees for gladioli, lilies, and chrysanthemums, and a third kept at 55-60 degrees for tropical flowers. As this may not be practical, one refrigerator set at 36-40 degrees would accommodate most flowers. Tropical flowers, due to their natural habitat are the exception to this guideline. They respond best to refrigeration temperatures no lower than 55 degrees.

An accurate thermometer is an essential tool for the proper care and handling of cut flowers and foliage. Measuring the temperature in the refrigerator is critical for optimal flower longevity. The use of a "high/low" thermometer that registers the highest and lowest temperature over a specified period of time will give a clear indication of the range of temperatures the flowers are exposed to. These are available from many electronic retail stores or from greenhouse suppliers.

Humidity

Temperature is not the only life-extending factor in the cooler. Humidity plays an important role in extending the vase-life of cut flowers by helping to conserve water loss from transpiration. A relative humidity of 90% is rec-ommended for most flowers stored in the refrigerator. Low humidity can actually pull moisture from your flowers and the shock of this dehydration will accelerate the aging process. This "pull" exists due to the fact that any high concentration of a substance diffuses down to equilibrium with a lower concentration. In plants and flowers, the substance is water and its high concentration inside plant tissue is "pulled" out (transpiration) to the lower concentration outside the plant. Thus, the higher the humidity around the plant, the less is the "pull" to equalize (transpire).

Ethylene

Even though cut flowers may be in a proper holding solution under ideal refrigeration, they are still susceptible to the death-inducing ethylene gas. Sources of ethylene gas include the normal healthy tissue of the flower, damaged foliage and diseased tissue, fruits, and incomplete combustion of fossil fuels. The symptoms of ethylene damage are... downward bending of leaves; premature withering or rapid development and aging; dropping of leaves, florets, or berries; yellowing of foliage; changes in petal coloring; and inward curving and closing of opened petals (sleepiness in carnations).

Carnations, roses, snapdragons and several varieties of orchids are sensitive to ethylene gas and fade as a result. Not all flowers fade in response to ethylene gas. Gladioli and chrysanthemums do not fade but suffer from a reduction in overall vase life.

There are several things that can be done to minimize ethylene damage:

A. STS pre-treatment (see Additional Care and Handling Treatments).
B. Ethylene block Treatment (see Additional Care and Handling Treatments).
C. Removal of damaged and unhealthy tissue since they are big ethylene producers.
D. Keep the refrigerator clean; do not allow

old flowers and foliage to be kept past their usefulness.

E. Do not store fruits, vegetables, or large quantities of evergreens in the refrigerator as many are major ethylene producers.

F. Ethylene production is affected by temperature. At temperatures of 40 degrees F. and below, ethylene production is greatly reduced. Also at cooler temperatures, it takes longer for the gas to damage the flowers.

Microbial Activity

Microbial activity, if allowed to exist, can reduce the vase life of cut flowers considerably. The bacterial organisms do their damage by plugging the stem of the flower. This plugging of the stem reduces the water intake capacity, which in-turn, shortens the vase life. These stem blockages usually occur in the lower 1-2 inches of the stem.

To prevent or keep the damage to a minimum, the best practice is good sanitation. Flower storage containers should be clean enough so that you would not object to drinking from them! After each use, the buckets should be washed and disinfected with bleach or bucket wash. The refrigerator floor should be washed once per week. All foliage should be removed from the lower stem that would be underwater in the storage container. Foliage that stays underwater will rot, producing harmful bacteria and releasing ethylene.

Secondly, the proper use of a commercial floral food can significantly reduce microbial growth and subsequently extend vase life. (see commercial floral food section)

Commercial Floral Food

There are many commercial floral foods available on the market. They come in a wide range of formulations designed for different types of water - i.e. hard water, pure water, etc. Retail florists, wholesale florists, and growers can best take advantage of a floral food's life-extending properties for cut flowers and foliage, by first testing their water to see which type of floral food would be most suitable for them. The major floral food manufacturers will test water samples and make the correct recommendation.

Ingredients

There are three main ingredients in commercial floral foods; **sugar**, **bio-inhibitor**, and an **acidifier**. The sugar used in many commercial preparations is dextrose, however glucose is also sometimes used. Sucrose, common table sugar, is rarely an ingredient in commercial floral food due to its high cost. The flower is a living organism and, like all living things, it requires a source of energy or food to survive. Sugar is the **food** for the flower. Once cut from the plant, the flower has only a limited reserve of food to draw upon for that energy. The sugar, (dextrose), added to the water in commercial floral food, supplies that source of energy so that the flower may continue to mature and open properly.

The drawback of adding sugar to floral food is that bacteria also thrive on sugar. Bacteria are almost everywhere; on the flower stems, in the air, in the vase, on your hands, etc. Bacteria act as a plug in the bottom of the flower stem restricting water flow into the vascular system. The result is a wilted flower. Because of this, it is necessary to add a **bio-inhibitor** along with the sugar to prevent rapid and uncontrolled bacteria growth. The two commonly used **bio-inhibitors** in commercial preparations are 8-Hydroxyquinoline Citrate (HQC) and Physan.

The third major ingredient is an **acidifier**, usually citric acid or aluminum sulfate. The measurement of hydrogen ions in a solution is known as "pH". The correct pH of the floral food solution is essential for proper water uptake. Acidic water (a pH of 3.5 - 5.0 is ideal), moves more readily within the stem. It is important that the pH be reduced from its original level, but to over-acidify to reach a predetermined theoretical goal, can cause a toxic environment in the water. Citric acid also helps to control bacteria and other microbes in conjunction with the bio-inhibitor.

Procedures

It is important, when using a commercial floral food, that the solution be completely mixed. A lump of undissolved floral food can clog the flower stem just as bacteria and/or dirt do in unsanitary containers. Always start with a clean, non-metallic bucket or container. Metal containers react chemically with the acidifiers in the floral food and render them less effective. Fill the containers about 1/3 full if it is a container for storage and about 3/4 full if it is a vase for arranging. Use tepid water.

Cold water traps more air and this dissolved air can impede water flow up the stems. Add the correct amount of floral food for the amount of water in the container, (check manufacturer's rate of use), and stir until dissolved. Mark storage buckets indicating a fill line that corresponds to the proper amount of floral food. If you are using a clear container and notice a white precipitate settle to the bottom, do not be alarmed. This is simply the floral food at work, combining with harmful salts and minerals and taking them out of solution. This is a little unsightly in clear glass containers, so mix the solution in one container and transfer after the precipitate has fallen to the bottom or use one of the commercial floral foods designed for clear containers. When adding water to vases, buckets, containers, etc., always replenish with a pre-mixed water/floral food solution to assure maintenance of the floral food concentration.

Why Use Floral Food?

Why should the retail florist, wholesale florist, and grower invest in a commercial floral food? First, a commercial floral food is scientifically blended to the correct proportions of **sugar**, **bio-inhibitor**, and **acidifier**. It is usually not feasible for the retail florist, wholesale florist, or grower who needs large quantities, to make their own floral food. Homemade floral foods are merely "rough" estimates and cannot compare to the accuracy of commercial brands. The wrong combinations and proportions can mean the difference between longer life and early death. The second reason; in a side-by-side test, commercial floral food will be 40-80% more effective in extending vase life than the best homemade types. This could mean anywhere from 3-8 additional days of vase life! The third reason for using commercial floral food is cost. Penny for penny, commercial floral foods are much less expensive to use, especially on a large scale.

Why should the retail florist, wholesale florist, or grower use a floral food if turnover of fresh flowers is rapid? The main reason is the customer. Retail florists are in business to serve and retain their customers. One of the best ways to keep customers satisfied is to provide an excellent product. To the consumer, excellence in cut flowers is not only their beauty, but it is their longevity, their vase life. If any step of the industry, from the grower to the retail florist, neglects to use floral food, they are decreasing the potential vase life of the flowers and short changing their customers. The general public is more educated now than ever before and will very quickly stop purchasing a poor quality product if not completely satisfied. Therefore, it is essential that a top-notch product be presented to the public. This means that the majority of the life of the product must be in the customer's hands!

Additional Care and Handling Treatments

Advanced technology in the specialty area of cut flower care and handling, developed through partnerships with industry and higher education, has created some exciting results. Pre-treatments such as citric acid hydration solution and post-treatments like EthylBloc have greatly increased the vase life potential of many cut flowers. "Pre-treatment" is a term used to describe a procedure used prior to the normal usage of floral food. "Post-treatment" refers to a procedure used after the flowers are already processed and in a floral food solution. It must be stressed that pre and post treatments must be used in conjunction with the use of a high quality floral food, otherwise the maximum benefit of the treatments will be lost.

Silver Thiosulfate (STS)

The purpose of using an STS pre-treatment is to inhibit the effects of ethylene gas. The unchecked effect of ethylene is different for each type of flower, but in general it causes rapid aging or deterioration of the flowers.

Commercially, STS is being phased out of the floriculture industry. As of the writing of this book, several manufacturers of STS have stopped production due to strict environmental regulations from the federal government. STS will likely still be available for a period of time as inventories are depleted, but eventually STS will not be commercially available.

Ethylene Block

MCP (1-methyleopropene) is an environmentally friendly treatment that prevents the negative effects of ethylene gas. Trade named EthylBloc, MCP has been shown to be nearly as effective in the post-harvest care of ethylene sensitive flowers as STS (silver thiosulfate).

MCP (EthylBloc) is easy to use and a large quantity of flowers may be treated at one time. The product comes in powder form and is mixed with a provided solution that releases the MCP into a gaseous form. The treatment must take place in an enclosed area, such as a cooler or portable plastic tent, to concentrate the gas around the flowers. Treatment time varies with temperature. Once treated, flowers are protected from internal and external sources of ethylene. Toxicity is minimal and generally not a consideration.

Ethylene Sensitive Flowers
Table 14-1

Agapanthus	Freesia
Alstroemeria	Larkspur
Baby's Breath	Lilies
Bouvardia	Monkshood
Campanula	Phlox
Carnation	Snapdragon
Montbretia	Stephanotis
Delphinium	Sweet Pea
Dendrobium	Sweet William
Foxglove	

Citric Acid (CA) Hydration Solution

Water with a lower pH tends to facilitate rapid uptake by the stems. Citric acid has the ability to lower the pH of the water without creating a toxic environment for the flower. Roses, due to their internal stem structure, and water-sensitive garden and wild flowers seem to benefit more from a CA pre-treatment than most other flowers.

The rapid hydration (water uptake), that occurs using a CA pre-treatment accomplishes two things. First, it assures that the flower will be completely turgid (full of water), in the shortest time possible, which is critical when processing dehydrated flowers. Second, since the flower is completely saturated with water, a clean, unobstructed pathway is created for the follow-up procedure of using a floral food. The first type of treatment procedure for CA takes about 1 hour. Simply place the freshly cut (underwater if possible) stem, in the CA solution, and let stand at room temperature for about 1 hour. Then place in a high quality floral food solution and put in the refrigerator. DO NOT re-cut stems prior to placing into floral food solution.

The second type of treatment for CA is called a "quick dip". As its name implies, the procedure is to dip the freshly cut stem ends into the quick dip CA solution for 1-2 seconds. Then transfer to a floral food solution without re-cutting stems.

It must be stressed that these two CA solutions are *not the same!* The quick dip is a much higher concentrate and leaving the stems in this solution for more time than the recommended time will cause severe stem burning. Follow manufacturer's directions carefully.

Flowers That Benefit From Hydration Solutions
Table 14-2

Alstroemeria
Baby's Breath
Bachelor Buttons, Cornflower
Bouvardia
Delphinium
Gerbera
Nigella
Queen Ann's Lace
Rose
Saponaria
Scabiosa
Snapdragon

Processing Procedures

Processing is the act of preparing flowers and foliages for use in designs.

There is a huge array of flowers and foliages commonly available in today's marketplace, many with a unique set of processing procedures. However, most flowers & foliage can be placed into one of the following categories; (1) regular processing (2) underwater cutting processing (3) soaking and submerging processing (4) woody stem processing (5) foliage processing (6) forcing processing.

Regular Processing

Regular processing encompasses the largest part of the flowers processed. **First**, open floral shipping box (or wrapping) and assess the quantity of buckets/containers needed. Prepare buckets/containers of floral food solution (see commercial floral food section) filling approximately 1/3 fill. **Second**, select those flowers that will need a citric acid hydration treatment and process them first. **Third**, "de-bunch" (removal of binding at the stem base) and loosen or remove the sleeve or wrapping which may not allow flowers to expand. Remove foliage that will fall below the water line in the buckets, then cut stems on a sharp slant 1 inch from stem base. Immediately place in floral food solution. **Fourth**, all flowers should remain in their tepid water/floral food solution *outside* the refrigerator for a period of time until they can absorb water and become turgid. This is called *conditioning*. Most flowers will absorb a maximum amount of water in one to two hours. You will notice that they feel fresh and "perked up" instead of soft and spongy. Some flowers that are shipped in bud stage such as gladiolus, lilies, alstroemeria, and carnations could sit at room temperature overnight (or even longer) to open and reach an optimum stage of maturity. Roses however should need only 15 - 30 minutes of conditioning. **Fifth**, when the flowers have absorbed the maximum amount of water and/or reached the preferred stage of maturity, they should be placed in the refrigerator. This act of cooling the flower so that it becomes "crisp" and hard is known as *hardening*. Hardening slows the transpiration rate (and respiration) and therefore increases vase life. Generally, a temperature between 36 to 40 degrees will suffice for most flowers, with the exception of tropical flowers (see Table 14-3).

Tropical Flower Storage
(55-60 Degrees F)
Table 14-3

Anthurium
Banana Flower
Bird of Paradise
Calathea
Ginger
Heliconia
Orchids

may cause flower spotting or discoloration (see Table 14-4).

Flowers That Benefit From Soaking/Submerging
Table 14-4

Anthurium	Hydrangea
Dendrobium	Lilac
Galax	Lily of the Valley
Gerbera	Oncidium
Ginger	Stephanotis

Underwater Cutting Processing

The process of underwater cutting is particularly effective for those flowers that are sensitive to stem blockage due to air bubbles. Roses and Gerberas are two dramatic examples, but remember, all flowers will benefit to a certain degree from underwater cutting. This procedure is actually quite simple. Place stem ends into a bowl, bucket, basin, or commercial cutter that is filled with water. Slant cut 1 inch of stem off underwater. This prevents air from entering the stem. A droplet of water will form over the stem end when transferring to the holding container, again preventing air from entering the stem. This procedure should be done not only during processing, but ideally again at the design table just prior to inserting stems into an arrangement.

Soaking and Submerging Processing

Some flowers not only benefit from the underwater cutting process, but also from *total submergence in tepid water*. The water should not contain floral food, as this will cause spotting on the flowers and foliage.

First, cut the stem ends underwater and then submerge the entire flower in water. This total submergence in water aids in the re-hydration process and often can mean the difference between a "fresh" looking flower and a soft wilted flower. Fifteen to thirty minutes should suffice for this process, as longer times

Woody Stem Processing

Outdated habits are sometimes hard to break. The old technique of smashing and/or crushing stem ends of woody flowers & foliage is by far the most prevalent unnecessary procedure still in usage today. This technique does more damage than good! The smashing or crushing actually closes, and worse, often destroys the vascular tissue, thereby *restricting* water uptake. The correct method for woody stem processing is to slant cut stem ends, with sharp pruning shears, as for non-woody plant materials. Place in warm water with a high quality floral food or one especially formulated for woody stems. Some people put an "x" or "t" cut, with a knife, in the stem end to help open the vascular system. This, however, has not shown to be beneficial.

Foliage Processing

Cut foliage is often neglected during the processing procedure. However, cut foliage should be given the same respect as flowers to insure maximum vase life. One of two procedures should be followed: (1) treat as a cut flower and place in buckets of tepid floral food solution. (2) moisten thoroughly and place in plastic bags or waxed boxes in the cooler. Round, fluffy types of foliages (oregonia, rhamnus, myrtle) should follow method 1, while flat types of foliages (leather leaf, commodore, flat fern, galax) should follow method 2.

Foliage Preferred Storage: Buckets or Covered Buckets
Table 14-5

Anthurium	Monstera
Areca Palm	Myrtle
Aspidistra	Oregonia
Bear Grass	Pittosporum
Bird of Paradise	Podocarpus
Boxwood	Rhamnus
Camellia	Ruscus
Croton	Sago Palm
English Ivy	Scotch Broom
Eucalyptus	Sword Fern
Flax	Ti
Foxtail Fern	Tree Fern (Asparagus)
Horsetail	Umbrella Grass
Ming (Asparagus)	

Foliage Preferred Storage: Moist Bags or Boxes
Table 14-6

Galax	Plumosis (Asparagus)
Huckleberry	Salal/Lemon Leaf
Emerald/Jade	Springeri (Asparagus)
Leatherleaf Fern	String Smilax

Forcing Processing

Many kinds of flowers can be forced into bloom from the bud stage. This requires holding the flowers in an optimal atmosphere. The ideal atmosphere is accomplished with warm floral *food* solution, high *humidity*, and *light*. The floral food provides nutrients and energy for respiration to occur (life processes). Humidity prevents dehydration of the bud and blossoms through transpiration. Creating humidity can be accomplished by covering the flowers with a clear plastic bag or by misting. Light is necessary for many chemical reactions

within the plant that are critical for proper bud opening and proper flower coloration. Place the materials that are to be forced in clean buckets containing a warm floral food solution. Mist with plain water and cover with a clear plastic bag. Place in bright, indirect light at room temperature until desired stage of opening.

Flowers That Can Be Forced From Bud Stage
Table 14-7

Alstroemeria	Forsythia
Amaryllis	Gladiolus
Carnation	Iris
Daffodil	Lily (most types)
Flowering Peach	Peony
Flowering Plum	Pussy Willow

Special Considerations: Flowers

Roses and Thorn Removal

The stem structure of a rose must be considered when attempting to remove the noxious thorns. Just beneath the surface of the rose stem is the xylem or water conducting tissue. If this layer is damaged during thorn removal, bent neck and/or a decrease in vase life is inevitable. The use of heavy gloves, mechanical strippers, or a potato masher should only dull the thorn tips and not make large open wounds. Caution should be taken when using sharp metal leaf and thorn strippers as they may cause considerable damage when used improperly.

Straight Stem Tulips

Tulips are frequently stored without water at 34° by the grower and/or wholesaler. This practice does not reduce vase life appreciably, but it does dehydrate and curve the stems from this horizontal storage. To straighten the tulip stems leave the stems in the plastic bundle sleeve and wrap tightly again with waxed paper or newspaper. Be sure that the stems are tightly packed and flower heads are straight. Remove the white portion of stem ends (for better water uptake) and place in tepid floral food solution. Condition at room temperature for 1-2 hours and then place in a 36° refrigerator. The tight bundling should be removed only after the tulips have cooled for 1 hour or more.

Daffodil Toxicity

The soft fleshy stems of daffodils exude a gelatinous sap toxic to many other flowers. Tulips and anemone are especially sensitive to this sap. Always condition daffodils in a separate container, never mixing freshly cut daffodils with other flowers. After conditioning, however, daffodils may safely be used with tulips, anemones, or most any other flower, especially when designing in foam.

Protea Refrigeration

Most of those flowers loosely referred to as "proteas", should not be treated as tropical flowers, but refrigerated at 38-40°. The pincushion protea *(Leucospernum)*, sugar bush protea *(Protea repens)*, King protea *(Protea cynaroides)*, and several *Leucodendron* varieties ("Safari Sunset") should all be stored at 38-40°. Leaf blackening on these species is due to a lack of carbohydrates (sugar), lack of light, and high temperatures. Use floral food and place proteas near light sources in the refrigerator to prevent leaf blackening.

Stems with Latex Sap

Stems that exude a white latex sap when cut may contaminate the holding water and clog stem ends. Euphorbia, dahlia, and poinsettia are examples of this type of plant. Some recommendations suggest dipping the stem ends into hot water or searing the stem ends in a candle flame to stop the flow of latex. These may or may *not* help with flower longevity, as both techniques may cause damage

to the stem from the heat. Another method is to pre-cut the stems to the proper length needed for designing and place them in a mild bleach/water solution (1 teaspoon bleach per 1 gallon of water) for 15 —20 minutes. Though this is not a foolproof method, is does work especially well on poinsettias.

Deep Water Solutions

Some flowers seem to respond well to a deep water holding solution. Instead of the typical $1/4$ to $1/3$ of a bucket of floral food solution, these flowers should be placed in a floral food solution $3/4$ the length of their stems. Amaryllis and lilac are two notable examples for this treatment.

Baby's Breath

Baby's breath sometimes arrives with the lower leaves beginning to decay and stem bases covered with odiferous slime caused by bacteria. This is more common on field-grown plants as the wind and rain inoculate the stems and leaves with microorganisms. To counter the unusually high bacteria; 1. thoroughly wash the stem ends in tepid water, 2. dip stems in a hydration solution, and 3. add two or three drops of bleach to the floral food solution.

Alstroemeria Dermatitis

Many flowers have toxic substances contained within them. Most never cause any human reaction, unless there is a natural sensitivity or an allergy to a specific chemical. Alstroemeria plants contain glycosides, which may cause skin rashes on people with sensitive skin. In super-sensitivity cases, the rashes may become chronic and cause skin lesions. A physician should be consulted if any skin problems arise from the use of alstroemeria or any other cut flower or foliage. Wearing protective gloves while processing flowers may prevent this problem from occurring.

Special Considerations: Specific Foliage

Aspidistra is the cast iron plant and available in solid green or green/white variegated forms. This plant takes much abuse as a cut material and it is also a favorite potted plant in buildings that have little light.

Boxwood is small-leafed woody foliage that is used in both large and small designs as filler and/or mechanics covering. It is available in green or green/white variegated forms. *Oregonia* is used similarly, but is slightly more coarse-textured.

Beargrass is slender-leafed grass-like foliage about 18-24 inches long. The narrow leaves naturally arch gracefully from designs or they may be tied into specific shapes or forms, (hearts, circles, etc).

Caladium comes in many varieties and color combinations. It is a favorite potted plant in southern areas and is frequently grown outdoors for its interesting foliage. It also makes a good cut foliage if sprayed with an anti-transpirant to prevent wilting.

Chamaedorea or Jade or Emerald is standard "background" foliage in many large designs. It is imported form Mexico and Central America. Jade has a wide leaf blade while Emerald has a narrow leaf shape that can be trimmed with scissors into triangles or other shapes. Ends of the leaf tips may also be trimmed with pinking shears for a fishtail effect.

Croton foliage provides colors of bright yellow, orange and red. The thick leathery leaves will last longer if sprayed with an anti-transpirant prior to use.

Eucalyptus is available in many forms. Spiral, silver dollar, willow and seeded eucalyptus are some of the most popular forms. Most eucalyptus will air dry by hanging it upside down or treating with a glycerine solution (see Chapter 18).

Galax, native to the eastern United States, has a beautiful heart-shaped leathery leaf. The leaf color varies with the season, but is typically green or a green/bronze combination. Leaves are used at the base of a design to conceal mechanics or they combined together to form rosettes for use on wreaths, large designs or table decorations. Galax air dry easily or they may be glycerinized (see Chapter 18).

Horsetail or *Equisetum* is unusual hollow tubular-shaped foliage that adds strong line to any design in which it is placed. Stems are typically 2 to 4 feet in length.

Huckleberry is a product of the Northwest United States. This woody stemmed foliage may be purchased throughout the year and is especially useful as filler material or covering a trellis or screen as it is flat and one-sided

Leatherleaf Fern is probably the most commonly used florist cut foliage. It has very good vase life, especially if treated with an anti-transpirant, and is readily available throughout the year.

Lemon Leaf or *Salal*, also a product of the Northwest United States, is another woody stemmed foliage with 2-3 inch oval, leathery bright green leaves. Branches may be used as background foliage in large designs, or individual leaves may be glued onto a fabric or polyfoil backing to create table runners and mats.

Monstera are large (12 to 24 inches) flat leaves with irregular holes and splits. They are used in large tropical designs, contemporary arrangements, or as table mats and design bases.

Myrtle is available in both tall varieties (2 to 3 feet), or short varieties (12 to 16 inches). Myrtle leaves are aromatic when disturbed, giving off a pleasant spicy fragrance. May be dried and used in potpourri.

Oregon or *Flat Fern* is typically shipped in bundles of 50 stems. It is used as a background foliage in large designs or to make fern plants/trees for weddings and stage decorations. Store in buckets covered with plastic and spray with an anti-transpirant for best vase life.

Pittosporum a versatile foliage that may be used in designs for filler or mechanics covering or individual leaves may be used in corsages and wedding bouquets. Available in green and green/white variegated forms.

Plumosus adds softness to designs. It is also effective in making garland streamers to drape banquet tables or in wedding decorations. It is not advisable to use plumosus in corsage or table arrangements (especially cake decorations) because of its tendency to shatter. Springeri is used in a similar manner.

Scotch Broom is one of the few foliages that is both linear and flexible. The grooved stem and leaves can be massaged and manipulated into almost any curved shape.

Smilax is available in two types. 1. Bridal, which is small leafed, delicate, and is commercially grown on a string (sometimes referred to as String Smilax or Table Smilax), and is typically used to adorn bridal cake tables as garlands or as table runners along with candelabra. 2. Southern, which is harvested from the pine woods of the Southern US, has larger leaves, and is typically added to arbors, gazebos or used gracefully cascading over wall paneling or railings for weddings.

Ti is tropical foliage that is available in green, green/white variegated, green/white/pink variegated, and bronze colors. It is similar in shape and use to aspidistra, but it is not a durable.

Tree Fern, of all the cut asparagus foliages, looks the most like garden asparagus. It is light and fluffy, and less apt to shatter than the other cut asparagus (foxtail, plumosus and springeri).

Mosses and Lichens

The use of different types of moss and lichens as mechanics covering or as decorative additions to designs is quite common. Moss is a small spore-bearing plant that is seldom over $1\frac{1}{2}$ inches thick while lichen is a thin plant composed of a symbiotic relationship of a fungus and algae. There is a myriad of different forms, colors, and textures of these plant materials. Most are available in a dry form that may be used dry in silk and dried flower designs or they may be briefly soaked in warm water to be revitalized for fresh arrangements. A few mosses are available in fresh, or "just picked" form. These are stored in the refrigerator to maintain freshness.

Mosses and lichens may be anchored into place with greening pins, hairpin wires, or by one of several adhesives.

Chapter 15
DESIGN MECHANICS

All who work with flowers soon discover that natural materials are not as cooperative as might be desired. Sometimes the materials shift out of place or curve in the wrong direction. Good designers do not leave the stability of a design to chance. They anchor each flower and each foliage stem as securely as possible. The mechanical construction (such as wiring, taping, etc.) should be concealed, but not to the detriment of the design. In flower shows, points are discounted for mechanics being evident, and to the retail customer, the design may appear unfinished.

This phase of designing is not art; it is craftsmanship and must be mastered.

Container Mechanics

A flower stem holder, sometimes called a "frog," is any object or substance that is used to hold stems securely in position within the container. There is no limit to the types of materials to serve this purpose. In addition to the well known floral foam, pin/needle point holders, chicken wire, hardware cloth and floral cages are also used as "mechanics" with varying success. The selection depends on the type of bowl or vase, the kind of flowers, and the manner in which the arrangement is being used.

Floral Foam: The most common type of container mechanic is floral foam, sometimes referred to as "wet foam." It has the unique ability to hold water in its cell structure, yet release it to flowers as needed. Stems should be cut at an angle and inserted into the floral foam at least 1 to 2 inches. Available in cases of 36 or 48 bricks (special orders of other sizes are also available), floral foam's density and texture varies by brand and intended purpose. Dense, hard floral foam is used for large stemmed, heavy flowers while soft textured floral foam is used for smaller delicate stemmed flowers. An all purpose floral foam is adequate for most typical floral designs. Floral foam should be thoroughly soaked in tepid water containing a floral food prior to use. For best results, place the bricks in a large sink or basin and let the foam absorb water slowly, never forcing the foam under water as this may cause an air pocket to form in the middle of the foam. There should always be a reservoir of water surrounding floral foam in the container. Floral foam may be secured into the container with waterproof-tape, pan glue, or wedged tightly so as not to wobble or dislodge when transported.

Wet foam is also available in geometric shapes such as spheres, cones, cubes, circles, half circles and elongated bars. These items are very useful for providing a water source in all kinds of floral decorating.

Dry Foam: This type of foam is commonly used for silk and dried flower arrangements. It will not absorb water like floral foam does. It is available in several densities for use with larger or smaller stems. Case size varies with the manufacturer, as does the size of each brick, although it is usually similar in size to floral foam. Unusual shapes such as orbs and cones are also available pre-made from dry foam, or they be carved from large bricks. Attach dry foam to containers with hot glue, pan glue, anchor pins, anchor tape, or wedge tightly so as not to dislodge when transported.

Styrofoam™: This trade name foam is used primarily as a silk flower foundation or as a pre-made, rigid base for numerous fraternal emblems and specialty shapes. It may be purchased either green or white and either in a one-inch or two-inch thickness. The standard size sheet of Styrofoam™ is one foot wide by three feet long, but it is made in larger sizes. Styrofoam™ will melt if hot glue is used directly on it to attach materials and a heavy coating of aerosol paint will dissolve the outer layer. Attach Styrofoam™ with low temperature pan glue, anchor tape, or wedge tightly so as not to dislodge when being transported.

Floral Cages: Numerous cages made of floral foam or dry foam surrounded by a plastic grid, are available for use in lieu of, or with a container. These may be used for wall hangings, attached to wreaths and other forms, easel designs, etc. They vary in size from the small, single use 1" domes to large 10" to 12" cages that may be re-used with the addition of new foam. Some of the cages may be wired to objects by using taped # 24 or #26 wire, while others contain a suction cup for attachment to mirrors or glass. Security is essential and the addition of waterproof-tape around the cage is highly recommended.

Bridal bouquet holders comprise another special type of floral cages. They too, are made of floral foam or dry foam surrounded by a plastic grid, but they also have a handle for carrying. These handles may be straight, angled, round, flat, or a combination of these attributes. The foam size varies from small, for junior attendant's bouquets, to the extra large for over-sized bridal bouquets.

Grid Lids or *Tape Grids*: Plastic grid lids may be purchased for many of the popular utility containers. These lids snap into place over the container opening, providing a series of small square openings to brace flowers upright in the container. The same effect may be accomplished by taping waterproof or clear tape in a grid formation across the container opening. (Figure 26)

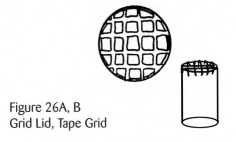

Figure 26A, B
Grid Lid, Tape Grid

Pin or *Needle Holders*: Pin holders (known as kenzan in Ikebana) are a metal mechanic frequently used in Oriental designs and commonly used by garden clubs for contests and shows. Flower and foliage stems are impaled securely on the needles for precise placements. It is advisable to purchase only those having brass points attached to lead bases that are flat on the bottom. These metals will not rust while in water. Inexpensive pin holders have steel points that soon rust and may ruin the container. Flat, heavy lead bases on pin holders are important for securing frogs to containers. Holders for temporary designs of no great height or weight can be placed on wet paper in flat containers, and this is enough to prevent slippage. To fasten a pin

holder permanently, a piece of floral clay is worked with the fingers until it is soft and pliable; then it is rolled between palms of the hands or on a flat surface until it is formed into a roll. This roll is placed on the bottom of the pin holder around the outer edge, forming a complete circle, Figure 27. Then the pin holder is pressed firmly on the bottom of container with a twisting motion; the clay flattens out, forming a slight suction cup which holds the pin holder securely (both pin holder and container must be DRY and dust free). A glove, hot-plate pad or thick towel over the points prevents injury to the hand. If difficulty is experienced in securing the pin holder by this method, the bottom of the holder and the surface of the container may be rubbed with clay before applying the circle of clay. Some brands of floral clay should not be used in silver containers because they leave a stain that cannot be removed. Use a smaller container inside the silver, as a liner, for protection.

Figure 27
Applying a circle of floral clay to hold pin frog securely

Chicken wire: Container mechanics may be made of 1" or 2" mesh chicken wire. The 1" mesh chicken wire 12" wide is the most convenient size. A strip may be cut long enough to brace against the ends of the container and then forced within a short distance of the bottom of the container; the rest of it can be folded across the top or near the top. Thus the stems of the flowers will go through two thicknesses of wire. The wire must be fastened securely to the container as follows:

1. Chicken wire can be secured to papier-mâché containers or to plastic containers with wire clamps (hog rings) which are clamped to

the edges with a pair of pliers made especially for this work (Figure 28). These clamps may be purchased from a farm supply store or a hardware store.

2. For a low bowl, a small piece of chicken wire may be rolled into a ball, wired onto a rubber suction cup, and placed on the bottom of the container (Figure 29). The container and suction cup should be wet before securing the cup to the bottom.

3. When securing chicken wire in a bowl or tall vase where suction cups will not fit, another piece of wire may be used to tie the chicken wire around the top edge of the container. This tying wire should be floral taped so that it will not rust the container.

4. For clear glass containers chicken wire may be secured to cover the mouth of the container. Tape two pieces of heavy florist wire (Gauge # 16 or # 18) with green floral tape and make a "saddle" of the two taped wires across the opening of container, clamping onto the sides. Shape the chicken wire to conform to the opening and secure it to the "saddle." The stems of the flowers will go through and form a part of the floral pattern (Figure 30).

Hardware Cloth: This is another type of wire mesh that may be used. It is cut the width of the top of the container and is crimped over the edge. This wire is very stiff and cumbersome, and it cannot be manipulated as easily as chicken wire. Candles may be secured into needle-point holders by tying a circle of hardware cloth (approximately 2" wide) around the candles and letting it extend one-half inch below the candles (Figure 31).

Natural Mechanics: The simple placement (kubari), tying or fastening (armature) or weaving of natural twigs, branches or stems, constitutes natural mechanics. They are often visible as a point of interest in the design.

Japanese Methods: Japanese methods are useful in many instances for special effects. Those wishing to follow strictly the Oriental custom of Ikebana will naturally use the accepted ways. Japanese methods are excellent for many free form designs.

1. A "kubari" is either a "Y" shaped branch or a twig that has been split in two pieces and tied at one end, forming a "V." This figure is fitted across the opening of the container. Flowers and foliage are placed in the crotch of this holder and are held in place with a crosspiece of twig called a "komi." This is an excellent way of holding the "nemoto" in position. The stems of the materials are cut on a slant to press against the sides of the container and extend through the "kubari." Oriental containers have rims inside the opening to prevent the "kubari" from slipping (Figure 32).

2. A second method of holding stems in place is to split the stem for 1" and 2" and insert another stem into the split, perpendicular to the main stem. Tie the crosspiece in place if it is loose.

Figure 28
Wire clamps (hog rings) applied with special pliers (hog ringer) holds chicken wire in a container

Figure 29
Ball of chicken wire held to a low, open bowl with a suction cup

Figure 30
Chicken wire is secured to opening with a "saddle" using heavy gauge taped wire (No. 18)

Figure 31
A circle of hardware cloth for candle holder used on pin frogs

Figure 32
A kubari made of a "Y" shaped branch, stems are held in place with a cross piece– komi

The inserted crosspiece holds the flower very steady (Figure 33).

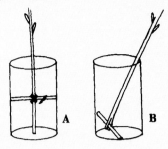

Figure 33
A – twig tied perpendicular to main stem for support
B – twig inserted into split section of stem used as a brace

3. To hold long stems in a cylindrical vase, a bend is made up the stem (it may break, but must not sever) approximately the diameter of the container, and the stem is wedged across the bottom of the container. The now "L" shaped stem holds the upright blossom in place (Figure 34).

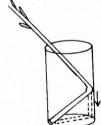

Figure 34
Stem broken into "L" shape hold blossom in place

4. Japanese knots for tying stems are serviceable. A loop is made and held onto the stems; then with the long end of the cord, the loop is bound to the end of the stems, leaving the loop free above this circling cord. This tying end is run through the loop. The short end (which formed the loop) is pulled tightly downward, binding the cord securely (Figure 35).

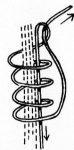

Figure 35
Japanese knot for tying stems

Miscellaneous Design Mechanics

Wire: Two types of wire are used in floral work. Eighteen-inch lengths of wire are sold in lots of twelve pounds to the box; such wire may be purchased plain or enameled green. The gauges vary from #16 through #30 for most floral work; like thread, the larger the number, the smaller the size. Practice in the use of wire will enable one to judge its approximate gauge and whether or not it has sufficient strength to serve one's need. Often one needs the flexibility of a small wire but more strength than the small wire affords. In such instances, two smaller gauge wires can be used. Wire is also sold in bulk on spools, sometimes referred to as spool or paddle wire. There is one-quarter pound on each stick (spool), and the length varies according to the gauge.

Because each designer has his own preference, the methods of wiring vary greatly. One should use the method that best serves his purpose according to the type of flower and design. A rose is wired with a specific gauge of wire for funeral work, another gauge for flower arrangements, and still another gauge for corsage work - and the method varies in each case. Funeral sprays are handled much more roughly than corsages and so their wiring must be sturdier. The method of wiring is determined to a large extent by the type of flower and its use in the design.

Uses of wire:

1. To curve a stem into the position or line desired.
2. To straighten a crooked stem.
3. To strengthen a weak stem and prevent drooping.
4. To group small stemmed flowers into mass effects (binding, bunching, tufting).
5. To stabilize the arrangement - some flowers tend to vary their position
6. To construct a composite flower, e.g., glamellias, galax, and ivy rosettes, Victorian roses and tulips
7. To reduce weight in corsages and wed-

ding bouquets by replacing stems.

8. To prevent flowers from showing wilt in arrangements made up without water. (This is very important in some funeral designs.) Flowers may have stiff stems when we work with them, but when they remain out of water for several hours, they begin to show wilt. Roses show wilt in the portion of the stem just under the blossoms; the heads of stock blossoms fall forward; carnation stems become very weak.

9. To add strength and rigidity to stems.

Wiring Suggestions

1. When using mass type flowers in arrangements of baskets or bowls, the insertion method is employed. Insert the wire into the head only; no hook is necessary. The remaining portion of wire is brought down around the stem with a few turns, care being taken not to damage the foliage (Figure 36).

2. For roses, carnations, and similar flowers, the wire is run into the calyx or seed pod by inserting it parallel to the stem and with a few turns, continued down around the stem, as in Figure 36. The wired stem should not look like a barber pole with many spirals visible. *A more discreet method is to hold the wire still while turning the stem one or two revolutions.* This method is used for arrangements when stems need strengthening or need to be curved. For funeral work, the wire should be inserted in the seed pod or calyx perpendicular to the stem rather than parallel to it; it should be pushed through about three inches and bent downward, forming a hook. This short length is secured with the longer remaining portion of wire, twisting downward around the stem (Figure 37).

3. On fleshy-stemmed flowers, such as callas, tritomas, daffodils, and gerbera - use the insertion method shown in Figure 38. To wire in this manner, leave the flowers on the work bench, out of water, allowing them to become flexible by being at room temperature. Once wired with a #20 or #22 gauge wire, shape the stem into the desired curve; complete the design and harden the arrangement in the refrigerator (Figure 38, Plate 59). This method will not reduce vase life by damaging internal stem structure.

4. Lilies - these blossoms, if damaged, often shed their petals at the point where they are attached to the stem. In funeral and wedding work additional support is sometimes needed.

Figure 36
Wiring insertion method – for general use in flower designing, e.g., asters, roses, chrysanthemums, carnations

Figure 37
Wiring hook method for funeral work – through seed pod, e.g., roses, carnations

Figure 38
Wiring hollow stems, e.g., daffodils or the fleshy stems of Callas, etc.

(Plate 59)
Crescent Callas.

Figure 39
Wiring line flowers

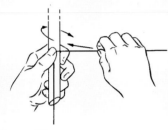

Figure 40
Wiring extension method –
Wire held under thumb at bent
corner and one end extends
downward.

Figure 41
Wiring extension method –
completed

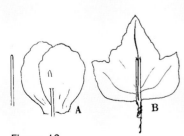

Figure 42
Wiring hairpin method –
B–foliages or A–petals

Use a rather soft wire, gauge #26 or #28, inserted on the petal midrib perpendicularly through, just above where the petals join the stem. Push through about four inches and fold down parallel to the stem; repeat this one or two more times, to gently "sew" each petal onto the stem. The 4-6 wires parallel to the stem may then be corsage-taped to the stem to disguise them.

5. Line flowers (e.g., gladioli) for funeral work - insert a heavy wire, gauge #18, into the stem of the glad just above the partially opened buds and parallel to the stem. A second heavy wire is grasped under the thumb against the stem below the first blossom; this wire should extend about two inches beyond the top of the first wire. Hold the stem and the second wire in your left hand. With the right hand grasp the second wire, and with the index finger guiding it between the blossoms, circle it up and around the stem and the first wire, binding them together. This second wire will extend beyond the first wire; bend the extra portion into a hook around the stem. By using this method, glads or other line flowers may be shaped into graceful curves, which are especially needed in casket work (Figure 39).

6. Tying or extension method - is used for extending short-stemmed flowers in designs with no water source, to add strength to garlands, and to tie the parts of a wedding bouquet or tie stems in corsage work. Hold the stem in the left hand. Pick up a piece of wire near its center with the right hand and bend over the thumb at a ninety-degree angle. Lay one- half of this wire parallel to the stem pointing downward. Use the thumb of the left hand to hold it securely while the right hand circles the remaining half of wire around and down the stem (Figures 40 and 41).

7. Hairpin method - In Figure 42, a method is illustrated for wiring foliage and petals for corsage and wedding work. The wire is folded double over the blade of a knife into the shape of a hairpin. The ends are cut evenly. Single petals or groups of petals are wired by inserting points of wire into the back of petals approximately midway of the petals and pressing the wire downward through the base. Victorian roses and "Duchess" tulips are made in this fashion (Plates 109, 110 and 111). Easter lily petals for design work are divided into groups of two petals each and are wired as described (Plate 110).

Plate109   (circa 1952)
Juliet Bouquet
Wiring techniques: hook and tubular methods, Figures 37, 43.

Plate 110   (circa 1986)
"Duchess" Tulip
Gluing technique: floral adhesive, page 142.

Plate 111 (circa 1973)
"Duchess" Lily
Wiring technique: hairpin method, Figure 42.

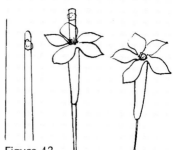

Figure 43
Wiring tubular or trumpet-
shaped blossoms, e.g.,
stephanotis

Figure 44
Wiring lily-of-the-valley

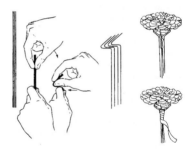

Figure 45
Wiring camellia

Figure 46
Wiring flowers for corsage or
wedding bouquets, e.g., roses,
carnations, spray mums

Plate 112   (circa 1966)
Crescent shoulder design—
spray chrysanthemums

8. Tubular or trumpet-shaped blossoms (stephanotis, tuberoses, hyacinths, etc.) Make a wire hairpin (#28 gauge) and push the wire down the throat of the flower completely through its base so that the wire ends come out parallel on each side of the stem. Tape securely (Figure 43, Plate 113).

9. Lily-of -the-valley - Cut a strip of floral tape lengthwise into three or four narrow strips; use these narrow strips to tape fine wire (#30 gauge). Run your fingers over the tape after wrapping the wire to smooth it out. Hold lily-of-the-valley and wire in one hand. Circle the wire up the stem between the florets with the other hand; fold the end of the wire over the top of the stem, hooking around this stem. Cut off the surplus (Figure 44). This small wire will blend into the stem.

10. Camellias - Camellias are wired with gooseneck hooks made of #26 or #28 wire, as shown in Figure 45. Four or more hooks are inserted evenly around the blossom of the camellia. The wires and stem are then taped together; no twisting is necessary. The old method of crossing wires through the blossom sometimes causes the flower to shatter by damaging the center crown to which all petals are attached.

11. Gardenias -Remove the green calyx from the base of the blossom. Insert two pieces of #22 or #24 wire through the stem of the blossom beneath the petals. These wires run in opposite directions and form a cross. Fold three ends downward and allow the fourth end to bind the wires and stem together. Staple the foliage to a gardenia collar, place the blossom in the center, and tape. If you have no gardenia collar, one may be prepared from a circular piece of thin cardboard which has a small hole cut in the center for the blossom. The hairpin method discussed above may be used on the foliage instead of a collar.

12. Small flowers (Figure 46) This method may be used in wiring small blossoms such as stock, spray mums and asters, bachelor buttons, daisies, and roses in wedding and corsage work. Remove all but three-quarters to one inch of the stem from the flowers. Insert wire into the base of the blossom parallel to the stem; tape wire and stem together tightly, but do not twist the wire (Plates 112, 113 and 114).

Plate 113   (circa 1986)
Informal cluster of lily-of-the-valley
and stephanotis with embroidered
ribbon.

Plate 114   (circa 1966)
Miniature roses in Hogarth curve
corsage.

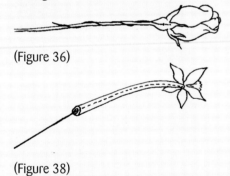

(Figure 36)

(Figure 38)

13. Dense mass type flowers such as cush-ion, daisy, and button spray mums and large asters should be wired for corsages and wed-ding bouquets using the insertion method as illustrated in Figure 36. This method helps pre-vent shattering of the flower head that hook wiring may cause.

14. Hollow stemmed flowers, such as lark-spur, narcissus and daffodils - run the wire up the center of the stem into the head (Figure 38).

15. For sympathy sprays, extra security of mass-type flowers whose petals are attached to a crown, such as asters and mums, is needed. Use the fish hook method. Hold the stem of the flower between the thumb and middle fin-gers; use the index finger to brace the head of the blossom to prevent it from snapping off when the wire is inserted. Insert the wire into the head of the flower parallel to the stem and extend it approximately six inches beyond the head, as shown in Figure 47. Bend about 2 $1/2$

Figure 47
Wiring fish hook method for funeral work — flat head flowers, e.g., asters, chrysanthemums

Figure 48
Picking — first position (rat trap used as pick holder)

inches of the wire downward, forming a hook; pull the hook back into the head of the blossom on the opposite side of the stem, thus securing the head on the stem. With the long end of the wire, make a complete circle around the stem and the hooked end that was pulled down through the flower; twist remainder of wire down around the stem.

16. Tulips continue growing (elongate) after they are cut. They may be wired on the outside of their stems to prevent internal damage, and in such a way that allows the stem to continue growing. Use light green corsage tape on a #20 or 22 wire, make a circle around a pencil on the end of the wire and bend it into a horizontal plane. Place the stem along the wire and inside the circle keeping it loose enough for the stem to grow.

Picks and Pins

Wooden picks are small wooden sticks, either wired or unwired, which are used to provide a stem or a point to a stem for sticking in foundations. They range in size from 2 to 7 inches in length and are either plain wood or dyed green. A large rat trap is one of the most economical and efficient means of holding a bundle of wired picks (Figure 48).

Method of picking: cut the flower stems the required length, removing leaves and small branches that will interfere with the pick. Place the wooden pick along the side of the stem, (Figure 48) use only one-third of the length of the pick to fasten to the stem and leave two-thirds free to stick into the foundation. Hold the stem and pick in the secondary hand. With the primary hand grasp the stem and the pick,

twisting outward one or two complete turns pulling the wire down to the bottom of the stem. Finish by using the surplus wire and twist around the bare pick (Figure 49).

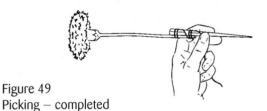

Figure 49
Picking — completed

In picking large, fleshy stems, such as glads, it is best to force the pick one-third of its length into the stem (Figure 50). Lift up with

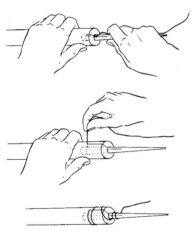

Figure 50
Picking — fleshy stem flowers — force pick up into stem

the wire, cutting the stem. Then use this wire to bind the stem tightly. The additional wire used in wiring the glad is brought down around the stem and pick, making a complete turn with the wire on the pick just below the end of the stem (See Figure 39 for wiring line flowers).

Water tube picks are small plastic vials of water intended to supply a small quantity of water to one or two flowers for a short period of time. Water tubes are available in several sizes, each containing a rubber cap with a small hole for inserting the stems into the tubes. The spike on the end of the tube is inserted into the foam or other foundation.

Steel picks are a small barbed piece of steel, dispensed through a picking machine. The pick clamps onto stem ends or other material and is then inserted into foam. Steel picks are frequently used with silk and dried materials.

Greening pins resemble hairpins, although the tops are flat. The best variety has an "S" curve across the top. They are used to apply greenery to wreaths and anchor moss to various foam bases. For heavy materials, angle two pins at a 45-degree angle opposite each other, making an "X" after inserting in the foam.

Bank pins, commonly known as "straight" pins, size 24, are useful to apply flowers on set piece designs for funeral work. They are also used to hold parallel flower stems together in arrangements (replacing wire as in Figure 51).

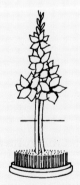

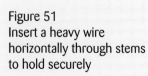

Figure 51
Insert a heavy wire horizontally through stems to hold securely

Anchor pins are small plastic disks with four prongs. The disk is secured to a container with a floral adhesive leaving the four prongs protruding upward. Floral foam or styrofoam is then impaled on the prongs. This mechanic lessens the need for, the sometimes obtrusive, anchor tape. Use more than one anchor pin for large blocks of foam.

Dixon pins are a strong anchoring device made of wooden picks attached to opposite ends of a flexible metal strip. They are used to attach Styrofoam™ (to easels as well as to attach small objects to foam mechanics.)

Corsage and *Boutonniere Pins* are much like straight pins, but have a glass or plastic bead attached to the end for decoration. They are used to attach corsages or boutonnieres to clothing, hats, purses, etc. and range in size from $1\frac{1}{2}$ inches to 3 inches in length.

Adhesives and Tapes

Anchor tape, also called waterproof tape, is an adhesive tape used primarily to hold floral foam in place. Anchor tape must be applied to a dry surface, but it will withstand moist conditions after attachment. It is available in white or dark green and $\frac{1}{4}$" or $\frac{1}{2}$" widths.

Clear tape is similar to anchor tape, except that it is transparent. It is most useful on clear glass containers where regular anchor tape would be distracting. Clear tape is not waterproof and even small amounts of moisture may cause it to release.

Corsage tape/stem wrap is used to cover the wires and bind wired flowers together, typically for corsages, boutonnieres, and bridal bouquets. It is rather like wax-coated crepe paper, not really adhesive in nature, but is sticks to itself when stretched and applied properly. It comes in a variety of colors.

Hot melt glue is a solid glue that when heated to high temperatures (400 degrees F), is used to adhere material together or to fasten materials to a foundation. Though seemingly secure, temperature extremes sometimes cause this glue to release. It is typically dispensed through a glue gun from round 4" or 10" sticks.

Low melt glue is a solid glue that when heated to relatively low temperatures (compared to hot melt) is used in much the same manner as hot melt glue. The adhesive qualities are much the same as hot melt glue, though maybe not as strong, and it has the same tendency to release with temperature extremes. It is typically dispensed through a glue gun from oval 4" or 10" sticks.

Pan melt glue is a solid adhesive that when melted in a pan, is used for gluing materials to a container or foundation. Melting of pan glue is lower than hot melt glue and can be controlled by the thermostat on the pan. Pan glue is generally considered stronger than hot or low melt glue and does not have the tendency to release with temperature extremes. It is available in glue pillows, pellets, or pads.

Floral Adhesive is liquid glue used to secure fresh flowers or foliage to containers or to a foundation. It is also very useful for repairing damaged flowers in corsages and is frequently used to attach flowers and foliage to corsage frames. It is waterproof after becoming completely dry. It is available in small bottles with a re-closing lid and user–friendly tubes.

Spray adhesive or *spray glue* is an aerosol spray used to attach lightweight materials together or to a container or foundation. It is available in different strengths for heavier or lighter applications.

Bouquet glue is an aerosol spray that is applied to the foam foundation of a finished bridal bouquet. It glues the flowers and foliage into the foam for security as well as acts to prohibit evaporation of water from the foam, allowing the flowers to last longer. Care must be taken not to use excessive amounts of bouquet glue or large strings and globs will run onto the flowers, or worse, cascade out of the bouquet.

Floral clay is a soft putty-like material commonly used to anchor needle holders to containers. It is available in either green or white and is sold in small bricks or thin strips rolled between waxed paper. Care should be taken when using floral clay not to stain or damage expensive containers.

Candles

Candle adapters are plastic holders that hold the candle upright and secure in floral foam. The base is constructed so that it does not create a large hole in the foam, therefore giving the candle a great deal of security. Candle adapters are available in several sizes to fit the commonly used candles in floristry.

Candle picking is a technique use to secure odd sized candles or when candle adapters are not available. Using 4" or 6" unwired wooden picks spaced around the base of the candle, wrap several layers of anchor tape around the picks and the candle. Insert the wooden picks into the foam, leaving the candle to rest on top of the foam. Disguise the candle base with greens and/or moss.

Mechanical Problems

The use of wire, picks, foam, etc., is a matter of craftsmanship. There are certain practices that may be learned by experience and observation. Flowers must be conditioned to conform to one's desires. The following suggestions may help solve many mechanical problems:

1. Flowers must be removed from the refrigerator several hours before stems are to be curved. Flowers that have been cut for a day or so are more flexible than freshly cut flowers. They can be shaped into pleasing curves by flexing the stems gently with the fingers. Stems may be made more flexible by massaging them gently. Both flower stems and foliage may be curved in this manner (Figure 52).

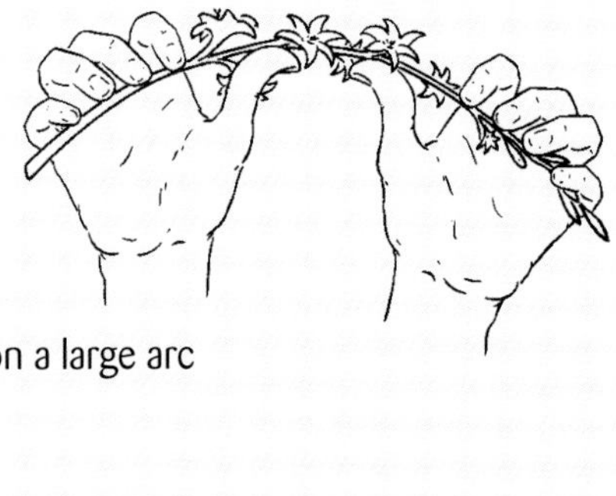

Figure 52
Flex stems by
applying pressure
gently lengthwise on a large arc

2. When a gladiolus stem does not bend correctly, the stem tissue may be split lengthwise by pressing with the fingers or palm (Figure 53). Do not break the stem crosswise, or the flow of water will be impeded.

3. To straighten succulent stems of callas, tritomas, and tulips, roll them tightly in newspaper and place in tepid water for several hours. Then place in the cooler to harden.

4. When using a low container with shallow water, it is important to cut flower stems with a long slant and to place cuts downward so the stems can take up water. A cut in any other direction may not be covered by water. When securing slanting stems to pin frogs, the fingers are never used to press stems in place; another stem may be used to do the pressing without injury to the person (Figure 54).

5. One line flower may be placed next to another line flower to continue the length of the blossoms; they are positioned first, and then a rather stiff wire (gauge #18 or #20) is run horizontally through the stems (Figure 55).

6. Brace wire large stems together using a #20 wire (Figure 56). Start by making one revolution of the wire around the tallest flower/stem, then brace it by attaching to other large flowers on either side of it. This makes a "unit" that is less likely to shift or become dislodged.

7. When extra height is needed in an arrangement, stems may be inserted in water tubes or water picks and then tied to sticks or other stems and placed in position (Figure 57). This is only for short-term designs.

8. Cable ties (indestructible plastic strips with a buckle on the end — just like a man's belt) are excellent mechanics for securing funeral sprays to easels, tying hand-tied bouquets and many other needs.

Ribbon

Ribbons used by florists today vary greatly in materials and patterns. Many novelty ribbons reach the market each year, following the fashion trends. Standard types, however, are always popular. Satin ribbon is used for wedding, corsage, and funeral work. Velvet ribbon enhances the beauty, texture, and quality of the blossoms in wedding and corsage work, adding a touch of luxury and building a reputation of quality. Wired edge ribbon creates graceful lines and flows beautifully in many designs while cotton ribbon tends towards the rustic and informal look. The initial use of ribbon in floral work was to tie the stems of flowers together. Its value has increased during the years with the ingenuity and artistry of floral designers. Though its value is appreciated in completing a design, it should never be allowed to dominate.

Figure 53
Crush stems lengthwise to bend easily

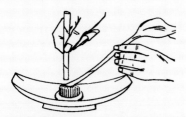
Figure 54
Place slanting cut face down toward water; use another stem for pressing

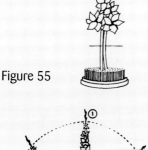
Figure 55

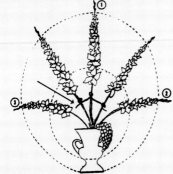
Figure 56
Brace large stems by attaching a No. 20 wire to other large flowers on either side of it

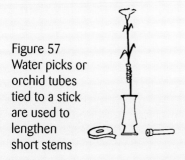
Figure 57
Water picks or orchid tubes tied to a stick are used to lengthen short stems

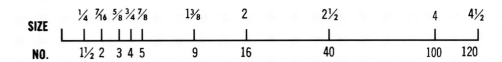

SIZE	¼	⁷⁄₁₆	⅝	¾	⅞	1⅜	2	2½	4	4½
NO.	1½	2	3	4	5	9	16	40	100	120

Figure 58
Measurement of ribbon sizes
with corresponding number

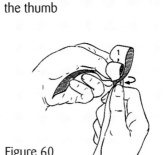

Figure 59
Tying bow – make loop over
thunb and gather ribbon under
the thumb

Figure 60
Twist ribbon
of first loop

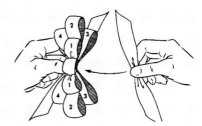

Figure 61
Loop No. 4 added to opposite
side and extra piece ribbon
added into bow (later to tie back
to cover construction)

Ribbon width is expressed in numbers ranging from No. 1, the narrowest, to No. 120, the widest. The widths may vary slightly according to the manufacturer (Figure 58).

The bow should be in proportion to the size of the design. Its loops should fit beneath the blossoms with streamers extending a little beyond. In bridal bouquets the streamers may extend farther, adding line to the design. Bows in football corsages carry the theme of the school colors and, therefore, are as prominent as the blossoms.

The question is often asked, "When are bows placed in arrangements?" They are used in arrangements for special occasions and often used to complete the "gift wrap" on potted plants. Many people now express that any gift, including flower arrangements, could contain a bow. However, since a bow is basically a tie (its purpose was to tie the stems), it is, best therefore, to be placed where the lines of the stems converge, at the center of interest.

The bow maintains its shape much better when it is tied with a piece of wire. Each loop of the bow can be pulled into position when so tied. Tying with another piece of ribbon causes a clumsy appearance, and the individual loops slip when they are adjusted. The bow is secured to the design by slipping the two ends of the wire around the design at the focal area or by attaching the bow to a wooden pick and inserting the pick at the focal area.

Types of Bows

Corsage bows - The ribbon is held between the thumb and, forefinger of the left hand. A streamer four to six inches long extends downward. The ribbon is brought over the thumb and under it, where it is gathered, thus making a center loop (Figure 59). (It is not necessary for the thumb to remain through this loop.) A pair of loops, approximately 1 to 1½ inches in length, is gathered. A second pair of loops is made under the first and extends beyond the first pair by approximately one inch; these loops are gathered beneath the thumb.

Should one be working with a single-faced ribbon or two-toned ribbon, it will be necessary to twist the finished face outward each time a loop is made (Figure 60). A third set of loops, longer than the first pair but shorter than the second, is placed off to the side; this arrangement prevents a stacked appearance of the loops (Figure 61). The fourth pair, a little longer than the third pair yet shorter than the second pair, is placed opposite the third pair.

Should a fifth and sixth pair be desired they are proportionately longer than the second pair, adding width to the bow. Another piece of ribbon approximately four to six inches in length is added to the back of the bow. This piece is to be tied later in a single knot, covering construction after the bow is placed. The size of the bow is determined by the size of the design. The quantity of ribbon should not overbalance the size of the blossoms. Ribbon is intended to enhance the beauty and be a part of the design, not to be the dominant feature.

The bow is tied with a taped wire. This wire is run through the loop that was originally formed over the thumb (Figure 62). Both ends of the wire are pulled to the back of the bow. The index finger of the right hand is slipped in between these two wire ends. The other fingers grasp these ends, pulling the bow tightly down on this index finger (Figure 63). Gather the loops in the left hand, still holding the wire with the right hand; then give one complete turn, tying the bow tightly (Figure 64).

Place the bow adjacent to the focal point of the corsage (toward the face) and tape it on securely with corsage tape.

Knotted Corsage bows - a different style of corsage bow is shown in Plate 115F. This example is more controlled and will appear very elegant in a corsage. Two lengths of #3 ribbon are held together with their shiny sides out. Simple loop-knots are tied and spaced according to the size of the bow, with the first knot being spaced 1-2" longer than the other spaces. This longer space will accommodate the small center loop of the bow (Figure 59). Then each knot should be centered in its own loop when the length of knotted ribbons is fashioned into the bow.

Figure 62
Inserting taped wire through center loop to secure ribbon

Figure 63
Index finger between wire, bow is on top of finger, pull wire tightly

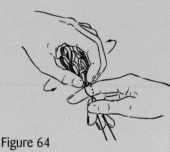

Figure 64
Grasp all ribbon loops and twist bow firmly

Plate 115
Types of bows
A–Spray   B–Radiating
C–Sparkle   D–Rolled ribbon
E–French
F–Knotted Corsage

Spray Bows -Spray bows are made similar to corsage bows, their loops being in proportion to the size of the design (Plate 115A). An extra piece of ribbon may be added to the back forms of the finished bow. Three streamers will prevent the formation of an "X" which would result if four streamers are used.

Bustle bows are close groupings of small loops used to cover construction on the back of designs and are made in much the same manner as are spray bows. They may be used on wedding bouquets, fans, etc., to cover the hands and unite the design with the gown.

French bows/Composite bows - French bows are made from single or double loops; each is pleated and wired on picks. The single loop for the center is a very short piece of ribbon attached to a pick. The streamers, if used, are made with one piece of ribbon tied individually and placed on a pick. To assemble this bow, place the individually picked loops opposite each other; position the streamers at the center. The small center loop, which gives the appearance of tying the bow is placed to cover this union. The finished bow gives the impression that the bow has been tied, but it is much easier to integrate the ribbon into the flowers. (Plate 115E).

French bows are excellent to use on funeral sprays and wreaths, especially tailored, satin-wrapped wreaths. They are also used on large wedding hats, but the sections are sewed together instead of wired.

The Radiating bow is effective on tailored sprays, some types of pot plants, and other designs where it is not worked into the blossoms but remains an individual unit (accent) in the design. It is made of a small center loop gathered tightly under the thumb, with another loop on either side. The streamers are strips of ribbon cut on the diagonal and gathered under this center rosette. This is an effective way of using odds and ends of short pieces of ribbon. A rainbow color combination can be developed

Plate 116 (circa 1966)
A presentation bouquet for the sports arena — carnations and trimmed foliage are tied with rolled satin ribbon.

beautifully in this type of bow. A quick way to make this bow is to simply make a regular bow and cut the loops. (Plate 115B)

Rolled ribbon bow (Plate 116) Many designs, especially those using solid-type blossoms, e.g., callas, or those that are sharply angular, need carefully planned ribbon treatment. Ribbon can enhance the texture of blossoms and design shape, but it must not compete with the blossoms.

Some bridal bouquets and tailored funeral wreaths need the rolled ribbon bow. Wide ribbon, preferably #40 or larger, is rolled on the diagonal. Plate 115D shows sections rolled and picked for use in a design. The length is determined by the size of loop or tail desired. It is then bent into an asymmetrical triangle and placed on a wooden pick. Place in the design as for a French bow.

Sparkle bow. This is an effective use of ribbon, again using odds and ends and various colors, if a person so chooses. This bow is excellent in some types of pot dressings, especially on cyclamen plants. The bow is made and worked into this plant, the ends extending beyond its foliage. When the plant has few open blossoms, a ribbon of the same color as the blossoms, used in this manner, increases the value of the plant. This bow is also good used in combination with the rolled looped ribbon, with these sparkle points radiating out of the center of interest. It is excellent for Christmas designs, especially when the edges of the ribbon are edged in gold or silver.

The ribbon is cut in short strips and the ends cut on opposite diagonals, as shown (Plate 115C). Each rolled piece is gathered in the center and is tied into the cluster.

Accessory Materials

Satin leaves (Figure 65) -'The size of the leaf is determined by the width of the ribbon, with the strips cut twice its width for a leaf. Fold the two upper corners down to the center forming a triangle. Hold the triangular piece of ribbon in the center where the two corners meet and fold double having the smooth face inward. Gather the ribbon from the center straight across the bottom out to the tip of the point. Complete one side of the triangle at a time. Tie with wire. These may be made of graded sizes to use in wedding work and silk flower designs (Plate 117A, 1-5).

Glamour leaves - Glamour leaves may be in outline form or this form may then be filled in with additional material, e.g., satin, net, etc. Use satin-wrapped wire or metallic cord reinforced with wire for the frame. Shape wire into the desired form, e.g., maple leaf, lance leaf, etc. Use a quick-drying glue or fabric adhesive on one side of the cord forming the outline of the leaf. Press down on the material that is to form the body of the leaf (satin, net, etc.) When dry, trim off the surplus material. These may be used in corsages and wedding bouquets (Plate 117B, 1-4).

Folding corners downward.

Figure 65
Satin leaf construction, gather from center outward

Plate 117
Types of Accessories –
A. Satin Leaves
 1. Fold first
 2. Pleated, wired
 3. Taped, finished
 4. Miniature size
 5. Branch
B. Glamour Leaves
 1. Satin tubing
 2. Finished on ribbon
 3. Finished on ribbon
 4. Applied to ribbon
C. Alençon Lace
 1. Clipped, starched, wired and taped
 2. Original piece
D. Pearl Leaves
 1-3. Pearl beads strung on a wire, shaped, taped
E. Ribbon Roses
 1-4. Folded petals, Benz Method, Figure 66
 5. Started with Benz method, then stitched underneath with needle and thread for extra security
 6. Stitched
 7. Pulled, stitched, pale edge of ribbon out
 8. Pulled, stitched, dark edge of ribbon out
 9. Pulled technique – pale edge pulled, knot is the starting point
 10-12. Pulled, stitched technique repeated.

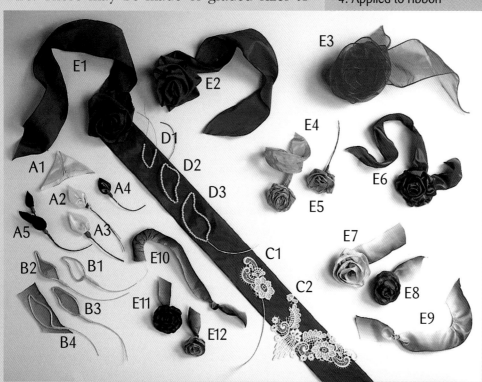

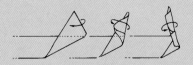

Figure 66
Fold and roll ribbon to form center.

Fold ribbon outward forming triangular petals.

Continue folding ribbon same direction for petals alternating each fold.

Use pin or glue to secure finished rose.

Ribbon rose second method — fold each end of ribbon at right angles from center outward.

After alternating folds, release top and pull one end downward.

Alternate ribbon points forming rose.

Alençon lace leaves - Select a lace pattern that coordinates with the garment and cut out a piece of the pattern; stiffen it with starch, spray adhesive or diluted liquid glue solution; wire, tape and use in corsage or bouquet designs (Plates 117C, 1-2, 262 and 283).

Pearl leaves - Strands of pearls may be purchased and strung onto No. 24 wire and shaped into leaf outlines (Plate 117D, 1-3).

Satin roses - Ribbon roses are useful as decorative items on packages or to add special color or texture contrast on Christmas designs. Benz method: Fold the end of the ribbon over itself several times forming the center of the rose. Holding the center in the left hand, fold the ribbon towards you at right angles with the right hand thus creating a pointed petal (Plate 117E, 1-2). Continue this process circling the center with right hand folds thus increasing the size of the blossom. Second method- Start with a piece of ribbon approximately thirty inches long. Fold it at a right angle in the center (Plate 117E, 3-4) and continue folding each end over the other at right angles (Figure 66), stacking the folded ribbon between the forefinger and thumb until all the ribbon is used. Hold both ends tightly and let go of the folded section. Pull one end of the ribbon down until the first fold almost disappears in the center. Slightly twist the petals to adjust the formation of the rose. Twist the base securely with #26 or #28 wire and add velvet or satin leaves if desired (Figure 66).

There is another quick and easy method of making ribbon roses using wire-edged ribbon. (Plate 117E, 9-10) Tie a knot in one end of the wired ribbon. From the other end securely pull the wire on one edge of the ribbon while pushing the fabric toward the knot, causing the ribbon to gather. Then hold the knot like a stem while encircling the gathered ribbon around it to form a rose. Use the exposed wire to wrap around the new calyx of the flower. Gently caress the ungathered edge into the shape of curling petals. A more detailed technique, stitching, is to secure each fold or gather with needle and thread. A stem may be added by wrapping a suitable gauge wire around the knot or calyx of the rose and taping its full length. This pulled and stitched rose is shown in Plate 117E, 7-12.

Raffia - Raffia, though not technically a ribbon, is frequently substituted for ribbon in many informal and rustic designs. Raffia may also be used to tie material together or create armatures for design use (binding) and for encircling cylinder containers for pure decoration (banding). It is a natural material made from palm trees, though is available in many assorted colors. Raffia bows are usually either tied directly to the container or base or attached to a wood pick, with the pick then inserted into the design.

Chapter 16   DESIGN TECHNIQUES

Creativity in floral design has advanced in recent years, due to the abundance of new *ways* of presenting material in designs. These techniques are demonstrated and explained all over the world by designers, commentators and educators, therefore it is of great importance for all professionals to be knowledgeable and accurate in their communication skills. The American Institute of Floral Designers has published an excellent reference book of florist-related terms entitled, "Book of Floral Terminology". This book is a dictionary of over 1200 vocabulary words with internationally accepted correct definitions. It is an excellent resource for everyone in the floral industry, and it serves as the basis for the information presented in this chapter.

Design Techniques

Mechanics and techniques in floral design, while closely related, have different meanings. **Design mechanics** as shown in the preceding chapter: are *devices that help to secure materials and create stability in a design; they are normally concealed but they may be deliberately exposed for artistic effect.* Mechanics are always functional. **Design technique**: is *the manner with which a designer implements specialized procedures and methods for placing plant materials and decorative accessories into a composition.* Techniques are usually decorative, sometimes functional and occasionally both.

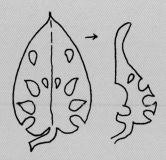

Figure 67
Abstracting

Abstracting (decorative): This is the act of changing a type of plant material so that it looks unnatural. Parts of a flower or leaf, for example, may be removed, clipped, folded, twisted, tied and even painted to aid the designer in achieving a special effect. Plant materials may also be positioned in unnatural ways.

Armature (decorative and functional): This is a structure that is constructed of natural or man-made materials and is used to support all or part of a floral composition. Armatures may be decorative or utilitarian, and they may be of any size and orientation.

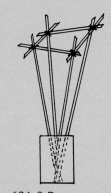

Figure 68A & B—
Naturalistic & Man-Made

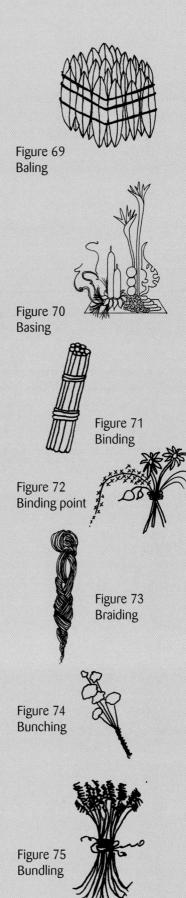

Figure 69
Baling

Figure 70
Basing

Figure 71
Binding

Figure 72
Binding point

Figure 73
Braiding

Figure 74
Bunching

Figure 75
Bundling

Baling (decorative): This is the simulation of a bale of grass or hay by compressing and tying plant materials together. It is often used as a means of creating an accessory for a larger composition. Compare and contrast this term with bundling (below).

Banding (decorative): Encircling plant or man-made materials in concise and consecutive rings with decorative appointments such as gold wire, raffia or silk cording is known as banding. This technique is ornamental rather than mechanical.

Basing (decorative and functional): This is accomplished when techniques such as clustering, layering, terracing and pavé are used to make a decorative surface for the foundation from which a floral composition emerges. Basing is particularly useful in parallel and vegetative designs.

Binding (functional): Tying materials together for the purpose of holding them in place. This is a mechanical technique, which is necessary for the stability of the design - even when it looks attractive. Compare and contrast this technique with banding (above).

Binding Point (functional): This is the place where the string is tied on a hand-tied bouquet. It is any point or area where stems are tied together.

Braiding/Plaiting (decorative): Strands of fiber, ribbon, foliage etc. are interwoven to create a decorative accent or accessory in a floral composition. Various maneuvers such as folding and pleating may be incorporated in making a braid.

Bunching (functional): A great deal of time can be saved when tiny or delicate materials are gathered and bound together before they are inserted into a design. Bunches can be tied with wire, cord, wired wood picks or they may be inserted into a picking machine.

Bundling (decorative and functional): Firmly tying like or similar materials together so that a radial stem pattern is created above and below the binding point. A sheaf of wheat is a good example of this technique. A small bundle may be a component of a large composition or a large bundle may be a freestanding design and serve as the foundation for a decoration.

Clustering (decorative): Placing a collection of small textural flowers or foliage of a single kind close together so that the individual component becomes indistinguishable from the mass. This technique is useful in creating forms and textures in abstract work. Compare and contrast this term with grouping (below).

Collaring (decorative and functional): Surrounding a flower, bouquet or container's rim with natural or man-made leaves or other decorative materials to create a finished appearance. This technique is often used in finishing wedding bouquets.

Figure 76
Collaring

Facing (decorative and functional): Directing or turning a flower head in a certain way in order to increase interest and provide visual movement within a design. This technique can help in achieving balance, emphasis, repetition, transition, harmony, contrast, variation, opposition or tension. Compare with mirroring.

Framing (decorative): Using branches, foliage or man-made materials to enclose, partially enclose, delineate or showcase the material within. Framing defines space and may call attention to the focal area or other facet of a design.

Gradation/Sequencing (decorative/functional): The placement of like materials in an ordered sequence, from largest to smallest or darkest to lightest etc. Used to create rhythm.

Grouping (decorative): The placement of identical materials within a specific, limited area, with each piece maintaining its individual identity. There is usually space between the groupings. The grouping of materials is often used in vegetative, formalinear and parallel designs.

Hand-tying (decorative and functional): Arranging the stems of flowers, foliage and accessories in the hand using a disciplined method of diagonals and spiraling around the center of the design where the hand grasps the stems (binding point). When the bouquet is completed, the stems are bound with string, raffia or binding cord at the binding point, thus creating a hand-tied bouquet.

Figure 77
Hand-tying

Lacing (functional): A method of crossing and interlocking stems to form a framework for holding other plant materials in place in a vase. Successive stem placements result in a mechanically sound vase design that is deliverable.

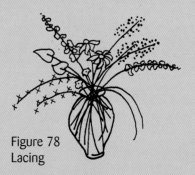
Figure 78
Lacing

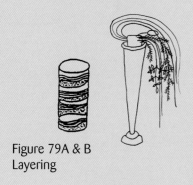

Figure 79A & B
Layering

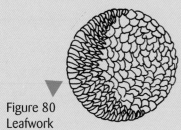

Figure 80
Leafwork

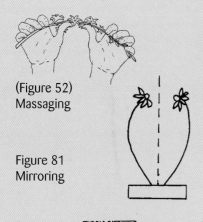

(Figure 52)
Massaging

Figure 81
Mirroring

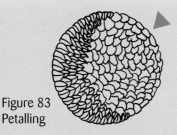

Figure 82
Pavé

Figure 83
Petalling

Figure 84
Pillowing

Layering (decorative): Covering a surface with foliage or other materials horizontally placed, by overlapping the individual units leaving little or no space in between them. An example of this would be the nice decorative effect that can be made by layering different colors and textures of sand inside a glass cylinder. Foliage, bark chips etc. could also be layered on the base of a design. Compare and contrast this term with stacking (below).

Leafwork (decorative): The process of creating a decorative surface by applying foliage (small sprigs or individual leaves) in an overlapping manner to give texture and visual interest to the outside of an object. The leaves are usually glued into place, but in interpretive and abstract designs, they may be sewn with thread, wire or long thorns. Compare and contrast this term with pave and petalling (below).

Massaging (decorative and functional): The bending or curving of a flower stem by applying gentle pressure and warmth with the thumbs, fingers and hands. Working with plant materials at room temperature facilitates this process. Anthurium, aspidistra, calla lily, pussy willow and Scotch broom respond well to this technique.

Mirroring (decorative): The placement of materials in a composition such that one appears to reflect the other (mirror image). Mirroring may be accomplished with the technique of facing.

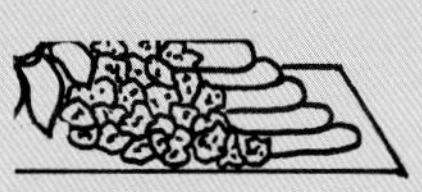

Pavé (decorative and functional): This is a term borrowed from jewelry making which refers to setting gem stones so close together that no metal shows. In floral design it is usually a basing technique using parallel or surface contoured insertions, which creates a uniform surface area with little or no variation of depth.

Petalling (decorative): Covering the surface of an object such as a wreath ring, block of foam or container with individual petals in an overlapping manner. The petals may be held in place with glue or by wrapping metallic thread (gold bouillon) around the object as the petals are applied. Compare and contrast this technique with leafwork (above).

Pillowing (decorative): A tightly organized and controlled radial placement of clustered materials into a composition. The clusters may range from tight basing to taller dimensional contours with emphasis on color and texture. When clusters of materials are pillowed at the base of a design, the result is like a cushion, which, at intervals is depressed and looks similar to rolling hills, clouds or pillows, emphasizing the color and texture of the sum, rather than the individual blossoms.

Pruning (decorative and functional): This technique reveals a stronger line or a more interesting shape by selectively removing branches, foliage, florets or petals to create desirable negative space and produce materials that appear more sculptural.

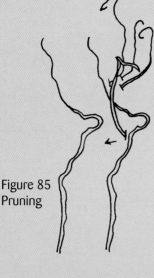

Figure 85
Pruning

Reflexing (decorative and functional): To reflex petals, place the thumb against the outside lower center of the petal; then with the index and middle fingers, gently pull back the petal causing it to reverse its natural curve. This practice increases the size of a flower such as a rose or tulip. In carnations the same action is used on approximately one fourth of the calyx allowing the petals to expand outward.

Plate 118
Reflexing

Sectioning/Zoning (decorative): Confining like materials to specific areas within the composition. This is larger scale treatment than either clustering or grouping.

Figure 86
Sewing

Sewing (decorative and functional): Fastening materials together by piercing them with needle and thread or wire. This technique is most commonly used in the construction of casket covers, horse blankets, leis, table runners or wall hangings.

Shadowing (decorative): Giving a composition a three-dimensional appearance by the close placement of one identical material directly behind another - either lower or higher. This results in the appearance of a shadow or echo of the original. Compare and contrast this with facing and mirroring (above).

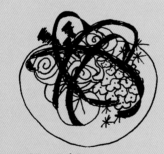

Figure 87A and B
Sheltering (above and below)

Sheltering (decorative): Placing one or more materials over or around another, lightly enclosing the materials within, to create an impression of protection.

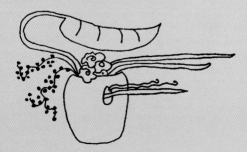

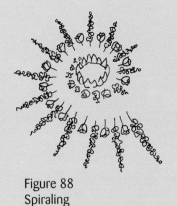

Figure 88
Spiraling

Spiraling (decorative): A clear line movement circling around a central point in a flat curve that is constantly increasing or decreasing in size.

Stacking (decorative): Placing pieces of the same material in similar sizes on top of, or against one another, without space between each component, in an orderly (usually vertical) fashion. Compare and contrast this technique with both layering and terracing.

Terracing (decorative): Placing like materials in stair-step fashion, creating spaced horizontal levels. This is a way to create depth within the concept of basing.

Tufting (decorative and functional): The placement of tufts – radial clusters of short elongated materials tied together at a binding point – into a design, often at the base, to create interest and variation in the surface area.

Tying (functional): A practical way of securing or fastening materials together with raffia, cord, rope, straps, etc. See hand-tying, binding and bundling for contrast and comparison.

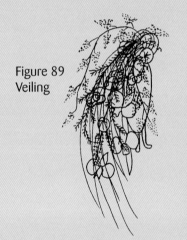

Figure 89
Veiling

Veiling (decorative): Layering light materials such as bear grass, springeri, plumosa, metallic threads, angel hair, etc., over more solid forms creating a light, almost transparent screen. This is often used in the waterfall style design. Compare and contrast with sheltering and layering.

(Plate 10)

Weaving (decorative/functional): Interlacing materials to create a new dimensional texture or pattern. Compare and contrast this term with sewing.

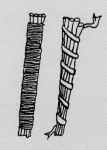

Figure 90
Wrapping

Wrapping (decorative): Covering the length of a single stem, bundle of stems, dowel rod or cylinder, etc., by encircling it with decorative materials such as ribbon, raffia or cording. Compare and contrast this term with banding.

155

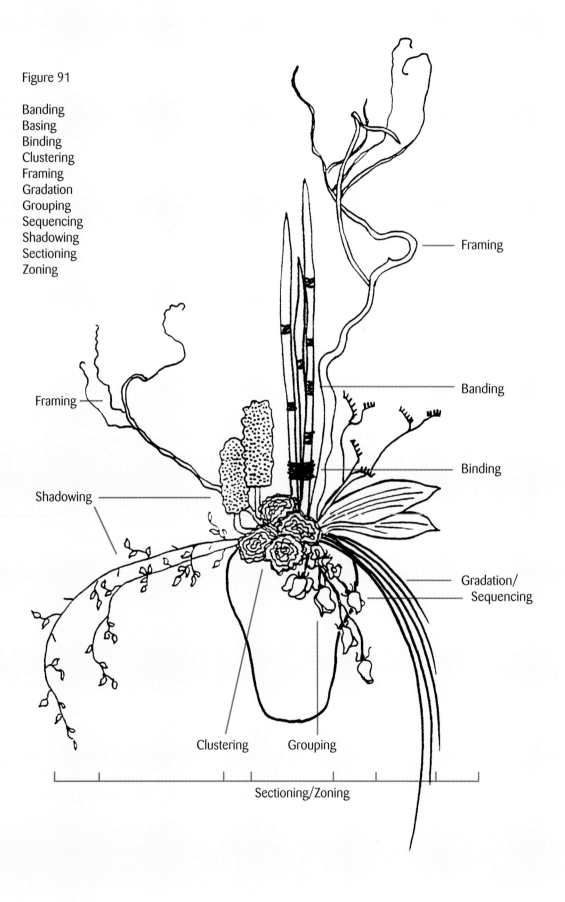

Figure 91

Banding
Basing
Binding
Clustering
Framing
Gradation
Grouping
Sequencing
Shadowing
Sectioning
Zoning

Framing

Framing

Banding

Binding

Shadowing

Gradation/
Sequencing

Clustering   Grouping

Sectioning/Zoning

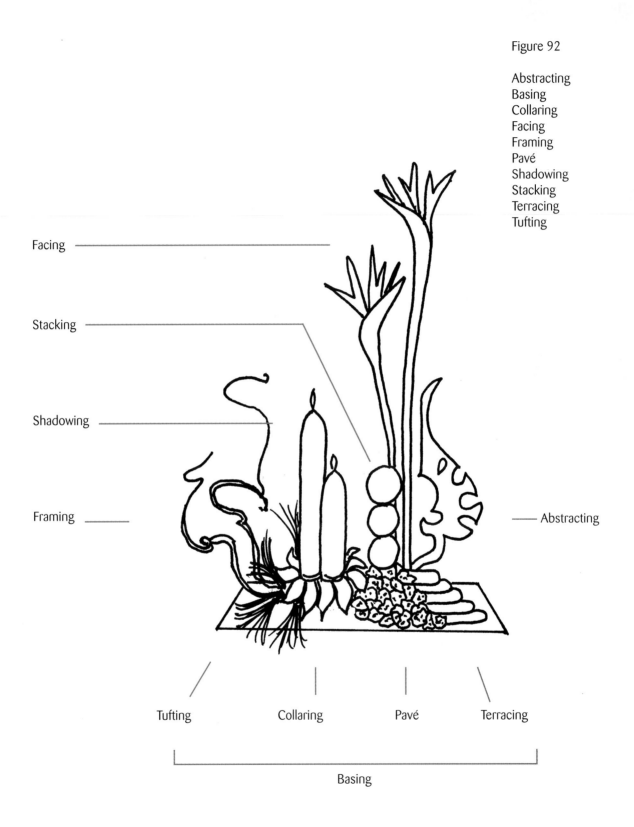

Figure 92

Abstracting
Basing
Collaring
Facing
Framing
Pavé
Shadowing
Stacking
Terracing
Tufting

Facing

Stacking

Shadowing

Framing

Abstracting

Tufting   Collaring   Pavé   Terracing

Basing

Chapter 17 Color Alternatives

Aerosol Paints

There are two types of floral aerosol paints: (1) Tints and (2) Paints. Tints are always pastel - they will never be a dark color even if you spray a whole can on one small basket. The color range in tints is somewhat limiting (blue, pink, yellow, green, burgundy), but they are mixable (see double spraying technique) to obtain many other pastel colors. Tints are most often used to make white or ivory objects a pastel color or for subtle color changes on colored materials. (For more details see 'Techniques').

On the other hand, floral paints are much heavier in pigment content than tints. Therefore, they can drastically alter the color of the material being sprayed - such as changing red to black or blue to orange. The color choices for floral paints are quite extensive (over 60 colors), and constantly changing with the color trends.

Both floral paints and tints can be used on fresh flowers and foliages without harm if applied according to manufacturer instructions. Each manufacturer has a different spray nozzle and spray pattern, so what works well for one brand will not necessarily work for another. It is easy to "freeze" the petals of flowers if the can is held too close to the flower. This is caused by the propellant as it exits the can and distributes the paint. Brown tips and/or brown spots on the petals, is an indication that the flower was painted too closely and "frozen".

The secret to proper painting with aerosols is movement. Move both the object being sprayed and the paint can. The speed which the paint is propelled can cause runs and/or drips if you should stop moving even for a moment. Start the spray off to one side of the intended object and move onto it. This helps prevent spotting from the first few large droplets of paint that come out of the can. Also do not stop the spray on the object, but move off to one side to prevent runs and dark spots. Floral sprays dry quickly, (30 - 60 seconds), so it is better to give several light coats than one heavy coat that might run.

Techniques

Double Spray
Spraying the same flower or container twice with different colors of spray, usually a tint.
Step 1 -   Start with a white carnation (as an example) and spray with a yellow tint. Let dry.
Step 2 - Then spray with pink tint. The result should be a peach or apricot colored carnation.

Faux Antiqued
This technique will give baskets, containers and other material an old "used" look. This technique can be done with one color or double spray and wipe the top color only.
Step 1 - Spray paint onto a small section of an object, usually containers or dried material, then quickly wipe the paint with a soft cloth before it dries.
Step 2 - Repeat step 1 as you rotate the object until totally antiqued.

Back Spray
Technique of spraying the back edges of a flower (usually orchid or similar form flower) to cause a wrap-around effect of the paint onto the front face of the flower. Normally done with a tint for only a subtle color addition.
Step 1 - Prepare orchid (as an example) and turn flower over with the back facing the aerosol can.
Step 2 - Direct the aerosol at the flower petal edges and lightly spray, being certain not to over spray and damage the flower.
Step 3 - Check the front of the blossom and determine if more color is needed. Compare with un-colored blossom for accuracy.

Leaf Stencil

An interesting way to make containers have a bontanical or garden appeal.

Step 1 - Start with an interesting shaped leaf as a pattern (maple, oak, etc.) and adhere it to the container with bits of rolled tape.

Step 2 - Lightly spray the leaf edge with an appropriate paint color. Let dry.

Step 3 - Remove leaf and re-apply in different position.

Step 4 - Repeat steps 2 and 3 to create as complex or simple a pattern as you desire.

Faux Gold Gilding

A useful technique when creating Christmas decorations, renaissance motifs, or opulent party decorations.

Step 1 - Fill a large bucket lined with a trash bag (to prevent paint from sticking to the bucket) 3/4 full of tepid water.

Step 2 - Heavily spray an aerosol sealant onto the water surface. Let dry 5-10 minutes or to expedite the drying process, use a hair dryer on its low setting.

Step 3 - Repeat heavy sealant application 3-4 times being careful not to break the film coating from previous applications. Dry 5-10 minutes between coats.

Step 4 - Then spray 2-3 coats of gold paint onto the sealant letting it dry between coats. After last coat of gold paint, let dry 30-45 minutes.

Step 5 - Finally, gently remove the thin gold gilding from the water surface and place topside down on a soft cloth to dry. Carefully transfer and adhere the gold gilding to containers, leaves, fruit, etc. with spray glue.

Faux Birch Branches

Create your own birch branches from ordinary sticks and twigs for Holiday decorations.

Step 1 - Start by spraying dried sticks with flat white paint. It may take two or three coats to make them completely white.

Step 2 - Then spray the sticks with black Deco Lace® or flat black paint using a splattering technique for the horizontal "Birch" lines.

Silver Undercoat

Silver aerosol paint has a very heavy pigment, but it is also a neutral color. It will cover most other colors with one coat and most colors will cover silver with one coat. Therefore, use silver aerosol paint as the first coat when drastically changing colors. There is also a silver/gray colored "primer" that may be purchased for altering colored material.

Dip Marbleizing

This finish may be used on many different items such as containers, dried material, fresh material, candles, etc. The effect is to add depth and texture, while at the same time creating a unique combination of colors.

Step 1 - Place a trash bag in a large bucket (to prevent paint from sticking to the bucket) and fill 3/4 full with tepid water.

Step 2 - Choose paint colors for the marbleizing. Experiment to determine which colors look best together. Three to six colors are typical for dip marbleizing.

Step 3 - Spray the first color onto the water surface, heavier in some places, lighter in others, creating different pigment concentrations and patterns.

Step 4 - Dip the object into the water letting the floating paint envelop the object. Note that the object should be completely submerged into the water to avoid blank or bare places. Try twisting the object as you begin to submerge it for a swirled effect.

Step 5 - Remove the object from the water and gently pat dry with a soft cloth. Let dry several minutes or use a hair dryer to completely dry the paint.

Step 6 - Repeat steps 3 to 5 with other paint colors to achieve the desired effect. Always let the paint dry between coats for best adhesion.

Step 7 - After the last coat, let the paint dry 1 to 2 hours (or use the hair dryer). Then spray with an appropriate sealant to prevent paint chipping and scratches.

Inside Marbleizing

This variation of the dip marbleizing is great for use on clear glass. All the painting is done on the inside of the vase and is thus protected from outside chipping or scratching. This technique is ideal for containers that will hold permanent designs. However, for fresh designs it is recommended that a liner be used inside the marbleized glass vase to protect the new paint finish from stems and moisture.

Step 1 - Thoroughly wash the inside of the vase with warm soapy water to remove any dirt or residual oils. Dry completely.

Step 2 - Choose which colors of paint to use. Experiment to determine which colors will look best together. Typically there are 3 to 6 colors used for this technique.

Step 3 - Holding the vase on its side, place a puddle of tepid water in the vase. Larger puddles of water tend to make delicate marbleizing while smaller puddles make heavier marbleizing.

Step 4 - Spray the first color onto the puddle of water, creating floating paint that resembles heavy spider webbing.

Step 5 - Rotate the vase letting the paint adhere to the sides of the vase. Just before the water is free of paint, add more of the same color or choose a different color. Keep rotating and adding paint until the entire inside of the vase is covered. Do not try to repeat past the starting point, or the paint will float off of the glass.

Step 6 - Gently pour out the water and use a soft cloth to pat and adhere the paint to the glass sides.

Step 7 - Let dry several hours or use a hair dryer to thoroughly dry the paint.

Step 8 - Repeat steps 3 to 7 as many times as needed to reach the desired effects.

Step 9 - Again, dry thoroughly, and then apply a solid background color by over spraying the entire inside of the vase. Do not use water for this step! Typically the background color is black, white, hunter green, or a metallic color.

Step 10 - Dry thoroughly and then spray with a sealant to protect the finish.

Step 11 - Optional - As a finishing touch, rim the opening of the vase with gold or another metallic paint color. Use a small paint brush or your finger tip and dip into paint sprayed into a paint can lid. Carefully apply this to the rim of the vase.

Monet Blending

This technique causes the paint colors of a previously marbleized object to blend together, giving it the look of an impressionistic painting.

Step 1 — Elevate a previously marbleized object over several layers of newspaper so that the base is not in contact with the newspaper. Use a bud vase, paint can lid, or other object that is smaller than the base of the marbleized object as a stand.

Step 2 — Using a spray sealant or clear porcelain spray, heavily spray the marbleized object, letting the excess drip off the bottom onto the newspaper.

Step 3 — Continue spraying the sealant or porcelain until the marbleized paint begins to melt. Stop spraying when the desired amount of dissolving and blending has occurred.

Step 4 — Carefully wipe the bottom of the object to remove any excess sealant or porcelain drops.

Step 5 — Let dry for several hours or overnight prior to use.

Deco Lace® Texturing

This technique is similar to the Monet Blending, but uses the product called Deco Lace as the base coat. It can be used to salvage scratched or damaged vases, and at the same time, create a wonderful deep texture.

Step 1 — Select a vase, choose an appropriate color of Deco Lace, and choose the color of the aerosol paint that will eventually be the dominate color of the vase. For best results, the aerosol paint should contrast with the Deco Lace. Both plastic and glass vases that have a "shoulder" (like a ginger jar) will work with this technique.

Step 2 — Heavily spray the rim area and/or shoulder of the vase with Deco Lace, allowing it to form pools and small rivulets that run down the side of the vase. Use the directional spray of Deco Lace to encourage rivulets down the sides. The Deco Lace should bubble up and look very bumpy. Let dry completely 30 to 45 minutes or use a hair dryer to speed up the drying process.

Step 3 — Spray the entire vase, including the Deco Lace with the aerosol paint chosen in Step 1. Let dry thoroughly.

Step 4 — Optional — Spray another coating of aerosol paint contrasting with first. This will then become the dominate color, but it will blend with first coating to create interesting color contrasts in step 6.

Step 5 — Elevate the vase as with the Monet Blending technique.

Step 6 — Using a spray sealant or porcelain spray, heavily spray the Deco Laced area. Let soak for a few seconds, then spray again at close range. The aerosol paint should start dissolving away leaving the Deco Lace bumps and ridges exposed.

Step 7 — Continue spraying the sealant or porcelain until the desired amount of Deco Lace is revealed. Carefully wipe the bottom to remove excess sealant or porcelain drips. Let dry several hours or overnight prior to use.

Powder Texturing

This is a quick and simple method to either "age" something, like a terra cotta pot, or give texture to smooth objects, such as wooden cattails.

Step 1 — Paint the object the chosen color, or paint in blotches to resemble an aged, discolored container.

Step 2 — Before the paint dries, dust it heavily with baby powder, letting the powder stick to the wet paint areas.

Step 3 — Spray again, over the baby powder, with the aerosol paint, and again dust with the baby powder while still wet.

Step 4 — Repeat step 3 up to 6 times to achieve the desired texture and colors. At anytime, substitute spray sealant for the paints to keep the baby powder white (such as for terra cotta pots)

Step 5 — After the last coating of baby powder/paint or baby powder/sealant has been applied, apply a final heavy coat of sealant to assure proper adhesion and to protect the textured finish.

Specialty Aerosol Sprays

Anti-transpirants - Used for all fresh flower designs but especially on corsage and wedding work. Spray both the top and bottom surfaces of the material to greatly reduce water loss due to transpiration, which occurs mostly on the bottom of petals and leaves.

Spray Sealers - Used on dried material to help prevent shattering and loss due to high humidity and insects.

Mum Glue - Sprayed on the back of football mums to prevent shattering.

Glitter Glue - Sprayed on surfaces before applying glitter, diamond dust, etc.

Spray Glitter - Aerosol spray that has very fine particles of glitter.

Pearl/Opalescent Spray - Aerosol spray that adds a "pearl" or opalescent finish. Usually does not change the existing color, but masks it slightly.

Web Spray - Web-like spray that comes in red, gold, black and silver. Both "high tech" and "antique" finishes are possible with this product.

Porcelain Finish - Clear aerosol spray with a high gloss finish.

Color Washes - Thinned down version of aerosol paints to create "white washed" or "pickled" effect. Works best on dark colored materials.

Always remember to spray all aerosols in a well-vented area, preferably outside. When finished spraying, clean the nozzle by holding the can upside down and spraying for 3-5 seconds - until no color comes forth. This will prevent the nozzle from clogging.

Liquid Dyes

There are two major methods of dyeing flowers: (1) absorption method, and (2) dip and rinse method. Both methods are more time consuming than aerosol painting/tinting, but when large quantities of flowers are needed, the dyeing methods may be much more time and cost efficient.

Absorption Method - Dye is absorbed by the flower through the stem. The freshly cut flowers are allowed to soften a bit from need of water (de-hydrate). The stems are then re-cut and are immediately placed into the dye solution. As stems absorb the liquid, tepid dye is transported into the petals. It is first noticed in the large veins and soon spreads over the entire petal. This process usually requires 1 to 4 hours at room temperature. Remove flowers from the dye just prior to desired color since dye in the stem will continue towards the petals. Do not refrigerate until desired color has been obtained. Caution must be used when designing in clear vases with flowers colored in this manner. The dye may bleed into the water from the stem ends causing unsightly colored water.

Dip and Rinse Method - When using this method, the blossoms and solution should be at room temperature. The dye may be thinned with a special thinner to obtain the exact tint desired. After dipping blossoms into the dye solution, rinse them briefly in a bucket of tepid clear water. Should the flowers not dye evenly, it is probably because of the residue of grower chemicals or natural waxes on the blossoms. If the first blossoms tried do not dye well, rinse the others in clear tepid water and allow them to dry for thirty minutes before dipping them into the dye solution again.

Chapter 18
PRESERVING FLOWERS AND FOLIAGE

Preserving Foliage with Glycerin

Glycerin is a chemical emollient that helps preserve foliage in a pliable and supple stage. The glycerine actually replaces water in the plant cells causing them to remain soft and flexible, instead of becoming totally dehydrated (dried). Properly glycerinized foliage can last many months depending upon type and variety.

Foliage that is treated by this method will generally turn a brown or brownish-black color, unless absorption dye is used along with the glycerinizing .

Use the following step-by-step procedure as a guideline for creating glycerinized foliage.

1. Solution should be: 30-40% pure glycerine, 60-70% water and floral absorption dye (if color is desired); experiment to get preferred amount of dye.
2. Harvest leaves and small branches after the leaves are mature, otherwise the tips may wilt.
3. Bunch and place freshly cut *stems* only (not the entire plant) in solution immediately. Foliages left out of water for long periods of time lose their ability to take up solution.

4. Be sure to let the materials set in bright light (not direct sunlight) during the absorption process. Light is needed to draw up the solution through the transpiration and respiration processes (solution should be at room temperature; 60-80°F).

5. Let plant "drink" until evidence of dye or glycerin can be seen (2-4 days). The process will vary according to the variety, climate and solution. Remove plant material and hang bunches upside down or place individual leaves on wire racks to complete the process. Do not over glycerinize or leaves and stems may ooze glycerine.

6. Let foliages stand for 1-2 weeks after removing from glycerine solution to complete the process. This allows for shrinkage as well as final color determination. Store in a cool, dry, area with good air circulation.

7. Expect a 20-30% loss of material that will not absorb the glycerine properly.

Foliage Suitable for Preserving With Glycerine
Table 18-1

Anthurium	Holly-grape	Poplar, White or Silver
Aspidistra*	Lemon	Purple leaf plum
Beech	Magnolia*	Quince, flowering
Cotoneaster	Maples*	Russian Olive
Crabapple	Mountain Ash	Salal (Lemon leaf)*
Dracaena	Oaks*	Spirea
English Ivy	Orange	Sweet Gum
Eucalyptus*	Peony	Weigela
Galax*	Periwinkle	

*highly recommended

Drying Flowers and Foliage

Foliage and flowers may be dehydrated and still retain much of their natural beauty. Most florists have an abundance of odds and ends that could be turned into profit with only a few minutes of attention. Arrangements of naturally dried materials are popular, easy to create and long lasting.

Selecting Materials for Drying

Flowers and other plant materials for drying should be chosen or picked that are close to their prime. Flowers continue to open as they dry, and therefore should not be fully open at picking.

Always collect more material than is needed, to allow for damage. Use only the most perfect forms. Poor shapes dry as poor shapes. Use only plant material free of insect and disease damage and moisture. Place stems promptly in a container of tepid water to prevent wilting if gathering or collecting.

It is sometimes difficult to develop graceful lines when making dried flower arrangements. Therefore, while collecting, look for branches and stems with sweeping curves or lines that will add distinctiveness to arrangements. If none can be found, curves or other lines can be made by shaping the branches or stems into the desired positions while they dry.

Methods for Drying Plant Materials:

The Hanging Method. The oldest and simplest method of drying flowers is by drying them in the air. By hanging them upside down, gravity keeps the stems straight. Remember, as the material loses its moisture, the stems will weaken and wilt.

1. Choose a warm, dry (and dark) room.
2. Stretch a wire or clothesline across.
3. Group stems into small bunches and bundle with a rubber band—secure to the clothesline with "s" hooks or similar wire attachment.
4. Check occasionally for dryness. Stems of different sizes and densities will require different lengths of drying time.
5. Once completely dry, remove material from drying area and spray with a sealant to prevent moisture re-absorption and to retard shattering.
6. Store in a cool, dark, dry area with good air circulation.

Materials Suitable for Drying by the Hanging Method
Table 18-2

Baby's Breath	Bells of Ireland
Cornflower	Cockscomb
Globe Amaranth	Larkspur
Lemon/Salal	Beargrass
Mini Calla	Yarrow
Roses	Aspidistra
Sage	Statice
Strawflower	Mini Carnation

The Standing Method. Any materials that are stiff and not given to wilting may simply be placed into containers and left "standing" in a corner.

1. Select clean, dry containers such as tall vases, baskets, etc. and stand loosely grouped bunches into them.
2. Be sure that "branchy" materials are not tangled. Once dry, they are difficult to separate without shattering.
3. Once completely dry, remove from drying area and spray with a sealant to prevent moisture re-absorption, and to retard shattering.
4. Store in a cool, dry, dark area with good air circulation.

Materials Suitable for Drying by the Standing Method
Table 18-3

Cattails	Ginger
Grasses	Heliconia
Lotus Pods	Montbretia Pods
Poppy	Teasel

The Racking Method. Many things such as bunches of grasses and small tree branches may simply be laid out on a rack made of wire or wood slats.

1. Take care to place these materials carefully so the heads do not get mashed.
2. Place some materials partially over the rack's

edge to create curves and interesting lines, if so desired.
3. Once completely dry, remove from the rack and spray with a sealant to prevent moisture re-absorption and retard shattering.
4. Store in a cool, dry, area with good air circulation.

Materials Suitable for Drying by the Racking Method
Table 18-4

Beargrass
Cottage Yarrow
Dock
Grasses
Seed pods

The Pressing Method. Pressed flowers and foliage are especially suitable for flower pictures, as well as for decoration on note paper, place cards, lamp shades and many other items.

Use flowers and foliage for pressing that are in prime condition. Also, use flowers with different stages of development for more variety when designing. Avoid plants with fleshy stems and leaves as well as flowers with very thin petals. Do not try to press wilted materials. Flowers that are flat, such as pansies, press best.

1. Select materials for your plant "press". Two 12"x12", half inch plywood boards, several sheets of corrugated cardboard, newspaper and non-quilted paper towels to layer between the plant specimens, is ideal. Do not place newspaper against delicate petals because the ink sometimes transfers to them. Telephone books and catalogs work pretty well also, but they don't allow for good air circulation, which is important to prevent mildew. Plant presses may also be purchased at many craft stores.
2. Sandwich your flowers and leaves between the plywood boards using the sequence of stacking; 1 cardboard, 2-3 layers newspaper, 1 layer paper towel, flowers, 1 paper towel, 2-3 layers newspaper, 1 cardboard,

and so on. Stack only 6-8 layers of flowers per press or uneven pressure will cause improper drying.

3. Select weights (brick)—or tie your layers tight with cord or large rubber bands, and place your press in a warm well-ventilated place. Do not over press the materials with too much weight or pressure. They will dissolve into the paper towel and be impossible to remove.

4. Drying time varies with material used, so plan layers with similar materials. Check periodically for dryness.

5. Once completely dry, remove materials from the press and spray with a sealant to prevent re-absorption of moisture and retard cracking and breaking. Store flat, between layers of tissue, in a cool dry area.

Materials Suitable for Drying by the Pressing Method
Table 18-5

Alyssum	English Ivy	Maidenhair Fern
Begonia	Galax	Pansy
Boston Fern	Geranium	Periwinkle
Bougainvillea	Hydrangea	Phlox Salvia
Buttercup	Larkspur	Priumla
Candytuft	Leatherleaf	Queen Annes's Lace
Croton	Lemon/Salal	Sweet Pea
Cosmos	Lily of the Valley	Verbena
Delphinium		

Drying with Granular Agents. Blossoms may be dried in their natural three-dimensional form by burying them in a mixture of absorbent granular agents. Several authorities have recommended the following mixtures:

With Cornmeal & Borax	With Detergents	With Silica Gel
1 part borax	2 cups dry detergent	Silica gel in
2 parts cornmeal	4 cups cornmeal	sufficient amount
3 tablespoons uniodized	1 cup borax (optional)	to completely
Salt per quart of mixture		cover flower (to
		preserve color)
Drying time: 6-12 days	Drying time: 4-7 days	Drying time: 2-14 days

Silica gel is a commercial product sold in craft stores. It can be reused for years if it is dried out before each use. Simply place a cookie sheet with the silica gel in an oven for 30 minutes at 250°F or until the pink crystals (moist) have turned blue (dry). Stir the crystals several times while they are drying. Always keep used silica gel crystals in air-tight containers. For best results, follow these steps:

1. Choose a container that can be tightly sealed, such as Tupperware, plastic margarine cups, ice cream or milk cartons, coffee cans, fruit juice cans, mason jars, and cardboard boxes. When using containers other than those with plastic seals, you will have to seal all seams and the top with plastic wrap and masking tape. This is to make certain no moisture is allowed to seep in and no agent drains out of the container.

2. Line the bottom of the container with a thin layer of the agent and place the flowers in the agent face-up. Clip the stems to a length of one-half inch.

3. Cover each petal of the flower (specimen) with the drying agent being careful to keep the petals separate—to retain its natural shape. Several layers of flowers may be placed in each container, leaving at least one inch of crystals between each layer.

4. Test for dryness. The time will vary depending upon the flower and agent used. Check the recipes above for approximate times. If the silica gel is pink, you'll know it is void of dehydration capability. As a rule of thumb, you can generally tell if the specimen is dry by feeling it. It is "silky" to the touch.

5. Remove flower from agent and tap free of granules. Use a soft brush to completely clean the powder from materials.

6. Add florist wire of proper gauge (#26-#20) and tape with floratape before arranging.

7. Spray with a sealant to prevent re-absorption of moisture and retard shattering.

8. Store all unused dry materials in airtight boxes.

The Microwave Oven. The following information was tested and prepared by the late Grace Rymer, AIFD, a leading expert in this field.

Besides the many conveniences of microwave cooking in your kitchen, the microwave oven enables a person to dry flowers in a matter of minutes.

This new technique gives fresher appearing, more colorful materials for use in floral designs.

Preparation for microwave drying requires a supportive substance (granular agent) for flowers that wilt. The drying substance, or agent, absorbs moisture so the flower can dry in its natural three dimensional shape as described above (see Granular Agents).

In addition to the three drying agents listed above, a fourth agent, which is inexpensive and very easy to use, is kitty litter. Use a brand that is made of ground clay as it has great absorbing quality. Sift the kitty litter to remove the larger granules. For delicate and smooth-surfaced petals such as orchids or daisies, silica-gel is most satisfactory. All of these agents can be used over and over again.

Containers for drying can be any size of glass or paper dessert, cereal size bowls, shoe boxes and cardboard platters. Here is a step-by-step procedure for drying flowers in the microwave oven:

1. Select fresh flowers or leaves you desire to make permanent.

2. Select container deep enough so the agent (litter, borax solution or gel) can cover the entire bloom.

3. Place a one-half inch layer of the drying agent in container. Clip stem of flower about one-half inch long. Then place flowers in agent, face up. With a spoon, sprinkle granules of the agent gently between petals of flowers making certain every petal is covered and not bent out of shape by the weight of the agent. Petals should be completely covered so that they are not visible.

4. After the flowers are carefully covered by the agent, set the dish into the micro-wave oven along with a cup of plain tap water. Set the oven timer about one to three minutes, depending upon the characteristics of the particular flower or leaf you choose to dry.

5. After flowers have been cooked, remove

from oven and leave in agent for at least 36 hours. When removing flower from agent, gently tap the flower until all granules of the agent are removed.

6. One of the most important considerations is storage of these beautiful blooms—until they are needed in your designs. Plastic shoe and garment boxes with tight fitting lids work fine. Place a thin layer of styrofoam in the base of the boxes—then place flower head into position on the foam with a long corsage pin. Small bank pins are sufficient for smaller flowers. These boxes can then be stored until needed.

7. Stem extensions can be added to the flowers as needed in design, by using florist wire of the appropriate gauge. Floral tape the entire length, forming a loop on one end, then use a quick drying glue spread lightly over the circle and place flower into position. Cut the wires according to the length needed in your arrangement.

8. After the flowers are dry—they sometimes become brittle and may shatter when placed in the design. A really remarkable way to avoid this problem is by using a humidifier or clothing steamer. Wave the flower through the steam and it will become pliable as in the fresh stage. After you have placed the flowers in the arrangement, it will again become dry and retain the original form.

Flowers dried in this manner are not as dry looking nor are they as perishable as flowers dried by other methods. They feel and look more like fresh flowers. While the agent is drying the flowers, it is also drying our hands so it's wise to use rubber gloves, regardless of how you dry your flowers.

The microwave process is very quick and intense, therefore a glass container filled with water and set inside the oven can protect the flowers from becoming too dry and disintegrating. This is a must!

Like everything else worth doing at all,

drying flowers must be done properly to get the best results. All flowers should be picked just as they are reaching their peak of bloom. If picked past their prime, when they have already started to turn brown, flowers will continue the browning process and nothing will successfully prevent this. Correct timing, therefore, is the first requisite.

When drying miniature roses and smaller flowers such as Pansies, approximately $1^1/_2$ minutes baking time is all that is necessary, with about 10 hours set-up time. Daisies, small Dahlias, Black-eyed Susans, Zinnias, Marigolds, Carnations and small type Chrysanthemums, require $2^1/_2$ minutes—with about 10 hours cooling off period. Large Dahlias, Peonies, Chinese Peonies, and large Chrysanthemums bake approximately three minutes—and let stand in drying agent about 36 hours. Orchids should be baked in silica-gel for approximately (according to size) $1^1/_2$ minutes with set up time of 24 hours.

Foliage can be microwaved dry, particularly beautiful types with interesting color and texture that are available in the fall. Leaves can form the major part of winter arrangements, with just a few flowers used in the focal area. Microwave-drying fall leaves allows their beautiful colors to be retained.

1. Place a shallow box lid or platter in the bottom of the oven, with a paper towel over it. Then start layering your leaves with paper towels. Use as large a spray of leaves as will easily fit in the oven. The oven can be almost full. (Clean the leaves before placing into the oven.)

2. Turn the microwave oven to $1^1/_2$ minutes and when the bell rings, turn leaves and towels completely over and repeat same process, giving total of three minutes in all. Remove branches when bell rings and the leaves are dry and beautiful—no setup time is needed—they are ready for placement in your design.

Magnolia branches and leaves, ferns of all types, Camellia foliage—all these may be dried by the same method and timing.

When the need arises for a larger branch of blooms or leaves with a long stem, it is best to place it in a large container of the granular agent and let it stand over night in your gas oven with only the pilot light. Then your material is ready for placement in the arrangement, without any setup time.

A wedding bouquet may be preserved by first taking it apart, then immediately drying the individual blossoms. The flowers must be dried while still fresh looking, for the finished product to look beautiful! Then reassemble the bouquet for display in a shadow box frame or glass dome for years of enjoyment.

It is wonderful to discover a new use for the microwave and at the same time gain a new means of speeding up the process of drying flowers. Dried arrangements by this new method are as colorful as fresh flowers and, needless to say, the results are beautiful. Any flower may be dried in this manner, but some of the most obvious choices are listed below:

Flowers Suitable for Microwave & Granular Agent Drying
Table 18-6

Anemone	Hydrangea*
Begonia	Lilac
Columbine	Lily
Coralbells	Marigold
Daffodil	Orchid
Dahlia	Pansy
Delphinium*	Poppy
Dill	Rose
Feverfew	Stock
Foxglove*	Tulip
Hollyhock*	Zinnia

*whole flower stalk or individual blossoms

Storing the Finished Product

The final step in preserving flowers and foliage is storage. First, spray the dried material with a moisture preventing sealant. This not only inhibits re-absorption of moisture from the air, but also adds a small amount of strength to delicate materials. Do this to materials whether storing them for use later or for designing immediately. Allow sealant to dry completely. Several commercial products are available from your local wholesaler or from craft stores. Do not use hair spray as a sealant as it attracts dust and frequently causes delicate material to stick together during storage. Place finished material in shallow boxes, hang from the ceiling, or lay on mesh/screen shelves.

Second, proper storage humidity is critical. Air moisture levels should be below 30 % relative humidity or loss of dried material may result from mold and flower disintegration. Air temperature is not as critical as humidity levels during storage, unlike during the drying process when temperatures are much more important. A cool area with low humidity will work just as well for storage as one that is warm with low humidity.

Direct sunlight will fade colors of preserved materials very quickly. Store dried products away from direct sunlight and do not display the finished designs near bright sunlight. Finally, to prevent insect damage to dried material, place moth balls or cedar shavings in the storage area.

Plate 119
Four methods are used for drying these materials: Hanging method – mass and filler materials; Standing method – straight grasses; Racking method – wisteria vine, pods, curved materials; Granular agent method – lotus leaves.

Part 4
Special Event Designs — Weddings & Parties

Chapter 19 INTRODUCTION

Weddings are one of the most interesting and fascinating phases of the floral business. They are pageantry in full array. The ceremony is based on tradition handed down through the ages. Though custom has dictated certain procedures, we must keep in mind the wishes of the bride and groom and incorporate their ideas in the plans. Make weddings personal. One is not bound by rules or by tradition. In today's weddings, the traditional ceremony may be completely changed to follow individual inspiration, and to illustrate how different one can dare to be. The couple may write their own vows and dictate place and procedure to their liking.

Well-planned, beautifully decorated weddings definitely establish the name of a florist in a community. No other work expresses quality design and service as do lovely weddings.

Write down all details on a wedding form; the plan should be clear concerning the approximate size and type of wedding the bride has in mind. Show pictures of weddings in order to help her make decisions about bouquets and decorations. Pictures from magazines or books devoted to this subject aid in the discussion. Every florist should subscribe to various bridal magazines and fashion periodicals to stay abreast of the fashions. Know the recommendations of style experts and bridal consultants. After the wedding order has been given to a florist, full responsibility is placed in his hands. He must be an authority on all details of etiquette, wedding procedure, decorations, etc.

For the final discussion of details concerning floral decorations and flowers for the bridal party, it is best to meet at the place of the wedding (home, church, etc.), and review each phase, painting a word picture of the scene. At this meeting have printed copies of church or hotel wedding rules.

Plan to service the wedding from the first meeting with the client until the last guest has departed after the ceremony. The florist should tabulate the number of hours spent in consultation and planning, in addition to the execution of the wedding. This practice will help the florist price future weddings more accurately.

To service the bridal party, the florist should deliver all flowers to the location of the wedding. This includes setting up the decorations for both the ceremony and the reception, as well as handing out all of the personal flowers. The bouquets may be boxed separately and addressed to each attendant with a card: "To Mary on my wedding day, love, Jane." This note gives a personal touch and at the same time prevents the bridesmaids from picking through the flowers to find the ones they prefer. An additional benefit is that each bridesmaid will have an envelope with the florist's name printed on it, should she wish to contact the same florist for her own wedding.

The corsages and boutonnieres are pinned on the proper people by the florist. The mothers' and grandmothers' corsages are the first to be pinned on, followed by the other members of the wedding party. The bridesmaids then receive their bouquets and are shown the proper way to carry them. Hold the bouquet in front of each girl for a second or two for her to enjoy a moment of anticipation. Have her relax her shoulders and drop her hands to her side; then raise her hands to her waistline, keeping her elbows close to her body without raising her shoulders. Slip the bouquet into her hands. Make any adjustments necessary to the bouquet. Tell her how lovely she looks and how beautifully she carries the flowers.

The bride is the last one to receive her bouquet; she has been enjoying the thrills of each bridesmaid. The climax comes in presenting her the most beautiful of all the bouquets. In the meantime, the florist's assistant is pinning the boutonnieres on the men of the wedding party. In military weddings, men in uniform do not wear boutonnieres. However, men in civilian clothes participating in the bridal party do wear boutonnieres. It is never proper to pin a boutonniere or corsage on clerical or choir robes. Flowers for these people may be pinned on their street clothing at the reception.

A make-up box containing cosmetics, smelling salts, and sewing essentials, etc. may be provided by the florist for the attendants' use. It is wise to suggest that the bridal party dress at the church. A protective floor covering may be put down in the dressing room to prevent their gowns from being soiled while they are dressing. These extras in service will be appreciated by the customer and will distinguish this wedding as the "perfect" one.

Garden wedding plans are sometimes upset by rain. A secondary plan must be made at the garden scene in order that decorations may be moved indoors without confusion.

Generally, the florist is brought into the confidence of the bridal couple. He will know where they are spending the first night of their honeymoon. It is a nice gesture for the florist to send a flower arrangement to greet them when they arrive in their suite, with his personal card attached expressing his wishes for their happiness.

If the groom's parents are from out-of-town, the florist may suggest the bride have a flower arrangement sent to their hotel room to greet them. The bride's personal card is enclosed.

Chapter 20 ETIQUETTE

Type Of Wedding

The season of the year often determines the place. For summer weddings, the garden may be the ideal location. Or, in case of inclement weather, it may be best to use a church, home, or hotel. The hour of the wedding is influenced by the locale and religion, and will many times indicate the formality of the occasion. Evening weddings generally are the most formal, however most large Protestant weddings in the East and North take place in the afternoon at four or five o'clock. In the South and West it is more fashionable to have the wedding scheduled for eight o'clock in the evening. Protestant weddings in the morning are usually informal.

The *ultra-formal* wedding is a lavish affair that may be held in a church, a home, in a garden, or even at a club or hotel. It has regal magnificence and achieves awesome dignity and splendor through many accents of elegance. The floral decorations are spectacularly beautiful and they add much to the impressive scene. The guests rise and remain standing as the wedding party passes in review. The mother of the bride is the cue for this courtesy. The bride wears a full length, formal bridal gown with a long veil; her attendants, generally 6 to 12 in number, will be dressed accordingly. The bridegroom and his attendants are attired in corresponding formal dress, tails or striped trousers and cutaways. This wedding is followed by a large reception held at the place of the wedding or in the home or club. These festivities have a catered dinner lavish with food and champagne. There will be an orchestra and dancing. The duties of the maid of honor, the best man, and ushers are carefully prescribed as explained in this text.

The *formal* wedding is not as large as the ultra-formal wedding or as costly, but it is as beautiful and in good taste. The degree of formality depends on the choice of the bride. Her gown may have a formal train or short sweep; it may be without a train, contemporary ankle-length or ballerina style, with long or finger tip length veil. The men wear formal attire.

The small, intimate, or *informal* wedding is also dignified and impressive. It aspires to rich simplicity and unostentatious beauty. Many circumstances rule out large weddings: a recent death in the family, a second marriage, the bride's family of modest circumstances, or the young couple simply preferring the intimate small wedding. The term "informal wedding" covers a wide range of circumstances. The decorations and ceremony are formal though somewhat simple. The informal wedding may have only one attendant or as many as three in the party. The bride may wear a simple street-length dress or suit. She may also choose to wear a fingertip veil and a wedding dress without train. The attendants are dressed accordingly.

Wedding Party

The BRIDE, in consultation with her fiancé and parents, decides three of the most important details: the date, time, and form. A resumé of wedding forms and variations in religious faiths will be discussed separately.

With these questions settled, the bride will then select her attendants, decide on their dresses (her parents may provide them when circumstances permit), and select the attendants' accessories. Gifts for her attendants are given them at a special party or at the rehearsal dinner. The bride, her mother, and usually with the groom, consult the clergyman (who will officiate) about the date, the hour of the wedding, and the time of rehearsal. The minister may set a time to review the wedding vows with the bride and groom and to discuss regulations concerning their church and faith. Many churches have printed copies of the rules and regulations governing this subject, including specific rules regarding the floral decorations and use of candles. These rules must be carefully studied and followed. The mother of the bride may be a constant companion to the bride, guiding her in the various decisions. She will select her own dress, according to the formality of the affair, and let the groom's mother know her choice by phone or letter, thus enabling her to select a dress of harmonizing shade and type. The bride's mother must consult the florist with her daughter about decorations, flowers, etc.

The bride's mother may ride to the ceremony with her husband and the bride, or with the bridesmaids or she may be escorted by a close member of the family. It is the duty of the bride's parents to see that the groom's parents, if they are from out-of-town, have an escort to guide them to the church and to the reception, to prevent any delay.

The last ones to arrive at the church are the bride and her father. She is instructed to wear her engagement ring on her right hand. Or it is a thoughtful gesture to let the bride's mother wear it during the ceremony. It is then given back to the bride at the reception. If the bride wears long gloves in the ceremony, the seam of the glove of the ring finger is opened so that the wedding ring may be placed on the finger without removing the glove.

Custom and etiquette through the years have divided the financial responsibilities between the bride's parents and the groom. The bride's parents are responsible for:
1. Floral decorations for the church and reception. Flowers for the bridesmaids, corsages for the house party, soloist, organist, and special guests, and boutonniere for the groom.
2. Rehearsal dinner, unless given by the groom's parents or a close friend. The flowers and corsages are often sent by the bride's parents for this occasion.
3. Church rental, and fees for the sexton, organist, soloist and choir.
4. Transportation for the bridal party and traffic policemen when needed.
5. In Catholic ceremonies, the offering for the Nuptial Mass.
6. The aisle runner, awnings, and other decorative items.
7. Photographs.

The groom's financial responsibilities are:
1. Flowers for the bride and the bride's "going-away" corsage.
2. Boutonnieres for the male attendants, including the bride's father, the minister, and any other men serving.
3. Corsages for both mothers, for grandmothers, and for special relatives. They are boxed separately. His personal card goes with each.
4. Gloves and ties for his attendants and a present to each attendant.
5. Clergyman's fee and the marriage license.
6. Hotel bills incurred by his attendants while at the wedding.
7. Bachelors' dinner unless given by a special friend.

The GROOM visits the florist prior to the wedding date to discuss his responsibilities and the costs involved. His personal cards are enclosed along with the mother's corsages. The going-away corsage is occasionally designed as a part of the bride's bouquet, for sentimental reasons and economy. The groom's visit to the florist is an excellent time during which to make the suggestion that a special corsage be designed as a surprise gift to the bride. A card is inserted with the inscription, "May I be the first to call you Mrs. John Jones? - Love, John." Most grooms will appreciate the thoughtfulness and sentiment of this little gesture; brides remember it always.

There are times when the groom is not financially able to furnish flowers in keeping with the wedding that is planned by the bride. In such cases, the bride's parents may assume part or all of this responsibility, which they will suggest during one of the consultations with the florist. When the groom is financially able and the bride's parents are in moderate circumstances, he may wish to assume the responsibility for all floral expenses of the bridal party, leaving the expense of the church decorations for her parents. These details must be carefully handled in order to avoid embarrassment to either side.

The MAID OF HONOR is an important person with specific duties to perform. The bride may choose a maid, or matron of honor, or both to serve. She is usually a sister of the bride or groom, or a very close friend. The maid/matron of honor takes the bride's bouquet when the marriage vows are spoken. She may adjust the bridal veil and see that the train is straight as the bride turns for the recessional. She will help the bride dress for traveling and may be responsible for the wedding dress and veil when the couple departs. In a double ring ceremony, the bride gives her honor attendant the ring for the groom. She will assist the bride in many details previous to the wedding date. Her dress is generally the same style as the bridesmaid's, although her bouquet may be a different design.

The BRIDESMAIDS add beauty to the wedding. Their duties are few unless asked to assist when the occasion arises. Often they will alternate at the bridal guest book or serving the cake. They may carry their flowers throughout the evening to distinguish them from the other guests or their bouquets may be placed in vases or laid on tables as decorations. Junior bridesmaids are usually between the ages of seven and fourteen. Their attire and flowers are similar to those of the bridal party. The bridesmaids may dress at the church or they may meet at the home of the bride, at which

time formal bridal photographs are made of this group. The bridesmaids are then taken to the church in a group.

A FLOWER GIRL will add greatly to a formal wedding; either one or two girls are used, depending on the size of the wedding. Flower girls are between the ages of four and eight and are usually the sisters of the bride or groom. Since they are unpredictable, it is highly important that they be well rehearsed in their role. They wear replicas of dresses in the bridal party or dainty party dresses of their own.

The RING BEARER at a large formal wedding is a small boy especially chosen to act in this capacity. He will carry a small white satin cushion to which a substitute ring is attached. Or, it is different and well received for the boy to carry a jewel box with flowers attached. This practice represents a servant of the chivalrous knight bringing in the jewel casket for him to select a ring for his bride. His costume may be a white satin suit with short pants and a page boy blouse. Very small children participating in the wedding should not enter the chancel for the ceremony, nor need they appear in the recessional.

The groom's BEST MAN is usually his brother, father, a very close friend, or he may be the brother of the bride. The role is an important one, for he is supposed to remember all details that the groom has overlooked, see to it that the groom is not late, and be equal to any emergency. He will be with the groom all the day of the wedding. The best man will have the bride's ring, the marriage license, and the clergyman's fee (which is sealed in a white envelope with his name on it). He checks with the ushers concerning their duties, their attire, and matching accessories. He will handle the luggage, help the groom dress, and accompany him to the church thirty minutes before the wedding. In ultra-formal affairs he goes with the minister to the vestry after the ceremony for the groom's hat and gloves. In formal weddings he will accompany the maid/matron of honor in the recessional and to the reception.

He proposes the toast to the bride and groom and reads special telegrams of congratulations, etc. He will precede the bridal couple through the rice and confetti as they leave on their honeymoon.

The USHERS and GROOMSMEN are selected by the groom. In formal weddings groomsmen will accompany the bridesmaids, while the usher's duties are to seat the guests. The groomsmen may also assist in these duties when needed. They are all dressed identical to the groom. They are to be at the church an hour before the appointed time. If the ushers are not acquainted with relatives and close friends who have invitations to sit in the reserve sections, a person familiar with these details may be there to assist. They are fully instructed at the time of the rehearsal about any special request made by either the parents of the bride or groom. In a large wedding, extra ushers may be used, but they will not be a part of the procession. They seat the guests only; one usher for every fifty guests is the usual ratio.

As each female guest arrives, the usher offers her his right arm and escorts her to her seat. If she is with a gentleman, he will follow a few steps behind. When two ladies arrive together, the usher will lead one and return for the other, or another usher may take the second lady to her seat. If several guests arrive in one party, the usher will offer his arm to the eldest lady and the other guests will follow.

When an aisle carpet is used in the wedding ceremony two of the ushers will step forward and pull it to the back of the church, covering the aisle. This action is taken immediately following the seating of the mothers, and signals the beginning of the ceremony. In more elaborate weddings the florist may pull the carpet and secure it before any guests arrive. Ribbons would then be tied across the aisle to prevent the guests from walking on it. In this scenario the guests would be seated from the side aisles. The head usher then removes the satin ribbons, thus opening the aisle and making way for the bride's mother and bridal party to enter. The head usher or the one of her choice will escort the bride's mother to her place. Her entrance is the cue to ushers that no other guests are to be seated; the wedding is about to begin.

Chapter 21 PROCEDURES

Rehearsal

In large congregations the wedding rehearsal is often conducted by a bridal consultant, but sometimes the minister of the church may consider this part of his duty. However, the florist must be knowledgeable in wedding procedure and be able to assist, since assistance is a part of the floral service. The florist knows the correct positions of the bridal party in relation to the candelabra, the floral arrangements, and greenery.

The rehearsal is influenced greatly by the religious faith, the clergyman's wishes, and the regulations set by the church. The regulations vary greatly even within the same faith. Before the decorations and rehearsal plans are made, regulations must be ascertained and carefully followed.

All details are discussed with the bride prior to the time of rehearsal; she must understand that she need not be bound by custom. Her wishes are to be followed. There are excellent books written concerning wedding procedure, which may be used as a guide. However, personal preferences in wedding procedure vary greatly. The most graceful gesture that fits the situation is usually the best course to follow.

Ushers are instructed to seat the bride's relatives on the left side of the church facing the altar, and the groom's relatives on the right side. Friends of either family are not divided as to the side on which they are seated. Several rows of pews are designated as the "family section" and are reserved for relatives and close friends. The two families decide whom they wish to seat in this section, and a list is given to

Figure 93
Key to Wedding Party –
    1 bride
    2 groom
    3 best man
    4 matron of honor
    5 maid of honor
    6 bridesmaid
    7 groomsman/usher
    8 flower girl
    9 ring bearer
    10 father of bride
    11 mother of bride
    12 father of groom
    13 mother of groom
    14 clergyman
    15 clergyman's wife

the ushers. These people are notified by verbal invitation.

Should candles be used as a part of the wedding ceremony, candle lighters are furnished to the ushers for the purpose of lighting all the candles at the altar. When many candles are used, only those placed near the altar should be lighted by the ushers. All the others are lighted by the florist or by someone designated to do so about twenty to thirty minutes before the first guest arrives. The timing is judged by the size of the wedding. The florist should place a square of matching carpet under each candelabra to catch any stray drippings and be sure that each candle is placed straight and secure.

Appropriate music is played ten to twenty minutes before the ceremony begins, or in large weddings it is started about thirty or forty minutes before the appointed hour. It may be played softly throughout the ceremony if the bride has permission from the minister.

The bridal march is reserved for the entrance of the bride and her father; this march should not be repeated over and over throughout the wedding procession. A few chords of this march will start the actual procession when the mother of the bride is seated and then will fade off to other appropriate music until the maid of honor reaches the altar. Her arrival is the cue for the organist to increase the volume and announce the arrival of the bride.

When conducting rehearsals, place the participants in their positions at the altar; mark these positions with chalk (Figures 93 and 94). Arrange members of the party according to heights, etc., and review the duties that each person is to perform. Tell the participants to walk gracefully in a natural manner to the tempo of the music and not to use a hesitating step. Then have the participants go to the back of the church to start the procession. Churches that do not have a center aisle have the participants go down the left aisle and out the right aisle. Never divide the party by using both aisles for the processional. The bride and groom's families will sit on the left and right sides, respectively, in the center section (Figure 97).

Processional

The groom's mother is ushered in on the right arm of the head usher a few minutes prior to the wedding. Her husband follows three or four paces behind; they are seated on the right side of the church, facing the altar.

The bride's mother is seated at the appointed time of the wedding. She is ushered down the aisle on the right arm of the head usher and takes her place on the left side of the church, second seat from the aisle. The entrance of the bride's mother is the cue to start the wedding. Guests arriving late will not be seated after the mother of the bride has been seated. They remain in the rear of the church or find their way to the balcony.

If the candle lighting is to be part of the ceremony, the two ushers designated go forward together immediately after the bride's mother is seated and light the candles; they begin at the lower ones and finish in the center. They about-face and return to the rear of the church.

Now is the time for the solo. There may be one or more selections. The second solo is sung after a short musical interlude, or at the end of the service as a prayer. "The Lord's Prayer" by A. Malotte is appropriate for a solo sung as a prayer. The soloist remains seated in the choir during the entire ceremony.

It is traditional at this time for the minister to lead the groom and best man in from the vestry at the right side of the altar, where

they take their places. A second procedure is sometimes followed, in which the groom, best man, and the minister make their appearances as the bride and her father, enter the sanctuary of the church. The groom, in this procedure, does not have to stand through all the preliminary ceremony. It is also correct for the minister to take his place at the beginning of the ceremony and for the best man and groom to enter when the bride and her father make their appearance.

The processional to the altar is shown in Figures 96 – 97. Ushers march down the aisle in pairs, divide at the altar, and take their places. The bridesmaids appear singly; if there is an unusually large number, they go down the aisle in pairs. The maid of honor follows the bridesmaids. She takes a position on the left side nearest the altar. Now is the time for the ring bearer to enter. He is followed by the flower

girl. In traditional weddings, it is customary for the two to follow the matron of honor. However, it is wise to put these two small children just before the matron of honor in order that she may command any situation that may arise should these children become frightened. Should they stop she can take them by the hand and lead them on to their places. When the matron of honor reaches the steps leading to the altar, she stops and turns slightly to face the entrance of the bride.

When the matron of honor arrives, the organist starts the wedding march. At this time the bride and her father make their appearance and come down the aisle. The sound of the wedding march is also the signal for the minister to lead the groom and best man in, if

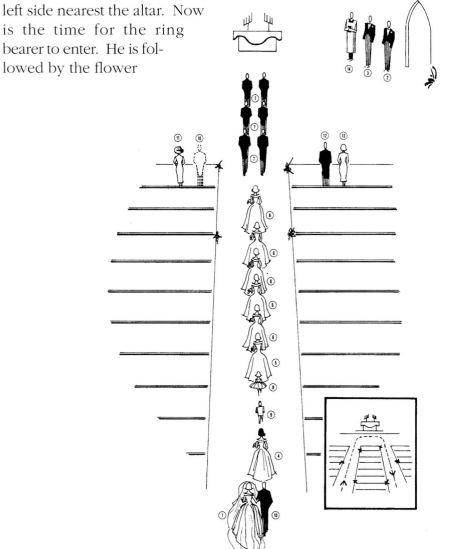

Figure 96
Processional –
Wedding party to the altar on central aisle.

Figure 97
Processional, Alternative –
Wedding party to the altar down left aisle, (for recessional, out right side) when auditorium does not have a central aisle. The location of only 6 pew bows (x) is shown properly spaced when they have to be spread out over two aisles.

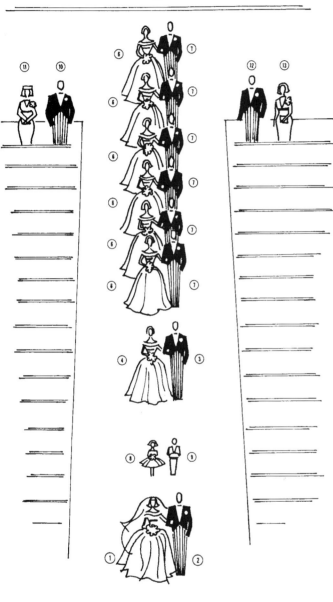

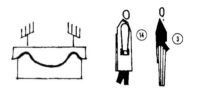

Figure 98
Recessional —
Formal wedding party
leaving altar;
bridesmaids and
groomsmen are in
pairs.

Figure 99
Recessional —
Ultra-formal wedding,
the best man goes to
the vestry with clergy;
groomsmen may
follow the bridesmaids.

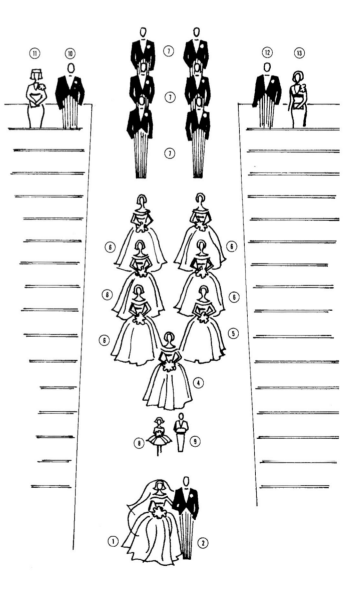

they have not already entered as explained previously.

The minister takes his place in the center of the first step. The best man and the groom form a semi-circle on the right side opposite the matron of honor and turn to face the bride.

The entrance of the bride with her hand lightly on her father's arm is the breathless moment of the wedding. The bride's father may be on the left or right side of the bride. Suggest that the father be on the bride's right side. This places him between the bride and the groom at the altar (Figure 94). When the minister asks, "Who giveth this woman to be married to this man?" the father says, "Her mother and I do." He kisses his daughter good-by and joins the hands of the couple, and he then takes his seat beside his wife. He may be on the bride's left, which causes him to reach across the bride when joining her hands with the groom's. This gesture appears awkward.

If the father is not available to give the bride away, a close relative or friend may perform this duty. If she does not wish a substitute, the bride may choose to come down the aisle alone, or an escort may accompany the bride to the altar and then take his seat beside her mother. The bride's mother stands at the appointed time and say's "I do." The mother may also remain seated and signify approval by nodding her head. When the parents are not present, it is proper for the bridal couple to enter together.

At the rehearsal, the father should be cautioned concerning the length of the bride's train so that it will not interfere with his taking his seat.

In the case of divorced parents who have remarried, the mother of the bride, is seated by the head usher in her usual place. Her husband, the stepfather, follows three to four paces behind and takes his seat beside her, or he may be seated prior to her entrance. After the father of the bride has given his daughter in marriage, he takes his place on the first seat, third row beside his wife, the stepmother, who was seated about five minutes before the ceremony began.

The minister may continue the ceremony from his present position or go to the altar, leading both bride and groom. The matron/maid of honor sees that the veil is not entangled on the steps, etc., and then she and the best man take their places by the bride and groom, respectively. During the ring ceremony the matron/maid of honor holds the bride's bouquet. This bouquet is returned when the ceremony is over.

After the last prayer the groom lifts the bride's veil and embraces her. The train may be lifted by the matron of honor, or maid of honor if she is serving the bride. The bride may lift her own veil if she chooses, or she may prefer her father to do so when he embraces her at the altar.

Recessional

(Figures 98 and 99) - In some instances church bells or chimes ring, and lighting is increased, in addition to the usual music to signal the recessional. The bride and groom turn in their places to leave the altar. The matron of honor straightens the veil and train and sees that the couple is not entangled in them. The bride receives her bouquet from the maid of honor. The bride must be cautioned at the rehearsal not to rush from the altar, or she may trip and fall. Rushing destroys all the serenity and beauty that has been created. The bride and groom are followed by the flower girl and ring bearer a few paces behind.

In ultra-formal weddings, it is the duty of the best man to go out with the minister, pay him his fee, pick up the groom's hat and gloves, and meet the bride and groom at their car. The matron of honor follows the bride and groom without an escort. The maid of honor and her escort fall in line and are followed by the bridesmaids and ushers. After the bridal party is in the vestibule, the head usher returns for the bride's mother. The bride's father follows. The usher then returns for the groom's mother and takes her out. To avoid prolonging this phase of the recessional, after the head usher has escorted the bride's mother, a second usher may follow him to escort the groom's mother. No wedding guests should leave their seats until the bridal party and the parents of both bride and groom have left their places.

Formal and informal weddings follow the same recessional procedures as in ultra-formal weddings, with the exception of the best man who will escort the matron of honor. In some weddings the ushers do not escort the bridesmaids out of the church in the recessional. In this case the bridesmaids come out in pairs, followed by the ushers in pairs. The parents of the bride follow, and then the groom's parents and special guests. In situations where the vestibule is too small to accommodate a crowd of people, the ushers may return to the aisle and release the guests, one pew at a time. This allows people to wait comfortably while seated rather than stand in a bottleneck at the back of the church.

Religious Variations

With rapid advances in the social sciences, in our thinking, and in our own manner of living, many changes have occurred in our way of life. With these changes, custom and tradition are rapidly being broken; we accept new ideas. We find these changes in religious rituals, especially pertaining to marriage ceremony. There are many variations within the same faith. Nationalities influence regional preferences. One should confer with the clergyman in preparation for the bridal consultation.

CHRISTIAN SCIENCE faith does not have ordained ministers; therefore, a minister of another denomination conducts the ceremony at a place chosen by the bride. When decorating for an EPISCOPALIAN church service, the florist quite often must arrange to have a member of the altar guild place the flowers. The florist is not allowed behind the altar rail. Artificial flowers or greenery may not be used in the floral designs for many Episcopalian churches.

When servicing a GREEK ORTHODOX wedding, flowers are normally placed on the solea located immediately in front of the altar, which is secluded behind the icon screen. Floral personnel may place the flowers on the solea but it is advisable to stop by the church office for instructions and/or permission to do this. Women are not permitted to enter the Holy of Holies behind the icon screen.

JEWISH faith is divided into three divisions: Orthodox, Conservative, and Reform. Their wedding rituals vary slightly; therefore, it is best to consult the rabbi about these differences. Jewish weddings are never held on the Jewish Sabbath, which begins Friday sundown and ends Saturday sundown. Very religious Jews do not marry on specified high holy days.

The ORTHODOX JEWISH wedding is based on ancient tradition. The bridal pair is wed under a chuppa symbolizing the new home. It is a part of the furnishings of Orthodox and Conservative synagogues. With permission from the rabbi, the florist may use an umbrella or pergola canopy, if it is properly covered with material, flowers, or greenery. The seating arrangement of the parents is reversed; the bride's parents are seated on the right and the groom's parents on the left. The procession is led with the rabbi, followed by the best man who waits for the groom on the left side. (Or the best man may come in at the usual time). The ushers come down the aisle in pairs; the bridesmaids walk singly unless there is a large number. A ring bearer enters if one is used. The best man is next, unless he entered with the rabbi. He is followed by the groom, with his parents on either side, his mother on his right, and his father on his left. The flower girl then precedes the maid of honor. Last to enter is the bride with her parents on either side. They take their places under the canopy. There is no formal giving away of the bride.

As the ceremony begins, the maid of honor is on the bride's right, the best man at the groom's left. The other attendants stand outside the canopy in the usual grouping. The ceremony of the Seven Blessings proceeds. In the ring ceremony, the rabbi gives the gold band to the groom, who places it on the bride's right index finger. (Later she changes the ring to her left-hand ring finger.) The ceremony continues with the Three-Fold Blessing to the High Priest, the drinking of the ceremonial cup of wine, and a benediction. At the conclusion, the rabbi offers the groom the small glass, which he places on the floor and crushes under his heel. The recessional is led by the bride and groom followed by her parents, his parents, the flower girl, the matron or maid of honor with the best man, the bridesmaids and the groomsmen with them. The bridesmaids may come out in pairs, in which case the groomsmen follow in pairs.

The CONSERVATIVE JEWISH wedding ceremony retains much of the old form and ritual of the Orthodox. Men and women sit together. A choir and organ are permitted.

The REFORM JEWISH ceremony begins with the wedding march, which is the signal for the rabbi, the groom, and the best man to enter and take their places. The bridal party enters in the usual manner — the groomsmen followed by the bridesmaids, the maid of honor, and the bride on the arm of her father. The groom comes forward as the bride approaches, takes the place of her father, and the ceremony begins. The groom places the ring on the bride's left-hand ring finger. There is no ceremony or the breaking of the glass.

ROMAN CATHOLIC procedure differs little from the Protestant service. The father may, or may not, give the bride away, according to local custom. He stops at the chancel rail; the groom comes forward to meet them, and leads the bride to the altar. The father joins his wife in the first pew. The priest leads the couple into the sanctuary. The attendants may or may not follow, according to the priest. There are three types of Nuptial Mass. The first is Low Mass, offered by one priest, and traditionally held at eight or nine in the morning, requiring approximately half an hour to celebrate. The second is High Mass, requiring about forty minutes and sung by the priest, with responses from the choir. The third, Solemn Nuptial Mass, requires more than an hour, is said at more formal, elaborate weddings, and is held at noon. Three priests, a celebrant, a deacon, and a subdeacon chant their parts with a full choir singing responses. In recent years all of these ceremonies may be held in the afternoon. Floral decorations may be planned to surround both the main altar and the front altar making sure to not interfere with the necessary "traffic pattern" of the participants. Flowers are never planned for the center of the main altar; the chalice and tabernacle are used in the wedding.

Today there are many variations to all wedding procedures in all faiths.

Military Weddings

The traditions of military weddings are strict in peacetime. During periods of wartime emergency there is more latitude, and the Chaplain should be consulted. Custom and tradition in the branch of service of the bridegroom will influence the procedure. The men will be in full-dress uniform, with civilian personnel in formal dress. The most picturesque and striking difference between a military and a civilian wedding is the arch of sabers or swords formed by the male attendants under which the bride and groom pass at the end of the service. For the recessional, two lines are formed and the ranking officer gives the command, "Draw sabers." The bride and groom march through this arch alone. The command, "Return sabers," is given; the men sheath their sabers and escort the bridesmaids down the aisle. It is also proper for the men to leave the altar immediately after the ceremony, go to the back of the church, and form their line of arched sabers. In this case the bridal couple leads the procession down the aisle in the usual formation, with the maid/matron of honor alone and the bridesmaids in pairs. The command to return sabers is given when the last pair of bridesmaids is through the arch.

The arch of sabers is a rite only when the bridegroom and his attendants are commissioned officers. The bridal party and bride's family are seated at the head table during the reception; all other personnel are seated according to rank. The bride uses the groom's saber to cut the cake and is assisted by his hand, which is placed over hers.

Chapter 22
CEREMONY DECORATIONS

A note of formality is always desirable. Even though it may be a small wedding with the bride and her attendants wearing street clothes, formal balance in the arrangement of decorative material is often maintained. The place in which the bride and groom stand for their wedding ceremony should draw all eyes. This spot where they take their vows is the focal point whether it be located in a church, private home, garden or any other place. This focal area (altar, fireplace, staircase, arbor, etc.) should be emphasized by the decorations. The same elements and principles are followed when planning a wedding decoration for any setting. The altar, even though it may be improvised, is still the center of interest.

As stated before in Chapter 19, it is wise to meet with the bride and groom or the bride and her mother at the place where the wedding is to be held to discuss the final plans. Regulations, set by the church authorities or hotel managers, governing restrictions on wedding decorations, are discussed. These are carefully followed when the plans are being formulated to avoid any misunderstanding and confusion. Most churches and public venues have these rules printed and they may be obtained from their offices.

All mechanics must provide stability in the placement of the decorations and at the same time, protect against any kind of damage to the property. Decorations must *not* be held in place with any kind of sticky tape, clay or glue in churches or reception halls. *Never* use nails, tacks or staples on someone else's property. Taped wires, chenille stems, heavy rubber bands, velcro, plain ribbons, and even felt-lined C clamps can be used to hold decorations in place without leaving a mark of any kind.

When planning the decorations for any wedding ceremony or special event it is best to first establish a theme. This concept will focus all components in a cohesive direction and make a greater impact on the eye. A theme-based decoration always creates a lasting memory. A theme idea will emerge from the bride's personal preferences, the style of her gown or the location of the ceremony itself. The degree of formality, selection of colors, textures and types of floral materials follow suit.

The next step in creating the perfect decoration is to look at how the elements and principles of design can be used to increase the impact without necessarily increasing the budget.

Focal Point: The place to which all eyes are drawn can be emphasized with one large bouquet of flowers. A cross, communion table or mantel may be flanked with a pair of candelabra. A bird bath or garden statue may be decorated with flowers. A pair of columns, potted trees or spiral candelabra may be placed to frame this vital spot like a "parenthesis".

Balance: The decorations may be placed in symmetrical (mirror image) positions to enhance the existing architecture and décor, or they may be of unequal size and weight. Occasionally asymmetrical placement offers greater interest, even pizzazz, to a standard setting.

Proportion: For the greatest impact, the floral decorations should be designed in scale to the surroundings. High vaulted ceilings and long aisles demand much larger and taller arrangements than do more intimate areas. If the budget is low then put all of it into one spectacular bouquet that can easily be seen all the way from the back row!

Color: Be aware that aggressive (warm) colors can usually be seen from greater distances while receding (cool) colors often fade away — especially under soft lighting. Light colors will show up best in front of dark backgrounds while dark colored flowers and foliages show best against light backgrounds.

Space: In addition to the amount of space contributed by the building and occupied by the furnishings there is a more practical matter to consider. This is the amount of space required by the bridal party and then the space left for decorations, which must not impede the movements of those in the wedding party.

Harmony: Is there a pleasing interaction between the components of the decoration and the surroundings? This can be accomplished for one bride through the principle of Unity giving her a oneness of purpose, thought, style and spirit in decorating. A different bride, however, may respond to the principle of Contrast by emphasizing the differences between colors, styles and choice of materials in the given setting.

Several different styles of wedding ceremony decorations are presented here to offer some basic guidelines in planning successful designs for various situations.

Renaissance Theme: A rich harmony of colors creates a strong feeling of unity in the intimate, traditional setting shown in Plate 120. Symmetrical placement of the floral arrangements and garland frame the cross and Bible, drawing all eyes to this important focal area. The diagonal lines in the wood paneling and cabinetry strengthen this feeling. The bride and groom may stand before the communion rail and kneel here during the ceremony. The choice of colors and flowers along with the velvet drape remind one of medieval times. This historical feeling is strengthened as one realizes that the garland was popular in Greece and Rome, and the

Plate 120
Renaissance Theme, Traditional Setting — A bit of relief to the perfect symmetry has been provided by placing the Bible at a slight angle on the carefully gathered altar cloth. A few blossoms have been strewn to enrich the effect.

flowers lifted on wrought iron stands speak of the "eyes toward heaven" theme of Gothic architecture. Lifting the bouquets puts them in perfect proportion to the setting.

In Plate 121 we see the same floral decorations placed in a modernistic setting. Even though the symmetrical balance, use of color and height of the floral arrangements work well, the overall impact is not as strong as in Plate 120. This is because the first plate shows wonderful *unity* of decorations to setting, while the second plate shows acceptable *contrast*, it is not strong enough to have great impact on the eye. The modernistic background also competes to some extent with the flowers. It should be noted that the same garland, used in both settings, has much greater impact when hanging than when laid flat on the table top.

Tradition A La Mode: The basic round design shown in Plates 122, 123, 124 has its roots in the biedermeier, millefleur and colonial nosegay styles. This version speaks "2000 AD" because it is devoid of frills, yet romantic. The choice of open roses and hyacinth stalks offers the fragrance and feeling of a romantic garden, but the smooth curled flax leaves add a degree of modern sophistication. The romantic facets of these designs are heightened in Plate 122 by placing them in a traditional setting and by adding the plush altar cover. However, the more modern and sophisticated aspects are emphasized in the contemporary setting shown in Plate 123. These designs are equally at home in both scenes. Contributing to this is the use of the altar vases — correctly (as vases) on the traditional altar and upside-down (as pedestals) on the contemporary altar. The contemporary setting shows these designs composed for use as the unity candle with the bride's and groom's candles laid on the table within easy reach. One of the most meaningful things a florist can do for a bride is use some of her own family heirlooms in the decorations. In Plate 125 we see the same floral designs incorporating an antique stained glass panel into the center of the altar. Ironically

Plates 121,121a
Renaissance Theme, Modernistic Setting — Shown here with communion service for practical use and cherubs for decorative use.

Plate 122
Tradition A La Mode, Traditional — The asymmetrically gathered altar cloth provides contrast to the perfect symmetry of the other components.

Plate 123
Tradition A La Mode, Contemporary – The unity candle in this setting will become the memory candle that is lit on every future anniversary.

Plate 124
Tradition A La Mode, Contemporary – The technique of massing the blossoms in these small arrangements allows them to stand out and not be dominated by the background.

Plate 125
Tradition A La Mode,
Heirloom – Though
using a family heirloom
is meaningful to the
bride, permission must
be given by the clergy
before placing it on
the altar.

Plate 126
Baroque Beauty – The
intimate feeling and
intricate details and
textures in this
composition, will be
enjoyed only by
people viewing it at
close range, i.e., a
chapel or small room.

the squares of glass in the panel repeat the squares on the background and the colors are compatible. The placement of lighted candles behind the glass panel enhances its decorative value.

Baroque Beauty: Plate 126 shows a romantic setting for a wedding ceremony that could be created in any location. The use of a plain fabric-covered screen establishes the focal area and allows a feeling of intimacy by separating it from the existing background. Its lack of pattern, like you would have in trellis panels for instance, increases the impact of the floral decorations. These panels are very cost effective and simple to make. The three panels were cut out of foam board and covered with heavy muslin fabric. They are set into place and pinned together with corsage pins which allows for easy transport and set–up. With proper care and handling they can be used over and over again.

A baroque feeling is created with the combination of materials: cherubs and fresh grapes, open roses and pillar candles, and a generous amount of cascading foliages. The addition of the soft scrim drape and special lighting to paint a shadow of the cherubs on the right panel adds richness and romance to the overall composition. The wrought iron candelabras were designed by a floral artist and then hand-made in Mexico. This is an excellent idea for designers who specialize in weddings and wish to enhance their image of offering unique equipment along with their service. Plate 127 shows how well this type of decoration can work in a secular setting.

White – A Gentle Classic: The use of a single color always increases its visual impact. When this color is white (or ivory) the decoration will be very elegant, and it will stand out more than any other color under the soft lighting of candles or twilight. White flowers also extend the feeling of purity associated with a bride's white gown. Plate 128 shows a simple but elegant setting designed with only two kinds of white flowers — French tulips and

Plate 127
Baroque Beauty – These custom made candelabra are made in sections so the heights can be varied thus broadening their use.

dendrobium orchids. The contrast of textures among these flowers fills the need of creating interest in this monochromatic color scheme. Minimal use of foliage lavishes more style and attention on the elegant blossoms. The center arrangement is in proper proportion to its space and the wrought iron candelabras that flank it. The size of the candles and ribbons reflect the bold scale of the architecture and furnishings. Note how the combination of diverse textures in the ribbons softens and adds romance to this overall composition.

In Plate 129 a pair of green arrangements has been added to enlarge and increase the effect of the decoration. The three white arrangements now seem to frame and direct the eye upward to the cross, which would be

Plate 128
White – A Gentle
Classic – The center
bouquet is large
enough to anchor the
setting and is a good
choice for the focal
area when such an
impressive symbol is
on the wall above the
altar.

effective in a church with a vaulted ceiling. The positions of the white and green arrangements are reversed in Plate 130, and here we see a more horizontal orientation to the setting. This placement focuses attention a bit lower and may be especially pretty in a more intimate setting. A floral designer can use different placements to emphasize different aspects of both ceremony and architecture.

The Color Green: The combination of a creative designer and a bride with a strongly developed personal taste can result in a truly unique wedding decoration. A perfect example of this is shown in Plates 131, 132 and

Plate 129
White – A Gentle Classic – The addition of foliage arrangements enriches and freshens the setting.

Plate 130
White – A Gentle Classic – Notice how the white flowers continue to show up beautifully as the light progressively softens across these three pictures.

133. A generous mixture of greens and yellow greens with accents of candles, flowers and vegetables creates this unique yet harmonious scheme. Candles no longer need to be thin tapers in white or ivory. The candle industry is providing many new shapes, colors and finishes. Mottled chartreuse pillar candles are used here for impact and style. The textures in these arrangements are multiple and complex giving a great deal of interest to this setting. This complexity requires some plain surfaces where the eye can rest and these areas are provided by the candles, bird of paradise leaves and broccoflower. Can you imagine these materials pulled into the rest of the wedding? The bride's gown and the wedding cake may be enhanced with the delicate green bells of Ireland, viburnum blossoms and laurel — the colors of new growth celebrating a new life together. The bolder textures in these designs — salal, strelitzia, broccoflower and eleagnus could be used more appropriately on the buffet tables. The challenge for the florist — and the reward for the bride — is to interpret successfully this blend of tradition and innovation in the wedding flowers.

America In Bloom: What could be more beautiful or appropriate than bringing America's garden flowers indoors to the bride? In Plates 134 and 135 we see bountiful bouquets of spring garden flowers arranged in glorious colors for a seasonal setting. These companion pieces are presented in an asymmetrical manner to show that flowers arranged informally can be positioned informally as well, even in a formal (symmetrical) setting. The asymmetrical placement is unexpected yet compatible with both the background and the altar tables due to the strict attention given to visual balance by the designer. The two designs are similar in size but the lower one has more volume at its base while the other design appears visually lighter in weight due to its slightly extended height. These variations in size are emphasized, by lifting the taller design, in this case by placing it on an in-

Plate 131

Plate 134

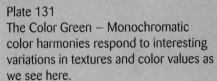

Plate 133

Plate 132

Plate 131
The Color Green — Monochromatic color harmonies respond to interesting variations in textures and color values as we see here.

Plate 132
The Color Green —The exotic "notes" in this symphony of greens are anchored in a cage of wet foam that is placed into the candelabra's center.

Plate 133
The Color Green — Euphorbia, viburnum and broccoflower are unexpected partners in this floral odyssey.

Plate 134
America in Bloom — These two designs appear to be full partners due to their overall mass, grouping concept and similar distribution of colors.

Plate 135
America in Bloom —
By grouping the delphiniums, Bells of Ireland, anemones, tulips, irises, lilacs, forsythia and pussy willow with their own kind, each makes a greater impact on the eye — especially from a distance.

Plate 136
Country Casual —The iris, myrtle, eryngium, monte casino, sweet pea and Indian hawthorne could easily be replaced with wildflowers or native plants that are compatible with the bride's chosen colors and season.

Plate 137
Fantasy of Nature — The focal area must be very strong to hold its own with these unique attention-getting candelabras. Monkshood, roses and Crown Imperial lilies work together making a very bold statement in this composition.

Plate 138
Fantasy of Nature — Clay pots with heavy gauge taped wires threaded vertically through the drainage holes are tied into the tree branches. Plastic-wrapped blocks of wet foam are dropped into the pots to hold the fresh flowers

verted maple syrup pail.

Country Casual: Occasionally a bride comes along who loves flowers but doesn't relate at all to design. She likes both her lifestyle and her flowers to be relaxed, informal and loosely structured. We may expect to develop this kind of theme outside in a garden, on a ranch or at the beach, but it is perfectly possible to bring this considerable degree of informality into a chapel or church. Plate 136 shows this effect with several monofloral bouquets (one kind of flower per container) grouped on the altar. Loose flowers were just dropped into the old weathered containers. The centerpiece has candles mounted in moss-covered wet foam in a wooden trug, which blends well with the other components. The little jar of sweet peas and the birdhouse appear as logical accessories in the overall composition. The checkered cloth ties everything together and repeats the wall

Plate 136
Country Casual —The iris, myrtle, eryngium, monte casino, sweet pea and Indian hawthorne could easily be replaced with wildflowers or native plants that are compatible with the bride's chosen colors and season.

Plate 137
Fantasy of Nature — The focal area must be very strong to hold its own with these unique attention-getting candelabras. Monkshood, roses and Crown Imperial lilies work together making a very bold statement in this composition.

Plate 138
Fantasy of Nature — Clay pots with heavy gauge taped wires threaded vertically through the drainage holes are tied into the tree branches. Plastic-wrapped blocks of wet foam are dropped into the pots to hold the fresh flowers

pattern — all in the bride's chosen colors.

Fantasy of Nature: There are a few times in every designer's life when words like *imagination, ingeniousness, ingenuity,* and *innovation* describe the best response to a design challenge. Occasionally a customer of the same disposition appears and when the two get together something wonderful can happen! Today's bride, more than ever before, can "step out of the box" — abandon the rules of tradition — do her thing. The open-minded designer leads the way by turning vision into reality. Plate 137 shows such a fantasy of nature — come true. Just as the past can inspire an infinite variety of wedding styles, so too can an eye for putting together so-called incompatible materials. Here we see copper tubing swirling through bare-branches as an apparent accent in completely unexpected altar candelabras. The branches, mounted in terracotta rose pots, extend the lines of the pots. This V-shaped pattern is repeated and actually strengthened by the hanging glass votive candles of the same shape. Cohesiveness is gained through the matching colors of the pot and tubing, glass, moss and background. The center grouping of potted bouquets repeats the same elements thus causing diverse materials to create unity!

In Plate 138 we step back and see the same altar flanked by taller trees made into similar shapes. The same elements — copper tubing, bare branches, potted bouquets and the V-shaped outline — are repeated, again for unity. Notice how

the same diagonal lines are present in the ceiling and in the shadows on the floor. This is an example of "..an eye for putting together.." as mentioned in the previous paragraph. Of course special lighting is used to create just the right shadows. Another variation on this theme is shown in Plate 139. A very naturalistic arbor has been made, by laying long branches across the top of the two trees, and tying them securely in place with raffia. These materials are heavy enough to support the weight of additional potted bouquets. The two large altar tables were removed leaving the smaller square stand to hold a single candelabra and a communion service thus providing the necessary focal point. Imagine how this decoration could be expanded to create a chuppa with the small table prepared for the Breaking of the Glass ceremony. In fact it is important to note here that all of these props could be used in various combinations in almost any setting. Plate 140 shows the same set-up with the votive candles suspended in the top of the arbor and the copper tray of potted bouquets in the center.

The construction of these trees was done by nailing the tree branches to a 4' x 4" wood post that was bracketed to a 22" square piece of 3/4" plywood. Sheet moss was then stapled over the post making the whole effect look more naturalistic. Note how well the square terracotta tiles with moss in between hide the plywood base. The most time-consuming part of this project was selecting branches that would fit the plan. However, once made, these trees become reusable props. To make the candelabras, selected branches were put into containers of plaster of Paris that fit inside the terracotta rose pots. Gravel was added to the pots to provide extra weight for stability. The top branches were secured in many places with raffia to provide stability and security for the hanging votive candles, which added a lot of weight high above the center of gravity.

High Tech Revisited: Our introduction to the new millennium includes the resurgence of interest in the design styles of the mid-1900s, i.e. "Retro". The use of industrial materials in wedding

Plate 139
Fantasy of Nature – Every time a designer develops a creative idea that includes the use of candles, the mechanics are of critical importance – to prevent a fire hazard. The finished product must always comply with church (or any venue) regulations, and ease of delivery and on-site setup must be planned ahead.

Plate 140
Fantasy of Nature – The designer would have a plan for lighting the votive candles, in this setting, as it would be too awkward for the ushers to attempt in front of an audience. We remember that in all creative endeavors, the mechanics will be designed so that no "mark" of any kind will be left behind when the decorations are removed.

decorations takes us back to the 1970's when High Tech became fashionable as a style for the home, with people buying restaurant cutlery and warehouse storage systems. The American fascination with things industrial goes further back to the popular glass brick vase of the 1950's and even further to 1936 when the Museum of Modern Art in New York mounted an exhibit that extolled the virtues of laboratory glass for the home. In Plate 141 we can see aluminum conduit used to make the armatures that support some of the flowers in the altar vases. The metal containers used on the altar are finished to look like lead, emphasizing the industrial theme. Such strong materials require bold flowers — powerful in both color and form.

The vertical, horizontal and diagonal lines found in the interior of this church are all repeated in these altar designs. The lines and forms of the floral materials are used in the formalinear style of design. The spheres pavéd in kumquats provide distinctive accessories in this setting. Another industrial detail is the technique of using exposed mechanics. The armatures are tied with gold cord and the kumquats are attached with bare wires that give the effect of lacing, all exposed.

Plate 142 shows the complete set–up for this formalinear High Tech decoration. Tripods of conduit approximately seven feet tall flank the altar. In general they repeat the spare look of the interior furnishings. Even though they are four feet across at the base there is plenty of space for several people to stand for the ceremony. Alternative materials for the conduit could be dowel rods, bamboo, straight tree branches, and even lengths of rusted iron.

Minimalism: A very stark environment may not be everyone's preference for their wedding but it opens up another direction for the floral artist. A space like this is a bare canvas, so extravagant decorations are often chosen to disguise the empty look. If, however, one approaches such a venue with the same critical eye for suitability that might be applied to

Plate 141
High Tech Revisited – The very word "industrial" evokes the concept of precision. Formalinear designs are precise in line, balance and repetition of forms – note the perfect parallel lines in the altar piece, the position of the spheres and the clear delineation of each flower.

Plate 142
High Tech Revisited – This setting of formalinear designs really speaks the language of the geometry in this building. Points and edges need the right kind of home, and here they found it. This is a good example to show how important compatibility is, between decoration and setting.

a historical setting, equally interesting and perhaps even more striking results may be achieved. Such is the case in Plate 143. Minimalism — the reduction of design to its essential elements — is explored here in the use of potted azaleas. Far from decreasing the impact, simplicity with an emphasis on a single flower creates a surprisingly dramatic effect. The potted plants shown here in their greenhouse plastic pots and the candles in pink ribbon banding, are used solely as elements of design, not as an extension of the garden as is so often seen. Asymmetrical balance and strong color help to implement this effect. In this decoration the unity candle is lifted on a clear acrylic stand, which adds impact at first glance, as it seems to float above the table. This display technique mirrors the upper left azalea. The precision of the wall design is repeated in the exact placement of the potted plants and candles. The real key to this design is in the meticulous selection and placement of the plants. It is easy to pull plants off the shelf, but they must be identical in size, shape and amount and position of flowers. And then they must be spaced perfectly.

Plate 144 shows a comparable decoration but with potted gloxinias and variegated English ivies, two plants whose color and texture express strong contrast. Once again, the careful selection and orderly placement of the components creates a very distinctive decoration. Both of these settings require some real design sensibilities, but the set–up time on the busiest of days is also minimal. Our bridal clientele will continue to increase its level of sophistication and interest in design and this will give designers more opportunities to practice high style design.

Back To Basics: There are some basic thoughts about planning and installing wedding ceremony decorations.

Entrances. The importance of doors is one area that many decorators overlook. Handrails festooned with ribbons, doors decorated with swags or wreaths, even a bowl of flowers on a table or pedestal announces what's to come! Like an appetizer for a meal, a decorated entrance piques the senses — creates anticipation. In addition to aesthetics, entrances also affect the flow of traffic. Some churches have the altar located at the main entrance. In such a situation, the doors should be locked if possible, and the guests rerouted through a different entrance.

Aisle cloths. Today's bride uses a white aisle carpet to increase the royal and ritualistic effect of her wedding ceremony, but in historical times a carpet was necessary for the protection of regal gowns from dirty floors. Aisle carpets made of sturdy cotton canvas may be hemmed in any length that suits the aisle. They are costly to purchase and maintain but they last for many years. Less expensive disposable aisle runners made of synthetic cloth or white plastic may be purchased at the florist supplier. These are used

Plate 143
Minimalism – Azaleas
Precision again! Perfect placement of the plants, clean lines, visual balance, color distribution, textural contrast – between flower and pot, flower and candle, flower and table, flower and background. These are the ingredients of this distinctive composition.

Plate 144
Minimalism – Gloxinias
Each plant appears as a living sculpture thus increasing its visual impact and monetary value. Plants hold up well, transport easily and would be eagerly accepted gifts to members of the wedding party.

only one time. An aisle carpet will make the aisle look like a grand promenade. When there is a center aisle the runner can be laid before the guests arrive and the aisle closed off with ribbons. Guests may be seated from side aisles. The head usher opens the aisle at the appointed time for the bride and her attendants. Everyone can exit this way following the ceremony.

Florists must secure the aisle runner to the floor so that it will not "walk" with the attendants. It is usually attached to the church carpeting with corsage pins. The pins are inserted horizontally pointing away from the altar. Installation to a smooth surfaced floor is with double-faced carpet tape, which can be purchased in white.

There are many weddings at which the aisle carpet is attached only at the front of the church leaving the main aisle clear for seating the guests. Canvas aisle carpets are usually folded (accordion style) with the top corners doubled over. After the mothers are seated two ushers may come forward, grasp the corners and pull the carpet all the way back to the foyer where the bride enters. The end is fastened down to eliminate the danger of people tripping. A disposable carpet is pre-rolled on a cardboard tube with a rope "handle" looped through. One usher simply holds the rope and walks backward watching the carpet unroll. The end is fastened down securely.

Aisle Decorations. Pew decorations add a beautiful touch of color or candlelight to the bride's entrance. Creative use of materials will be appreciated in clusters attached to pews or on tall standards. Secure attachments and protection of church property are vital. Never use bare wire, adhesive tape, clay, or glue on church pews. Plastic clips with or without foam cages, felt-lined clamps, ribbon-wrapped wires, and large rubber bands make excellent and safe attachments (Plates 145 –151). When the church seating is done with chairs or open-ended pews the decorations must be free standing designs.

Kneeling Benches. Should the bride and groom wish to kneel for prayer or the receiving of communion during the wedding ceremony, a kneeling bench of some type will be required. Many churches use their own "kneelers" that match their furniture or small gates in the communion railing will be closed for this purpose. Quite often, however, the florist is called upon to provide this equipment. Plates 152 and 153 show a typical set of individual kneeling benches, which can be positioned according to the bride and groom's preferences so that they face each other or the altar. Decorating this intimate focal area without interfering with the bride and groom's movement greatly enhances the beauty of the ceremony.

Lighting. In many weddings, electric lights ruin the soft

Plate 145 (circa 1986)
Aisle Decorations
Aisle standard with nerine lilies and dendrobium orchids arranged in a foam block placed over a candle cup (afternoon wedding). Looped pampas grass and painted soapberries add a contemporary accent.

Plate 146
Aisle standard showing a traditional cluster of lilies, alstroemeria and spray mums with cascading springeri.

Plate 147
An exotic color scheme is achieved with anthurium, red ti leaves and painted bamboo; these materials are placed in a small block of wet foam held in a commercial plastic clip-on holder.

Plate 148
Cascade of dendrobium orchids, baby's breath and ivy in a clip-on holder.

Plate 149
A votive candle is securely anchored into dry foam in a custom-made metal clip-on holder, and is surrounded by mixed foliages in this simple cascade design.

Plate 150
Mixed foliages cascade from a commercial clip-on holder with wet foam.

Plate 151
Aisle standard with candle and glass hurricane globe. The arrangement made in a dome-shaped cage of wet foam is attached at the pew clamp instead of at the top.

illusion created by candlelight. Flow of light should be from the rear of the church to the altar, with just enough light to compliment the candles and illuminate the bridal couple and surrounding flowers. In churches that have rheostat-controlled lighting, the system is tested and light levels established during the rehearsal, and a special person is designated to set or operate the lights during the wedding.

Candles. A beautiful and romantic atmosphere for any wedding can be the result of candles properly installed. Candles may be lighted on the altar and flanking the bride and groom at any time of day, but more extensive use of lighted candles to decorate the chancel, aisle and windows must be done after 5pm – for evening weddings. Fans and air-conditioning units cause trouble by creating drafts on candles, making them flicker or burn rapidly and smoke. This disturbance even causes the dripless candles to run wax onto the carpets of the church. These units should be directed away from the candles or turned off for the duration of the

Plate 152   (circa 1986)
Traditional Decoration I –
Formal balance is maintained by exact placement of candle trees and foliage arrangements on either side of the focal point created by the mantelpiece and kneeling benches. A garland of mixed foliage, baby's breath and spray mums, adds delicate refinement to the kneeling bench.

Plate 153   (circa 1986)
Traditional Elegance —The large center arrangement of laurel, salal, springeri and caladium with open roses anchors this setting. The glass hurricane globes have been removed (scc Plate 163) from the wall sconces to allow placement of companion pieces to each side. Kneeling benches placed side-by-side are flanked with foliage and touched with the romance of roses.

ceremony to prevent any trouble. Matching squares of carpet or sheets of clear plastic under the candelabra provide necessary protection. Metal candles with spring-loaded wax inserts may be used as a rental item. They are safe and their height remains uniform. Never store them in a warm place.

To remove wax from carpets, place several layers of paper towel over the wax and use a warm iron on the towels to absorb the wax. Be certain that all aisle candelabra are securely fastened to the pews so that the guests will not tip them over. The lighted candles must be above shoulder height.

Candles may cause trouble in hot weather by becoming soft and leaning over. It is a good idea to store candles in a refrigerator before using them. Glass votive candles with a peg on the base fit most wedding candelabra. Many churches prefer them because they are both beautiful and safe. Another advantage is that votives are much easier to keep straight than candles, which often "prefer" to lean. We must always remember that the photographer puts our work on record for posterity!

Trees. Decorative foliage trees are effective for wedding backgrounds. Foliage tree stands are wooden dowel rods or posts of various heights painted brown or green, and mounted in paper mâché or plastic pots filled with plaster of Paris (Plates 154 & 155).

Drive a nail at the top end of the pole and tie a wet foam floral cage to it. The nail prevents the foam from slipping. Styrofoam may be used instead, but only for foliages that will hold up without moisture. The foliage is then inserted into the foam with the branches facing the front for a one-sided design, or they are inserted all the way around for a free standing tree that will be viewed from all sides. It must be kept in mind that the branches radiate from the crown as though they were growing. Boxwood, Chamaedorea (emerald palm), magnolia, sprengeri, salal (lemon), and pittosporum

Plate 154   (circa 1986)
Easy-to-make Topiary Tree —
The foliage tree standard (Plate 155E) is filled with fresh salal (lemon leaf) and variegated pittosporum to create a ball. Additional foliage is placed at the base to add balance and elegance. A papier-mâché pot is placed inside the basket.

Plate 155   (circa 1986)
Wedding Equipment — Detail
A – bare-branch tree mounted in plastic bucket of plaster of Paris (Plate 158)
B – aisle standard prepared for flowers (Plates 145,146,151)
C – candle tree prepared for flowers (Plates 152,156,159)
D – candle spiral prepared for flowers (Plates 160,164)
E – topiary tree, dry foam (Plate154)
F – palm tree holder
G – foliage stand (2 sizes) and foliage arrangement dish with wet foam

are all long lasting choices for these decorations. A mixture of foliages that have contrasting colors and textures will look splendid. Fresh flowers may be added to radiate from the foliage for a more expensive look. A matching cluster at the base will give a beautifully finished piece.

Another type of foliage decoration is the palm tree that is made by inserting Chamaedorea leaves into a wire tree frame. Two leaves facing apart placed in each receptacle give a full and natural look (Plate 155F). Greenery mounds are low arrangements of foliage made in plastic bowls of foam, and strategically placed to hide the base of a candelabra, soften the corner of an architectural feature, or hide a floor light (Plates 152, 153, 156). These are very useful and inexpensive to make, and they give a luxurious effect to the overall decoration. Greenery mounds may be placed on easy-to-make pedestals of different heights and grouped for different effects (Plate 155G).

The use of bare-branch trees is a very cost efficient way of creating an impressive decoration (Plates 137 – 140 and Plate 155A).

The trees are selected in the field for their attractive branching patterns, stripped of foliage, and mounted in buckets of plaster of paris or concrete. They may be decorated in numerous ways depending upon the need. Water tubes or plastic-wrapped blocks of wet foam may be tied in the branches to hold graceful clusters of flowers or foliage. A matching cluster at the base will give a beautifully finished piece. For a different kind of impact votive candles may be suspended or placed on picked rings to give the soft glow of candlelight (Plates 140, 157). Twinkle lights may be strung in the trees or sprays of autumn foliage or silk dogwood would give different seasonal effects. The possibilities are endless (Plates 158 and 137, 138, 139).

(Plate 140)
Fantasy of Nature –
These bare tree branches are mounted as described on page194

Plate 159
Candle tree with votives; the asymmetrical triangle of gladioli, carnations and spray mums with clipped Chamaedorea foliage provides both flowers and candles in one unit. Care is taken that no flower is near a flame.

Plate 160
This graceful design of eucalyptus, variegated pittosporum, oak and galax roses, follows the curve of the spiral candelabra. A pair of these would be positioned like a parenthesis framing the bride and groom. This type of design detail would be most appreciated from a close-up view in a small chapel.

Plate 161
A free-standing trinity (unity) candle decorated with mixed foliage would be lighted by the bride and groom using the two outside candles.

Plate 162
This trinity candle is embellished with a cascade of dendrobium orchids, soapberries and English ivy.

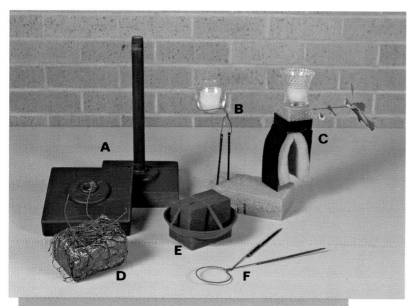

Plate 157   (circa 1986)
Mechanics – Detail
A – plant stand made of 2 blocks of wood, 3/4 inch threaded pipe and 2 pipe flanges
B & F – heavy gauge wire votive cup holder
C – custom-made pew marker base with foam rubber liner (Plate 150)
D – wet foam wrapped in polyfoil and chicken wire (Plates 156,159,160)
E – Foliage arrangement dish with wet foam (Plates 152,153,156)

Plate 158   (circa 1986)
A Contemporary Chapel Setting
A 10' bare-branch tree draped with fresh yellow acacia is placed on the left, and is repeated on the right with a shorter version, to complement the asymmetrical balance of the chapel architecture.

Plate 163 (circa 1986)
Asymmetrical Balance—
A contemporary Flemish
look is achieved with similar
but unequal designs. The
bride's color selection is a
perfect complement to the
oil painting. Candles were
chosen to match.

Plate 164 (circa 1986)
Symmetrical Balance –
Variation –Necessary
interest is provided by the
unusual placement of the
foliage arrangements above
the mantel. One of two
existing wall hangers holds
the top design while the
foliage reaches across
hiding the other hanger.
Should there have been a
mirror above this mantel, a
suction cup holder would
work – on the glass.

Figure 100
The Receiving Line – If the bride's father chooses, he may fulfill his duties as host and mingle with the guests instead of standing in the receiving line.

Chapter 23
RECEPTION DECORATIONS

Receiving Line

The reception is a gala affair. Guests should allow plenty of time for the bridal party to arrive at its destination. Photographs are usually taken before guests are admitted. The receiving line is formed conveniently near the entrance so that the guests may pass without creating confusion in the area where refreshments are served. Free, easy circulation of guests must be maintained to control the situation.

The bride's mother is first in the receiving line, followed by the groom's father, the groom's mother, and the bride's father. If the bride's father chooses, he may fulfill his duties as the host and mingle with the guests instead of standing in the receiving line. The bride is next in line and then the groom. The matron of honor, maid of honor, and bridesmaids follow in the order named. It is not necessary for the maids to be in line either. Ushers do not participate (Figure 100).

One or two close friends of the bride are asked to assist in registering the guests in the bride's book. Many guests overlook registering. This oversight can be prevented by having the book placed on a table near either end of the receiving line. In weddings where there is a large number of guests at the reception, close friends of the bride's family may be asked to assist in serving refreshments. They are usually provided with corsages. After all the guests have been received, the bride and groom enjoy visiting with the guests. When dancing is planned, the bride and groom have the first dance alone on the floor; they are joined later by the immediate family. The father cuts-in on the bride and groom; the groom will ask her mother to dance, and then the groom's parents dance with the bridal couple. The best man and the matron of honor begin dancing, followed by the bridesmaids and ushers.

After the bridal couple has mingled with the guests for a while, the bride will let the bridesmaids know she is leaving to change clothes. They group around the stairs to catch the bouquet when the bride tosses it. A sentimental gesture is made when the young lady who catches the bouquet gives it to the bride's mother for a keepsake. Guests wait for the reappearance of the couple before throwing rice and confetti. Rice tinted the color of the maid's dresses and tied in little bags of tulle, carries out the color scheme to the last item. In recent years, rice and confetti have been replaced by fresh or dried potpourri, birdseed or the blowing of bubbles over the bride and groom. Local custom and the rules and regulations of the local venue may dictate what can and cannot be thrown over the bride and groom as they leave the reception.

Bride's Dinner

The dinner following the wedding ceremony is a joyous affair and is given by the bride's parents. The guests may be served buffet style when the wedding ceremony is informal, or the guests may be seated (Figures 101, 102 and 103) . After the main course has been served, the best man rises and offers a toast to the bride. The groom replies quickly by thanking everyone. The other members of the party may then offer their toasts.

After a morning wedding, a breakfast menu is served; at high noon, a luncheon menu or brunch may be served; at afternoon weddings, a reception menu is served. It may include punch, cake, coffee, mints, and open-faced sandwiches. For evening weddings, the reception menu may be used, or the bridal seated dinner may be served.

Figure 101

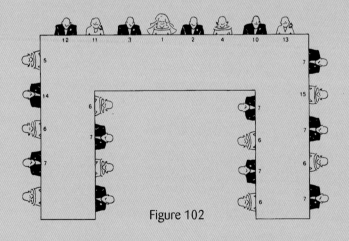

Figure 102

Figure 103

Figure 101
Semi-formal Dinner – Seating arrangement, head table.

Figure 102
Horseshoe Table – Seating arrangement, "U" shaped table suitable for a reception or a rehearsal dinner.

Figure 102A
Rectangular Table – Seating arrangement, intimate setting.

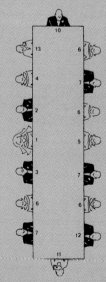

Figure 103
Formal Dinner – Seating arrangement, parents of the bride and groom are seated at another table.

Bride's Cake

The bride's cake is a specially decorated tier-on-tier cake, which is cut and eaten at the wedding dinner or reception. It dominates the table and may be flanked with candelabra or arrangements of flowers. Garlands of flowers and greenery may also adorn this table (Plate 166). This table may be the central feature of the wedding reception with no other decoration planned. A cake knife, festive with satin ribbon and fresh flowers, is provided for the cutting of this cake (Plate 170). In military weddings, a saber may be used to cut the cake. The bridesmaids and family are grouped around the couple. The bride cuts the first piece of cake from the bottom tier with her husband's hand over hers. It is shared with the bridegroom, signifying that they will share life together, now and forever. The bride may cut two more pieces of cake. The groom will give one piece to the bride's mother while the bride gives the other slice of cake to the groom's mother. This gesture is a thoughtful one that is appreciated by both parents.

The bridesmaids may draw ribbons from the cake for their small favors, which have special meaning. When punch or champagne is served after the cake is cut, toasts are offered. Small cocktail napkins are provided for those sentimental guests who wish to take home a memento of wedding cake.

The double tiered bride's cake shown in Plate 166 creates a perfect centerpiece on a very elaborately decorated Victorian table — a thrilling focal point of the reception. Thrilling in part because sentimental family heirlooms collected over many years by the bride's family are used in the decoration. The cake top is an antique tussie mussie holder filled with fresh pansies, ranunculus and miniature carnations. This unique holder with spring-loaded legs that open, allowing it to stand freely on any flat surface is shown in detail in Plate 165. The tussie mussies on the table are detailed in Plates 167 and 168. They could have been the bouquets carried by two bridesmaids and later used as cake table decorations, or they could be intended as decorations only for the cake.

This presentation solves the age-old challenge of harmonizing ivory with white. Since the bicolor cake is finished with a white ruffle at the base, it must be separated from the white tablecloth for maximum effect. The hand crocheted doily provides the perfect transition in color, texture and *feeling* to harmonize the various components of this composition. The garland of fresh string (or table) smilax with its lacy bows repeats the garland design on the cake and supports several dried and pressed dogwood blossoms, a reflection of a favorite Victorian hobby. The antique gilded cherub candlesticks lend vertical emphasis to the entire setting. The soft white candles are "exclamation points" that emphasize the

Plate 166
Victorian Sentiment —
The "Language of Flowers"
popular in the Victorian
Period, speaks a sentimental verse at this table:
Fern — sincerity
Pansies — thoughts
Ranunculus — radiant
    charm
Roses — love
Roses, China — beauty,
    always new
Roses, cream — purity
Tulips, red — Declaration of
    Love

Plate 166
Victorian Sentiment

Plate 167
Antique carved ivory supports this cluster that includes a dark wine colored inflorescence of the evergreen wisteria.

Plate 168
Victorian Tussie Mussie –
China roses, the pink single
petal clusters, carry a
romantic message in this
bejeweled holder with chain
and finger ring.

lines of the cake columns and the table skirt pleats also calling attention to the table.

A more contemporary expression of decorating a bride's cake and cake table is shown in Plate 169. The clean lines of the 5 tiered cake are repeated in the clean sweep of the silk satin table overlay, which matches the bridesmaid's gowns. However, the juxtaposition of the frilly Corelli Lace cake frosting on the clean–shaped cake is repeated by tying the satin overlay with tulle bows. The cake is studded with simple wired and taped clusters of the bride's chosen flowers that have been carefully attached to the cake with sanitized corsage pins. They can be removed as the cake is cut without leaving any mark whatsoever on the cake. This design is a very sophisticated solution for the bride who prefers simplicity of design yet needs a feminine touch of softness.

Plate 170 shows a bride's cake that is both sophisticated and youthful in its effect. The cake is literally draped with a "cloth" of Rolled Fondant, each gather accented with a cluster of fresh wired and taped hyacinth blossoms, again pinned to the cake with a clean corsage pin. It is imperative to lift a single layer cake to greater heights so that it won't be overpowered by the size of the table, itself. This cake is presented on a pedestal cake plate that has been wrapped in tulle to give the effect that the cake is floating on a cloud. This tulle "cloud" repeats the effect of the gathered tulle table skirt. The pedestal cake plate is sturdy enough for the cake to be cut without tipping. Ribbons of the bride's chosen colors complete the picture.

A collection of cakes is presented in Plate 172. The satin striped table cover repeats the architectural aspects of the composition of cakes, which includes both a fountain and a "sky-bridge". The cakes are separated from the same color tablecloth by wreaths

of fresh greenery. The mechanics for this design are shown in Plate 171. Note that the four blocks of wet foam are placed on edge on a clear liner, which protects the silver tray. The flowers on top of the two cakes are arranged in white plastic spray-can lids, which have been thoroughly cleaned. This mechanic gives the flowers a source of moisture and prevents making a hole in the top (anniversary) cake. A bit of shredded coconut is sprinkled on the cake frosting before placing the small floral arrangement. This prevents the icing from sticking to the bottom of the spray can lid. Another spray-can lid is used for the small bouquet on the "sky-bridge". Weight, balance and symmetry are critical factors in this composition. The symmetrical balance of this overall composition has been eased by designing an asymmetrical cluster of flowers in a low plastic dish, and placing it in front of the center cake. A meeting with the cake designer before the wedding will help the florist know how to proceed with his designs from the standpoints of both design and mechanics.

Plate 171
This simple, quick and cost effective mechanic is a good way to lift any cake, especially a small one above the table allowing it to look more impressive.

Plate 172
Stairway to the Stars – This is a very complex composition that could easily become cluttered. The round silhouette of the roly poly votive cups repeats the curving lines on the cakes and bridge while the solid flower clusters unify the entire composition with the table.

Plate 173
Sheffield Candelabrum –
Traditional beauty is always in
good taste. The cascading
foliage unifies the top and
the base of this composition.

Candelabra are often used as accessories to the bride's cake. They may be used to enhance the formality and grandeur of the occasion or they may simply add visual interest. Three examples are shown here. The first is an antique Sheffield Silver five-branch candelabrum. This versatile holder has removable arms; it can be used to hold five, three or a single candle or bouquet. A traditional symmetrical design is shown in Plate 173. The center candle cup holds an epergnette — a plastic or glass dish with a rubber-encased peg on the bottom, which fits the candle cup (Plate 176). When creating a design such as this, it is important to have the candles in place while designing so the flowers can remain low and centered enough to not catch fire as the candles burn down. Good mechanics prevent a fire hazard.

A single candle is included with fresh flowers in a spring arrangement (Plate 174). This is easily accomplished with an

Plate 174
Spring Fling – Flowering quince, ranunculus, anemones, solidaster and honeysuckle are arranged in an epergnette, a glass dish with peg to fit the candle cup, see Plate 176.

Plate 175
Classical Elegance —
Rich harmony.

Plate 176
Candelabra mechanics —
These safe/secure mechanics (glass and plastic epergnettes) will help prevent a fire hazard; may adapt to any candle holder.

epergnette and candle pick, both of which are available at the florist supplier. This design shows each delicate bloom grouped with others of its own kind, which gives each more impact on the eye. The tall branch of flowering quince is kept well away from the candle flame. The height of a design such as this allows the honeysuckle vine to cascade gracefully.

The antique gilded cherub candlestick shown in Plate 175 is designed with a similar mechanic — a standard wet foam bridal bouquet holder (with its handle cut to a short peg) is used to hold the flowers. This holder has a smaller diameter and is therefore easier to hide without creating a bulky look. Due to its weight, the cluster of fresh grapes was tied to the cherub holder first (not the wet foam device) followed by inserting the smilax stems into the foam. The snapdragons and roses were added and all mechanics were covered with foliage. The fresh rose petal potpourri would be an added touch at the last minute. The mechanics for these three candelabra arrangements are shown in Plate 176.

Two other table arrangements that would be very appropriate for decorating wedding receptions are the classical topiary tree and a table centerpiece that holds a candle in the center. The lifted horizontal candle arrangement (Plates 17 and 177) could easily serve as the memory candle at the reception or even as the nuptial candle in the ceremony. The mauve colored stock flowers have been cut with both ends inserted into the foam to look as if they extend all the way through the design. This "just gathered from the garden" look is a little bit more interesting and romantic for an informal wedding reception. Should a commercial candle pick not be available for mounting the candle, a piece of styrofoam can have the candle countersunk and hot glued into it. The dry foam is picked onto the top of the wet foam for complete security. Again, the mechanics for securing candles must never allow them to be a fire hazard.

Plates 179 and 180 show a very romantic interpretation of the topiary and its mechanics. The old Belgian clay pot holds a few tortuous curly willow stems that serve as the trunk of the topiary. The main stem pierces a plastic covered block of wet foam that will supply the roses with moisture. This block has been further secured by wrapping two taped wires around it and tying

(Plate 17)
Monochromatic Color Harmony – The bare stems of the stock are inserted into the design separately, but they look as if the flower goes all the way through.

Plate 177
Monochromatic Mechanics – This custom-made dry foam candle holder is secure and will not become a fire hazard. It is also excellent for making "containerless" Christmas designs.

Plate 178
Wedding Treasure – Another family heirloom, this antique Sheffield silver biscuit box holds twelve roses – a perfect accent to a gift table or a guest register table.

Plate 179
Neoclassic Topiary – Traditional roses
with non-traditional curly willow trunk
and ribbon suggest that the formal
topiary is reborn.

Plate 180
Topiary mechanics – In lieu of a pre-
made cage holder, this custom-made
plastic wrapped foam block works well.
The thin plastic wrap reduces dripping
and prevents moisture from evaporating.

them to the trunk. Since topiaries are usually top heavy, a bag of sand was put in the pot underneath the foam in which the willow stems are hot-glued. A length of wired ribbon has been rippled and tied through the design for a romantic finishing touch.

Topiaries are making a strong comeback as we head into the new century. There are many interpretations and some are quite unexpected! Shown here are a collection of table centerpieces that are assuredly unique and bold. In Plates 181 – 183 several spheres and a cube of wet foam have been covered with various flowers and mosses and used without trunks as components of groupings that center the guest tables. Plate 186 shows another variation — several agapanthus flowers bunched together and mounted on a pin holder. The stems are wrapped with crisscrossed ribbons for both security and eye appeal.

A floral finial suitable for decorating the top of a column or post inside or outside the reception hall is presented in Plate 184. The large dry foam sphere covered in moss, literally floats on a raft of flowers and foliage that have been casually arranged in wet foam. The clean and bold form against the soft and frilly blossoms produces a delicious tension in all of these designs. This topiary decoration would make a lovely greeting to arriving guests.

Topiaries are generally thought of in today's design work as having a trunk or a stem,

Plate 181
Volumetric Designs –
The design techniques of
sectioning, pavé and spiraling
have been used in this table
composition.

Plate 185
Pavé is the technique with
which this cube has been
covered in hydrangea florets.
The shape of the hydrangea
floret makes this look like an
example of petalling, but
technically the entire blossom
is used so it is pavé.

Plate 182
Clustering, collaring, pavé and
wrapping have been used in
this group of designs.

Plate 183
We see clustering, pavé, zoning
and shadowing in this
composition. The glass ball
shadows the floral sphere and
the circular tray frames both.

Plate 184 (far left)
A perfect finial for the top of a
column, pedestal or post.

Plate 186
This parallel bundle of
agapanthus and the moss-
covered cube are decorated
with ribbon in the manner of
wrapping. The strewn florets
and petals constitute fresh
potpourri.

creative though it may be (Plate 179). However, a new concept, gaining acceptance, is the "topiary without a stem". This is known as a volumetric design. A volumetric design is defined as *a three dimensional composition consisting of a clearly defined geometric form which is wholly or partially filled or covered with plant or other materials.* The addition of accessory material must not violate the integrity of the form; e.g., cone, cube, funnel, obelisk, sphere, etc. Plates 181–185 show a number of these designs. Volumetric designs may be used

Plate 187A, B, C
The Look of Luxury —Flowers used in this way give a feeling of great extravagance, but in reality they are the odds and ends of left over materials from creating all of the wedding decorations. It is a creative interpretation of the pavé technique.

Plate 188
Renaissance Topiary I — This is a three-piece 7-foot tall design that comes apart for easy delivery. The mossing and ribbon wrapping of this extruded foam cone was labor-intensive, but it becomes a durable prop that can be stored and used many times over. Since the flowers are used in only one area, a luxurious combination was selected. They are placed in a tray of wet foam that sets on top of the metal urn (Plates 189, 191).

(Plate 188)
Renaissance Topiary I — Detail.

with or without containers. Many design techniques such as baling, banding, binding, bunching, bundling, clustering, collaring, layering, leafwork, pavé, petalling, sectioning (zoning), spiraling, tufting, tying and wrapping are used to create and decorate volumetric designs.

The guest book table has not been forgotten. Plate 187 presents silver candelabras fitted with single topiary-shaped blossoms of hydrangea and viburnum and a mini topiary of roses. The guest book would be propped up on the edge of the silver tray that holds a tapestry of leftover blossoms inserted into a thin layer of wet foam.

This decoration of understated chic extends to the cone topiaries displayed in Plates

Plate 189 (opposite page)
Renaissance Topiary II –
5-foot buffet table size.

Plates 190,190a (above, right)
Renaissance Topiary III –
Another version, a pair could
flank an entrance, stage
or altar.

Plate 191
Mechanics – A close view of
the tray of foam used in
Plates 188, 189, 190.

188 -189. The topiary in Plate 188 is a floor piece that stands approximately seven feet high. It's partner in Plate 189 stands at five feet and would be perfect to decorate a buffet table. The topiary in Plate 190 extends also to five feet in height, but has a different character with it's trunk covered in French knotted satin ribbons. Each form is made by covering an extruded foam cone with sheet moss, then applying the ribbons with great precision. A pearl headed corsage pin anchors the ribbons at each cross point. The flowers are inserted into a "platform" of wet foam that is placed on a large tray (Plate 191).

Groom's Cake - Wedding Cake

Tradition indicates that the true "wedding cake" is traditionally the "groom's cake." It was always a dark fruitcake, slices of which guests were given as mementos to take home. However, current tradition regards chocolate and other flavors as appropriate for the groom's cake. It is customary for the wedding cake (groom's cake) to be sliced and packed in small white or silver boxes, tied with ribbon, and placed at each plate at a seated breakfast or dinner. If the reception is a buffet affair, the boxes are put on a silver tray conveniently located near the entrance for the guests to help themselves. This cake service may also become part of the ceremony, and is cut by the groom with the bride's hand over his. It is done after the bride's cake ceremony. This cake may or may not be iced; however, the table provided for it is beautifully decorated with flowers, etc. Coffee is served with this cake.

Many wedding couples take the opportunity to develop a theme around the groom's cake, which depicts his background, university affiliation, hobbies or special interests. This decoration can be challenging, but it can also be a lot of fun. The groom's cake shown in Plate 193 celebrates his ranching heritage. The cake itself is a true feat of engineering; it has three layers, which can be cut and served at the reception. It is completely edible — including the thorns! The desert sand upon which it rests is really a drift of unrefined sugar in a sanitized terracotta saucer. The yellow roses (of Texas) growing up through the barbed wire express that "Don't fence me in!" feeling so typical of the wide-open spaces. All of this is encircled with a giant bandana and rests upon the quintessential denim fabric of the cowboy's daily outfit.

Memory Candle

The lighting of a memory candle is a pleasing addition to a wedding. This candle is a large, decorative white candle secured with hot glue or melted candle wax in a permanent container. It may be decorated with garlands of the chosen blossoms of the wedding and is placed on a special table. It is lighted by the groom, with the bride's hand placed over his. This candle is used on their future wedding anniversaries. Current preferences allow this candle to be lighted by the bride and groom together during the wedding ceremony. When used this way it is known as the nuptial or unity candle. It may be transferred to the reception area and used again. (Plates 123, 124).

Plate 193
Don't Fence Me In!
A groom's cake and table with a Western theme,
developed to create an unforgettable memory.

Part 5

Personal Flower Design

Chapter 24   INTRODUCTION

Corsages may be thought of as *living jewelry*. They are accessories that accent a lady's charm. A corsage must "do something" for the person who wears it, like the favorite hat or scarf that gives an added lift when worn. It must be light, airy, and so much a part of a lady's costume that she is unaware of its presence.

Corsages should be like pearls around the neck, or a watch on the arm. The wearer knows that they are there, but their presence is not felt. (Plate 194).

Since many corsages are not designed for shoulder wear, make it a practice to place a card with the corsage, telling the customer how it was designed — for the wrist, waist, hair, or to be worn as a necklace. The card may read: "This corsage was designed for you to be worn as a... " Also, a card with this quotation will subtly suggest the proper way to wear the flowers :

"Wear the flowers the way they grow;
Never let them dangle by their toes."

The *occasion*, the *costume*, and the *individual* will be the deciding factors in the selection of flowers, ribbon, and design of the corsage. For formal occasions the flowers should be of fine texture, the ribbon, if used, of top quality, and accent materials may be desirable. Semi-formal and tailored costumes do not require this "dressy" look. Foliage often replaces accessory items and ribbons.

Considering the costume: its design and color greatly influence the design and color of the corsage. The individual's type and size have to be considered also. Fashion and style of dresses that are in vogue will influence the designs and accent materials. It is imperative that florists keep abreast with fashion, remembering at all times that they are selling creative ability and craftsmanship as well as flowers.

The elements and principles of all art, previously discussed, certainly apply to corsage work. They cannot be ignored merely because corsages are small. Some important elements, principles and concepts which apply specifically to corsage designs are listed here:

SECURITY: the mechanics of flowers and accent material used in a corsage must be secure. Falling petals and leaves, or flowers working out of position are indicative of poor workmanship.

PROPORTION: the units of the corsage must not only be in proportion to each other but also to the person wearing the corsage. Flowers smothered in too much ribbon or foliage do not show to full advantage. Some corsages have so much ribbon, tulle, and accessories, that it appears the florist is selling these instead of flowers. This excess is particularly tragic when flowers such as orchids are involved. Football corsages are another matter, for in them, the ribbon and accessories carry the school colors and are a vital part of the corsage.

COMPACTNESS: the spacing of flowers into tight wads or loose, floppy designs are inexcusable. There is a happy medium, which we must learn, that will allow each flower in a corsage to stand out as an individual and yet blend with the foliage and ribbon into a harmonious design. Corsage flowers should never be pressed together; there should always be a slight space between the petals.

FOCAL POINT: the focal point of a corsage is that place (binding point) at which the stems of the flowers come together. In practically every case, the "stems" are taped wires.) It is also the center of gravity. At this point the stems are taped together. The largest, heaviest or most intensely colored blossoms are placed in the focal area, and the ribbon is added here, adjacent to the focal point. The stems of certain corsage flowers, particularly in contemporary designs, are important in that they add line and rhythm.

BALANCE: the corsage should be so constructed that it may be worn with ease and comfort. The flowers lie on the shoulder (not the chest) in an easy, natural manner to become a part of the attire. Never do they protrude like fingers - this is called "goose-necking." The focal point is the governing spot affecting balance. Flowers extend above and below this point, giving balance; the smaller ones are placed on the edges and the larger ones toward the center of the design. Never design a corsage with flowers at one end and a bow at the other.

WEIGHT: weight in a corsage is of particular importance since it may be worn on lacy, fragile materials. It is imperative that corsages be as light and airy as the designer can make them. Consequently, all material not absolutely necessary to the construction of the design must be eliminated. In preparing flowers for corsage work, remove all but 3/4 inch of the stem from the flower. The purpose of using wire and tape in corsage work is to reduce weight and bulk. Insert a No. 28 or lighter weight (Figure 104) wire into the base of the flower, parallel to the remaining stem ; then floral tape it. No twisting of wire around the stem is necessary; tight taping will suffice to hold the flower firmly. Also when it is necessary to have a long line in a corsage, as for a circular hairpiece, tape the stems together — do not twist. Refer to Chapter 15 DESIGN MECHANICS for proper wiring and taping techniques.

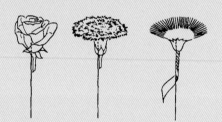

Figure 104
Corsage Stem Wiring -
Insertion method.

Chapter 25 CORSAGES, BOUTONNIERES, HAIRPIECES

Design of corsages follows closely the geometrical patterns in regular flower arrangement. Carefully review the elements and principles of design in Chapters 2 and 3, especially those principles applying to corsages at the beginning of this chapter. Similarities in all aspects of floral design should be clearly understood to increase efficiency. In flower arranging, wedding bouquets, and in corsage work, one should have a definite picture in mind and should visualize the placement of the corsage on the shoulder before assembling it.

Crescent Designs

The most popular place for flowers to be worn is on the shoulder. Generally, the left shoulder is preferred; however, depending on the dress design, or whether the flowers are to be worn dancing, it might be best to design the corsage for the right side. The shoulder design is similar to the crescent. The upper portion is longer and is curved backward over the shoulder in order to fit the contour and lie snugly in place. The lower section of the corsage is formed below the center of gravity (focal point) where all stems are taped together. This design prevents the mistake of having flowers at one end and the bow at the other. (Plates 194, 196, 198).

Number 1 blossom and/or leaf is held between the thumb and index finger; it is the smallest to be used. Number 2 blossom and leaf (also small), whose stem is shorter than that of No. 1, is held between thumb and index finger and is pulled down over the thumb nail (Figure 105). Additional blossoms are added under the thumb: the size of these blossoms increases as the center focal area is approached. The thumb always remains in the original spot, so that all stems meet at this point. The longer outer stems, which may move out of position, can be taped together smoothly (never twisted), and added in small groups.

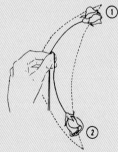

Figure 105
Crescent Design – Placements of No.1 and 2 stems establish points of the crescent.

Plate 195
Casual Crescent – Alstroemeria, cottage yarrow, "Eric John" waxflower, and grapevine tendrils are combined with eleagnus leaves.

Plate 196   (circa 1962)
Crescent, Shoulder Design – Button mums with ribbon integrated adjacent to the focal point and without foliage, express a bit of formality.

To secure the stems: tape very tightly with floral tape to gain a smooth and stable binding point. Make final adjustments by gracefully curving the components into the crescent shape and at the same time, arch its back to fit the contour of the shoulder.

If adding a bow: position it on the lower side of the corsage toward the face of the wearer. The taped wire that ties the bow is taped tightly at this center point where the stems are bound. Work some of the ribbon loops into the flowers on the side next to the face. Do not place the bow straight across the center of the design thus dividing the corsage in half, but rather let the bow be parallel to the design to accentuate its curve and length.

The finished corsage should have the shape of the new moon or crescent, being tapered at either end and widened at the center. The "spine" of the corsage will be bent backward to follow the curve of the shoulder gracefully and not be a straight exclamation point. Remember that a light weight corsage that follows the contour of the shoulder will feel comfortable and never bother the wearer. It truly will be living jewelry!

Triangular Designs

In a triangular shoulder corsage, the small sections or buds form the three points of the design (Figure 106). Hold the flowers between the thumb and forefinger of the left hand. Give the wire stems a graceful curve, picturing them lying over the shoulder (Plate 197, 198, 199).

The No. 1 blossom (lies over the shoulder) pointing upward; No. 2 blossom, shorter than No. 1, points downward; No. 3 blossom also shorter, points horizontally to the left, adding the third point of the triangle. This No. 3 blossom must be shorter so as not to tickle the wearer's neck, which can easily be a problem for a lady of delicate stature. Each stem being added is held under the thumb and forefinger; this central point is never changed while assembling the corsage. Though some flowers do point downward they are assembled with heads above the thumb and then bent downward over the thumb. *Do not have stems running in two directions!* Use the remainder of the blossoms to fill in the design (Figure 107).

Plate 197 (circa 1986) Triangular Design – Agapanthus and variegated pittosporum leaves accent a single fuji spray mum. The individual taped stems are left exposed to give the effect of a bouquet.

Plate 198 Triangular Design – Cushion spray mums and white waxflower work well together in this shoulder corsage.

Plate 199 Triangular Design – Rolled rose petals, cottage yarrow and inverted eleagnus leaves accompany three "corsage size" roses in this design. The stems are taped in black, which matches the grosgrain ribbon and will disappear against a black gown.

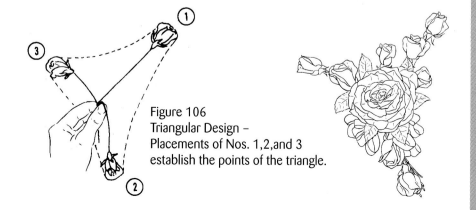

Figure 106
Triangular Design –
Placements of Nos. 1,2,and 3
establish the points of the triangle.

Figure 107
Triangular design, completed – Bow may be added at point of thumb.

Keep, in mind that all the material that is added is not to extend past the imaginary boundary lines that unite the three points of the triangle; it should form a graceful curve uniting these points. Avoid having the points equidistant from center. The stems are taped together tightly at the binding point.

To complete the corsage, the mechanics at the binding point are hidden by adding extra filler, leaves, or by adding a bow, and any of these would be taped in securely at this point. The wired stems may be trimmed into a graceful tapered point and taped as a single unit, or they may be cut individually at various lengths, then each given a graceful curve, flowing into the lines of the corsage. The petals of the flowers lie on the costume. This type of corsage may be worn in any position on the shoulder or waist, across the front of a dress, or pinned to a handbag.

Round Designs

The Round corsage is informal; it is similar to a cluster of violets that have just been gathered. For suits and other casually styled clothing, this design attracts attention by its charm and simplicity. The flowers are grouped together so that they radiate from one point. The ones in the back are straight up from the central point, and the ones in front flow over the thumb to hide the binding point. The bow is placed at this spot. Galax, camellia, English ivy or other similar foliages are excellent for backing (Plate 200, 201). The wired and taped stems may be individually clipped at different lengths to simulate the look of a gathered bouquet like a nosegay or tussie mussie.

Corsages may be carried in the hand. This works well for a person whose costume or occasion won't permit the wearing of flowers. The traditional hand-held "corsage" or small bouquet is a nosegay, posey bouquet, or "tussie mussie", which is a round cluster of flowers similar to the tailored bunch of violets mentioned above. However, they may be formal or informal and are often more delicate and feminine. Historically, laces, tulle, pearls, velvet or satin leaves, and other accent materials were used to outline the design, but in today's fashion world all fresh materials are preferred. There is usually one conspicuous central flower, e.g., a rose or lily encircled with delicate flowers, then a circle of carnation petals etc., and the design is completed with the accent material (Plate 224). A flowing velvet ribbon bow with streamers is tied to the design. The nosegay is Victorian; its popularity reached its peak during the time of Mrs. Mary Todd Lincoln. She was photographed in her inaugural gown holding a perfect example of one. The "tussie mussie" was first noted in England in the Oxford Dictionary, dated 1585. A beautiful example of one is in the portrait of Marie Antoinette by LeBrun, which indicates its popularity in France where this design

Plate 200   (circa 1952) Round Design – Nosegay or posy of stock florets and galax leaves surround an open pink rose.

Plate 201   (circa 1986) Round Design – Pixie carnations, Kalanchoe and alstroemeria with ming and galax foliage surround a miniature amaryllis flower in this update of the Victorian tussie mussie.

Plate 202 Interpretive Round – Gerbara and pixie carnations with oak leaves.

Plate 203 Round, New Millennium – Hydrangea and delphinium florets are paired with a Stargazer lily and variegated English ivy.

was perfected. Both clusters of flowers were originally meant to be very romantic with certain flowers carrying messages of love via the "language of flowers".

Informal Clusters

The informal cluster departs from the geometric shapes previously discussed. The materials themselves dictate the design shape or style as defined in Free Form — Interpretive Design, realistic interpretation. In Plate 204 the immature dogwood blossoms are left attached to their natural twigs, the shape of which determines the design. The small cattleya orchid in Plate 205 has been backed with wired and taped eucalyptus leaves whose stems are cut off at the binding point so as not to interfere with the more interesting curly willow stems. Plate 206 illustrates how tiny discarded twigs have been put to artistic use in the construction of a delicate armature that accents the dendrobium orchids. These three designs are excellent examples of living jewelry. For the person who prefers traditional design but doesn't wish to be restricted to the typical geometric patterns, we show two informal clusters in Plates 207 and 208. These examples both depend on the use of color and texture for interest and satisfaction.

V-neck Designs

When the design of the dress permits, the "V"-shaped corsage is most becoming. It will accent perfectly a "V" or sweetheart neck line or fit nicely in one corner of a square neck line. When a scarf is being worn, this design can be pinned at the knot. It is versatile. For a strapless dress this corsage may be worn on the top of the shoulder, being held in place with neutral-colored adhesive tape. The ends will flow to front and back from the top (similar to an epaulet Figure 108, Plate 210).

The flowers are wired and taped one to the other as in any other corsage slightly elongating the shape and forming a garland. The length of each "arm" of the "V" will depend

Plate 204
Naturalistic Design – An informal cluster is created by leaving the dogwood flowers attached to their natural stems. Four Burford holly leaves are placed to hide the binding point.

Plate 205
Orchid Solitaire – Curly willow brings a line of interest to this informal cluster of ming and eucalyptus backing a very special single miniature cattleya.

Plate 206
Constructive Cachet – A tiny armature strikes a charming pose in this unique example of living jewelry.

Plate 207
English Garden – A casual gathering of garden blossoms speaks with a wistful yearning for times past.

Plate 208
True Blue – Blue can be a difficult color to match, but these "Bella Donna" delphinium florets rise to the occasion.

Figure 108
Epaulet Design – Three garlands brought together are used on top of the shoulder.

on the amount of flowers used and the design of the costume. Bring both "arms" together and add flowers to form a focal area. The last flowers will flow over the thumb hiding the binding point. Tape the stems at this point. Be sure the mechanics of the binding point under the focal area, are hidden with additional foliage. (Figure 109, Plate 209).

Strapless Dress Designs

Strapless evening gowns offer the designer opportunities to create unique, personalized, one-of-a-kind living jewelry. One idea is to wire the flowers together in sequence and use them over the shoulder as a shoulder strap for the dress. Another practical idea is to purchase from the variety store hair clips that are used to hold curls in place. A single blossom, such as an orchid or camellia, is fashioned into a corsage and secured to this device (Figure 110). It may be used to clamp at the neckline, in the hair, or on a scarf. Delicate flowers such as small orchids may be fashioned into an epaulet (Figure 108, Plate 210) and taped to the shoulder with flesh tone adhesive tape, available at a pharmacy or medical supply store.

Floral chokers and necklaces offer another opportunity for creative personal adornment. Plate 212 presents a floral choker with very simple mechanics: the choker, made of braided grosgrain ribbons knotted on both ends simply encircles the neck, crosses and is pinned at a comfortable length. The flower cluster is simply pinned to the ribbon braid. This jewel can also be worn in reverse, with the flowers in back. An elaborate floral necklace is featured in Plate 211. These delicate blossoms are wired on the thinnest wire and taped into a softly flexible garland. The taped wire is shaped into a sturdy hook on one end, and the garland simply loops the neck and hooks over itself at any point that is comfortable to the wearer.

Floral jewelry of this caliber depends entirely on the personality of the wearer.

Figure 109
V-Neck Design – Wired and taped materials may be shaped to the exact contour of the neckline.

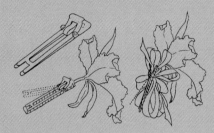

Figure 110
Strapless Gown –
The mechanics for a strapless gown may be as simple as attaching a flower cluster to a hair curl clip.

Plate 209   (circa 1986)
V-Neck Design – A small cattleya orchid with "Rosario" alstroemeria and touches of ming to add softness.

Plate 210   (circa 1986)
Epaulet Design – Daisies, agapanthus and ming work well to create a light weight epaulet corsage that may be worn without interfering with arm movement.

Plate 211
Floral Necklace –
Dendrobium orchids and
cottage yarrow are used in
this living necklace. A hair
piece has been fashioned to
match.

Plate 212
Floral Choker – Cottage
yarrow, delphinium and
foxglove trumpets work
together in this decorative
personal adornment.

Consultation is a must! Fabric samples and knowledge of the occasion would be very helpful in making suggestions.

Hairpieces

Coiffures vary greatly in design according to the fashion trends in hair styling. Regardless of the style, the flowers should fit closely to the hair and follow the curvature of the head. Two designs that generally fit with any hair style, the crescent and informal cluster are shown in Plates 211, and 213 – 216). The smaller blossoms form the points just as in designing the crescent corsage; additional flowers increase in size, thus adding width. Tape all stems tightly and smoothly together as you go, keeping the design as light in weight as possible. It is vital that the flowers lie flat to the head unless the coiffure is quite bouffant. This is achieved exactly as in fitting a corsage to the shoulder — by arching its back. Be sure all mechanics remain hidden under the blossoms or leaves. Since the flowers will create a focal point in the hair, it is imperative that they snuggle into the side of a French roll or bun, or be placed into a wave that forms the style. This type of corsage if very light weight, needs no frame; the wire stems of the flowers are support enough. Bobby pins hold the design in place or it could be attached to a comb. The figure eight or bow tie armature made of a taped wire or a chenille stem as described under wristlets, to which the hairpiece may be attached, will provide security when the flower stems are too thick for a bobby pin to close.

Many varieties of flowers are excellent for fashioning coiffure designs. An orchid used for this purpose will fit more beautifully if its lip lies flat on the hair and its other petals float softly close to the hair. This requires careful wiring in order to bend the stem into the position that will allow the orchid to fit as described. See Plate 214. Foliage may be used with caution in hairpieces. It can be used as a dramatic accent as in Plate 214 or it can be secondary

Plate 213 (circa 1986)
Coiffure Design –
Ventura lilies are paired with alstroemeria. Inverted eleagnus leaves will contrast beautifully with dark hair.

Plate 214
Butterfly Orchid – This singular phaelaenopsis orchid floats above ruscus foliage issuing a graceful trail of bear grass.

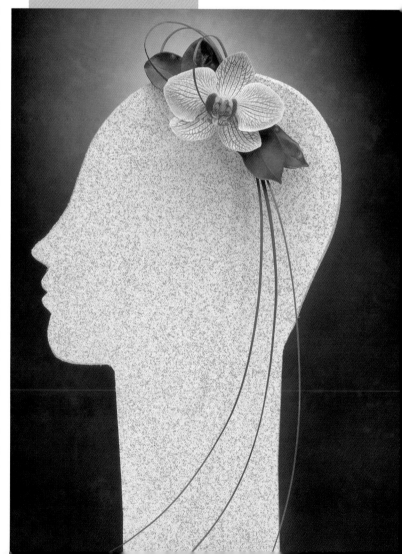

to the flowers with only suggestions of it showing as with the roses in Plate 215. Hydrangea and delphinium florets gathered with French wired ribbon in Plate 216 make a beautiful statement without any foliage. Feathers and many other accessories may add interest and variety in these designs.

Wristlets

Wrist corsages vary with the trend of fashion. They are popular with teenagers for dancing because they are not so easily crushed as are shoulder corsages. Wristlets must be so constructed that they will feel comfortable and secure. All wires that are used on the flowers

Plate 215
Simple Cluster – Champagne roses, variegated English ivy and tiny unopened solidago buds create an unpretentious hairpiece.

Plate 216
Monet's Garden – Rippling wired ribbon decorates a cluster of water lily-colored blossoms.

must have the ends turned upward into the flowers; never allow one to protrude, for it might injure the wearer.

This design is traditionally made in two sections, each tapering from a point to a wide end, similar to a bunch of grapes. The two sections are then tied together and the bow is added (Plate 217). Do not make the corsage too long, for it will overlap when it is brought together under the wrist. The flowers lie on the arm and follow the curvature of the wrist. This design may also be shaped into an "S" curve and be placed on the diagonal on the top of the wrist, rather than encircle the arm.

A wide variety of commercial wristlet forms may be purchased, or a wristlet armature can be made from three chenille stems (Figure 111). One stem is shaped into a loop on the end, and the others (No. 2 and No. 3) are placed to either side of this loop. Tie these together tightly with a No. 28 wire, leaving the loop standing free. Now extend stems No. 2 and No. 3 outward from No. 1. Fold these over the thumbnail or knife blade back toward the center stem (No. 1), starting a criss-cross pattern. The No. 28 wire is brought down from the first tie to this second crossing and is tied by making a complete circle where No. 2 and No. 3 cross No. 1. Do not cut off the tying wire. Continue the process until you have the length desired. Cut the surplus of No. 2 and No. 3, leaving No. 1 long. The No. 1 extension is used to circle the wrist and fit into the loop which was made first at the opposite end. The flowers are secured to the armature using taped wire in three places.

A second wristlet frame is the "figure-eight" clamp. Wrap a heavy wire (No. 18 or No. 19) with tape; then wrap, this taped wire with satin ribbon. Bring the two ends together forming a circle and tie them with taped wire. Hold the circle at the intersection of ends and grasp the opposite side; bring to-

gether and tie or twist one turn. This forms the figure eight. Flowers are secured to the twisted section. Both ends of the loop of the figure-eight are bent around the wrist forming a clamp. This frame may be made of satin or metallic cord which has wire reinforcement.

In addition to the design ideas just covered, a designer may be innovative and use other materials at hand such as the plastic spools inside the rolls of corsage tape. By cutting through a spool then rounding the corners of the fresh cut, a suitable bracelet form can be made. This bracelet form is then covered with velvet ribbon attached with hot glue. A small wired and taped corsage may then be glued to the bracelet and, at the same time, tied on with matching ribbon for double security, Plate 218. Another method of designing a floral bracelet is by hot gluing each blossom into the loops of French wired ribbon that has already been hot glued in serpentine fashion to the bracelet form, Plate 219. This method is time efficient and allows the finished product to be less bulky.

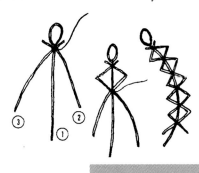
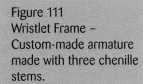

Figure 111
Wristlet Frame –
Custom-made armature made with three chenille stems.

Plate 217 (circa 1962)
Wristlet Design –
Miniature roses with feathered carnations show the curvature of the design just before it is attached to the armature.

Plate 218
Rose Solitaire –A "Fire and Ice" rose with its outer petals reflexed, makes a simple but elegant statement.

Plate 219
Good Luck Charm Bracelet – Heather, the flower of luck, softens this bracelet, which is accented with a few single rose petals and a berry or two.

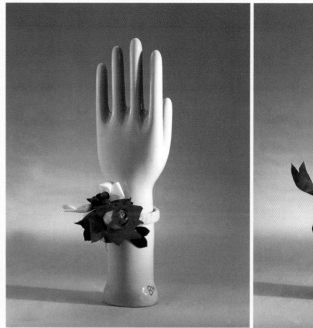

A selection of living bracelets is shown in Plates 220 — 223. Plate 220 shows a single exotic phalaenopsis orchid perched atop a cluster of foxglove trumpets with mechanics neatly hidden by a few hydrangea florets. This bracelet shows two kinds of ribbon,

Plate 220
Orchid Gemstone – The gluing technique of attaching blossoms into the folds of ribbon makes quick work of this ornate design.

one for the foundation and one for accent. The lovely bracelet in Plate 221 brings to mind an English garden with its collection of favorite Victorian blossoms and colors — hydrangea, delphinium and cottage yarrow nestled among the loops of French wired ribbon. The light-as-a-feather bracelet pictured in Plate 222 is very economical with individual rose petals tucked in among the hydrangea and cottage yarrow, all hot glued to a serpentine ribbon that ends in a romantic love knot. And lastly, we see a living jewel in Plate 223 that repeats the cadence of a real chain link bracelet. Each leaf overlaps the one before it in a subtle, yet sophisticated presentation.

Plate 221
Victorian Bracelet – Liquid glue allows these Pansies, delphinium, cottage yarrow and hydrangea to nestle among the loops of French wired ribbon.

Plate 222
Petalled Bangle – Just think of the many beautiful floral materials that could be substituted for the ones shown here.

Plate 223
Chain Link Bracelet – The orderly placement of materials reflects the look of a golden chain.

Leis

Leis carry with them the message of "aloha" from Hawaii, the island where this design originated. Leis are made by threading blossoms on dental floss, lei string (kite string) or fine wire, using a needle to thread the blossoms. Carnations must have the ovary (seed pod) removed, which frees the petals allowing the bottom of the calyx of one flower to be gently pushed into the center of the next flower. The floss is then threaded through the bottom of one blossom, out its face and into the bottom of the next. The number of blossoms required to make a lei may be reduced by assembling it with foliage, bows or tufts of raffia interspersed throughout. Small orchids of the vanda type are popular for this design. The needle and thread pierces the nose "bridge", enters its throat and continues on out through the point of its "chin". Sixty four vanda blossoms are required to make a standard size lei in this manner (Figure 86).

Individual Flowers In Corsages

CARNATIONS

Carnations are versatile and popular for corsage designs. The spicy aroma of the carnations distinguishes them from all other flowers. The long-lasting quality of these blossoms makes it possible to make corsages of them in advance of the rush holidays. Whole blossoms may be used in this type of design work, or unusual effects may be created by "feathering" the carnations.

"FEATHERING," (occasionally known as "Frenching") is a very popular technique for creating delicate corsages. The term, feathering means that a flower is cut into several pieces and each piece is wired and taped, then reassembled into a small version of the original. Many flowers lend themselves to feathering - carnations, chrysanthemums, marigolds, gerberas, iris, cymbidium orchids, birds of paradise etc. (Plates 224-227).

Fresh, crisp carnations may be divided

Plate 224 (circa 1962) Nosegay Style Corsage – Feathered carnations make the bulk of this round corsage. Note how beautifully the curly carnation leaves serve as an accent.

Plate 225 (circa 1973) Birds of a Feather – Birds of Paradise and carnations have been feathered to create a much more delicate composition than if whole blossoms were used. Even the carnation calyxes, sprayed gold, are used giving the effect of Christmas bells.

249

Plate 226 (circa 1962)
Feathered Crescent –
Carnation buds and glamour
leaves (Plate 117) complete
the design.

Plate 227 (circa 1980)
Peppermint Carnations –The
entire flower is used;
feathered petals, curled
foliage, and golden calyx-
bells make this a monofloral
composition.

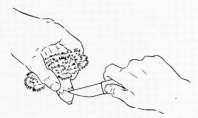

Figure 112
Feathering Cartnation –
Remove stem at base of calyx
and insert point of knife.

Figure 113
Feathering Carnation – Pull
the carnation apart by
grasping the two cut ends.

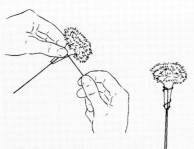

Figure 114
Feathering Carnation – One
section is held with thumb
and forefinger; wire by
extension method with No.
28 wire. (Fig 40, 41).

the day before using. They are wired and taped, and fashioned into corsages with or without bows and accessories. To preserve their freshness, mist them with anti-transpirant and water and store them in plastic bags in the refrigerator.

By studying the conformation of the blossom itself, one will find all the petals are attached just below the seed pod (ovary) inside the base of the calyx. To begin the simple process of feathering a carnation, first remove the stem where it meets the calyx. Then insert the point of a knife into the small calyx and push downward, cutting the base of the flower in half. (Figure 112). Pick the carnation up by the cut ends, pulling it apart (Figure 113). Place the two halves on the table with the cut faces upward. The seed pod is visible and is removed at this time. Do not remove the green calyx. By cutting a carnation in this way, the petals remain attached to the base under the seed pod and will not fall out when made into a corsage. It is imperative that the petals remain attached to the calyx. When a blossom is large, divide the halves into quarters or even into more sections, giving four to six feathered pieces per blossom. To remake this cut section into a miniature flower, hold the cut section upside down and gently shake to fluff the petals into a circular shape. Then enfold the green calyx around the delicate petals in the manner of a tiny envelope. Shape the petal section into a circular unit. Make any necessary adjustment to the petals at this time, being sure each petal shows. Do not let one petal cover another.

For wiring: with the right hand pick up a No. 28 wire in the middle and bend it over the thumb to a ninety degree angle. Place the angle of the wire with the flower under the thumb. One-half of the wire extends down the calyx, forming a stem. The other section extends outward (Figure 114). Slip the right hand out to the end of the wire and circle it above the thumb, binding this section snugly. Bind high under the petals to keep them from drooping. One complete circle with the wire holds the petals in place. Continue spiraling the wire down to the bottom of the calyx. This wires the section securely. It is not necessary to continue twisting the wire. The tape will suffice to hold the wire and form a stem. Wire all pieces in the same manner.

For taping: tape high under the petals, letting them remain in a natural position. Do not flatten the petals, or the size of the "new" blossom will be reduced. Petals that flop have not been taped high enough. This fault can be corrected by taping higher under the petals. Graceful, smooth taping, accomplished by practice, adds a beautiful finish. Since the larger, feathered sections will be used close to the binding point, it will not be necessary to tape these wires as far down as the smaller ones. When taping blossoms, learn to arrange them in sequence of size - small, medium, and large; then efficiency and speed are gained in assembling a corsage.

Note that throughout this entire process no tools were used, other than the knife to cut the carnations in sections. Learn to "let the scissors lie." They are not used for cutting tape; this is simply "pulled in two" with the fingers. Wire cutters will be necessary for cutting the wires.

ROSES

Roses - truly the queen of all flowers, are admired and loved universally. Their uses are unlimited. This flower is at home in the most humble of places and is elegant in the most fashionable home. They lend themselves to all types of floral design work and are suitable for every occasion.

The rose growers have increased the color range and lasting quality of these beautiful flowers and made them available year around. This assures their continued popularity. The various color tones assure the designer of almost any color combination.

Roses have always been popular for corsage designs. The triangular design (Figure 106) has unusual versatility; it may be used as a shoulder corsage, or pinned to the waist, or used on a handbag, to name a few possibilities.

When working with roses that are approximately the same size, remove some of the outer petals from the buds. These petals can be rolled to simulate small buds and are used on the outer edges of designs. To aid in wiring and taping these petals, a small rose leaf may be rolled with the petal. It will look like a true calyx. These petal buds will last as long as the individual flowers.

The larger rose used at the center of interest (Plate 228), has the outer petals reflexed (turned backward) to add the weight needed in tying in the focal area where the lines of this corsage come together. It is called a "camellia" rose because of its resemblance to a camellia when the petals are reflexed. The roses are graded in size from the ones at the points to the central rose.

The VICTORIAN ROSE (Plate 229) is

glamorous and is always a conversation piece. It flatters the person who has the joy of wearing it. For other descriptive names this design may be termed Edwardian, Empire, or Regency Rose but do not use the name of "Cabbage" rose. The corsage is made using a three-quarter-opened blossom for the center. Petals of the more-opened roses are wired and taped with No. 28 wire by the hairpin method in groups of twos and threes and are assembled around the central rose. In assembling these petals around the rose, place them higher on the back and somewhat lower in the front, shaping the corsage to fit snugly when pinned to the shoulder. Natural leaves are used to cover the mechanics beneath this blossom; small rolled petal buds may add accent and line in this design. Wedding bouquets, debutante and style show flowers are beautiful when made with Victorian roses.

GARDENIAS AND CAMELLIAS

Gardenias and Camellias are two of the most beautiful and traditional of corsage flowers. Their velvety texture and ethereal quality enhance the beauty of any gown. In a corsage, they may be fashioned for a tailored effect or they may be designed with accent materials so that they blend with the most elegant of gowns. For the tailored corsage, natural foliage, seedpods or berries could be used in lieu of ribbon.

For evening wear, silk, satin, lace, tulle, velvet or jewels are appropriate accent materials. When two blossoms are used together, the bow is placed at the side of the second blossom, never between the two, this would divide the design in half. Curve the two blossoms so that one rests over the shoulder. Do not have them one above the other in a straight line, which would produce an ungraceful, manufactured appearance.

Plate 228   (circa 1986)
Empire Rose – This "20 carat solitaire" rose with its outer petals reflexed, is joined in perfect harmony by several rolled rose petal "baguettes".

Plate 229   (circa 1952)
Victorian Rose – A composite blossom is made from the petals of a number of fully developed roses (Fig. 42).

Plate 230
Gardenia wedding corsage– white dendrobium orchids and satin ribbon with love knots.

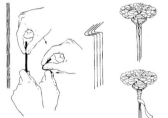

Figure 115
Wiring camellia, see Plate 231

The wiring of camellias for both corsage and wedding work is illustrated in Figure 115. Gardenias are generally purchased already tailored, on the wholesale market. However, if wiring them yourself, the calyx is first removed from the blossom. A No. 28 or 26 wire is run through the floret stem. A second wire is run through in the opposite direction, forming a cross. The wires are bent downward parallel to this stem and then taped. A gardenia collar is then placed up under the blossom. The foliage may be wired by the hairpin method, or it may be stapled to this collar before it is placed under the blossom. The stems are then taped together.

A   B   C   D   E

Plate 231
A– Wiring method: Use goose–neck shaped (#24) wires to insert into petals and also to form the flower stem. (See Fig. 73)
B– Wired satin tubing form hearts for a valentine camellia.
C– Pink perfection camellias with podocarpus foliage and butterfly accent.
D– Two camellias (variegated M. "Buddy" Benz) with glamour leaves of gold cord. (See Plate 117)
E– Variegated camellias with velvet tie.

GLADIOLI

Gladioli are admired and loved by all flower lovers. These blossoms have become a standard in the florist shop today, for special event and sympathy work, due to their stately and long–lasting qualities. They are available on the market throughout the year. It is an inspiration to work with the many beautiful colors. This beautiful flower is not often thought of for corsage work, but a number of different designs can be created from the florets of a single spike.

SINGLE BLOSSOM IN DESIGN - The individual florets of the gladiolus may be used for corsage designs. They are always removed from the stem for corsage work. The calyx remains on each floret. The single flower and buds can be used to fashion the corsage, or one can add small blossoms to the center of the floret, e.g., miniature roses and carnations and other small varieties. When small roses are used in the center, the result is called "glad-rose." (Plate 232).

In wiring the individual florets for this design, run a No. 28 wire through the base of the petals just above the green calyx. Fold both ends down (hairpin method), parallel to the trumpet, and press firmly with the fingers and then tape. There is no twisting of wire. The blossoms should be graduated in size as they are on a stem. Start with a small bud for the tip of the series; then add a slightly larger blossom so the upper petal covers about one-half of the bud. For a regular shoulder design, add two more florets, making a total of four, increasing their size. The lower blossoms are then curved into position over the thumb; their stems will run in the same direction (Plate 233). This extremely cost-effective corsage will be mistaken by many for orchids! The single blossom florets may be fashioned into any of the corsage styles previously mentioned.

BUDS - Buds make one of the most beautiful and unusual of all tailored corsages (Plate 234). Since they are buds, they do not show wilting and, with proper care, may be worn for several days. This corsage is ideal for a person who is going on a trip. Tightly closed buds are used and are wired (hairpin method) in the same manner as single blossoms. Use No. 28 wire through the bud, press downward, and tape without twisting the wires. Some of the larger buds used at the focal point may be cut horizontally in half, producing a rosette effect. Line is the most important element in this design. The bow, if used, must be tailored.

GLAMELLIA - BENZ METHOD

Glamellia-This word is a combination of two words, "gladiolus" and "camellia" (gla-mellia). Glamellias are among the most glamorous flowers that the designer can make. They fit beautifully into many occasions (Plate 235 and 236). They are as much at home on a suit as a tailored corsage, and yet they have the delicate quality and elegance that is needed in bridal work. A single glamellia

Plate 232 (circa 1973) Glad-Rose – Small roses (wired and taped) have been inserted through individual gladiolus florets to form "glad-roses".

Plate 233 (circa 1966) Single Gladiolus – Individual florets and buds are accented with glamour leaves.

Plate 234 (circa 1973) Sport Corsage – Gladioli buds with a looped dracaena foliage French bow create a tailored effect. The larger center buds are clipped to give the effect of rosettes.

Plate 235 (circa 1973) Glamellia – Always glamorous, always new and fascinating, this versatile blossom may be casual or elegant, and should be considered the "cadillac of the line" of your corsages.

used as a corsage is a conversation piece.

A glamellia is made from the petals of graded sizes of gladiolus florets; the completed blossom resembles that of a formal type of camellia. When made from fresh, crisp blossoms, they last for several days. After the glamellia corsage has been worn, let it float face down in room temperature water for a minute or two. Replace it in a plastic bag and store it in the refrigerator.

There are several methods of making this beautiful flower. The classic and most efficient method is developed from a botanical study of the individual floret. Select a stem that has four opened blossoms and several buds of graded sizes. By selecting a single good stem for making a glamellia, one saves the remaining stems for other uses. Do not make a habit of picking florets from a number of stems.

Plate 236
Glamellia – Queen of corsage flowers, always available and economical, yet of great value because of your artistic and "surgical" expertise!

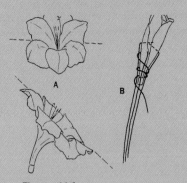

Figure 116
Glamellia –
A – Note the gladiolus floret
has three dorsal (upper) petals
and three lip (lower) petals. It
is flat across the face.
B – The 1/4 opened bud is
wired.

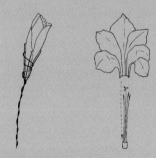

Figure 117
Glamellia – First floret is
divided between lip petals;
green "button" at base is
removed.

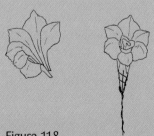

Figure 118
Glamelia Construction –
Second floret divided on right
side to be joined to left side of
glamellia.

STEPS TO FOLLOW

1. Remove the blossoms from the stem keeping them in sequence as they were grown. Do not vary this sequence.

2. Start with the largest bud that does not yet have an open center. This will become the center of the glamellia. In wiring this bud run a No. 28 wire halfway through and press one end tightly down the side; wrap the other end snugly around the bud in a downward spiral to its base (Figure 116B). Note that this wire was inserted slightly above the point where the petals are joined together.

3. Nature has grown these blossoms in perfect shape and in graduated sequence of sizes perfect for this use. Viewing the florets from the side, they are flat across the face; three upper petals (dorsal) are standing erect; and the three lower petals (lip) are curved downward in the front (Figure 116A). It is vital to realize the importance of this division, for the lip petals MUST remain toward the lower portion of the blossom in order to maintain the natural appearance of the flower.

4. Cut floret according to position needed. Look at the center core and decide where it needs floret petals to maintain a circular flower. Pick up the first blossom in sequence (small to large), remove calyx and "green button" at the base of the floret; hold it together with the center core facing you in the position that nature grew it, the lip down, the dorsal petal up. Cut this floret between the petals on the opposite side from where it is needed. Should the center core need dorsal petals, then divide the floret in front between the lip, petals (Figure 117). Do not damage the portion which is needed. Use a knife or thumbnail to cut between the petals. The cut floret is placed around the core, circling as far as it will. Usually the first floret completely circles the center core.

5. Keep the glamellia flat across the face. Raise the floret that is being added until all petals appear even across the face. If the center is too high in the beginning, the glamellia becomes cone-shaped. Look at it from the side. When the petals are in the correct position, insert a wire halfway up the floret into the petal at the cut edge. Do not wire low, for support is vitally needed. Direct the wire at a downward angle through the center core and out the opposite side. Then circle the other end of this wire around the floret again piercing the petals at a downward angle (Figure 118).

6. Make sure that at least one-fourth to one-half of each added floret is visible from the front. A larger, more beautiful glamellia will result with fewer florets if all petals show to their best advantage. Looks-value and light weight are needed, not numbers of petals.

7. To add the second floret, remove the calyx and the little "green button." Hold the unfinished glamellia and the floret side by side in

the correct position (lip petals down). Assume that petals are needed on the left side (Figure118); cut the blossom on the opposite side (right side), and place the blossom on the left side of the center core. Be sure that it is flat and that petals show to full advantage. Insert a No. 28 wire downward through one side of the floret; loop it around the same group of petals and insert it on the other side of them; pull so that it binds them snugly as before. No circling with wire is needed; the hairpin loop, holds.

8. To add the third blossom, assume that the glamellia needs petals on the right (Figure 119). Slit the blossom on the left side and add it to the right side of the center core. Wiring is done in the same loop manner as just stated; work with straight, smooth pieces of No. 28 wire so that they will slip through the petals without cutting. Direct the inserted wire downward toward the stem each time.

9. Adding the fourth blossom: this time lip petals are needed (Figure 120). Cut this last floret in the back side. Study carefully where to cut this floret so as to throw the top dorsal petal either to the right or left, according to the need. This fourth blossom is wired in the same manner as the others. However, the wire ends are pointing upward and the loop is holding the petals on the lower side. Bring each end of the wire around and down, joining them into the stem, or insert the ends back into the flower, pulling them down and sewing the glamellia.

10. Cover the construction work with any flexible broadleaf evergreen such as English ivy, pothos, galax, etc. The front side of the leaf faces out and the back of it is against the flower. Cut pieces out of the lower section of the leaf if it is too large. Insert a No. 28 wire through the base and circle above the other end that is protruding. Cut off the protruding end leaving a quarter inch to turn up, holding the circling wire. Tape over the wire construction. (Figure 121).

Two closed buds are now added to the glamellia. Do not remove the calyx. They are wired with No. 28 wire, and taped. The position of these buds is important. For a short person, the buds which form the line through this blossom point upward curving over the shoulder. They add height to the person by peeking out from underneath the glamellia (Plate 236). If the person is tall, then these buds are placed on the lower side of the blossom pointing downward. They should not point toward the neck.

Any foliage that accents the glamellia beautifully may be used as long as it doesn't overpower the flower. Line foliages may be looped like ribbon to achieve a tailored look. In using solid leaves similar to ivy or lemon, have only three leaf points arranged forming a graceful triangle. The leaf used directly under the lip, or the lower side of the glamellia, is hairpinned high and shaped over the thumb so that it follows the curvature of the petal. Additional

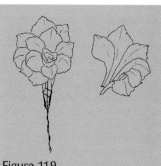

Figure 119
Third floret divided on the left side to be joined to the right side of glamellia.

Figure 120
Fourth floret divided on the top to be added on the bottom.

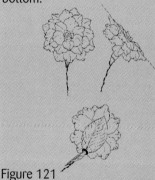

Figure 121
Construction is covered with a pliable broad leaf, top-side out.

(Plate 236)
Glamellia – Buds positioned for a person of short or average height.

foliage may be needed at this point to hide the mechanics of the binding point.

The leaves are taped to the glamellia and gracefully curved outward from the binding point and the stems are taped together in a gracefully tapered single stem. (Plate 236).

When making a glamellia larger than those required for corsages, use only the large petals. Split each floret in the front and continue adding the petals until the desired size is achieved. Additional florets are added by the hairpin method with No 26 or 24 wire, which gives them stronger support.

Gladioli are available in many varieties, and the conformation of florets in each is different, causing a variance in cutting them. By following the steps above, difficulties should not arise. When large unopened buds for the glamellia center are not available, simply roll the individual petals to form a center.

Plate 237 (circa 1962) A Presentation Gift – This glamellia is tied to an ivory fan as a presentation gift. It would be equally at home laid at the base of a silver candelabrum or crowning a wedding cake.

GLAMELLIA - QUICK METHOD

Another method, less time consuming, is simply gluing the florets together. All materials would be removed from the stalk and laid out just as before. A large bud would be glued into a small open floret and that one in turn would be glued into a larger floret etc. This method is adequate for glamellias that would be inserted into large topiary trees, tucked into garlands, or used on reception tables. In other words these glamellias due to their lack of having a truly natural shape and stem, are used where perfection of detail is not needed.

Glamellias if properly cared for, will last as long as any other flower. As soon as the glamellia is finished, spray it with anti-transpirant, mist with water and store in a plastic bag in the refrigerator.

CALLA-GLAD, a man-made flower, receives this name from its similarity to a calla lily. It is made of a single gladiolus petal taped around a tight bud. They are formed by using a very tightly closed bud, wired and taped (No. 28 wire). One of the large petals is then placed behind this bud and wrapped around the bud with tape so that it forms a miniature "calla" blossom. The petal of a gladiolus makes the corolla of the calla and a tight gladiolus bud the spadix (Figure 122 and Plate 238). Do not allow this petal to become bruised or let the bud turn. The flowers are then fashioned into a design. Calla-glads are used in wedding bouquets, corsage work, baby funeral work, and any place that requires delicate, small callas. They also make exquisite formal boutonnieres for men.

MISCELLANEOUS FLOWERS

A great many flowers, foliage and other plant parts are adaptable to corsage work. However, the making of corsages does depend on the creative ability and imagination of the artist and the selection of materials. Corsage flowers must have long-lasting qualities to withstand the abnormal conditions under which this fresh material is worn. Flowers that wilt quickly and those past their prime must not be used.

STATICE, KALANCHOE, FREESIA (clustered flowers) look delicate in corsages. Insert the "hair pin" wire over the stem between the florets (Plate 239).

STRELITZIA REGINA, the bird-of-paradise, makes one of the most beautiful and exotic of all corsage flowers. They create allure no other flower can. Divide the florets into segments (feathering), being sure to open the calyx (the boat-shaped portion of the stem) and use the pale delicate buds too. Each piece is wired, No. 28, by the hairpin method. When assembled, the sections radiate from one point (Plates 19, 194, 240).

TULIPS may furnish an interesting corsage variation. The whole flower may be used,

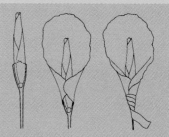

Figure 122
Calla-glad – Construction.

Plate 238   (circa 1966)
Calla-glad Corsage – Calla-glads grouped with glamour leaves (Plate 117) make a charming corsage.

(Plate 194)
Enchanting Jewel

Plate 239 (circa 1986)
Summer Mixture – Lily,
kalanchoe, freesia and ming
come together in an alluring
triangular corsage.

Plate 240 (circa 1966) (see Plate 19)
Strelitzia (Bird of Paradise) – Feathered blossoms have been grouped
with lycopodium foliage and blue petals toward the center.

Plate 241 (circa 1986)
Duchess Tulip – The focal flower in this bouquet is made by wiring
or gluing clusters of petals to the base of a single blossom.

or the flower can be divided with a knife into two or three segments. This division reduces the weighty look that the solid blossom sometimes has. Assemble the petals into the desired pattern. Tulip petals may also be designed into a composite blossom for corsage and bridal work, as shown in Plate 241. This is explained in the section on wedding bouquets.

IRIS blossoms may also be divided into three sections, with the petals wired and taped by the hairpin method. In assembling these sections into corsages, use the buds that are encased in the sheath. The sheaths themselves are turned backward, wired and taped in order that the silver lining of the sheath is exposed; they are then used as accent foliage.

POTHOS IVY leaves and CALADIUM foliage are excellent for making a foliage calla. Their stems may be wrapped with ribbon or painted or glued and covered with metallic dust. The stem is then turned back over the face of the leaf. The sides of the leaf are wrapped around this stem, simulating a calla. It is wired and taped. These foliage-callas are excellent for sport corsages and holiday wear when sprayed in brilliant colors. They make unusual and exotic wedding bouquets.

SMALL FLOWERS, such as stock blossoms, agapanthus, alstroemeria, hydrangea and hyacinth, are excellent in all corsage designs.

The flowers must be graded in sizes from the smaller buds, which add much interest in designs, to the larger blossoms used at the focal point. About one-half inch of the stem remains on the flower. The wire, No. 28, is inserted into the base of the blossom parallel to the stem and then taped. Do not twist the wire around the stem (Plates 197, 200, 201, 210 and 213).

NOVELTY CORSAGES add interest, but they must fit the occasion if it is for a specific affair: e.g., holly berries and miniature cones for Christmas corsages (Plate 242).

The calyx cup of carnations may be sprayed gold and the pointed tips turned backward. A small Christmas ball or berry is inserted deep into the cup to form a living Christmas bell. Holly leaves are excellent to use with this design. The points of the leaves must be clipped. In Plates 225 and 227 calyx cups are used.

When feathering chrysanthemums for a corsage, take a pinch of petals, reverse them and wire the tip ends, letting the green ends show. The effect is unusual and creates a new type of blossom.

DAFFODILS are interesting in corsage design. The whole blossom is usually too large to use; however, "feathering" the trumpet will change its appearance. Insert the point of a knife at the base of the trumpet and split upward dividing each scallop at the rim of the daffodil (Figure 123). They are then used in fashioning corsages. It is also interesting to remove the trumpet; wire and tape this piece. Fill the

Plate 242
Foliage Corsage – Miniature English ivy and red berries make an attractive long-lasting Christmas corsage.

Plate 243
Contemporary Cluster – Lily-of-the-valley, stephanotis and lilac (flowers from the bride's bouquet) make a wonderful "going away" corsage for the bride.

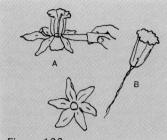

Figure 123
Cutting Daffodil
A–the trumpet is cut upward at large scallops; released sections will curl downward
B–trumpet removed, wired, and taped; perianth is filled with other flowers

Figure 124

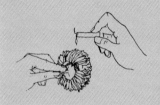

Figure 125

Plate 244
Football Corsage – School colors, multiple ribbons, braid and trinkets are represented in this example of a "Homecoming Mum" corsage. Missing are students names and more novelties.

perianth (or lower portion) with euphorbia, acacia, cornflower, or any other small blossoms. These divisions are then fashioned into a corsage.

FOOTBALL CORSAGES — Classic method: Wire the large chrysanthemum heads using the hook method (Figure 124). After the flower is securely wired and taped, drop melted candle wax (Figure 125), or use spray adhesive on the back of the blossom at the base of the petals where the wire extends through the head. This prevents the petals from falling. Foliage wired with the hairpin method, and taped, may outline this blossom to add support. Loops of satin-wrapped wire will also give added support (Plate 244). The ribbon represents the school's colors and should equal the size of the blossom, or be larger, with long streamers.

Current method: Glue the flower head (stem removed) to a cardboard mum collar that has been outlined with ribbon loops stapled to it. Additional trinkets tied on ribbons, ribbon braids and personalized ribbon streamers may also be stapled or glued to the backing before the flower is glued on. Permanent flowers have largely taken over this design, allowing the work to be done further ahead and giving the recipient a lasting keepsake.

BOUTONNIERES have a tremendous commercial value, which is still not fully developed. Men are self-conscious about wearing flowers because they feel that it sets them apart. However,

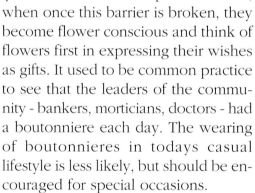

when once this barrier is broken, they become flower conscious and think of flowers first in expressing their wishes as gifts. It used to be common practice to see that the leaders of the community - bankers, morticians, doctors - had a boutonniere each day. The wearing of boutonnieres in todays casual lifestyle is less likely, but should be encouraged for special occasions.

Boutonnieres are often too large or crudely made. Many discerning men much prefer to be without a boutonniere rather than wear one with a stem unwrapped or too long. When making a boutonniere for evening wear or morning weddings, use a white or ivory flower, such as a carnation, small gardenia, rose, stephanotis, lily-of-the-valley, or calla-glad. For informal wear almost any flower may be used, even in combination with foliage, berries, twigs, etc. in any color which harmonizes with

Plate 245
Formal Boutonniere –
Agapanthus, tiny green buds
and ivy. Imagine stephanotis
or rolled rose petals as
substitutes.

Plate 246
All-Occasion Boutonniere –
Miniature carnation, bud and
leaf with eucalyptus (could
be 1/2 carnation feathered).
Almost anything could
substitute.

Plate 247
Traditional Boutonniere –
The proverbial rose with
cottage yarrow. Could be
made in any color with any
kind of filler.

Plate 248
Classy Boutonniere – A small orchid with ivy. Why not try alstroemeria or bird of paradise?

Plate 249
Exotic Boutonniere – The curled dendrobium orchids are unusual. Always test unusual blossoms for lasting quality before sending them out to a customer.

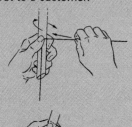

Figure 126
Wiring, Extension Method.

the attire. The groom's boutonniere may be made of the same flower used in the bride's bouquet. His boutonniere should be different from the other boutonnieres worn in the wedding. Various foliages are used with boutonnieres to lend stability or add interest to informal occasions, while the plain flower is preferred for ultra-formal situations. Do not use ribbon with a boutonniere! Flowers for men should look masculine. A selection of boutonnieres is shown in Plates 245– 249.

CONSTRUCTION - To make a carnation boutonniere, divide the blossom in half should it be a large one. Remove the seed pod and any imperfect petals. Hold the blossom downward and fluff into their original shape. Place the petals between the thumb and index finger and by the extension method, wire these petals together (Figures 126 and 127). Keep them in place by circling the petals three or four times with wire; then bring the wire on down,

Figure 127
Wiring, Extension Method.

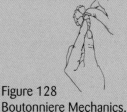

Figure 128
Boutonniere Mechanics.

binding the petal-stems together. Tape high up under the petals, but do not flatten them. This reduces the stem to a small bundle. Catch the circling wire with the thumbnail on one side of the blossom beneath the petals and brace the other side with the index finger. Lift the wire up with the thumbnail, forcing the petals forward over the index finger (Figure 128). The flower will fit closely to the lapel or easily slip into the buttonhole.

Boutonnieres of all flowers are wired and taped, leaving only a short stem. The buttonhole of the lapel on many suits is not cut. Do not cut this buttonhole unless it is the wish of the owner. By proper wiring of the flower it can be pinned to the lapel and look as though it goes through the buttonhole. The pin can come from behind the lapel into the stem and back underneath allowing the boutonniere to look nice without any part of the pin showing.

ORCHIDS

Orchids are always glamorous. They are the prestige flower and hold an allure as no other blossom. Many people have not yet had the pleasure, the thrill, of receiving their first orchid. The glory of this versatile flower should be maintained. It is always in good taste, always fits the occasion, whether it is tailored for suits, or embellished with elegant accessories for evening wear.

When fashioning one orchid into a corsage, the lip (labellum) should be facing forward and the petals erect (Plate 250 and Plate 251). Proper wiring will enable one to position the orchid correctly. A graceful "S" curve, fastened to the back of an individual flower, will give a decorative brace to prevent it from moving side to side. This brace, made by wrapping a taped wire with satin ribbon, need not be prominent or detract from the orchid, which so many curlicues often do.

When two orchids are used in a corsage, each is prepared individually. The stems are then taped together. These are form flowers and must be so spaced that they can retain their individuality. One orchid may face over the shoulder, the second one facing the front, as would a single orchid. The "S" curve is not needed in this design. A corsage fashioned in this manner will be lovely viewed from any angle (Plate 252 and Plate 253).

A second way to arrange two orchids in a corsage is to place one above the other. However, the top one should face outward, to the side away from the person's head. The second is placed below it and faces forward. Do not place one directly above the other in a straight line. The ribbon bow, if used, is tied closely under the lower orchid; do not place a bow of ribbon between two orchids. A third way as seen in Plate 254, is to allow the two blossoms to face each other — as if they were having a conversation. The orientation of the flower on its stem will determine placement.

Plate 250 (circa 1952) Cattleya Orchid – The "S" curve armature with ribbon-wrapped stem, braces the corsage.

Plate 251 Lady Slipper Orchid – Waxflower and dendrobium buds are combined with this exquisite blossom for a special occasion.

Plate 252 (circa 1966) A Matched Pair – The orientation of the flower on its stem usually indicates its position in a corsage.

Plate 253 Butterflies Floating – Exquisite blossoms become living jewelry without any accessories.

When three orchids are used together, each is prepared as a single orchid. The first takes the position over the shoulder and the second faces forward ; the third one is placed a little to the outside and in between the first and second orchids, thus forming a triangle. The orchids are placed close together, but they still retain their identity as individual blossoms. The ribbon bow goes up under the base of the lower orchid, if ribbon is used.

THE SELECTION OF RIBBON for an orchid corsage will vary according to the color of dress and the blossom. It may be desirable to choose a color that contrasts with the orchid but blends with the costume; however, its color should complement the orchids. When the orchid petals are wide and full, the ribbon may match the lip and throw full emphasis to the value of the orchid petals. However, when the petals are narrow, it is best to use a ribbon that exactly matches these petals to increase their impact. The size of the bow is determined by the size of the flower and is kept within the width of the petal range. The ribbon should not overpower the size of the blossom; ribbon is an accessory (Plates 251 – 254).

The bow should be placed high enough on the stem to give the appearance that the loops and the petals of the orchid originate from the same spot (binding point). Placing the bow too low gives the effect of two separate units.

WIRING ORCHIDS FOR CORSAGES - There is some controversy over the proper wiring of orchids for corsage work. Some authorities contend that wire inserted into the stem shortens the life of an orchid; others disagree. Experiments showed no noticeable difference whatever in the life of the orchid blossom whether or not the stem was punctured.

There are two methods commonly used in wiring any variety of orchid for corsage work. The choice of either method is the personal preference of the designer and not the type of orchid. Cut the stem slanting so that it tapers neatly. A blunt, horizontal cut gives a stubby appearance when the stem is taped and wrapped

Plate 254 (circa 1986) Cymbidium Orchids – These two orchids are having a conversation, no doubt about the oak leaves and ixia buds that accompany them.

Plate 255 (circa 1973) Phalaenopsis Orchids – These butterflies are hovering over a "bow" of live ribbon – chlorophytum foliage.

Plate 256 (circa 1973) Dancing Orchids – A triangle of butterfly orchids and glamour leaves with English ivy.

with satin. Though orchids vary quite a bit in appearance, their basic conformation remains the same. The column (pistil) is the hard portion of the center, joined stiffly to the stem.

Method A: utilizes a wire, No. 24 or 22, bent double, hairpin fashion. This hairpin is placed, points down, on either side of the stem, with the curved portion of the wire fitting snug under the head of the orchid. The stem and hairpin wire are taped together.

Method B: on large orchids (cattleya types) a No. 22 wire is inserted into the stem about one-half inch below the head of the orchid and forced upward until it enters the hardened portion of the pistil. A second wire, No. 28 or No. 30, is used for binding the stem and the first wire together.

All orchids may be wired by one of these two methods, whether they are cattleyas, cymbidiums, paphiopedilums (lady's slipper orchids) or phalaenopsis (butterfly or moth orchids). In wiring the smaller orchids such as vandas or dendrobiums, insert a No. 28 or 26 wire into the crook of the stem at the base of the head and push just into the hardened portion of the pistil. The stem and wire are then taped together; no other wiring is necessary. Many florists prefer to hairpin phalaenopsis through their faces. This is a questionable practice because it may deface the blossom and should not be used unless the flower is broken from the stem. The stem is then taped and the wire stem cut in proportion to the design of the corsage.

Stems of orchids should be wrapped in satin to give a finished look to the corsage. Tape the wired stem with floral tape of the same color as the satin, before wrapping the stem with the satin ribbon. Start the satin one-half inch from the bottom of the orchid stem and roll tightly to the end. Then reverse the direction, keeping the ribbon almost parallel to the stem while rolling toward the blossom. The end of the ribbon is brought forward through the last loop, and tightened. The finished knot will then be at the binding point beneath the petals. Security will be improved if this knot is stabilized with a drop of hot glue. Fresh foliage of any type compatible with the flower

and design, wired and taped, will serve as a backing for any corsage. This construction method makes the flower a pleasure to wear (Plate 250).

The "S" curve also shown in Plate 250 would be comfortable if the corsage was to be worn as a hairpiece. The brace could be shaped to the curve of the head and secured with bobby pins. A No. 19 or No. 20 wire is taped and wrapped with ribbon of a compatible color. Start the wrapping about one inch from one end of the wire and wrap outward beyond this end about half the width of the ribbon. Immediately reverse the ribbon by pulling downward, continuing to wrap in the same direction. Keep the tension on the ribbon taut and almost parallel to make a smooth surface on the wire. Finish with a single knot: stop wrapping about one inch from the end of the wire leaving the last turn open. Bring the end of the ribbon up, through this loop, and tie the knot. To fashion the "S" curve: hold the end of the wrapped wire tightly between the tip of the fingers and bend in a circular motion. Practice will give an even curve to the brace. The "S" curve should be taped to the orchid at the binding point, having the upper portion of the curve pointing away from the face and the lower portion inward.

BRIDLING The conformation of most orchids grows naturally so that orchids can be fashioned into corsages without changing the petal arrangement or "bridling." Generally, orchids sold on the commercial market are open-faced. However, because of improper packing or the inherited quality of the blossoms, the petals may fall to the front, closing down over the lip (labellum) of the orchid. These flowers require "bridling" to show to full advantage (Figure 129).

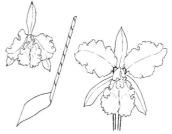

Figure 129
Bridling an orchid petal-rolled tape or ribbon forms the bridle to hold the petals back.

The blossom needing this bracing is first wired and taped. The bridle may be made of a piece of floral tape twisted to the size of a small piece of twine, or a ribbon may be rolled in the same manner. This tape or ribbon should be the same color as the petals. It is looped over the base of the petal and pulled down, forcing the petal backward into the position desired. This bridle is applied to each petal on either side of the labellum, which gives the orchid an open face. It is then taped to the stem, and the corsage is completed as previously described.

REPAIRING A PETAL - When it is necessary to use an orchid with a broken petal, some simple repairs are possible. The orchid stem should be wired and taped in the usual manner for a corsage. Method one: Make a small hairpin crutch of taped No. 28 wire the color of the orchid. Bend this wire over the thumb so that it will follow the contour of the petal; make it long enough to extend just beyond the break in the petal. This crutch is fitted snugly under the broken petal with the wire ends parallel to the stem and then taped to the stem (Figure 130). Method two: Should the petal be broken completely off it may be glued with floral adhesive to a wired and taped leaf. That leaf is then snuggled into the position of the missing petal and taped to the stem.

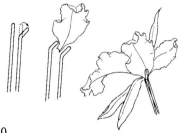

Figure 130
Repairing broken petal – No. 28 wire is taped and bent "U" shaped to fit under curve of broken petal; a second "U" may fit on top to clamp petal.

COVERING DEFECTS - When it is necessary to use an orchid which has off-colored spots, the spots may be covered in a number of ways, depending upon the occasion for which the flower is to be worn. The quick and easy way is to simply spray the back of the petal with the matching color. Another way is to cover the spots with a thin floral glue or clear plastic from pressurized cans, and then dust with chalk dust the same color as the orchid. In the case of white orchids, talcum powder is effective. Should the corsage be made for an evening affair, either glitter or sequins are suitable to cover defects. Commercial floral sprays are available for this use.

Chapter 26
WEDDING BOUQUETS

The bride selects the flowers and the style for her bouquet, assisted by the florist. Her gown and stature will influence this choice greatly.

The bouquet of flowers should enhance the beauty of the gown and not be the dominant feature. Even though most flowers are available year-around, it is better to sell the bride on a design rather than on a specific flower. Make every effort to get the flowers of her choice, but explain that flowers are perishable and if substitutions have to be made, the style and color of the bouquet will remain the same.

In formal weddings the bride generally carries white flowers and the floral decorations are white. However, she may select accents of her chosen wedding colors. In these instances the floral decorations, flowers, and candles may be of the same color.

When the bridesmaids' dresses are of many colors, one option is to have all flowers the same color in order to create a feeling of unity. Another option is to stress each bridesmaid's individuality by selecting flowers that match each particular gown. Rainbow effects in wedding parties are being replaced today by monochromatic or analogous color combinations. These two color harmonies are sometimes stressed in both flowers and accent materials in order to give unity. During a holiday season, such as Christmas, the flowers may be of strong contrast and brilliant coloring. The season influences the choice of colors for the bridal party. The ribbons on the bouquets may match the dresses or be of a lighter or darker hue.

When the wedding is informal, the bride may select a corsage for her suit, or she may wish to carry a tailored bouquet with flowers that harmonize in color and texture.

Bridesmaids' bouquets are often similar in design to that of the bride's. However, the designs may vary according to the preference of the bride.

In the same wedding it is not necessary that bouquets repeat the same design, e.g., the bride may carry a cascade bouquet while the bridesmaids carry arm bouquets. The matron of honor may have a bouquet of a different design, such as a crescent.

When white flowers are chosen, study their degree of whiteness. Gardenias and callas have a creamy tone. Therefore, select an antique white or eggshell ribbon for the bouquets. Many white flowers are pale green or chartreuse deep in their throats. With these flowers use fresh foliage throughout the bouquet. This practice will intensify the whiteness of the flowers and give a more elegant and fresh appearance to an all-white bouquet.

Very few flowers are true white. White roses for example, have an underlying tinge of green (Polo, Tineke), yellow (Champagne, Virginia), or pink (Ariana, Bridal White). The ones with a soft yellowish cast are called "ivory" and the ever so slightly pinkish ones are called "blush". From our study of the color wheel we know that certain colors are regarded as "cool" and others as "warm". This knowledge is important because it will help a designer to coordinate warm white flowers (ivory, blush) with warm white fabrics. Conversely, the greenish, bluish and silvery white flowers will complement cool white fabrics. A bride will usually select a gown that enhances her own skin tone. The floral artist will then complete the picture

with appropriate guidance in the selection of flowers, foliage, ribbons and metallic accents. Foliage is available with warm tones of yellow, gold, orange, red and burgundy as well as the cool hues of blue, violet and gray. Gold metallic ribbons, cording and boullion always enrich the warm whites while silver and pewter metallic accents will intensify the crispness of cool white gowns.

Most white flowers can have their hue changed to match a particular fabric, by the use of spray dyes or various dipping techniques as presented in Chapter 17.

In designing bouquets consideration must be given to the stature of the individual and the line of her gown. Crescent and cascade bouquets with long graceful lines can add an illusion of height to a short bride; line in these bouquets will cause her to appear taller. A round bouquet, e.g., colonial, ballerina, and Juliet, or an arm bouquet is better for a tall, slim girl. The flowers of a bouquet should follow the contour and line of both the bride and her gown, creating unity. It should also cover the hands neatly and appear finished and attractive from all sides.

The traditional way of constructing a bridal bouquet is with the wiring and taping method. This method offers some distinct advantages. It is possible to create a bouquet of greater delicacy and less weight by using this technique. Wired and taped stems also allow the designer much more leeway in bending them into desired positions. Two disadvantages to this method would be additional design time and the lack of a water source. In recent years a practical device has been introduced that decreases design time and provides a water source for wedding bouquets. This device is a plastic bouquet holder with caged foam (wet or dry) for holding fresh or silk flowers. The advantages of using this bouquet holder include moisture for the fresh flowers and the elimination of time consuming wiring and taping. However, the finished bouquet is quite a bit heavier, and in poorly constructed designs, flowers may loosen and fall out.

Study the four parts of a wired and taped wedding bouquet as illustrated in Plate 257. It is the combination of any one or more units that create the geometric designs in Plates 257A, B, C, and D. Before beginning the design of a bridal bouquet, the flowers and foliage must be fresh, of high quality and subjected to proper care and handling techniques (Chapter 14). For quality, fine workmanship and beauty, all flowers and accessory materials must be wired and taped before being assembled into a design. It is helpful at this point to spray the fresh materials with and anti-transpirant, especially on the underside of their leaves and petals. To make each unit, tape the wired stems together; do not twist one on to the other. When forming either the cascade, crescent or triangular designs, a No. 20 wire, extension method, MUST be added to each stem of units No. 2, 3,

Plate 257
Divisions of a wired and taped Wedding Bouquet – Illustrated are the four primary units that comprise the Benz Method of developing a wired and taped bridal bouquet. Various combinations are shown in Plates 257A–D.

Plate A
Section 1, Round – This part, completed by itself may be round, oblong, or it may be an informal cluster.

Plate B
Section 2, Cascade – Parts 1 and 2 together may create many different cascade designs.

Plate C
Section 3, Crescent, Hogarth – Three sections combined may develop any interesting line through the center.

Plate D
Section 4, Triangle – This small addition is placed to create a triangular design. There are many variations.

and 4, for strength and security. The length of the various stems to be used in unit No.1 will be determined by the height of the bride and the ornamentation on the front of her dress. By today's standards depth in a bouquet is very desirable, but one does not want to interfere with the beauty of the gown. When assembling unit No.2, the cascade, to unit No.1, hold them both at arm's length so as to see the best position. While holding them firmly in place, squeeze the two stems together with a pair of pliers. This technique flattens the stems to each other and will prevent the cascade from twisting and turning in the bride's hands. Tape these units together making several revolutions, which holds the units firmly in place.

The handle of all wedding bouquets should be wrapped in satin by using the method for wrapping a wire with satin as described in the section on orchid corsages. The mechanics of the back side of the bouquet must be hidden with extra foliage. A small bustle bow may also fill the back of the bouquet neatly covering the construction. The bow need not show from the front; however, it may be an integral part of the design and have flowing streamers. A tiny blue bow may be tucked in for that "something blue" or a sprig of heather for "good luck", to give an extra bit of pleasure.

BRIDE'S CORSAGE

For sentimental reasons, the bride may request that her going-away corsage be a part of her bouquet. It can be incorporated into the bride's bouquet in several ways. The first method is done by curling a heavy satin-wrapped wire around a pencil. The corsage stem is then placed in the spiral and is held in place with corsage pins. A second method utilizes a ball of cotton or a piece of styrofoam on a heavy wire. Cover this ball with satin and place it in the desired position; pin the corsage to it. A third method is achieved by

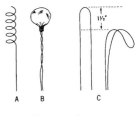

Figure 131

using a taped wire (No. 18). Bring the two ends together, forming a loop. Bend the top of the loop down about 1 1/2 inches, forming a hook or cradle. The two side pieces which form this cradle will hold the corsage in place when they are pressed together (Figure 131). Regardless of the method used, the corsage is inserted in the bouquet on the upper side of the focal point, in full view of the bride. It should nestle into the flowers and become a part of the whole design (Plate 258). A corsage pin will help to secure the corsage in the holder. It is a loving, sentimental gesture to have two extra flowers in the bouquet, free and easily removed. In the processional, as the bride reaches her mother, she pauses and gives her mother a kiss and one of the flowers. In the recessional the bride pauses at her mother-in-law, greets her and gives the other flower.

Plate 258 (circa 1952) This bouquet of lily-of-the-valley and tulle has a removable orchid "going away" corsage.

Geometric Designs

Circular - Round Bouquets

Even though geometric designs remain constant, the names of bouquets must keep abreast with fashion. For example, when ballerina and waltz-length dresses became popular, the round design, so well-known as a "Colonial" bouquet or "nosegay," was perfect in form but not in name. It was necessary to call this bouquet either "Ballerina," "Juliet," or to give it a French connotation, "Tussie Mussie." This bouquet, though traditional in design, is perfect for today's fashion trends. It may be a dainty modern cluster of assorted blossoms and foliage with emphasis on texture and fragrance that accents perfectly the bride's gown, or it may be designed with flowing lines of carefully selected ribbons to maintain the old-fashioned appearance (Plates 259, 260). The selection of unusual accent materials and artistry in designing will give this bouquet distinction. This design is an excellent choice for informal weddings in the home, garden or chapel and is suitable for a wide

Plate 259
A luxurious combination of cymbidiulm orchids, gardenias and stephanotis is further enriched with a plush ribbon treatment.

Plate 260
This entirely different round bouquet is made of roses, scabiosa, corn flower, seeded eucalyptus, dusty miller and silverleaf protea, creating a tapestry of textures.

range of semi-formal and informal gowns and dresses.

This bouquet is round in outline and is mound-shaped on top (Plates 261 – 271). Start with center flowers about three or four inches high and hold the stems together firmly with the thumb and forefinger at this point. Add the other blossoms, bending the wire stems so that flowers will extend slightly, forming a dome. When the finished bouquet is held, the flowers will look attractive all around, including the portion toward the body. The handle will be straight and pointing downward, keeping the weight and balance on top of the bride's hand. It

Plate 262   (circa 1952)
This Juliet bouquet of roses, stephanotis, tulle and Alencon lace (Plate 117) returns to the scene with ballerina gowns.

Plate 261
The monofloral bouquet is captured here with three tints of roses, a pretty palette encircled with French wired ribbon loops.

Plate 263   (circa 1986)
Tulips and begonia leaves march through this fountain of lilac and ming creating a bit of a cascade in lieu of ribbon streamens.

Plate 264   (circa 1986)
This veritable "painting" of spring blossoms takes one into Monet's garden.

Plate 265   (circa 1986)
Heather, leptospermum, waxflower and kalanchoe, all fillers, dance in this garden of anemones.

Plate 266   (circa 1962)
Roses, heather and pearl glamour leaves float on a cloud of tulle.

is important for the bouquet to feel comfortable and well balanced, not front-heavy. A poorly balanced bouquet will produce tension in the bride's arm and cause her great discomfort during the ceremony. This design is easily assembled so that it is unnecessary to bend the handle when the bouquet is complete. Bending the handle will cause the bouquet to be front-heavy. To finish the bouquet, it may be placed in a colonial bouquet collar or outlined with accessory materials, such as satin leaves (Figure 65), lace, tulle, natural flower petals or foliage, pearl loops, etc. The round bouquet may also be left unadorned, especially if the blossoms are full and luxurious, such as hydrangea, peonies or open roses.

Plate 267 (circa 1973)
A round bouquet of roses, orchids and caladium – variety "Buddy Benz". Hybridized by L. L. Holmes.

Plate 268 (circa 1980)
Seashells have been drilled, wired and taped and positioned to frame a "going away" corsage in this unusual bouquet, that is softened by the ribbon and ivy streamers.

Plate 269   (circa 1973)
Feathered carnations and bird of paradise are
combined with juniper in this unusual design.

Plate 270   (circa 1968)
Concentric rings of roses and stock are outlined with
feathered carnations and velvet leaves, reminiscent
of the Biedermier style.

Plate 271   (circa 1970)
Very Victorian is this posey of roses, stock and satin
glamour leaves. It seems very modern with its
satellite cluster.

Cascade Bouquets

Many brides often picture the cascade bouquet as the one being carried down the aisle. Its extensive usage through the years has made this design traditional.

When the bridal gown is formal, with a full-skirt and a beautiful train, this type of bouquet is most suitable. It adds the proper floral accent, which enhances the beauty of the chosen gown.

The cascade design is the combination of the center circular grouping (Unit No. 1) and the lower garland (Unit No. 2) as shown in Plates 257B, 273. The circular center portion is as-sembled as a round bouquet explained in the preceding design. By making these two units separately and then combining them, the designer has complete control over shaping the bouquet to its need. In other words, unit No. 1 doesn't have to be perfectly round; it may be designed of a considerably irregular shape, but the other units are still attached to it.

The cascade garland is assembled, using the small buds and leaves first, increasing their size and spread as they are added. The stems are taped, not twisted together, to a taped No. 18 or 20 wire, which will serve as the backbone of the cascade. Accessory materials if used, are taped to the main stem of the garland as flowers are added. The length of the garland depends on the size of the bouquet which must be in proper proportion to the bride and her gown. The handle of each garland including its extension wire (No. 18 or 20) gives strength and keeps the garland in place when the bouquet is assembled. When these two sections are completed, they are fitted together, squeezed with pliers and taped to the center unit keeping the tape as tight and wrinkle-free as possible. Additional materials may be added as needed at the juncture of the two units and underneath the bouquet to hide mechanics.

The cascade bouquet may have several garlands of varying lengths; it is not limited to a single, main garland (Plate 272). The garlands shown in this bouquet are made by

Plate 272
This bouquet of 'Casa Blanca' lilies and seeded eucalyptus is combined with garlands and sprays of hyacinth blossoms in a very artistic presentation. The French wired ribbon reflects the movement of the hyacinth showers.

Plate 273
The beautiful orchids are left on their own stems, which are wired and taped at the lower ends allowing them to float above the other blossoms in this traditional cascade. The camellia with its own buds and the red roses are placed deep in the design to provide depth.

Plate 274   (circa 1973)
English ivy is integrated
throughout with roses and
feathered bird-of-paradise to
give a dramatic and colorful
cascade.

(Plate 111)   (circa 1973)
A spectacular "Duchess" lily
bouquet is centered with
feathered bird-of-paradise
florets and fitted with a
cascade of buds.

threading individual hyacinth blossoms on a
No. 24 wire, adding the No. 20 extension at the
base and taping each garland to the main handle
of the bouquet. Foliage garlands or streamers
of ribbon may be used to add line, though restraint must be the guide in the use of shower
effects (Plates 274, 111, 275 – 277).

Plate 275 (circa 1986)
Alstroemeria with acacia and lycopodium foliage, create a graceful cascading Hogarth curve.

Plate 276 (circa 1986)
Freedom of movement is expressed in this design of nerine lilies, roses, kalanchoe and suspended spider plants (chlorophytum).

The most popular mechanic for bridal bouquets at the present time is the pre-made bouquet holder. It is a plastic cage attached to a handle that is either straight or angled, and it is available with wet or dry foam for both fresh and silk or dried materials. One advantage of this holder is economy of time as the labor of wiring and taping is eliminated. The wet foam holders may be prepared days in advance, and they allow the use of flowers that require more water. However, these holders are successful only when the mechanics are absolutely secure. Most large or heavy blossoms and all cascading materials should be cross-pinned to keep them from falling out of the holder.

Cross-pinning is the act of pushing a wire or corsage pin

crosswise through the flower stem once it is deep in the foam. After feeling the wire go through the stem, and it is certain to be locked in, cut off the excess wire or pin head. Another aid for this need is pressurized foam designed to lock stems into place. Designers must keep abreast of new products always considering their cost, practicality and reliability. In looking through the gallery of bouquets in this chapter, it may be assumed that all designs with natural stems visible are made in bouquet holders.

Figure 132
It is more comfortable for the bride to hold the slant-handle bouquet holder with the handle toward her, as if she is "shaking hands" with it. This position also allows the bride to see beautiful flowers when she looks down into the bouquet instead of looking at the back of it.

Plate 277 (circa 1980)
Sea shells create an exotic cascade expressing the waves of the sea and fitting for a mermaid. The seemingly impossible-to-use shells are easily drilled with an electric drill, wired, taped and fashioned into the cascade.

Figure 133
Cross-pinning is a quick and secure way of locking the cascading stems into place and preventing the force of gravity from "pulling" them out. Be sure the pin is inserted behind the grid, and be equally certain its point doesn't emerge from the base of the holder and injure the bride.

Crescent Bouquets

Crescent bouquets are lovely for almost any type of girl, and they blend with most bridal fashion trends. This design is ideal to use when bridesmaids in a bridal party are of various heights. Place this bouquet almost vertically in the hands of the short girl; it will add line which gives height to her appearance. The taller girls will carry their bouquets horizontally, with the points of the design downward, to soften the line of height. The other bridesmaids will have their bouquets adjusted accordingly. These bouquets will give unity in design and will complement each bridesmaid's stature (Plate 278).

This bouquet consists of the center circular grouping and two garlands. The assembly is the same as that of the cascade bouquet with the addition of Unit No. 3, Plate 257C. The three sections are brought together, the lower one forming the cascade, the upper one changing the design to a vertical crescent. Both garlands are curved. The upper and lower garlands may be used to make the crescent, omitting the center section (Plates 279 – 281).

Plate 278
This graceful crescent of traditional flowers used with delicate diosma and genista is made in a bouquet holder. The concept of developing sections 1, 2, and 3 however, still applies, even though the stems go directly into the wet foam (see Figures 132 and 133).

Plate 279   (circa 1966)
An all-foliage crescent of ivy, tradescantia, acuba and caladium centered with galax rosettes.

Plate 280   (circa 1966)
Brilliant red anthuriums and lycopodium are "tied" with a bow of dracaena leaves (individually wired in the manner of a French bow).

Plate 281   (circa 1986)
This deeply curved crescent is designed in a wet foam holder.

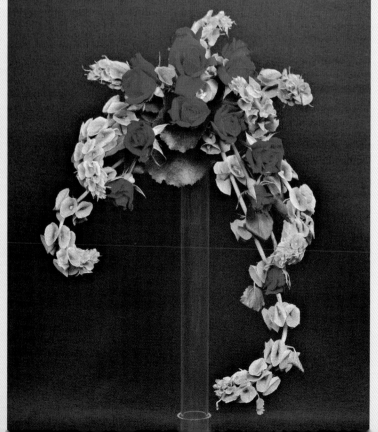

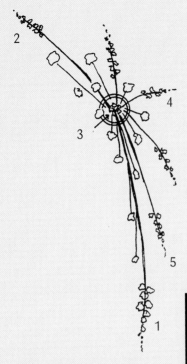

Triangular Cascade Bouquets

The large, formal cathedral wedding, with the pomp and ceremony that tradition dictates, suggests this lavish bouquet. The cathedral wedding is pageantry in all its glory, and the flowers must be fitting for such an occasion. Good design and carefully chosen blossoms should be skillfully blended with accent materials (Plates 282 – 286).

The bouquet consists of the center circular grouping and three garland sections (Plates 257D). Before assembling the four parts, add an extension wire (No. 20) to each segment to strengthen the handles. The units are brought together into their positions, squeezed with pliers one at a time, and then taped very tightly.

Assemble the units as in making the crescent' design, adding Unit No. 4 to the opposite side to form the triangle. Note carefully that the two upper units are not on the same level. Unit No. 3

Figure 134
Stem placement for a bouquet holder begins by establishing the outer points: No. 1, the longest line (cascade); No. 2, the opposite dimension (height); No. 3, the focal point (also depth); No. 4, the width. The difference in designing a crescent or triangle is determined by the length of the No. 4 stem placement.

Plate 282
This contemporary cascade made in a wet foam holder has materials grouped in the manner of a formalinear design. Even so, the various sections previously mentioned are visible and establish perfect balance and proportion.

Plate 283   (circa 1952)
This Alencon lace bouquet of roses and stephanotis is the classic design of a bygone era (see Plate 117, lace leaf technique).

Plate 284   (circa 1986)
The dracaena and aglaonema leaves establish the pattern of this triangular Cathedral bouquet; the lilies and button mums complete the composition.

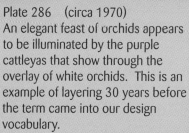

Plate 285   (circa 1986)
Rich color emanates from the golden callas, Ventura lilies, pink syngonium and kangaroo paws against cascading sprengerii, in a foam holder.

Plate 286   (circa 1970)
An elegant feast of orchids appears to be illuminated by the purple cattleyas that show through the overlay of white orchids. This is an example of layering 30 years before the term came into our design vocabulary.

flows toward the elbow, and Unit No. 4 points somewhat lower. These two units curve, backward toward the person, covering the hands, and provide comfortable balance. In Plate 286, the three sections are blended into a single unit.

Miscellaneous Designs

A young woman associates herself more closely with flowers at her wedding than at any other time in her life. Flowers can visually express her personal feelings and style better than any other aspect of the wedding. The floral artist must gain an understanding of the client to be able to bring her feelings and ideas into being. Design in wedding bouquets is limited only to the imagination of the artist and the wishes of the bride.

The wired and taped crescent bouquet shown in Plate 287 has traditional roots in its radial stem placement, but inserting the equisetum through the center, combines parallel stem placement and gives the design a fresh new look. The unusual combination of materials brings many interesting textures into this monochromatic color harmony.

Plate 288 shows a waterfall design. The hallmark of this romantic bouquet is the technique of layering materials. The eye is drawn into this design through layer over layer of delicate and even transparent materials. This historically European design concept requires many different materials, textures, colors and accents. It is made in a bouquet holder with wet foam.

Plate 287
Tuberose, delphinium florets, equisetum, seeded eucalyptus, 'Fluffy Ruffles' fern and variegated ivy make interesting partners in this charming design.

Plate 288
This sumptuous waterfall design displays current layering and veiling techniques. The purposely tangled gold bouillon adds twinkle to a very organic composition.

The unexpected color intensity causes the bouquet in Plate 289 to literally jump, but one of its most important aspects is the use of two traditional flowers, gladiola and carnation blossoms, in a very non-traditional manner. This design also combines fresh and dried materials arranged appropriately for the autumn season. The preserved sea grape leaves are wired and taped and spaced so that the other wired and taped flowers can easily fit in between. The long stems of the orchids are wired and taped at the end of the main stem thus preserving their natural beauty.

Plate 289
Color Saturation –
This combination of "James Storey" orchids, gladiolus, carnations, hypericum berries and sea grape leaves produces an intense color shock!

Plates 290, 291, 292 are representative of the formalinear style. These designs are for the contemporary taste. Drama is present in each of the flower forms, colors and spacing. Each of these designs is assembled in a bouquet holder, allowing for uncluttered development in the focal area. The lines that extend outward are anchored deep in the foam and tied to the grid or crosspinned for extra security. The grouping of materials and separation of textures provides distinction and individuality.

Plate 290
The "Pink Ice" protea directs this play while the alstromeria, gerberas, aglaonema, leucadendron and kiwi vine play their parts to perfection.

Plate 291   (circa 1986)
Fresh, silk and dried materials come together in this early formalinear design for a casual wedding.

Plate 292   (circa 1986)
Natural growth patterns are emphasized in this simple design of dendrobium orchids, freesia, gerbera and native oak foliage.

Topiary designs show man's inherent desire to control nature. The topiary in Plate 293 is an interpretation of a scepter. A bouquet holder was attached to a satin wrapped dowel to create the foundation for this design. The veiling of silver bouillon and white tulle softens this volumetric form with an air of mystery and romance. (Note additional Topiary designs, Plates 297-299)

The "Gift of Love" wedding bouquet, depending on the selection of materials, would be suitable at any time of the year, but the one in Plate 294 is designed for a holiday wedding. Simple construction includes a cardboard box of the appropriate size and shape, with an opening cut for flower insertions. A bouquet holder is placed on a plastic liner inside the box, which is then wrapped in metallic fabric, Plate 295. The ribbon is tied around the box and the flowers are inserted. This makes an interesting design to display at the reception. Plate 296 shows the design to be beautifully finished on all sides. It is important that the bride sees beauty when she looks down into her bouquet, as well as the wedding guests attending both ceremony and reception.

Plates 294, 295, 296
"Tis better to give a flower than a jewel". Lily-of-the-valley, gardenias and stephanotis are the real jewels in this "Gift of Love."

Plate 293
Our most common flowers: roses, carnations, chrysanthemums and baby's breath take on an air of romance and intrigue when veiled to emulate the bride herself.

Plate 297   (circa 1966)
A suspended topiary (snowball) of white chrysanthemums with an accent of Christmas holly is ready and waiting for the bridesmaid.

Plate 298
Two snowballs linked with tubular velvet for a winter wedding.

Plate 299
An even more elaborate example for the bride or matron of honor marrying in a winter wonderland.

The bouquet holders described in this chapter and shown in Figures 132 and 133 are manufactured with straight, flexible or sharply angled handles. When the angled handle version is held in the obvious handle-down position, the weight of the wet foam is front-heavy, falling forward as the bride's wrist gets tired. It is recommended that before placing the first flower, the holder should be inverted so the handle points toward the body and the foam faces upward. The bride will carry it with her hand in a natural palm-up position under the bouquet. Her arm will look more graceful, and she can manage her bouquet more easily in this position (Plates 302-306, 284-285, 290, 292).

The show stopper bouquet pictured in Plate 300 is designed for an individual with taste for the glamorous, the dramatic, the daring!

Prayer Book

When a Prayer Book or white Bible is to be carried, a cluster of blossoms as simple as a corsage may complete the design (Plate 301). The bride may prefer shower ribbon with love knots tied into the ribbon, lace, or cascades of flowers or ivy. Prayer books may be used in formal or informal weddings. When the prayer book is read in the ceremony, the passages to be used are marked with streamers. Should the bride have a beautiful piece of fine antique lace, which is an heirloom in the family and carries much sentimental value, it may be appliqued to a satin streamer and used to mark the verses of her choice in the Bible. Any favorite passage of the bride's or groom's may be marked or the florist may suggest the passage in the Bible from the Book of Ruth, Chapter I, Verse 16, "Entreat me not to leave you or to return from following you ... for where you go, I will go, and where you lodge, I will lodge; your people shall be my people, and your God my God."

The question of whether or not each member of the bridal party should carry a prayer book sometimes arises. It is best for them not to do so, since the practice detracts from the bride's prayer book. The use of the prayer book ends with the wedding ceremony. It is not

Plate 300
A highly personal design of cattleya orchids, ostrich plumes and specialty ribbons.

Plate 301
A modest cluster of lily-of-the-valley with an orchid is pinned to a ribbon that ties around the Bible.

held in the receiving line at the reception. The flowers are either held or are worn according to the design or wishes of the bride.

There are several ways to attach the flowers to the book, the simplest being to tie a ribbon around it in both directions and pin the flower cluster to the ribbon. This technique would be suitable only for a ceremony in which the Bible would not be used to read from. When it is opened and read during the ceremony, the ribbon would be tied through the inside of the book at the page

that is to be read, with the flowers still pinned to the ribbon. In situations when the reading requires a page to be turned, the hard cover of the book may be slipped into a tailor made overlay of white satin or lace. Flowers are attached to this keepsake covering; they are never pinned or taped directly to the front cover of a prayer book or Bible. A protective shield of cardboard, covered in satin: may also be made to fit a soft cover prayer book. The flexible covers of the prayer book are slipped into this prepared one. Flowers are pinned to this cover, or a wire clamp can be made to hold the flowers. Tape a No. 18 wire and wrap with satin; tie the ends together, forming a circle. Twist the circle into a figure eight; clamp, the ends over the edges of the cover. The flowers are then pinned to the clamp.

Plate 302 (circa 1986) "Apple Blossom" gerberas and pixie carnations lend distinction to a traditional crescent.

Plate 303 (circa 1986) Spathiphyllum flowers and foliage provide a distinctive background for the exquisite cambria orchids. Bear grass streamers replace traditional ribbons.

Fans

Fans of many types are used at any time of the year to
enhance romantic themes. Their designs vary greatly; some are
made entirely of flowers, while others have a lace or net background (Plate 307). The wire frame for a floral fan may be purchased from wholesale houses. Oriental fans made of silk or rice
paper with beautiful scenes hand painted on them are very lovely
to carry. Tubular velvet, into which No. 18 or No. 19 wire has been
inserted, can be shaped into loops or hearts and makes a beautiful
frame for fan arrangements. Flowers are wired and taped as for
corsages and are pinned to the foundation. In fashioning flowers

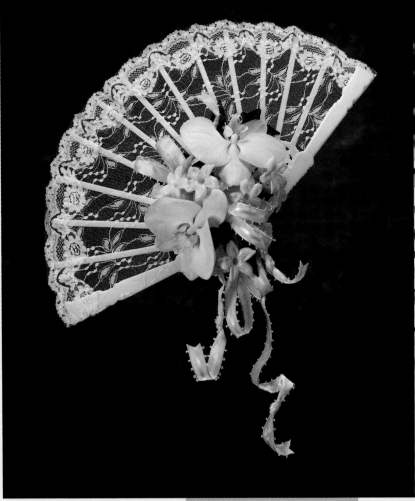

for the fan, curve them gracefully to complement the contour of the fan, with some flowers, foliage or ribbons cascading downward to hide the bride's hands, complete the design and unite the bouquet with the gown.

Heart Designs

The single Heart is another romantic design favored by many brides. Others prefer a double heart, one interlocked with the other. Frames for these may be purchased from the florist supplier. Interpretations of the heart can be fashioned of curly willow and other natural materials. Plate 308 illustrates the extent to which creative use of color and material can create an unforgettable living memory of this romantic theme.

To make a traditional open heart when no frame is available, use two, taped No. 16 or No. 18 wires (Figure 135). Hold these together and curve them into the shape of half a heart. After shaping, turn up three-fourths of an inch of wire at each end, forming hooks. Open the two wires, placing them opposite each other. The hooks at each end will overlap, forming the complete heart-shape. The frame is tied tightly with a fine wire at the hooks and is taped. The handle is made from a heavy wire added to the upper

Plate 306   (circa 1986)
For something different, pincushion proteas are placed with various foliages, moss and dried kelp to form a collage of rustic textures.

Plate 307
A romantic lace fan in the Southern or Spanish tradition is complemented with a cluster of orchids and stephanotis and delicate picot ribbons.

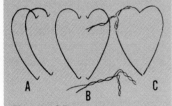

Figure 135
Heart, wire frame.

left side and secured tightly in position. Cover the framework with any manor of fabric or ribbon treatments, or sheath the wire frame with a covering of natural sheet moss by tying with raffia, or entwine the frame with delicate honeysuckle vines.

Add blossoms to the upper left portion, where the handle is located, and a small grouping on the diagonal at the lower side of the heart. Be careful in placing the blossoms; do not to cover too much of the heart — keep it light and airy. The heart shape must be clearly visible in order that it is recognized immediately. It is considered poor design to fashion the flowers directly into the center of the heart, for then it will create a bulls eye.

A bouquet using hearts as the main accent would be charming for a Valelntine wedding. Small hearts are made from taped and satin-wrapped No. 20 wire bent double in the center and shaped into half hearts, which are then opened. The ends of the wire form the handle for the hearts.

Parasols

Parasols — Garden weddings suggest parasols either opened or closed. They are decorative and are flattering to brides or girls in the bridal party. They are usually covered with lace or sheer material. Parasols of many different types are available at bridal shops and florist suppliers. Plate 309 shows a closed parasol that has been tied with a satin ribbon at the center. This holds the fabric in place and establishes the location of the focal point, which is the flower cluster. To achieve greater impact the edges of the parasol have been pulled open and the inside filled delicately with matching ivory tulle, combining varying "whites" and allowing an ethereal feeling to dominate the design.

Presentation And Arm Bouquets

Presentation Bouquets glorify an occasion as no other gift can. Both the recipient of the bouquet and the audience receive pleasure making the affair special. The celebrity, the girl graduate, the guest star of the evening, or the debutante may be consulted concerning her wishes. Should this bouquet be a surprise gift, then a responsible person must be contacted in order to coordinate the flowers and the design with the gown.

Arm bouquets differ from presentation bouquets according to the occasion of their use. These similarly-styled designs would be carried by a member of the wedding party with colors and materials selected in advance. The design techniques are the same for both.

Stems are generally left on the blossoms, for the flowers are put in water later. All limber and brittle-stemmed flowers must be wired to hold them in place. If ribbon is used to accent this bouquet, it is placed where the flowers are held and tied. The foliage must complement the blossoms. It is a poor practice to "choke" bouquets with long stems of plumosus, or other greenery, giving them the appearance of funeral sprays.

Stand before a mirror while assembling this bouquet. Lay each flower across the left arm, holding stems in the left hand, paying careful attention to the placement of the blossoms. When held correctly and tied securely, the arrangement of flowers will not be disturbed when

it is presented. Use only wilt-resistant flowers; it is often necessary for them to remain out of water a long time. Plate 310 shows a classic combination of white stock, roses and stargazer lilies. The white flowers are enhanced with variegated English ivy and ming foliages. The soft green ribbon matches the buds of the flowers, and the curving streamers repeat the curves of the ivy and lily petals, giving the entire design a feeling of unity.

Flower Girls

Junior Bridesmaids' and Flower Girls' bouquets are styled similar to those of the bridesmaids, or they may carry basket-type bouquets. However, it is not wise for them to scatter petals, since

Plate 309
A very feminine design captivates the spirit with the most traditional of bridal flowers – Gardenias and stephanotis enhance the dominate cattleya orchid.

petals may cause a guest or member of the wedding party to slip or may cause damage from stain. In Plate 311 Pansies and heather have been gathered into a charming tussie mussie for the younger attendants to carry. The asymmetrical balance gives this composition a little extra flair.

Ring Bearer

The Ring Bearer may carry a satin pillow to which a ring has been tied (not the ring used in the ceremony). Should there be a lovely jewel box in the family, he may carry this in the wedding. A small garland or cluster of flowers may be added.

Hand-tied Bouquets

This bouquet is *a group of flowers and foliage assembled in the hand instead of a vase, and when completed, the stems are tied very tightly together with a binding cord*. The history of this bouquet begins in central Europe where it is the most popular floral offering in Holland, Germany, France and Denmark. The designers in each country have their own favorite techniques, but the basic concept of construction is the same everywhere. Diagonal stem placement directed around a central core of flowers and foliage creates a unique spiral effect and is the key to designing a successful hand-tied bouquet. Pleasing visual balance and proportion, and stability depend on this particular idea of stem placement.

Plate 312
Hand-tied Bridal Bouquet – The mixed whites of "Porcelina" roses, alstroemeria and snapdragons achieve a rich look that would complement any white or ivory gown. Red huckleberry foliage provides contrast and springeri– adds soft flowing lines.

Plate 313
Satin Handle – After tying the spiraled stems as tight as possible they were taped together with corsage tape and wrapped with No. 9 satin ribbon. A second application of ribbon was French braided over the first wrapping. Ribbons are secured at critical points with drops of glue.

Figure 136
The first several flower and foliage placements are held in the hand (upright) to form the center of the bouquet. Try to hold materials deep between thumb and forefinger only, keeping the other fingers out of the way so the added stems can spread out to the sides. A right-handed designer would normally hold the bouquet in the left hand and vice-versa for the left-handed designer.

Plate 314
Hand-tied Garden Bouquet –
These jewel-tone blossoms:
"Caldwell Pink" roses,
larkspur, Sweet Williams, pixie
carnations, statice and
miniature calla lilies, all
garden flowers, make a
spectacular analogous color
harmony. The stems should
be subordinate to the flowers,
especially when viewed
against a beautiful gown.

Plate 315
Spiral Stems – The spiraling
of the stems is visible as is
the tightly tied raffia at the
binding point. The clean
stems are cut to comprise no
more than 1/3 of the total
height of the composition.

Diagonal (spiral) stem placement accomplishes two things for this design: 1) it allows the design to gain more width and prevents overcrowding the blooms, 2) the stems will not break when the binding cord is pulled tight. There are several advantages to making hand-tied wedding bouquets. Accomplished designers find them quick to make, and they can be made well in advance of the wedding and stored in vases of water until the hour of delivery. The bridesmaids may put their hand-tied bouquets in vases that are provided at the reception for decorating the tables.

The procedure for making a basic round bouquet of mixed flowers begins with careful selection and preparation of all flowers and foliage.

1. Select materials – rigid bunched greens like oregonia, boxwood or pittosporum serve well as "spacer" material placed between and under the flowers keeping their heads separated while flat leaves serve well to collar the bouquet. Flexible stemmed flowers and foliage will flow gracefully out over the sides of the bouquet.

2. Clean materials – remove all side branches and leaves that would end up below the binding point. This preparation is critical because once started the bouquet cannot be laid down until it is finished.

3. Organize materials - lay out all materials, cleaned and separated by kind, on the table so the designer can see what is available and pick it up easily.

4. Binding material - when finished, the stems are tied with waxed string, raffia, flat plastic packing cord, a heavy rubber band or cable tie; have it ready to use before starting the bouquet.

Figure 137
Begin adding materials at a 45-degree angle to achieve greater width. This diagonal stem positioning is the beginning of the spiral. Direct the stems in a counter clockwise manner if working with the right hand, or clockwise if working with the left hand. Never switch directions or crosshatch stems as these yield a disorganized look and prevent locking the stems tight at the binding point. Continue adding material in the spiral manner until sufficient size is achieved.

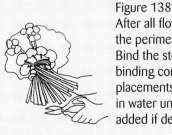

Figure 138
After all flowers are in place, add the finishing foliage around the perimeter to hide mechanics and create a finished look. Bind the stems as tight as possible with several revolutions of binding cord. Diagonal stems will not break, incorrect placements will. Trim the stems to preferred length and place in water until the bouquet is to be carried. Ribbons may be added if desired.

Part 6
Sympathy Designs

Chapter 27 INTRODUCTION

Flowers are the final tribute we pay our friends and loved ones. Funeral flowers are more than an expression of sympathy; they symbolize faith and respect. No other material thing can convey these emotions with quite the same beauty and appropriateness. Those who work with flowers professionally are very near to people in times of sorrow as well as times of happiness and celebration. The florist, when called upon by the family or the funeral director, may discuss appropriate designs and flowers for the family tribute.

An enclosure card must accompany each order, bearing the name of the sender(s) on the face and a brief description of the design on the back. The address of the sender must also be written on the back of the card. This practice will aid the family in acknowledging their floral tributes. Depending on the funeral director's preference, the enclosure card must be securely attached to the sympathy tribute so that it won't get lost during delivery and handling. It may be attached to a wired pick and placed at the focal point where it is quickly seen or it may be loosely tied to a sturdy flower or leaf. If it is tied to one of the flowers, be sure that it can be removed without disturbing the arrangement. Double perforated cards are best to use; one section remains with the flowers for identification and the other end goes to the family for acknowledgment.

Flowers for sympathy designs should be at the peak of their beauty; tight buds seldom show to full advantage. In the case of roses, the half-opened or full-blown rose is more beautiful than the bud. The florist should always find out the day and the time of the funeral service so that proper judgement can be made when selecting flowers. Over-mature flowers should never be used.

When orders are received too late for delivery to the service, the florist should consult one of the members of the family. He may suggest that the unfilled order be suitably designed to send to the home, to the family's business office or church, or to a charitable institution. In addition to these possibilities the order could be held until a later date when a suitable design could be sent to decorate the grave. These flowers then serve a double purpose; expressing sympathy and bringing joy to the living. The florist must also be sensitive to the individual's personal preferences, as some people would appreciate the sentiment of having flowers in their home in remembrance of a loved one, while others would abhor the thought of something 'funereal' being delivered to their door.

There is sometimes doubt about the proper etiquette when sending flowers to CREMATION or MEMORIAL SERVICES. When cremation takes place *after* the funeral service, there is a casket present for visitation. The family orders the casket piece accordingly, and other flowers are appropriate. When cremation takes place *before* the funeral service, then it is known as a memorial service. A memorial service is the proper name of any service being held in memory of a person when their body is not present. Memorial services may be held in many different formats, but floral tributes are usually appropriate. It is always best to contact the family or the funeral director to get the correct information regarding delivery and family preferences.

There are many different types of sympathy tributes, some of which are much more popular in certain regions of our country than others. Individual offerings may be arranged in baskets or vases, or they may be potted plants. They may be mounted on easels, or they may be religious symbols or fraternal emblems pavéd in flowers. Local tradition usually prevails when a customer is selecting a sympathy design, but there is considerable opportunity for creativity. The highest possible quality of both flowers and service will be appreciated and even expected by people when they are under the emotional strain of planning for a funeral. We see a contemporary sympathy design in Plate 316, in which the flowers are grouped, as a reminder of the deceased person's garden. Some of these flowers could actually have been brought to the florist from the client's garden as a special accommodation, which would create a wonderful memory for the family of the deceased. Flowering plum frames the column of burgundy stock that symbolizes the spiritual aspect of this family tribute. The joyful colors of the tulips, roses, gerberas and ginesta express hope, and even joy to the living.

Chapter 28
CONTAINER DESIGNS

Beautiful flowers arranged in containers have the distinct advantage of having a water source. Container designs often require less design time, have simpler mechanics, and they continue giving pleasure through longer visitation periods, even after the funeral. Standard disposable containers include those made of papier mâché, plastic and composition. Clear glass vases, wicker baskets with waterproof liners and metal basket-shaped containers with handles are other popular choices for sympathy containers. These so-called "stock vases" are cost effective; they hold plenty of water and they are usually designed with a wide base to be very stable whether displayed on a stand or on plush carpeting. Various decorative containers such as jardinieres, even family antiques, may be sent to the funeral service providing they have the aforementioned practical qualities.

Plate 317 shows a traditional

Plate 317
A Tradition Worth Keeping – The ti leaves add distinction to this traditional design, and the use of only three kinds of flowers, make it economical. A pair of these designs (mirror images) would be very impressive flanking a casket.

Plate 318 (circa 1986)
Flemish Bouquet – Flowers and colors are grouped for maximum effect in this Flemish Bouquet arranged in a wicker basket. The natural beauty of flowers may express sympathy without looking funereal. This design would make a lovely gift to hospital, nursing home or church after the funeral service.

bouquet of larkspur, roses and heather featuring ti leaves that add mass in a diagonal plane. The ti leaves have been looped to strengthen the focal area in lieu of ribbon. Traditional container and basket designs often follow the geometric patterns mentioned in Chapter 7, and usually originate from the triangle or the circle (Plates 318, 319).

There are several important points to remember when designing baskets. The first is to use approximately one-fourth of the material behind the handle of the basket (Plate 320). This precaution prevents the arrangement from being front-heavy and from falling forward. A second point well worth remembering is that the flower establishing the height of the arrangement should be six inches or more above the handle. Should line flowers be used, remember that only the open blossoms are counted in this measurement (Figure 139). The reason for the second point is that it assures good proportion; the handle of the basket becomes part of the whole composition and is included in the overall picture. The focal point of a design such as this should be at the upper edge of the basket rim, where all stems converge, and not on the handle of the basket where, so often, a bow of ribbon is placed.

Baskets with different proportions such as those with taller or shorter handles may be treated differently. The millefleur (1000 flowers) look is captured in Plate 321. The proportions are determined by the historical concept of this design style as well as the size and shape of the basket. A "basket" can also be made simply by creating a handle in a plain design. Compare Plate 320 with Plate 332 – the grapevine handle is inserted into moss-covered dry foam under the design. The added candle controls the height of both flowers and handle. These two designs would not be typical funeral offerings, but each could be a perfect solution to a given set of circumstances, which, of course includes customer preferences.

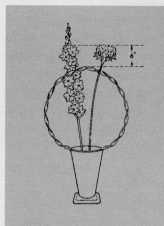

Figure 139
Baskets– line or mass blossoms are approximately six inches above the handle and to the rear to give balance. The buds of line flowers are not counted.

Plate 319 (circa 1986)
Sympathy Tribute – Gladioli, majestic daisies and pixie carnations create this unmistakable asymmetrical triangular design. The container has a sturdy base that does not easily tip over.

Plate 320 (circa 1986)
Sympathy Basket – A combination of line, mass and filler flowers characterize this traditional sympathy basket design.

(Plate 11)
Altar Arrangement – This horizontal design is suitable for a funeral service (see variations of this design in Plates 332 and 352).

Plate 321
Millefleur – Many customers request their order to not look like a typical funeral arrangement. This reenactment of a historical French design would be at home in any situation. It appears generous but not extravagant; charming but not quaint; complex but not labor intensive.

Chapter 29   SPRAY DESIGNS

The spray is the funeral piece ordered most frequently throughout the "Old West" and southern parts of the country. It originated from the old-fashioned cluster of flowers or sheaf of grain tied together with a ribbon. As the floral industry developed, people realized more and more the value of floral tributes as an expression of their love and respect for the deceased. Since the funeral director uses these floral tributes to paint a lasting memory picture of the loved ones, it became, necessary to develop a sturdy method of construction. Popularity of sprays increased because they were convenient to use as a background setting and they were within the price range of a great number of people.

Sprays may be either single or double, regardless of the manner of their construction. The double spray has a focal point in the center with flowers extending outward to either side. The single spray, which we diagram in detail, has a bow at one end with flowers extending to the other. The spray can be very effective even though few flowers are used. Whether the spray is large or small, the placement of the first eight blossoms establishes the pattern (Figures 140, 141).

Follow these design guidelines for the best result:

1. The placement of the first six blossoms is very important. The positions of blossoms No. 7 and No. 8 are variable. The placement in Figure 141 prevents the eye from picking out definite groups of two's and three's. Note from the figure that blossoms Nos. 1, 2, 3, and 4. form a diamond; No. 5 and No. 6 add the width to the spray and are on the diagonal in line with Nos. 2 and 3, forming an arrow. Avoid round, "bunched" designs or long, narrow ones. Oval or arrow-shaped ones are more desirable. Blossoms No. 7 and No. 8 are best placed between No. 5 and No. 6, and a little lower. They may also be placed below the bow, but this practice divides the flowers. The length and width of the spray should be in proportion to the number of flowers used.

2. In grading the blossoms, the buds and smaller ones (Nos. 1, 2, and 3) are placed to the outer sides and the more open blossoms (Nos. 4, 7, and 8) are used with the bow at the focal area, giving good proportion and balance.

3. A mound effect is desired; avoid flat sprays. In Figure 140, the outer blossoms are shown to lie almost flat on the background while the blossoms toward the center of interest gradually rise

Figure 140
Tied Spray – Eight blossoms emanate from the focal point (bow).

in height (approximately six inches), giving depth to the spray. This depth is filled in with other foliage. Do not allow this secondary foliage to choke or cover the blossoms.

4. When only a few blossoms are used, do not use two colors. This division of color reduces the impact on the eye. A spray of eight carnations, four red and four white, gives only half the value in appearance of a similar spray made from all white or all red flowers.

5. Do not divide the blossoms by placing a bow in the center, especially when the blossoms are few in number. A spray of eight blossoms so divided would produce four to either side, which would look very skimpy.

6. Greenery must be in proportion to the quantity of blossoms. When flowers are few in number, a great quantity of background greens will not improve the spray. It will overwhelm the flowers, making the spray look skimpy.

7. When the flowers are not fully opened or are few in number, the bow must be of the same color as the flowers. Do not use a contrasting color, for again, this reduces the impact on the eye.

8. The bow represents a tie. All lines of foliage and flowers radiate from this point and give the appearance that the ribbon is tying them together.

There are three basic methods used in designing funeral sprays: tied, picked and wet foam.

Tied Sprays

The TIED SPRAY, due to historical perspective, will be discussed first. It was very popular from the late 1800's through the mid-1900's. Florist thread or wire can be used for tying. Spool wire (No. 24 or No. 26) is the most economical to use. Wire is laborsaving because fewer circles of wire are required to hold the stems in place.

The use of a small stick one-fourth-inch square and approximately twelve inches long, wrapped in green paper, will aid tremendously in learning to tie a spray. These sticks may be cut at the lumber company, though cane stakes purchased from a wholesale house are commonly used. The support given by the use of the stick prevents the spray from having a weak back and breaking when handled. Poorly tied sprays have been the source of dissatisfaction and complaints from morticians.

All flowers are wired far enough down the stems so that both the wire and stems can be securely tied into the body of the spray. Broken blossoms in good condition may be used if they are wired with the hook method (on flat-headed blossoms, e.g., asters or chrysanthemums, or through the calyx (on roses or carnations). The wire is run halfway through the blossom and then both ends are turned down, pressing this wire close to the flower calyx. Force a second wire up into the bottom of the blossom and twist the wires together, forming a stem. This wire stem may be covered with a piece of looped fern before being added to the spray, or it may be covered with the foliage later in the regular make-up. The wire stem is bent into a "U" shape, with the "U" straddling the backbone, and is tied into position. Should the wire stem be left straight the blossom will fall to one side. On flower stems that are too short, an extension wire is also used, bent into a "U" shape, and tied in.

When making a tied spray, the first wired blossom is laid on top of a piece of greenery on top of the backbone stick, extending beyond the end of it at least 10 inches. The second flower with its foliage is placed lower and to the left side of No. 1. Then No. 3 goes lower and to the right, and so on. This pattern is continued as seen in Figure 141. Filler material is added as the design progresses because each and every stem must be tied in as the wire encircles down the central core. There is no going back to add something in.

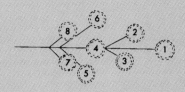

Figure 141
Flat Spray – showing placement of eight blossoms in diagram for tied and/or picked sprays.

Figure 142
Picked Spray – showing six blossoms, the depth of spray, and graded mound shape (flower heads are not bent forward, goose–necked)

The greatest advantage of tied sprays is that they are quick and economical to make. A significant disadvantage is that these sprays require a special display rack, and most of today's funeral homes do not have these display stands.

Picked Sprays

A PICKED SPRAY has for its foundation a block of plastic foam, or similar materials such as plaques made with wads of moss or pine needles wrapped very tight with wire or string to a backing of hardware cloth. These plaques (seldom used today) are never tied to boards because the morticians would be unable to hang the sprays on their display racks. In the picked spray the flowers are wired, secured to picks (wood or steel), and stuck into the foundation. Moss or needle foundations, often called "wet packs", were soaked in water hoping the flower stems could absorb a little moisture.

After the introduction of plastic foam the picked spray became extremely popular. Florists could then expand upon the size and creativity of these sympathy tributes. Chicken wire or florist thread may be wrapped around the plastic foam to reinforce it. The plastic foam foundation must be large enough to hold all the flowers used in the design (Figure 142). Do not economize on the size of the foundation. The numerous holes formed by picks will cause a small block of insufficient size to break apart.

All flower stems should be picked be-fore they are stuck into plastic foam. The stems are so smooth that they soon slip out unless they are picked. Foliages having strong or rough or serrated stems do not need to be picked. The lines of the greens must appear to radiate from the focal point. Do not place the greens perpendicular to the foundation. They will establish the radiating lines of the additional material. These greens are horizontal to the work table when added.

Blossom No. 1 is placed into position, extending straight out from the end of the spray bar, and is approximately four inches shorter than the background greens. Its stem is cut to this measurement. It is then wired, picked, and stuck into the spray bar, remaining horizontal.

Blossom No. 2 extends a little to the left and is approximately 3 inches shorter than No. 1. After deciding its length and cutting it, wire and pick it into place about two inches above greens.

Blossom No. 3 extends to the right of No. 1 and is one inch shorter than No. 2. When it is wired, picked, and placed into position, it is on approximately the same level as blossom No. 2.

Blossom No. 4 should be a very nice flower, for it is in a prominent position. It should be larger than the three previous ones if there is a size preference. It is shorter than No. 3, and when wired and picked, it is placed on a higher level than the previous flowers. This blossom establishes the depth of the spray. The four blossoms form a diamond shape, as in Figure 141. Should blossoms No. 2 and No. 3

be placed too far apart, then No. 4 would be forced up, between them to fill the void; the diamond shape would be lost. Note that No. 1 blossom is horizontal and parallel to the background. Blossoms No. 2 and No. 3 were raised an inch or two, and No. 4 gives the height (or depth). This arrangement produces a mound-shaped spray, as shown in Figure 142. Do not have these first stems too long, thus requiring they be stuck into the bottom end of the spray bar. Shorter stems placed at the top end are stronger and the flower heads remain at the correct position.

Blossoms No. 5 and No. 6 are to the right and left of No. 4, extending outward proportionately to the other blossoms. They are horizontal and in a diagonal line with Nos. 1, 2, and 3.

Blossoms No. 7 and No. 8 are added to the bar at approximately the same spot as No. 5 and No. 6 and extend upward to a height similar to No. 4. All the lines formed by the stems of the blossoms must appear to radiate from the center of interest, similar to the lines of the background greens. The addition of more blossoms (No. 9 to No. 12) may continue to make the spray longer or they may be grouped at the center of interest, the spot where a bow could be picked. Or they may be arranged in the same position as the first four blossoms, but at the opposite end of the spray.

Looped flat fern (or any other economical foliage of choice) is next added beneath the blossoms. With the heavier rib facing the foundation, bring the tip of the fern forward over the rib and secure it with a greening pin. Note that the foundation only is covered with this looped fern and that the flowers are not submerged. For a softening effect, plumosus fern or other delicate greens are added over the looped fern but are also kept under the blossoms. The stems of the plumosus may be secured with a pick, often attaching two or three of these delicate stems to one pick.

The bow, if one is used, will vary in size according to the quantity of blossoms. It may be made of looped foliage or ribbon (Plate 322, It should never be so large that it becomes the dominating feature. When one is using ribbon for the bow, the loops are made long enough to fit between and under the blossoms, the central loops being shorter than the outer ones. The bow is tied with a No. 20 or 22 gauge wire and secured to the spray foundation with a pick. When foliage is looped to form a bow, the loops should be picked individually. (See Plate 115)

Small filler flowers enhance the beauty and value of sprays. These may be evenly dispersed throughout the main blossoms or they may be grouped in one area (Plates 322 and 323). It is best to pick the fillers in small tufts. This technique increases the visual impact and decreases the labor.

Plate 324 shows a unique spray of dried materials most of which are picked into dry foam. The two clipped palm leaves have stems large enough to be cut to a point and inserted directly into the foam. Dried stems can be dabbed with hot glue before they are pushed into the foam, to increase their security.

Wet Foam Sprays

The recent introduction of wet foam contained in plastic grid cages and film-wrapped spray bars has greatly increased the ease and diversity in creating sympathy sprays. Designs of every style explained earlier in this book, can be easily adapted to these useful foundations. The provision of water and the elimination of labor-intensive picks are great advantages to the florist. It is vital that the stems of all flowers and foliages be cut to a point so that they will fit tight, like a wedge, when pushed deep into the foam. Conversely, blunt cut stems carelessly inserted will cause two problems: they wilt and fall out quickly. No way to please a customer — or funeral director, for that matter! We also highly recommend wrapping the caged block of foam in thin plastic to prevent normal evaporation of the precious moisture.

Plate 322 (left)
Asymmetrical Standing Spray –
Flowers are sectioned (zoned)
with snapdragons, liatris and
tulips, each forming a point of
the triangle. Open roses and
heather unite the three zones
at the focal area, which is tied
with a "bow" of looped flax
leaves.

Plate 323 (above)
Symmetrical Standing Spray –
Aspidistra foliage adds
distinction to a routine
combination of flowers in a
monochromatic color scheme

Plate 324 (circa 1986)
Standing Spray, Dried
Materials – An early example
of the formalinear design style.

Standing Sprays

Larger and more expensive sprays, either tied, picked or designed in wet foam gain prominence when they are mounted on easels (Plates 322–326). The easel, whether made of metal or wood, lifts a design for better display. A key point to remember is to always be sure the easel is strong enough to support the size and weight of the spray. A top-heavy piece will very easily fall over. Wet foam does add some weight to any design. It is also very important to attach the foundation to the easel in a completely foolproof and secure manner. Always remember that every sympathy design will be moved several times before it reaches the gravesite. Plate 325 shows a shallow wicker basket holding a cascading arrangement of garden flowers mounted on an easel. Perfect physical balance that assures overall stability is critical in this design. This easel is taller and heavier with its legs spread further apart, and this provides proper stability for its center of gravity (the design) which is so far above the floor.

A very creative design in which all materials are inserted into wet foam is shown in Plate 326. This is a great idea for a customer who would appreciate having a plant to keep after the funeral. The bromeliad can easily be transferred into a pot for enjoyment later, and the curly willow, which is beginning to leaf out, can be rooted in water or sand, or transplanted directly to the garden.

Plate 325
Garden Basket –
A challenging balance problem is solved with good mechanics and an easel large enough to support the weight of this design.

Plate 326 (circa 1986)
Standing Plantscape – The free and open effect of the curly willow as a counterpoint to the massive bromeliad and galax rose creates an impressive display for little expense.

Plate 327 (circa 1986)
Flemish Companions –
These two asymmetrical
compositions are balanced in
tandem by the mirror-image
placements of the eremurus
skeleton flowers, followed by
the various fillers.

Chapter 30   WREATH DESIGNS

WREATHS are circular in design. They invite a wide range of expression in both design and color combination. The circular foundation can be made of wet foam, pre-cut plastic foam or of a commercial wire frame packed with sphagnum moss. Should the plastic foam foundation be used, it must be reinforced with wire or placed on a substantial easel to assure its security. Plastic foam is fragile and will break easily if too many flowers are picked into a small area.

The wire frame wreath is packed solid with damp sphagnum moss and tied with green florist thread. These wreath frames can be prepared many days in advance and stored. When needed for use they are soaked in water and allowed to drain before they are delivered.

The foundation is covered with wreath wrap (green waxed paper), which is applied as you would a bandage, rolling it firmly onto the wreath frame from the roll. To tighten this wrap, slide the left hand over the paper in the same circular motion, taking up the slack as the wreath wrap is applied. Secure the end of the wrapping with a greening pin pushed horizontally into the frame. Only one layer of wrap is necessary except with satin-wrapped wreaths, where several layers may be needed to prevent moisture from coming through.

Wet foam wreath rings are available from the wholesale florist in many sizes, and of course they are quick and easy to use. They are thoroughly soaked in water with floral food solution and allowed to drain while the designer works. A beautiful example of this mechanic is shown in Plate 328. The solid floral circle becomes the dominant part of this composition, and the cluster is an accent. This floral tribute is intended to represent the many garden flowers so lovingly grown over the years by the deceased. Indeed many of these flowers could have been collected in a private garden — the rosemary and dusty miller foliages and all of the roses. In this presentation the easel is camouflaged with generous use of curly willow, which contributes to the garden effect.

There usually are two sections to a wreath: (1) the cluster which is the focal point, and (2) the remaining portion of the circle. The cluster may be at the top, bottom, or any place on the left side (Figure 143). There is no rule that the cluster should not be on the right side, but many of our habitual movements are from left to right. However, when there are orders for two wreaths of similar price, it is a good practice to have the cluster of one on the left and the cluster of the other on the right. This pair of wreaths can be used effectively at either end of the casket.

Figure 143
Wreaths — showing
location of focal point

Plate 328
Garden Wreath – Old fashioned garden roses, daisies, rosemary and dusty miller are brought in from the customer's garden. The commercially grown carnations, genista, beargrass and curly willow continue the "home garden" look of the design.

When the focal point is at the top, the flowers can radiate outward to create symmetrical or asymmetrical balance. This top cluster may also cascade down the right side giving the logical feeling of clockwise motion. If the cluster is at the bottom, it may flow upward, horizontal, or diagonally to either side. However, when the focal point is placed on the lower side of a wreath, the main portion of the blossoms will not be visible to the people seated at the service. When the cluster is on the side, the lines should flow upward, that is, the flower heads radiate up from that point and the stems downward.

When using stems in this manner they must continue the line of flowers through the focal point. A bow, if used, appears to tie the flowers to the circular foundation. The cluster should be mound-shaped and not flat. By being mound-shaped, it gains depth (Figure 143 and Plate 329).

In traditional or geometric design, line flowers are placed to create the skeleton, and they extend to the outer edges of the design (Plate 329). Mass flowers would be used toward the focal point, and form flowers in the center to give weight and emphasis where the bow is placed (Plates 329, 330, 331). The bow may be made of either ribbon or foliage loops. These loops are picked and stuck into the foundation to simulate a bow. Massed flowers may also be grouped into this cluster, giving weight and omitting the bow.

The second section of the wreath (circular portion not used by the cluster) allows for much expression in selection of materials. For a satin-wrapped wreath, the satin ribbon is applied first, leaving about one third unwrapped for the cluster. If a plastic foam ring is used cut the corners off on the front side and "sand" the edges with a piece of scrap plastic foam before wrapping with satin. Do not leave the edges square. Loops of ribbon or foliage may be applied to this circle, e.g., magnolia, galax, lemon (salal), or other broad- leafed evergreens. When plumosus fern covers this section, a flat green is generally applied first. This section may also be totally covered in moss or flowers. Gladioli and carnation blossoms are held with greening pins. Small blossoms (spray chrysanthemums and pompon asters) may be individually picked to the plastic foam with flat toothpicks through the center, or they may be picked in small clusters and inserted.

A cross section of the wreath would be mound-shaped in appearance. Do not apply foliage or flowers

Plate 329 (circa 1986) Dramatic Wreath – The wreath ring is wrapped with reversed satin ribbon in the "Austrian pouf" manner, and a dramatic vertical cluster is designed with liatris, dendrobium orchids and gerbera. The graceful bear grass is echoed with 1/4 inch ribbon.

Plate 330 (circa 1986)
Woodland Wreath – The
ring, covered in natural
sheet moss, provides an
appropriate foundation for
the cluster of rustic protea
and lilies. Honeysuckle
vines and ti leaves complete
the exotic-rustic theme.

Plate 331 (circa 1966)
Elaborate Pedestal Wreath –
Easter lilies form the
dominant floral interest on
both the carnation wreath
and at the base of the
pedestal.

so that they are flat across the face of the wreath. Flowers stuck in like soldiers (that is, straight up and down) show the sides of the picks, which is poor workmanship. The design should appear to wrap around three sides of the wreath. It should look attractive from all sides.

The design of the wreath must be decided upon before the application of any greens or flowers. Limit yourself to two or three colors and two or three materials. Keep the design simple. The use of too many colors and materials will be a hodgepodge, unless, of course, the materials are grouped in a way that lets each one show off to its best advantage (Plates 332, 333, 334). Do not fill the centers of the wreaths, for the result would be a solid mass.

Gold lettering is requested by some organizations and groups to identify their offering. These letters should be secured to a piece of ribbon with glue or staples; the latter method is preferred. Do not depend on the letters themselves to stick to the shiny finish of most ribbons. The lettered ribbon is used as a streamer flowing out of the focal point where it would be attached with a pick. However, if the design permits, the ribbon may be stretched firmly across the center and held in place with greening pins or picks at, or near both ends.

The circular part of the wreath construction is done on the work table, then it is firmly attached to the easel. When the wreath is in its upright position it is much easier to complete the design of the cluster. One must frequently step back from the design while working, so as to see that proportion and balance are correct.

The size of the easel is determined by the size of the finished wreath. The easel is generally three times the size of the wreath. In other words, the completed wreath will cover approximately one-third to one-half of its stand. All set pieces such as wreaths, pillows, and emblems should be mounted on easels. This mounting assures them of a rather prominent and secure location in the floral background of the funeral service.

Plate 332 shows an interesting exception to this rule. Grapevine is fashioned into a wreath and the ends are inserted into a dry foam base. A small tray with a candle securely mounted into wet foam is hot-glued to the top of the dry foam base inside the wreath. Flowers are inserted into the wet foam. The candle would be lighted for a prayer service. The design is suitable for placement on a table or altar.

Plate 332 (circa 1986) Grapevine Wreath with Candle – This idea incorporates a candle with flowers into an unusual wreath that sets on a table for stability. (For other adaptations of this design see Plates 11, 352).

Plate 333 (circa 1986) Pairs Repeated – The satin-wrapped wreath ring holds an exotic display of striking materials. All lines flow out from the focal area (eggplant). Compare with Plate 8.

Plate 334 (circa 1986) Spring Garden Wreath – The top of the easel is bent back at a 45° angle to allow the moss-covered wet foam wreath ring to be properly positioned. Assorted spring blossoms are then grouped in both parallel and radial (integrated) stem placements in this vegetative style design.

Chapter 31 SET PIECE DESIGNS: RELIGIOUS, CONVENTIONAL, AND FRATERNAL EMBLEMS

Religious and Conventional Emblems

Cross Designs

Crosses are popular emblems. Each type has definite proportions that make it a distinctive design and representative of the organization. These proportions must be followed carefully.

The LATIN CROSS is most often seen. The standard is two and one-half times the length of one arm. The width of the arms and standard varies only in proportion to the size of the cross (Figure 144). The focal point is the place where the arms cross. A cluster of flowers may be beautifully designed for this intersection. Garlands may circle down the standard of this cross. A dry foam cross may be satin-wrapped, covered with foliage or moss and decorated with a cluster of flowers at the focal point, whereas a wet foam cross may be a solid work of flowers or foliage. Regardless of the type of foundation, it should be securely tied on the easel at a slight angle to add grace and beauty. One placed straight up often has a stiff appearance (Plates 335 and 336). However, a cross that is presented as an architectural unit would be mounted straight. The cross in Plate 337 is secured to a foundation of dry foam that has been covered in moss. A flat tray holding a candle mounted in wet foam is placed at the foot of the cross and filled with flowers. This design is particularly well suited for use as the focal arrangement in a memorial service.

The RED CROSS is made of a series of four squares with a corner of each connecting to the others (Figure 144). It is solid in design, red in color, and does not vary. Flowers as a cluster are not added to the face of this cross as in the case of the Latin (Christian) cross. This design may be on a solid panel of white flowers or upright on a frame with flowers clustered at its base.

The TUBERCULAR LEAGUE emblem uses the width of the standard or arm for a unit of measurement (Figure 144). It is a double-bar cross with equal cross-arms, the upper standard being shorter and the lower standard longer than the

Figure 144
Crosses –
A – Latin or Christian Cross
B – Red Cross
C – Cross of Lorraine or Tubercular League Cross

Plate 335 (circa 1986)
Latin Cross, circa 1986 – Autumn colors enrich this simple design and the "Austrian pouf" manner of ribbon wrap softens the edges of this cross.

Plate 336 (circa 1986)
Monochromatic Greens –
The galax-covered cross
provides a cool background
for the serene curves of the
bells of Ireland, while the
green cymbidium orchids
establish a focal point and
the chlorophytum accent
adds a graceful cascading
line.

Plate 337 (circa 1986)
Symbolic Cross – A 3-foot
burlap-covered cross,
representing Christ's robe,
stands erect in a dramatic
asymmetrical triangle of
eremuris, gerbera and
miniature carnations. Flax
leaves emphasize height and
ascension while the candle
symbolizes eternal light.

cross-arms. The ends of both cross-arms and standards are pointed at 45° angles; they are not square. When solid, it is always red. If in outline, it may be done in any color.

The CROSS OF LORRAINE is a double-barred cross and may be called for in the service of a soldier who has served in France.

Pillow Designs

PILLOW foundations may be purchased from florist whole-sale houses. The foundations are made up of wet or dry foams, or they are the wire frames that can be filled with sphagnum moss. The sides are curved to add grace. Maintain this curve when applying flowers. The pillow design may be outlined with fresh or dried leaves, tufts of tulle or ribbon loops. Flowers are applied to dry foam with flat toothpicks, greening pins, or No 24 bank pins, or they are inserted directly into wet foam.

The focal point is usually designed on the upper left side. A properly proportioned cluster of flowers may form the center of interest. A pillow design is quite often a remembrance from a close friend or member of the family and is displayed on an easel. There are also soft satin and lace pillows that may have a corsage pinned to them. These pillows would be displayed inside the open casket by simply laying them in the corner at the base of the lid.

Plate 338A
Pillow 1 – Graduated salal leaves pinned to a styrofoam base provide a serene background for the delicate and free–flowing spray of oncidium and phalaenopsis orchids and freesia.

Plate 338B
Pillow 2 – A more stately look is given to the same pillow with a geometric cluster of yellow roses and tropical foliage.

Heart Designs

HEARTS may be solid or in outline. Wet foam, dry foam and wire frame foundations are available at florist supply houses. The grouping of flowers for the focal point is most effective when located on the upper left side. Place this design at a slight angle on the easel for a graceful effect. Plate 338 shows a solid heart design using a dry foam base. The edging is made with lemon (salal) leaves selected for uniform size and individually pinned to the back of the heart. Before covering the main portion of the heart with cushion spray chrysanthemums, the square edges of the heart form were rounded off and sanded to give a softer silhouette. Each blossom was attached with a flat wood toothpick pushed through its center into the foam. This "old-fashioned" technique works best because the toothpick is smaller than a florist pick and the wood won't slip out of the foam. The center of interest was formed with a cluster of red roses, thus the name "Bleeding Heart". The roses were arranged in a small dome shaped wet foam cage that was wired to the heart. Bear grass and narrow satin ribbons were added to increase the visual effect and repeat the lines of the heart form. This easel was spray painted burgundy to harmonize with the roses.

Star Designs

The STAR OF HEAVEN is an emblem used for the service of a baby. Tradition says that when a baby dies a star is added to the heavens. This design has five points with no definite specifications as to the placement of the points. It is beautiful combined with a crescent. The flowers must be small in size and delicate in texture and color. Tufts of tulle may be used in place of foliage, unless the foliage is very delicate, e.g., adiantum, plumosus, etc.

FIVE-POINTED STARS are positioned with one point straight up (Figure 145). This star is a patriotic symbol of the United States of America; it also represents the State of Texas, and may even be used at Christmas. Many business firms use a five-pointed star for their insignia. This star is also used for the funeral of a general in the military service. The flowers, foliage, and colors may be of the designer's choice.

The STAR OF DAVID is a six-pointed star consisting of two equilateral triangles, one pointing up, the other down (Figure 145).

All of these star forms are available from florist suppliers in both wet and dry foam of different sizes.

Fraternal Emblem Designs

Emblems are often ordered by fraternal or business organizations. Each floral emblem should adhere as closely as possible to the required design proportions, and colors of the symbol. It may be necessary to trim or manipulate the blossoms in order to finish the emblem in its proper shape.

Each emblem is fastened to an easel of appropriate size. (The easel stand should be approximately three times the size of the emblem.) Only emblems with specific color sequence or design specifications will be discussed.

When a FRATERNAL EMBLEM is not available in a manufactured form (wet or dry), a small printed insignia may be purchased from the wholesale house and superimposed on a background of flowers. Of course a floral artist may always cut the emblem out of sheets of foam and prepare it as needed.

The EASTERN STAR emblem is made in the shape of a five-pointed star (Figure 146). One point is downward, and it never varies from this position. This point is white and the following points, going clockwise, are green, red, blue, and yellow. The colors meet at the center.

Serious consideration should be given to the selection of materials so that the different textures will present a harmonious whole. It may be necessary to dye the flowers the desired colors in order to maintain unity in the design. When insufficient money is allotted to allow a lovely design, suggest that the emblem be made of satin ribbon tufts or tulle, or even dried flowers of the specified colors.

A corsage made with streamers and a bow of this fraternal organization's colors may be fastened to picks and secured to the center of the emblem. This corsage may be taken by the Worthy Matron to the home of the deceased; this practice has met with approval in many communities.

The MASONIC EMBLEM has exact proportions and details in design that must be followed accurately. It is a replica of the carpenter's square and compass. The angle at the arms of the square must be ninety degrees. The ends of the arms are cut square and point upward. The figure overlaying the arms of the square is the compass. Its legs are directed downward, and the ends come to a sharp point. The compass is placed on top of the square, as shown in

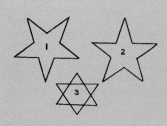

Figure 145
Stars
1– Eastern Star, one point is placed downward
2– Commercial star or Texas star, one point is placed upward
3– Star of David, six–pointed star made of two equilateral triangles

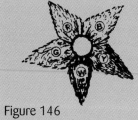

Figure 146
Eastern Star

Figure 147
Masonic Blue Lodge emblem

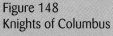

Figure 148
Knights of Columbus

Figure 149
Broken wheel
1– used to represent missing member of family or organization
2– lariat and spurs may be added when used for service of rancher

Figure 147. The letter "G" is centered in this design. It may be made of chenille over wire or cut from styrofoam. This is the emblem of the Blue Lodge. Many organizations prefer the emblem done in blue and white; others do not specify the colors. Generally, yellow is preferred for the square, white for the compass, and blue for the "G."

The KNIGHTS OF COLUMBUS emblem is made of a Maltese Cross, on which a shield is superimposed. The letters "K of C" and figures as shown in Figure 148 may be purchased or made from wire wrapped with chenille or ribbon. Two arms of the cross, the upper left and lower right, are white. The other two arms, the upper right and lower left, are red. The shield is made with bronze or yellow blossoms (to represent metal), and the letters are made with blue.

When applying the flowers, select those with solid heads, which will present an even texture over-all. This is solid work (pavé) where texture plays an important part in the final results. Have a convex surface for the completed over-all design.

The BROKEN WHEEL design is representative of the Brotherhood of Locomotive Engineers and the Brotherhood of Railroad Trainmen. Occasionally it is used to represent a member of a board of directors. It is excellent for the services of a deceased rancher. In the latter case, spurs and lariat are added. The dry foam foundation may be purchased from a wholesale firm or a regular wreath frame with spokes added may be used; each spoke represents a member of the organization. Where the membership is too large, add enough spokes for appearance only. One portion of the rim and its adjoining spoke are omitted (Figure 149), or they may be wrapped with satin; the remaining portion of the design is a solid pavé of flowers or foliage. The contour of the finished design, as stated before, must be rounded across the top and not flat, as this gives it a more "plush" appearance. Occasionally a family of several siblings will order a broken wheel design and have a spoke "missing" for each deceased member. The color choice is made according to the preference of the family or designer.

Door Spray/Door Badge

The DOOR SPRAY is placed on the entrance of a home or business establishment of the deceased to signify that a death has occurred there. It is an order requiring much conservation and distinction in design. Elaborate and flowing materials are not suitable. The flowers must be carefully chosen, with special attention being given to their lasting quality. Flowers that wilt quickly or shed their petals should not be used. Background greens are subdued and used sparingly.

A simple, single tied spray with flowers carefully wired in position is in good taste. White is the preferred color for flowers and black for the ribbon. A taped wire loop, by which it is hung to the door, is secured to the back of the design. A wall pocket type container with wet foam, or a wet foam cage make excellent foundations for this design. The flowers are placed into the wet foam and the finished design resembles a simple wall spray (Plate 340).

Chapter 32   CASKET DESIGNS

The CASKET COVER is generally the most prominent floral arrangement at a funeral. It may be a blanket, a spray, a pall, or in some instances, a soft, flexible wreath. This piece is usually ordered by the family, though a friend or business associate of long standing may ask for the privilege of sending this design. Current thinking allows that frequently the funeral director, in consultation with the family of the deceased, will place the order. In some religious ceremonies only the casket cover is allowed in the church with the casket. The other floral offerings are sent to the cemetery.

The family will not always know the correct name for the flowers they wish, nor will they know anything of your design possibilities. Therefore an album of photographs in combination with your detailed explanations of the various arrangements will help them in making the right selection. When the family comes in to discuss the piece, see that proper respect and quiet prevail in your shop during the interview. Loud talking and laughing, radios turned too high, or signs of merriment during this consultation are in poor taste.

The customer must be put at ease before discussing price. Express sympathy with sincerity. Do not become emotional or sentimental, but maintain proper composure. The tone of voice and choice of words can do more than any display of action.

The preference of the family or of the deceased must be given first consideration in choosing flowers or colors. Learn the type of casket, its color, and its lining as a guide to designing the cover. These facts will indicate the price range of the piece. Paint a word picture of

the design. Then the price of this design should be discussed. Do not let a customer leave without his knowing the approximate cost. Sometimes customers are prone to overspend at times of sorrow and later find it difficult to pay.

The casket piece is generally fashioned to soften the lines of the casket. Flowing lines that follow the contours of the casket will create a feeling of unity. Stiff, straight flowers, such as gladioli and various tropicals, though dramatic, may give the feeling of hardness and indifference. Such stems should be wired or massaged and given gentle curves. The foundation must not be bulky or cumbersome. All wire, construction material, and foundation must be covered in order not to mar the casket. The flowers should not be over ten to twelve inches above the casket, so they will easily fit into the funeral car.

When large, expensive designs are ordered it is a good policy to discuss the design with the funeral director. His suggestions should be considered. He will know the best time to deliver the piece, whether or not the casket will be opened, and other important details. Learn the size, color, texture and finish of the casket at this time.

Flowers to be attached to the inside lid of the casket must be delicate and carefully selected to express fine texture and quality. They are often fashioned in the corsage manner and are attached to the lining with corsage pins. It is important that the flowers complement the casket lining and the garment of the deceased. It is a good policy to accommodate the customer's personal and no doubt, sentimental wishes at this time. They may desire a corsage, a boutonniere,

Plate 340 (circa 1986)
Door Spray – A wet foam cage holds this graceful design of chrysanthemums, alstroemeria and ti leaves. The foam is wrapped in thin plastic to prevent the evaporation of moisture.

Plate 341 (circa 1986)
White Crescent – The simplicity of white carnations and lilies placed in a graceful and elegant curve creates a spray of distinction. The violet and burgundy ribbons (French bow, Plate 115) provide a rich transition between spray and casket.

Plate 342
Fan Casket Spray, Completed – Fresh red ti leaves have been used in place of ribbon, with a few looped at the focal area. Note how the line of the ti leaves flows from upper left to lower right in keeping with the normal movement of the eye from the open casket, which is always on the left. See Plates 345-347.

a small nosegay or single flower, or even a rosary to be placed inside the casket with their loved one. Maintaining good relations with the funeral director will be a great help in handling these needs.

Casket Sprays

Casket sprays soften the lines of caskets. Their flowers and foliage should flow gracefully over the edge. The sprays may be single or double. A SINGLE SPRAY can be made to cover one-half or three-fourths of a casket. Its focal point is either centered or placed to one end of the design, toward the head of the casket. Flowers flow toward the foot of the casket and are most effective in garlands or groupings forming lines. A single spray may be designed in the shape of a symmetrical fan, or it may be somewhat triangular in design with the long point toward the foot. The side points will not be as prominent. Smaller garlands are used to fill in between the main ones, with clusters of flowers used as fillers. The more prominent flowers should be used at the focal point. Ribbons may be interspersed with the flowers, and

Plate 343 (circa 1970) Full Couch Casket Spray – This casket spray is designed to cover the top of a closed casket. Long trails of plumosis extend outward and soften the edges of the composition.

love knots may be tied into the longer streamers to break the line and to add interest (Plates 341, 342).

When the casket is opened, the single spray is placed on the lower half with the focal point closer to the opening; flowers, foliage and accessories do not extend down into the casket, but do cover the edge of the opening. Under no circumstances should any designer use foliage or flowers that will shed petals, leaflets or spores (seed) into the casket. Use a spray sealer on questionable materials.

The DOUBLE SPRAY is larger than the single spray and has the focal point in the center with the flowers flowing out equally to either side. This design is proportioned to look well on a closed casket. However, when the casket is to be opened and the spray is of this double type, it is possible to construct this piece on two separate spray foundations. They are placed together during construction and are separated when the design is completed. Flowers, and especially foliage, are used to finish the division edges of each half of the sprays. The lower half is placed on the casket during the time it is open. The other portion is placed on a stand at the head of the casket ready to be placed on the casket at the close of the service (Plate 343).

In some funeral services the casket is placed against the pulpit or against a wall so only the front side of the casket is visible. In this case, for inexpensive casket sprays, flowers placed high on the far side of the casket and flowing over the near side will show to full advantage (Plate 344). The back of the piece can be finished with foliage and inexpensive filler blossoms that appear throughout the design. At the cemetery the minister, pallbearers, and morticians stand behind the casket; the friends see the full beauty of the piece from the front. It must be added, however, that during most funeral services, people will have some opportunity to view the casket from all sides. It is important then, to finish the casket spray beautifully on all sides even though the main emphasis remains on the front. Again, the florist needs to communicate with the funeral director and plan the design accordingly.

All casket sprays should be constructed on foundations called "saddles." These are devices made of wire (for dry foam) or hard plastic (for wet foam). The smaller ones are twelve inches long and range up to thirty-six inches in length. There is a size to accommodate any design and budget need. These saddles are made with curved legs that have rubber pads to prevent them from slipping or scratching the casket. All of the wet foam saddles have some water-holding capacity to prevent moisture from getting on the casket. It is imperative that the florist's mechanics can in no way damage the casket. A piece of soft mesh rubber matting may be hot-glued to the bottom of the saddle to finish this design and to provide extra protection from water or other damage. Since the casket spray often must look fresh for a few days, it is a good idea to wrap the wet foam block in thin plastic. This simple technique will prevent both dripping and evaporation.

Casket sprays generally have a base of flat fern or Chamaedorea used as the foundation green, which is placed into the base

Plate 344 (circa 1986) Chromatic Colors – This diagonal spray, designed to be viewed from the front side only, has slightly taller flowers placed in the back. The color-saturated irises, double tulips and acacia are anchored at the focal area with a concentration of cineraria blossoms.

Plate 345 – Casket Spray, Construction – A traditional fan-shaped casket spray shows the foundation of Chamaedorea softened with salal and leather leaf fern underneath a skeleton of larkspur flowers.

Plate 346 – Casket Spray, Construction – The mass flowers, carnations, have been added to the framework of the line flowers. Note the natural flow of stems and the even dispersion of blossoms.

Plate 347 – Casket Spray, Construction – Filler flowers, pixie carnations, have now been added to create overall fullness. It is easy to see from this picture just how many stems of flowers and greenery are inserted into a single block of wet foam. It is always wise to first wrap the foam in thin plastic, which prevents evaporation of precious moisture, and then to wrap it in chicken wire which will prevent a block of foam from breaking open from the pressure of so many stems. Stability is vital since sympathy tributes are moved many times. The finished spray with fresh ti leaf "ribbon loops" is shown in Plate 342.

(Figure 39)
Wiring line flowers.

at an angle so that it will drape over the edge of the casket. Long branches of plumosus are then added to soften this foliage. The outer flowers are wired and put into their places. When line flowers such as gladioli, larkspur, stock, etc., are used, they are wired so that the designer can curve their stems (Figure 39). Do not have straight "spikes" protruding from sprays.

Flowers such as carnations, roses, and tulips may be positioned between the skeleton flowers, inserted into the wet foam and allowed to curve naturally over the casket. Plates 345 — 347 and 342 show the step by step progression of designing a traditional casket spray. The foliage and skeleton flowers are placed first, followed by the mass flowers, which add volume to the composition. Then filler flowers and secondary foliages are added, followed by the "ribbon" ti leaves. A few of the ti leaves are looped at the focal area and others extend outward as streamers. Should streamers of shower ribbon be requested, they are fastened to picks and placed so that they flow with the flowers. The different types of flowers in this spray are evenly dispersed to create overall unity. The flowers in Plate 348 are grouped which gives a completely different look. The purpose of grouping flowers of like kinds is to increase the visual impact of each "personality", especially the more delicate ones. One group flows into the other and they are unified by similarity of color and texture.

When gold lettering is requested, it is stapled to a ribbon streamer. Do not depend on glue to hold these letters as changes in temperature and humidity in combination with the shiny finish of synthetic ribbons can cause the glue to detach. One of the ends of the ribbon is fastened to a pick and is secured to the foundation. Precaution must be taken to prevent any misspelled words or lost letters.

Casket Blankets For Adults

A casket blanket is similar in effect to a blanket on a bed; it will soften the appearance as it lies over the casket. The size will vary according to the wishes of the family. It can be one-half, three-quarter, or full size and can cover the casket completely, or it may lie just over the top of the casket (Plates 349, 350).

CONSTRUCTION - Cut a layer of green burlap the size of the design. Place a layer of two-inch mesh chicken wire over this for reinforcement. Add a second layer of burlap. Sew the layers together with No. 28 spool wire or green florist thread, using a curved upholstery needle. Place a layer of waterproof sheeting such as green waxed paper or plastic over this foundation to keep any moisture from seeping through. A large work surface will be necessary to hold this piece while it is under construction.

The foundation greens, plumosus, adiantum (maidenhair fern) or leather leaf fern etc. are now applied with the tips lying over the edge of the foundation for a softening effect. The greens are also sewed to the foundation. With practice they may be held in

place and secured when the flowers are applied. Flowers are wired (see chapter on wiring) with either single or double prongs (Figure 143). Small flowers are wired in clusters; medium-sized blossoms (roses, carnations) in groups of two's or three's; and larger ones (chrysanthemums, lilies, and orchids) are wired singly.

To use the single-prong method, leave one wire extending from the blossoms. This wire goes down through the foundation and is returned up through it and is folded over, thus securing the flowers.

When the double-prong method is used, two prongs of wire are left extended from the blossoms. Push the prongs through the foundation, twist them together with a single twist, bring them back through and flatten them. When applying the blossoms, position each so that it flows from the top center out to the edge. Even though a mass effect is desired and the flowers are to give a solid appearance, their heads must radiate from the top center outward to the edges.

Sew or glue a piece of felt or other soft but substantial fabric the size of the foundation to the underside after all the flowers have been added and the wire ends have been checked to see that none are protruding to mar the casket. Allow openings in this piece for the handles of the casket. A large blanket that is covered entirely with flowers may hang awkwardly at the corners. Remove a square from each corner, allowing the sides to meet (Figure 150). This type of piece is known as a "molded" blanket.

The designs in casket blankets are many. Some are solid compositions of graded blossoms, with small flowers on the outer edges and larger blooms in the center, e.g., pompon chrysanthemums edging, increasing to large mums on the top. Other blankets are made with heavy satin and an overlay of lace or net, or with garlands of blossoms around the edges flowing gracefully from the center.

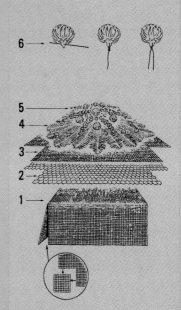

Plate 349A (circa 1958)
A Magnificent Casket Blanket– Garlands of carnations threaded on clear monofilament outlined with table (string) similax encircle the casket. Natural sprays of phalaenopsis orchids flow from the crest of white cattleya orchids. The foundation was made as shown in Figure 150.

Plate 349B
Detail – A detailed view of the casket blanket in Plate 349A. Rolled ribbon is used as an accent, (see Plate 115).

Figure 150
Construction of casket blanket
1– layer of burlap
2– layer of two–inch chicken wire
3– layer of burlap
4– layer of fern or foliage
5– flowers
6– wired flowers single or double prong method

Casket Blankets For Small Children

Casket blankets for small children are delicate in design and appearance. Since they are a great deal smaller in size than those for adults, the heavier foundation construction described previously is unnecessary. A heavy piece of satin or plush is excellent for this foundation. It is covered with lace or some other appropriate material.

The edging of each layer may be scalloped and finished with garlands of small blossoms interspersed with ribbon bows. Flowers at the center of interest are wired and taped and fashioned into large corsages-like clusters with ribbon streamers. They are pinned with corsage pins to the foundation.

Casket pieces for babies may be constructed in small wet foam holders about 3 inches wide and 5 inches long. Cover the base with a piece of soft open-mesh rubber matting. This will keep the foundation from slipping. Ribbon loops and streamers may be worked in with the blossoms.

Parents may like the idea of using the baby's own blanket as an underlay for the floral piece at the service - a beautiful, sentimental idea that is fitting for the occasion (Plates 350, 351). The blanket is folded into whatever position gracefully fits the casket. Flowers are wired, taped, and fashioned into clusters or corsages and are pinned into the folds of the blanket. Smaller clusters may

Plate 350 (circa 1986) Infant Casket Blanket I – Yellow roses with reflexed petals and rolled rose petal buds have been incorporated with agapanthus blossoms, all wired and taped in the manner of bridal work. The individual clusters have been pinned to the folds of the baby's blanket.

Plate 351 (circa 1986)
Infant Casket Blanket II –
Perfection of detail is shown
in this simplified version.
Many variations of color and
material would depend on
the family preference.
Sentiment may be ex-
pressed by incorporating a
favorite toy or stuffed
animal.

be individually pinned in other places adding interest and beauty to the overall composition.

It is usually appropriate in baby work to incorporate small tufts of delicate material and streamers of ribbon. Use a gauge wire that will be strong enough to hold the flowers in position but not so heavy that it forces the flower clusters to stick out stiffly. Baby casket pieces so beautifully made, should be delivered by a responsible person from the shop, who can see that they are properly placed on the tiny caskets.

Miscellaneous Casket Designs

THE ROSARY for the service of a priest, a nun, or a devout Catholic is appropriate. Florist suppliers carry metallic rosary "forms" in silver or gold colors that have the correct number of small clips for holding miniature rosebuds representing the beads of the rosary. This piece may be laid over the top of the casket, or fastened to the inside lid, or placed in the hands of the deceased.

CROSSES are beautiful and symbolic when used as casket pieces. The arms of a cross should be curved backward to fit the curve of the casket. Rubber matting secured to the back of a cross will help prevent it from slipping. The design is left entirely to the discretion of the floral artist concerning the choice of flowers and materials.

For baby services, pre–made satin and lace crosses may be placed on the casket. Garlands or clusters of flowers are fashioned into dainty designs and pinned to these crosses.

A WREATH can be contoured to fit the top of the casket. The mechanics for "bending" a wet foam wreath ring are simple. First, slice the foam with a knife at the exact places on each side where it is to be bent. Then heat the plastic backing with a candle flame at those same points and bend the wreath frame over the edge of the work-table. This procedure only takes a few moments. Cut two wedge-shaped foam plugs to fit the two openings in the wreath foam, pick them in, secure strips of rubber matting to its back, soak it in preservative solution and begin designing. The design of this piece, like that of the cross mentioned above, varies with the designer. Materials may express any season, theme or personal preference, but they must ultimately fit the contour of the casket. Stiff, bulky foliage and flowers are not appropriate for wreaths used as casket pieces.

PALLS are seldom requested. They may be made of a heavy piece of velour or satin, ten to twelve inches in width. They usually cover a casket from one end to the other and may drape several inches below the casket. A second piece may be used to form a cross. Flowers are attached at the center of the cross and at the ends. They may be wired, taped, and finished as corsages, or the pall can be solidly covered in blossoms. This piece is quite tailored in its effect.

The casket in a MILITARY SERVICE is covered with an American flag. No flowers are ever placed on the flag as long as it is covering the casket. The family piece may be any design they wish to select, such as a pillow, wreath, heart, etc.; the design is placed at the head of the casket. If the family prefers a spray, this piece can be placed on the casket before the flag has been placed there, and after it has been removed at the conclusion of the service. The flag is folded by military personnel and is presented to the family before interment.

A CANDLE may be positioned in a casket spray, as shown in Plate 352. The candle may be lighted before and during the funeral service. The florist must always be informed of fire regulations and have the funeral director or clergyman's permission for its use before suggesting the idea to the family.

Plate 352
Memory Candle– A new idea is presented with unusual materials and simple design. The candle could be lighted for prayer, rosary, or traditional services. Rubber matting is glued to the foundation for security.

Plate 353 (circa 1986)
Dutch Treat – Rex begonias, tulips, and ruffled kale share their home with fresh cut allium, broccoli, and asparagus tips—all safely tucked into wet foam. Onions and mushrooms develop the personality of this design.

FLORICULTURE
DEPARTMENT OF HORTICULTURE SCIENCES
TEXAS A & M UNIVERSITY

Part 7

Flowering and Foliage Plants

Chapter 33 INTRODUCTION

Potted plants may comprise a large percentage of the florist's volume of business. Flowering plants are popular because of their long-lasting qualities. They are being challenged in popularity by foliage plants, which offer even greater dependability. Florists should have a basic knowledge of the cultural requirements of plants to keep them growing and healthy. By giving this information to customers freely and accurately, good will is established, and a genuine service is rendered to customers.

Florists should know the common and botanical names of plants, in order to quickly identify a plant for a customer. All potted plants should be clearly labeled so that the customer may ask for plants by name. New introductions in the stock, particularly, should be labeled for the convenience of customers and shop personnel.

FOLIAGE PLANTS

Architects and interior decorators have learned to appreciate the value of foliage plants as decorative materials; it is no longer uncommon for these two groups to alter an architectural feature to use foliage plants more advantageously. Building plans have designed in provisions for the extensive use of these plants. Gardening and home decoration magazines have been influential in popularizing the use of green plants.

Most foliage plants are natives of the tropics, but they are generally adaptable to indoor culture. They vary in ability to endure neglect, abuse, and abnormal conditions. Florists should familiarize themselves with the characteristics of the most commonly used plant species-their habits of growth, their soil requirements, and the amount of light they need to maintain a healthy green color. With this knowledge florists will be able to help customers choose plants to satisfy their particular requirements. This information is available today from many sources-in garden magazines, in various professional journals, and in numerous fine books on plants. Newspapers are publishing this information about foliage plants on their gardening pages and websites.

FLOWERING PLANTS

Many flowering potted plants are seasonal while others are available year round. Sometimes temperamental and cantankerous however, they have been and always will be, a favorite of many flower lovers. Some of them have acquired through the years, a value beyond their natural beauty; they are symbols of various floral holidays and occasions. Can one think of the poinsettia without thinking of Christmas, or the Easter lily without thinking of Easter? There is one other advantage of flowering potted plants. After the flowering season is over many of them can be planted in the home garden, where they will flourish and give beauty for seasons to come.

Flowering plants are received from the growers in the containers in which they were grown. While these containers-pots, boxes, etc.- are acceptable for growing, they are not generally attractive and should be covered or decorated so they will not detract from the beauty of the blossoms. This pot decoration should be secondary to the flower. Do not smother the natural beauty of a plant with unnecessary decorations. Plants that are leggy or those with damaged foliage can be improved by decorations which cover these defects.

The region of the country in which one lives, and the taste of one's customers will influence greatly the selection of materials for pot decorations. The choice is enlarged each year by the introduction of new plastics, papers, foils and pot covers. Pot dressings help convey the message and express the holiday season or occasion for which the gift is being given. (See chapter 35: Decorating Potted Plants.)

Chapter 34
THE CARE AND HANDLING
OF FLOWERING AND FOLIAGE PLANTS

This chapter on the care of plants in the home and office is provided for those people who do not have a green thumb. It is not a substitute for experience or professional training, but will enable almost everyone to enjoy their plants without fear of losing them. In the following paragraphs, the prevention of difficulty rather than correction will be stressed.

SOIL

A good soil mixture is absolutely necessary for the growth of any plant, whether it be in the pot or in the field. It is the anchor and stability for the plant as well as providing the source of base nutrients for proper growth and development. If you have bought mature plants from a professional grower of flowers you will not need to worry about the soil until the plants need to be repotted. When you repot your plants, or pot rooted cuttings, give them a soil mixture that will provide adequate nutrients, high water-holding capacity, and good aeration. Most commercial soil mixtures will provide these things.

No plant should be potted in soil that is dried out. The soil should be damp enough to hold together when squeezed in the hand, but not so damp that it does not crumble when dropped on a surface from the height of one foot. If the soil is so dry that it is powdery, and it sometimes gets this way in storage, it should be sprinkled and turned over several times a few hours before it is used for potting. A soil mix containing peat moss should be moistened thoroughly before being used; otherwise it will compete with the plant for water during the first few days after potting.

WATERING

Watering is another element which is important to plant care and maintenance. "How often to water?" is a difficult question to answer. It can be answered, however, by observing plants carefully and remembering certain basic principles. Generally, most plants can withstand wilting better than over-watering. Plants with thick, fleshy leaves are more likely to withstand the hazards of dry soil. Plants with large, thin leaves lose water rapidly and since they have no water reserves, soon wilt if the soil does not supply more.

Plants nearing maturity and bearing blossoms require a great deal more water than young plants with smaller leaf area.

The most common watering malpractice is probably over-watering. This trouble is most pronounced when plants are placed in non-porous or non-draining containers. The possibility of over-watering can be reduced somewhat by providing drainage whereby the excess water will flow off. If non-draining containers are used, add at least one inch of gravel to the bottom. If you are planting an urn, jardiniere or similar deep vessel, add one inch of gravel for each four inches of container height.

Remember always to water thoroughly;

add enough so that all of the soil is completely soaked and drips from the bottom of the pot. Do not let plants sit in the excess water or root problems will develop quickly. Soil that has become very dry contracts and separates from the side of the pot; in this condition it is difficult to water well, as all the water drains around the soil out the bottom of the pot rather than being absorbed by the soil. When this happens, water the pots twice, allowing an interval between watering of at least thirty minutes. Or place the pot in a pail of water and let it soak thoroughly, but not longer than 5 minutes or root deterioration may occur.

LIGHT

Light is the most important factor in the growth of potted plants. Plants use the energy of light to convert various raw materials into simple sugars, carbohydrates, and more complex organic compounds in a process known as photosynthesis. If light is insufficient, the plants will starve, and they cannot be fed artificially. Chemical fertilizers, carelessly called "plant foods", are used by the plants as building blocks to manufacture food, but they are not food in themselves. More accurately, they are materials used by plants in the food manufacturing process.

Light, then, is absolutely necessary for plant growth. How much is necessary? Interior plants generally do not need full sunlight but, in spite of this, most of them would profit from more light than they get. If your plants are not growing properly and you know that the soil condition and water supply are adequate, light is probably inadequate. Gradually increase the amount of light each day, by moving the plants closer to the window or by drawing the curtains, or by whatever step is available. Do not place a houseplant in full sun after it has been in a dark room for several weeks or it will sunburn. Acclimate it gradually. Acclimation is equally important from the opposite point of view. Plants that come in from the high light levels at the grower's should be held at an intermediate light level (750-1000 fc) for two to three weeks before being delivered to the lower light environments of a home or office interior.

TEMPERATURE

Proper temperatures for plants are often hard to find in the house. A hot, dry atmosphere shortens the life of flowers. Flowering potted plants should receive temperatures from 65° to 76° during the day, and 55° to 60° at night. To get the most out of flowering potted plants in the home, move them to a cool spot at night.

Foliage plants are more tolerant of high temperature but they prefer temperatures between 65° and 70°. Avoid placing plants in front of heating or air conditioning outlets. Hot or cold air blowing on plants often causes an increase in the rate of transpiration and the leaves may get brown edges and drop or die.

HUMIDITY

Air in most modern interiors is extremely dry during the winter. A humidifier can help plant growth. If one cannot be used, water tight trays beneath the plants filled with constantly moist sand or gravel help increase humidity around the plants. Pots must be placed on, not in, the wet sand or gravel.

Misting with distilled water over the leaves daily can help a plant overcome the stress of low humidity. Simply grouping plants together will create a micro climate of increased humidity around the plants. Plants needing constant high humidity such as orchids or ferns are best kept in kitchens or bathrooms where humidity often runs higher. A relative humidity between 40% and 60% is best for most plants, but typically difficult to maintain in the house.

FERTILIZING

Newly purchased plants have been well fertilized in the greenhouse. They seldom need additional fertilizer for several weeks. If plants are to be discarded after flowering; there will be no benefit from fertilizing. Plants that are being kept on in the home should be scheduled on a regular fertilization program.

Fertilizing once a month is adequate for most house plants that are producing new growth or flowers. During mid-winter (December, January) when no new growth is apparent, fertilizer should be withheld.

Do not use fertilizer to stimulate new growth on a plant located in a poor growing environment. Lack of growth is more often due to improper light or water than to nutritional deficiencies. In such cases adding fertilizer may actually cause additional injury.

The dropping of lower leaves, an overall yellow-green color, or weak growth may indicate a need for fertilization. Since these same symptoms may result from poor light or overwatering, carefully evaluate all conditions before fertilizing.

Water-soluble complete fertilizers have been formulated for houseplants, and they are easy to use. Since formulations vary, be sure to follow directions carefully. Do not apply more than directed. The roots of potted plants are restricted and easily burned by the application of too much fertilizer at one time.

Never apply liquid fertilizers to wilted plants. Water the plants first, and apply fertilizer after the plants have recovered and the soil is still moist.

GENERAL MAINTENANCE

A plant's health also depends upon cleanliness and insect control. Keep all leaves free of dust, which can clog the stomata and eventually kill the plant. Dust can easily be removed from leaves with a smooth surface by wiping them with a clean cloth and tepid water. The insects most likely to affect interior plants are aphids, spider mites, scale, and mealy bugs. Mild infestations of these four common pests may be controlled by rinsing the affected areas of the plant with a mild solution of soap and water or by applying rubbing alcohol with a cotton swab. Commercial insecticides or insecticide soaps may be used in more extreme cases.

Chapter 35
DECORATING POTTED PLANTS

Before plants are decorated, the pots should be cleaned and the plants thoroughly watered. While the plants are draining, dead foliage and damaged blossoms should be removed. The leaves of the foliage plants should be cleaned at this time. There are several commercial preparations on the market that are useful for cleaning and shining foliage. Do not use oil on the foliage, it clogs the leaf pores (stomata) and collects dust. It is a personal aesthetic choice whether or not to polish the plant leaves. Some customers may find it offensive to have anything other than the natural plant, while others find the shiny leaves perfectly acceptable. Textured or fuzzy leaves of many flowering plants, e.g., gloxinia, African violet, geraniums, etc., should not be shined with these products.

The next important step in dressing plants is to decide on the "face" of the plant. There is usually one side of the plant that is prettier than the other side. Pot wraps are designed so that the prettier side of the plant is shown to the best advantage.

Pot trims enhance the beauty of plants and increase their sales value. Florists must be constantly alert for new methods and novel ideas for dressing plants, especially to convey holiday themes. Manufacturers present a great variety of ornamental containers from baskets to metal and pottery, which may be used to increase the attractiveness of plants. One may decide to transfer some of the plants from pots to these ornamental containers. After the plants are transferred, decorative accessories may be added according to the designer's wishes. Accessories such as branches, twigs, and bows are secured to picks and inserted into the soil.

Standard materials for pot trims are polyfoil, and preformed plastic covers. Novelty materials include burlap, cellophane, straw hats, fabric, and unique ceramic and plastic containers.

Plate 354 (circa 1986) Easter Lily – The four cornered foil treatment with folded edges described in the text is shown with a violet and white ribbon and raffia bow treatment.

POLYFOIL

Polyfoil is a very useful pot trim; and a large number of variations in color and texture are available (Plate 354). Variations of basic wraps can be made by allowing the four corners of the foil sheet to stand erect, as when decorating a tall plant, or the two rear corners may be up and the two front ones downward. To vary this design, pull the corners tightly, thus straightening the sides; a butterfly effect will result. The length of the foil is determined by the size of the plant and not by the size of the pot. Should the plant grow tall (Easter lily) the foil may extend rather high; if the plant branches low, the foil should be shorter and follow the curves of the plant. Study the proportion of the pot dressing in relation to the plant before cutting the foil. Foil may be lined with decorative cellophane for a variation or to fill in spaces between pot and leaves.

Place the pot on the foil a little forward of center with a flat edge forward. This will allow the back portion of the foil to extend higher than the front, giving more background. A neat finish is given the wrap by folding in the edges of the foil approximately one-half inch on all four sides. Pleat the flat edge of the polyfoil and pull it up on to the front face of the pot, folding it over the pot edge. Staple to the plastic pot. Repeat this procedure three more times, pleating and pulling each flat edge up and stapling midway on each side to the plastic pot. Finish the foiling process by smoothing each of the four corner pockets created; place middle finger of both hands on side-by-side staple attachments. Using index fingers, then pull the pocket sideways keeping it next to the pot, to smooth any wrinkles. Press pocket gently against pot. Finally, add a picked bow and stapled ribbon band around the pot if desired. (Figure 151B)

A three-cornered design is sometimes better for small plants, especially hyacinths, tulips, and most 4" pots (Figure 151A). The corner next to the face of the plant is turned in and folded down. The opposite corner extends high in the back of the plant and the two side corners extend outward. This design produces a Dutch cap effect and is very suitable for Dutch bulbs. It may also be shaped to resemble shamrocks on St. Patrick's Day.

WICKER BASKETS

Wicker baskets as containers for potted plants are beautiful to present as gifts. Their great variety in texture, color, and shape make them suitable for almost any personality or occasion. They may be used for many other things after the plants are gone. The most important factor to remember when using baskets is that they MUST BE LINED TO BE WATERPROOF to protect furniture from moisture. Many sizes and shapes of pre-made basket liners are stocked by florist suppliers for use in unlined baskets (Plates 355-362).

The practical waterproof liner is unattractive, especially in open weave baskets; therefore, different types of mosses have become popular as camouflage. Moss can cause problems for the innocent designer, so there are a few points to keep in mind. Shake excess debris from the moss and spray it with a floral sealer to prevent it from shedding further. Add a touch of moss green floral spray to keep its color from fading. Do not allow the moss edges to overlap the container, because it may act as a siphon and draw the moisture from the freshly watered plant. Remember, wet, soggy moss will smell musty and eventually support mold.

Ground moss (sheet moss) is the most practical liner cover, while Spanish moss is more useful as a decorative camouflage to hide mechanics above the container, such as attachments to a bare branch, etc.

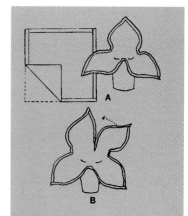

Figure 151
Polyfoil Mechanics – A – Three corner design using foil: 1) place pot on point of folded corner, 2) bring up folded edge to top of pot, 3) raise back point, 4) adjust side points. B – Four corner design with foil: Instead of folding the corner in as in (A), bring each side up and pleat, front first, then back, then sides and staple to the plastic pot.

Plate 355 (circa 1986) Whimsey – This playful puppy catches a mouthful of tulips in her spring garden of potted amaryllis and cut redbud.

Plate 356 (circa 1986) Cornhusk Bow – This plastic-lined hat basket with its edge frayed, is centered with a very authoritative cornhusk medallion, which creates a strong focal point on this chrysanthemum plant.

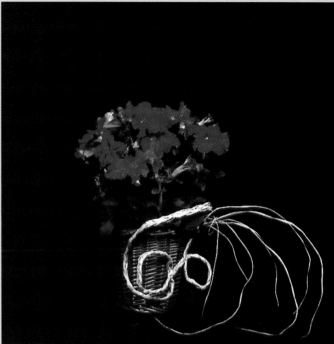

Plate 357 (circa 1986)
Petunia – This 4 inch potted petunia fits its basket perfectly, and the braided raffia continues in use after the plant is transferred to the garden.

Plate 358 (circa 1986)
Wolf in Sheep's Clothing – This big bad wolf is sneaking a Valentine through a forest of tulips and winged elm.

Plate 359 (circa 1986)
"Bird of Paradise" – This cheerful parrot perches in his nest of tulips, crossandra and petunia plants. Individual bulbs may be separated from a larger pot by gently washing the soil from the roots. Retaining the bulb assures the natural life of the blossom.

Plate 360 (circa 1986)
Easter Basket – After Easter the narcissus and petunias may be transplanted into the garden, while the green peperomia would be happy on the windowsill, keeping company with the duckling.

Plate 361 (circa 1986)
Living Treasure – Individually potted syngonium, zebra plant and daisy chrysanthemums fill this hand-woven carryall with living gold.

Plate 362 (circa 1986)
Stately Bromeliad – A wicker jardiniere with its wisteria vine and fungii add stately importance to this bromeliad. A plastic liner protects the furniture.

PRE-FORMED POT COVERS

Pre-formed pot covers made from cellophane, polyfoil, or other plastic materials are very quick and easy to use. They are available in most of the common pot sizes in a wide assortment of colors and patterns. Simply place the potted plant into the cover and secure with a couple of staples or dots of pan glue at the pot edge. Embellish with ribbons and accessories if desired.

MISCELLANEOUS POT DRESSINGS

BURLAP and fabric in various colors may be purchased by the yard from the display supply houses or fabric stores. It is an excellent pot dressing for holidays and theme events.

Cover pots first with polyfoil or plastic to prevent damage from drainage and apply burlap or fabric in the same manner that polyfoil is applied. The contrast of textures between satin ribbon and burlap or other fabric is excellent for pot dressings. Ribbon complements the texture of the blossoms while burlap repeats the texture of the stems or foliage of the plant, especially in the case of azaleas and hydrangeas. The cross threads of burlap may be removed for a frayed-edge effect. These threads can be tied into a bow or cut in short lengths and secured to picks for tassel effects as fillers.

JARDINIERES of ceramic, various metals, plastic and plastic compounds are labor saving pot covers. They also prevent drainage moisture from damaging furniture. When the plants arrive they can be cleaned, watered, and placed (pot and all) into the jardinieres; then the accessories may be added. Sheet moss, lichens, or bark chips, may be used to cover the soil, while tufts of cellophane or dried branches may be placed to fill the voids. The classic terra cotta pot and saucer adapt perfectly to many home décor themes, but they are not water proof and should contain a liner (Plates 364-369).

Fresh pine branches or prepared foliages add greatly to Christmas plants. The branches can easily be stuck into the soil. Decorative accessories are used to create a theme and may range from a simple bow, bare branches, silk or dried materials, and holiday "stick-ins," to add-on gifts such as a stuffed animal, corsage or potpourri sachet.

STRAW HATS with plastic liners are excellent for pot dressings at Easter, Mother's Day, and Father's Day. Place the plant in the hat and bring the brim up in the back and down in the front. Novelties such as rabbits, etc., nestled in a bed of shredded cellophane in the hat add interest for Easter (Plates 356, 357).

When the hat is used for dressing a Mother's Day plant, it may contain garden tools, packages of seed, or plants suitable for replanting. Stems of plants that root easily from cuttings may be added. Place the cuttings in orchid tubes filled with water to keep them fresh. Cuttings of coleus, various ivies, wandering Jew, geraniums, Chinese evergreen, etc., are excellent.

Plate 363 (circa 1986)
Geranium, Jardiniere – A wood-grained composition jardiniere holds this potted geranium, and the raffia-tied river cane armature adds interest.

Plate 364 (circa 1986)
Monkey Business – The armature becomes a trapeze for an active monkey.

Plate 365 (circa 1986)
High Tech – The philodendron is displayed in a mylar pot and decorated with clear acryllic "spaghetti".

Plate 366 (circa 1986)
Jungle – This incredible twisted vine holds the bromeliad in a moss-covered plastic pot.

Plate 367 (circa 1986)
Azalea – The decorative armature of pussy willow creates a natural accent that is compatible with the sheet moss and fresh mushrooms.

Plate 368 (circa 1986)
Incredible Rex – This rex begonia in a clay pot is dramatically accented with a piece of dried kelp. The rich satin ribbon provides a transition in color and texture from plant to pot.

For Father's Day a straw hat dressing may be decorated with garden tools, fishing flies, bobbers, hooks, etc. A stuffed animal may be incorporated with plants for the birthday of a young member of the family (Plates 359-361).

Chapter 36 DISH GARDENS

People yearning for a bit of nature, but limited in space, have turned to dish gardens in increasing numbers. Designing with living plant materials can present many challenges. It is easy to place a few plants in a container and call it a dish garden, but it requires careful planning and some knowledge of plant materials to exploit the full possibilities of plants in small containers.

A dish garden, properly designed, is a conversation piece. A well-designed dish garden may be an accident, but more likely it is the result of the application of the principles of good design discussed in previous chapters of this book. A good dish garden should have unity, balance, good proportion, and pleasing variations in texture, color, and line. Dish gardens are most successful when they are built around one specific theme or idea; if they are not, it will be difficult to give them a center of interest. Without a center of interest a dish garden is merely a collection of plants, and must rely on unique combinations of forms, colors, and sizes to look appealing.

There is one basic difference between designing a dish garden and designing a floral arrangement-the dish garden will grow and change its characteristics; the floral arrangement will not. For this reason, among others, plants for dish gardens should be selected carefully. For any given dish garden, the plants chosen should have similar growth rates and similar growth requirements. It is obvious that a fast growing plant will soon destroy all semblance of proportion in a planter if it is mixed with slower growing species. If plants that require a lot of water are used with plants native to the desert; both cannot be expected to thrive.

It does not make much difference whether the container is chosen to fit the plants or the plants to fit the container, but they should complement each other. Plants with strong, severe lines should be used with containers that have the same characteristics. Heavy pottery and simple brass or copper containers, for example, are suitable for such plants as sansevierias, dieffenbachias, Chinese evergreens, and peperomias. Baskets and woven woods offer a wide variety of textures and themes that go well with all kinds of plants – and interiors. Waterproof liners of plastic or galvanized metal should be used in all unglazed pottery, brass, wood and woven containers to prevent damage to both the container and the furniture that it is displayed on.

Some thought should be given to the eventual use of the dish garden and to the type of room or office in which it will be placed. Delicate ferns and lacy-leafed plants should not be placed in a dish garden designed for a modern office. Knowledge of the use of the dish gardens will also help you select the container and accessories. Figurines may be made a permanent part of an arrangement, setting its theme. Elves, pixies, and storybook characters can be used as the basis for an excellent dish garden that appeals to children and the young at heart. An old horseshoe may be combined with cactus and succulents for a Western arrangement for use in a ranch home or in a rustic environment.

Natural dried materials can be incorporated in dish gardens with success, either as accessories or as part of the major plan. Other choices might be shells, driftwood, grasses, blossoms, seedpods, unusual rock formations, and fresh vegetables such as onions, asparagus, and mushrooms—the list is almost endless.

Before you plant a dish garden, check the materials for the following points:

Will the plant materials grow well together? Is there sufficient variety in form, textures, and colors so that the arrangement will be interesting? Is there too much variety? Is the accessory material necessary? Is the container suitable for the theme?

The design of a dish garden will be determined to some extent by whether it is to be viewed from one side or two, from eye level or above. Coffee table pieces are viewed not only from above but also from the sides at a low level, and should display something of interest on all sides. Regardless of the problem of view, most dish gardens should have small plants in the foreground to tie the planting to the container and break the bare lines of the container edge; vines and trailing plants are good for this purpose. Tall plants should be placed in the background of a one-sided design or in the center of one that is to be viewed from all sides.

After the last plant has been added and the soil firmed around the roots, the soil may be covered with moss, crushed rock, bark chips, lichen, or colored sand to give a finished appearance. In elaborate dish gardens, paths and trails are sometimes made. These should be carefully executed for both stability and to give a natural look.

TRADITIONAL dish gardens are usually made by grouping a collection of tropical plants that enjoy the same growing conditions, i.e., light, water, and humidity. Ceramic containers and plastic terracotta colored saucers are especially practical and cost effective to use. If the container depth is greater than 3 inches, line the bottom with $1/2$ inch of pea gravel or crushed pottery to act as a drainage reservoir. If the container is less than 3 inches deep, do not add drainage material as there will not be enough soil to sustain the plants. In both instances, the addition of a small amount of activated charcoal to keep the soil "sweet" is advised. Fill the container above this drainage layer with the potting mixture most suitable for the plants. For most dish gardens, plants growing in 2 to 4- inch pots are about the right size. Remove the pots, taking care not to disturb or break the roots, and set them in holes scooped out of the potting mixture. Be sure that they are planted at the same level in the soil as they

Plate 369
Dish Garden, Construction –
All the components of this garden are ready and waiting. The branch is pan-glued into the plastic foam,which is pan-glued to the container. (Pan glue does not melt plastic foam.)

Plate 370
Dish Garden, Complete – The moss–covered pot of dwarfed iris is removable. The other plants may be allowed to spread or a new plant may be set into the same space. The winged elm branch arches over the plants to create balance and to draw the eye back into the design.

Plate 371 (circa 1986)
Anniversary gift – Several variegated peperomia plants are combined to give a mass effect in this basket. A cymbidium orchid corsage accents the handle and may be easily removed and worn to the anniversary dinner.

Plate 372
Tiptoe through …The tulips tower above begonias, pink arrowhead, and artillery plant, all nestled together with washed river stones.

Plate 373
Living basket – This basket of pothos is dramatically changed into a fantasy with its living handle of Scotch broom and fresh flowers– each side cluster is tucked into small containers of wet foam inserted into the soil.

were growing before, and compress the soil firmly around each plant.

The EUROPEAN-STYLE dish gardens (usually called European gardens) are different in that usually one or more blooming plants are combined with foliage plants. This gives a more luxurious display of colors and textures than plain foliage plants, but requires expertise in selecting plants that enjoy living together. In larger gardens, a blooming plant in a 4- inch pot may be left in its pot and placed into the garden. A good sales point is to advise the customer that he can easily retain color by replacing the 4- inch pot with a new one-just by lifting it out and setting in the fresh one.

Bare branches and dried materials offer endless possibilities for adding interesting lines and creative natural accents to dish gardens. Plate 369 shows how to stabilize a branch by placing it in

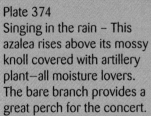

Plate 374
Singing in the rain – This azalea rises above its mossy knoll covered with artillery plant–all moisture lovers. The bare branch provides a great perch for the concert.

Plate 375
Container with accessory – The fluted ceramic pot is enhanced with honeysuckle vine hot glued to it in a manner that allows the rhythmic swirls to give motion.

Plate 376
Fluted container – completed Dieffenbachia and philodendron contrast beautifully with the container while the swirling vine adds interest to the composition.

a small square of styrofoam that is hot glued to the bottom of the container. The branch is pointed and touched with hot pan-glue before it is inserted into the foam.

When using facsimiles of nature (birds, mushrooms, etc.), be sure they are positioned to create harmony and to look as natural as possible.

Some designers include facilities for cut flowers in their dish gardens. Small plastic tubes filled with water can be inserted into the soil at strategic places for holding a few cut flowers, and for a larger grouping, a small block of wet foam wrapped in foil or thin plastic may be buried between the plants. Bromeliads have natural containers formed by their leaves that are suitable for holding a single flower such as an orchid spray, protea, or a bright nerine lily.

Chapter 37
SELECTED FLOWERING PLANTS:
Recommendations

AFRICAN VIOLET-Cold water on leaves causes yellowish blotches. Add tepid water from the bottom.

AMARYLLIS-Should be planted in pot 2 inches larger than bulb diameter. Leave 1/3 of bulb above soil level. Keep soil moist. No rest period is required. Pots moved outside in summer; can be moved inside for winter flowering.

AZALEA-Give bright, indirect light. Keep soil moist-cool temperature.

BEGONIA, REIGER-Susceptible to mildew and stem rot. Stake to prevent breakage. Use bright, indirect light.

CALCEOLARIA-Likes cool room-adequate but not too bright light.

CHENILLE PLANT-Prefers warm temperature and bright light. Can be used in summer outdoors-sun or partial shade.

CHRISTMAS CACTUS-Needs short days to flower; over-watering causes rapid deterioration.

CINERARIA-If possible, keep cool. Takes good judgment to avoid over-watering or under-watering.

CROSSANDRA-Give adequate light; pinch to cause branching.

CYCLAMEN-Keep cool if possible. Place in bright, indirect light.

EXACUM-Avoid over-watering. Give bright, indirect light. Can be used for summer bedding in partial shade.

EASTER LILY-Remove anthers before pollen sheds. Give bright light, cool nights. Keep out of drafts. Avoid dark storage-buds may abort, leaves turn yellow. Avoid over-watering.

GERANIUM-Needs high light. Avoid excessive dryness-leaf edges turn brown. Better on patios and porches.

GERBERA-High light-do not over-water or allow to wilt. Prefers warm temperatures.

GLOXINIA-Give bright, indirect light. Do not let water stand in crown of plant. If too dark, young buds will not develop.

HIBISCUS-Needs high light. Keep moist. Pots moved outside for summer can be moved indoors for winter flowering.

HYACINTH, TULIP AND DAFFODIL-Display when barely showing color. They open rapidly. Keep cool, avoid extreme dryness. Plant bulbs in garden after flowering. Retain leaves as long as possible to aid bulbs in storing energy for next year's blooms.

HYDRANGEA-Requires frequent watering, but avoid water-logging. If plant wilts, submerge entire pot in a pail of room temperature water then allow it to drain.

KALANCHOE-Keep in high light or under a reading lamp in the home, to retain original color. Avoid over-watering.

ORNAMENTAL PEPPER-Give high light; will tolerate low humidity.

POINSETTIA-For maximum keeping quality, give plenty of light. Protect from cold and drafts, by using a sleeve closed at the top, between point of sale and customer's vehicle. Remove from shipping boxes as soon as possible. Avoid temperatures below 55°F.

SELECTED FOLIAGE PLANTS: Recommendations

Plants That Will Withstand Most Adverse Conditions and Abuse

Scientific Name	Common Name	Scientific Name	Common Name
Aglaonema spp.	Chinese Evergreen	*Howea belmoreana*	Kentia Palm
Aspidistra elatior	Cast Iron Plant	*Pandanus veitchii*	Screwpine
Cissus rhombifolia	Grape Ivy	*Philodendron*	
Crassula arborescens	Jade Plant	*Oxycardium*	Heartleaf Philodendron
Diefenbachia spp.	Dumbcane	*Sansevieria spp.*	Mother-in-law's Tongue
Dracaena fragrans	Corn Plant	*Syngonium spp.*	Nephthytis, Arrowhead
Epipremnum aureum	Scindapus, Devil's Ivy	*Tradescantia spp.*	Wandering Jew
Hemigraphis colorata	Colorado Ivy		

Plants That Will Tolerate Low to Medium Light Intensities 100-500 fc

Scientific Name	Common Name	Scientific Name	Common Name
Aglaonema spp.	Chinese Evergreen	*Ficus spp.*	Rubber Plant, Weeping Fig, Fiddleleaf Fig
Anthurium crystallinum	Anthurium	*Fittonia verschaffeltii*	Nerve Plant
Aphelandra squarrosa	Zebra Plant	*Helxine soleri*	Baby Tears
Asparagus spp.	Plumosis, Sprengeri	*Monstera deliciosa*	Split-leaf Philodendron
Asplenium nidus	Bird's Nest Fern	*Nephrolepsis spp.*	Boston Fern, Fluffy Ruffle Fern
Brassaia spp.	Schefflera, Dwarf Schefflera		
Caryota mitis	Fishtail Palm	*Philodendron spp.*	Philodendron
Chamaedorea spp.	Bamboo Palm, Neanthe Bella Palm	*Pilea spp.*	Aluminum Plant, Artillery Plant
Chlorophytum spp.	Spider Plant	*Platyceriumbifurcatum*	Staghorn Fern
Chrysalidocarpus lutescens	Butterfly Palm	*Plectranthus spp.*	Swedish Ivy
Cyrtomium falcatum	Holly Fern	*Polypodium oreum*	Rabbit's Foot Fern
Dieffenbachia spp.	Dumbcane	*Spathiphyllum spp.*	Peace Lily, Closet Plant
Dracaena spp.	Marginata, Ribbon Plant, Corn Warneckei	*Syngonium spp.*	Nephthytis Arrowhead
		Tolmiea menziesii	Piggy Back Plant

Plants That Will Tolerate High Light Conditions over 500 fc

Scientific Name	Common Name	Scientific Name	Common Name
Aechmea spp.	Bromeliad	*Euphorbia spp.*	Milk Tree, Crown of Thorns
Araucaria excelsa	Norfolk Island Pine	*Maranta spp.*	Prayer Plant
Cacti spp.	Cactus	*Pedilanthus tithymaloides*	Redbird Cactus
Codiaeum spp.	Croton	*Podocarpus macrophyllus maki*	Southern Yew
Crassula argentea	Jade Plant	*Sansevieria spp.*	Mother-in-law's Tongue
Cryptanthus spp.	Bromeliad		

Plants with Colorful or Variegated Leaves

Scientific Name	Common Name	Scientific Name	Common Name
Acalypha spp.	Copper Plant	*Gynura auramiaca*	Velvet Plant
Aucuba japonica variegata	Gold Dust Plant	*Hedera helix 'Glacier'*	Glacier English Ivy
Begonia masoniana	Iron Cross Begonia	*Hemographis colorata*	Colorado Ivy
Begonia rex cv.	Rex Begonia	*Hoya carnosa variegata*	Variegated Wax Plant
Bromeliad spp.	Bromeliad	*Hypoestes spp.*	Polka Dot Plant
Caladium spp.	Caladium	*Maranta bicolor*	Prayer Plant
Codiaeum variegatum	Croton	*Pandanus vietchii variegata*	Variegated Screwpine
Coleus spp.	Coleus	*Peperomia obtusifolia variegata*	Variegated Peperomia
Dieffenbachia spp.	Dumbcane	*Polyscias balfouriana marginata*	Variegated Balfour
Epipremnum spp.	Devil's Ivy, Marble Queen	*Rhoeo discolor*	Moses-in-the-Cradle
Ficus elastica variegata	Variegated Rubber Tree	*Fittonia verschaffeltii*	Nerve Plant

Low Creeping Plants for Interior Plantscapes

Scientific Name	Common Name	Scientific Name	Common Name
Cissus rhombifolia	Grape Ivy	*P. minima*	Miniature Peperomia
Epipremnum aureum	Pothos, Devils Ivy	*P.pellucida*	Peperomia
Episcia spp.	Flame Violet	*Peperomia crassifolia*	Trailing Peperomia
Ficus pumilla	Creeping Fig	*Philodendron oxycardium*	Heartleaf Philodendron
Fittonia verschaffeltii	Nerve Plant	*Pilea involucrata*	Creeping Charlie
Hedera spp.	English Ivy	*P. nummularifolia*	Creeping Charlie
Helxine soleri	Baby Tears	*Tradescantia spp.*	Wandering Jew
		Zebrina pendula	Wandering Jew

Plants That Will Grow in Water

Scientific Name	Common Name	Scientific Name	Common Name
Aglaonema simplex	Chinese Evergreen	*Philodendron oxycardium*	Heartleaf Philodendron
Alternanthera spp.	Joseph's Coat	*Syngonium spp.*	Nephthytis, Arrowhead
Coleus bicolor	Coleus	*Tradescantia spp.*	Wandering Jew
Hedera helix	English Ivy		

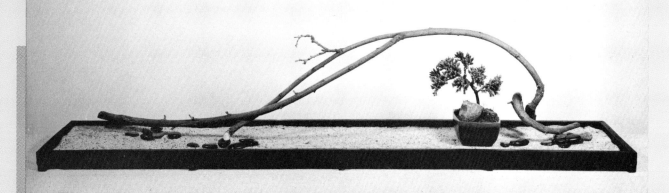

Chapter 38   BONSAI

BONSAI - the Oriental culture of dwarfing plants and recreating nature in miniature is a fine art in horticultural achievement. Bonsai is pronounced "bon-si"; 'bon' meaning tray or container, "sai" meaning trees or woody plants. They range in size from a few inches to several feet in height. This culture is several hundred years old. A number of specimen trees in existence today exceed 250 years of age. The practice of growing bonsai takes patience and time, but is most rewarding. Widespread appreciation of bonsai in America developed with Oriental influence in architecture, gardens, flower arranging (Ikebana), and other art forms about the year 1950. Through his devotion to nature, the Oriental's purpose is to express his "oneness" with nature, both in art and philosophy. The Westerner need not try to follow the traditional Japanese approach. He may create to suit his own taste and blend the trees with the decor of the office, home, or garden.

The source of the plants is either from the nursery or from the mountainous woodlands. Plants from the nursery are carefully selected for their form. The training for a specific shape is accomplished by wiring the trunk and branches, forcing the growth into the desired shape, and skillful selective pruning. Plants that are found in the forest, dwarfed naturally from the struggle for existence, are cared for in the nursery for a year or two and then potted.

The general rules of caring for most potted plants also apply to the care of bonsai. The pots must not be allowed to dry out causing the plant to wither from killing the roots. They must be fed periodically to keep them in a healthy condition. Repotting at least every two years is usually necessary. Use a good, loose potting soil mixture and sand. Root pruning is done at this time.

The artist's aim is to recreate in spirit the natural growth of each species and with the beholder's imagination, recall familiar scenes.

Bonsai are classified according to:

A. Types of growth:

1. Formal-in which the growth represents perfection in its habit according to the variety.

2. Informal - represented by the twisted, curving habit of growth.

B. Style of growth:

1. Formal upright - representing a specimen tree in a woodland, its trunk is straight with lateral branches.

2. Informal upright - the trunk of the tree may curve casually as an old tree in an orchard.

3. Slanting - the main trunk appears to slant at some forty-five degrees, showing the effects of the elements of nature.

4. Semi-cascading - the tree slants definitely to one side and is approaching a horizontal position.

5. Full-cascade - represents a plant hanging over a cliff.

C. Size of growth:

Mame - Lilliputian, not taller than five inches

Ko - Six to twelve inches

Chiu - Twelve to twenty inches

Dai - Two feet or more in height

Growing bonsai as a gift or as a hobby is quite rewarding. They are a challenge. The examples shown in Plates 377 — 379 are from Mr. Benz' own private collection, which he began around 1950 and cultivated for nearly 20 years.

Plate 378
Dai-Bonsai (Loblolly Pine) - This informal upright style bonsai developed with native pine, is twenty years old and approximately three feet tall. Its bark and root system show age.

Plate 379
Ko-Bonsai (Juniper) Shimpaku –
A – This slanting style juniper stirs imagination to a scene on a rocky meadow where prevailing winds have shaped the tree.
B – A miniature Shimpaku is in the Mame-bonsai size classification grown informal upright style.

Part 8
Glossary

The *Book of Floral Terminology* published by the American Institute of Floral Designers, serves as the primary reference for definition of terms in this book. *Merriam-Webster's Language Master* electronic dictionary and *The American Heritage Dictionary* are other important sources of reference.

Abstract (design style) – non-realistic use of natural or man-made materials solely as pure elements – line, form, color, texture, in space, evoking a well-thought out emotion.

Abstracting (design technique) – changing a type of plant material in such a way that it looks unnatural, e.g., clipping, folding, tying, twisting, painting, etc.

Accent (secondary principle) – detail added to a design providing additional interest, affecting the totality of the design.

Accessory – an object added to a composition to enhance its design.

Achromatic (color) – free of color, lacking hue; black, white, gray. Neutral colors; not on the color wheel.

Acidifier (care and handling) – any chemical that reduces the pH of a solution; citric acid is the most common acidifier in commercial preservatives.

Advancing (color) – colors predominantly composed of primary red or yellow; e.g., red violet, red, red orange, orange, yellow orange, yellow, yellow green. Also known as aggressive colors and warm colors.

Aesthetic – relating to beauty; visual or emotional.

Aisle – passage between sections of seats.

Aisle carpet – length of canvas or synthetic cloth, usually white, which lays over the aisle for the bridal party to walk on as they enter the wedding ceremony.

Altar – a table for sacred purpose in the focal area of a church or place of worship.

Altar piece – floral arrangement(s) designed for display on or beside the altar.

American Institute of Floral Designers (AIFD) – an organization of professional floral designers established to recognize and promote the art of floral design as a profession whose members set a standard for professionalism and inspire and nurture excellence in the field.

Analogous (color) – a color harmony featuring adjacent colors of the color wheel dominated by one primary.

Anti-transpirant (care and handling) – a spray or dip that slows the water loss from plant stomata, reducing the speed of transpiration.

Arm bouquet – a bouquet of bound flowers carried in the fold of the arm. Also know as a presentation bouquet.

Armature (design technique) – a decorative and/or supportive framework for a floral composition.

Arrangement – the orderly placement of plant and/or floral materials into a container.

Asymmetrical – without symmetry; not having a mirror image on both sides of a plane, axis or point.

Asymmetrical balance (primary principle) – a state of equilibrium where both sides of the arrangement are different and unequal and not a mirror image of each other, yet both sides of the vertical axis maintain similar visual weight. Asymmetrical balance is often referred to as informal or natural balance.

Attendants (wedding) – people who accompany the bride and groom and participate in the wedding ceremony. Bride's attendants are matron or maid of honor, bridesmaids, flower girl, ring bearer. Groom's attendants are best man and groomsmen.

Axis – a bisecting line, real or imaginary, that divides a building, room or floral composition at its central point.

Balance (primary principle) – the division of materials to either side of a central axis providing a feeling of equilibrium and stability. See asymmetrical, symmetrical, mechanical and visual balance.

Baling (design technique) – compressing and tying plant material into a geometric shape, like a bale of hay.

Banding (design technique) – encircling plant or man-made materials in concise and consecutive rings with decorative appointments such as metallic wire, raffia, silk cording, etc. for ornamental purposes.

Basing (design technique) – finishing the foundation of a composition with intricate, textured details, which provide a decorative surface from which the composition emerges. Accomplished with techniques such as clustering, terracing, pavé etc.

Beauty – qualities that please the senses or the mind.

Bent neck (care and handling) – stem wilt just below the head of a cut flower, caused by the lack of water uptake.

Best man (wedding) – Groom's first attendant.

Biedermeier (style) – a round bouquet similar to a nosegay and named for a German style of interior design. Usually designed with compact concentric or spiraling circles of contrasting colors and kinds of flowers.

Binding (design technique) – tying materials together, primarily mechanical.

Binding point (design technique) – any point or place where stems or materials are tied together, e.g., hand-tied bouquet.

Bio-inhibitor (care and handling) – any chemical that retards the growth and activity of bacteria and other microorganisms in cut flower water.

Bisect – divide into two parts.

Blanket – a design replicating a blanket for a bed, on which flowers and foliage are fastened. May be used to cover a casket, gravesite, or horserace winner etc.

Bleeding heart (sympathy) – heart-shaped design pavéd with individual blossoms, and centered with a cluster of red flowers, symbolizing the "blood of Christ" or "bleeding".

Bonsai – the art of dwarf tree culture developed by the Japanese. Roots and shoots of trees and shrubs are pruned to maintain dwarfing, and limbs are intricately wired to encourage graceful forms.

Botanical name – the universal scientific Latin name consisting of genus and species used to classify plants. The genus is always a noun and is capitalized; the species is always an adjective and never capitalized.

Bouquet – a group of flowers; a flower arrangement in a container; flowers and foliage designed in a manner that allows them to be carried. May be wired and taped, tied, loose, or in a foam-based holder.

Bouquet holder – a stem-anchoring device of floral foam (wet or dry), enclosed in a framework of rigid plastic, with a molded handle. Usually used for bridal bouquets.

Boutonniere (wedding) – a flower or cluster of flowers and/or foliage designed to be worn on the lapel of a suit. Usually worn by a man.

Braiding (design technique) – strands of fiber, ribbon, foliage etc. are interwoven to create a decorative accent or accessory in a floral composition.

Breaking of the Glass (wedding) – an act performed by the groom at the end of a Jewish wedding ceremony when he takes a glass wrapped in fabric and steps on it, breaking the glass. This act symbolizes the destruction of the walls of Jerusalem.

Bride (wedding) – lady getting married.

Bridal bouquet (wedding) – a bouquet carried by a bride.

Bridal party (wedding) – see wedding party.

Bridesmaid (wedding) – bride's attendant at a wedding.

Broken wheel (sympathy) – set-piece design composed of an outer circle and five spokes connected to a center hub. A portion of the rim and its adjoining spoke are omitted, thus giving the design its name. The foundation, usually made of plastic foam is covered with flowers.

Bunching (design technique) – several stems of small or delicate material are tied together so they can be inserted into a design as one item.

Bundling (design technique) – tying like or similar materials together so that a radial stem pattern is created above and below the binding point.

Cable tie (mechanics) – thin self-locking plastic strip with many applications for securing and attaching floral components.

Cake top (wedding) – a decorative ornamentation for the top of a cake. May be an heirloom or novelty figure, constructed of fresh or manmade materials.

Candle – wax molded around a wick, which gives light when burned.

Candelabra (wedding) – Ornamental branched candlestick for table or floor.

Care and handling – established post-harvest procedures and techniques based on horticulture research that increase the vase life of cut flowers and foliage.

Cascading bouquet (wedding) – a hand-held wedding bouquet style, in which a portion of the flowers, descend below the main part of the design.

Casket (sympathy) – a rectangular shaped case or chest made of metal or wood, and used to hold a corpse.

Casket blanket (sympathy) – see blanket.

Casket cover (sympathy) – any type of floral design created to cover a portion of, or the entire closed casket. Also known as casket piece and casket spray.

Casket saddle (sympathy) – a container or device, usually made of plastic or coated wire, specifically designed for arranging flowers for the top of a casket.

Chicken wire (mechanics) – pliable fencing wire also known as poultry netting that is used crumpled in a vase to support stems or wrapped over wet foam to provide added strength and security of both foam and stems.

Chroma (color) – the degree of intensity, strength, saturation or purity of a hue or color.

Chuppah (wedding) – a covering under which a Jewish wedding ceremony takes place. It symbolizes the nomadic tent of Israel for the couples new home.

Citric acid (care and handling) – a naturally occurring acid compound from citrus plants, present in many commercial flower foods (preservatives). This acidifier lowers the pH of the water facilitating water uptake.

Clustering (design technique) – the placement of several small textural flowers of a single kind so close together that the individual becomes indistinguishable from the mass.

Collaring (design technique) – Surrounding a flower, bouquet or container rim with natural or man-made leaves or other decorative material to create a finished appearance.

Color (element) – visual response of the eye to reflected rays of light.

Color chart (color) – see color wheel.

Color harmony (color) – the various compatible and/or useful combinations of colors.

Color spectrum (color) – linear diagram of the color wavelength system, in which all hues appear in their proper spectral sequence.

Color wheel (color) – circular diagram of the color pigment system, in which all hues appear in their proper spectral sequence.

Complementary colors (color) – a color harmony composed of any two colors opposite each other on the color wheel.

Composite flower – a hand-made flower created by reassembling detached petals, which are wired or glued together, e.g., glamellia, duchess rose, galax rose.

Composition – the result of organizing floral or man-made materials, according to the elements and principles of design.

Concept – thought or idea representing something comprehended.

Conditioning (care and handling) – the process of holding flowers at room temperature to take up water and insure maximum turgidity.

Construction – a composition that involves building a structure that will be an integral part of a design.

Container – a receptacle of any shape into which plant material is placed. Usually holds water.

Contemporary design – a generic term for any design, which is up to date or currently in favor.

Contrast (primary principle) – emphasis by means of difference. Contrast in a design adds impact through contradiction and opposition.

Cool colors (color) – see receding colors.

Creativity – artistic inventiveness.

Cremation (sympathy) – the disposal of a corpse by means of fire.

Cremains (sympathy) – the ashes remaining after a body has been cremated.

Crescent design – emphasizes the shape of a quarter moon. The design is usually tapered and extended at each end while the center is full and more compact. The crescent may be either symmetrical or asymmetrical in its configuration.

Custom-made – floral arrangements or mechanics designed to meet particular specifications.

Depth (secondary principle) – placement of materials at different levels in and around an arrangement.

Design – planned use of design components to complete an artistic composition suited to a purpose.

Design technique – the manner in which a designer implements specialized procedures and methods for placing plant materials and decorative accessories into a composition, e.g., binding, framing, etc.

Dimension – measurement of extension, e.g., height, width, length, breadth, depth.

Distinction – marked superiority in all aspects, achieved through craftsmanship, inspiration and proficiency; entails beauty, originality, and shows the result of uninhibited creative effort.

Dominance (primary principle) – the visual organization of a design that emphasizes one or more aspects; other components are subordinate.

Dynamic – energy in a design that visually creates a feeling of motion and force.

Easel (sympathy) – a three legged stand used to support set pieces and floral sprays for display at a funeral.

Element – the components or ingredients of design: line, form, space, color, texture, pattern and size.

Emphasis (secondary principle) – area(s) in a composition given special attention.

Epaulet – a corsage designed to flow over the shoulder in all directions.

Epergne – an ornamental stand with one or more separate dishes or trays, usually on arms, used for a table centerpiece for holding fruit and flowers.

Epergnette – small dishes with pegs on the bottom, that will fit into the candle cups of single or branched candelabra, making it look like an epergne.

Equilibrium – a state of balance between opposing forces.

Ethylene (care and handling) – a hormone that stimulates (accelerates) the aging process. Colorless and odorless, ethylene can damage many of our commonly used cut flowers such as carnations, snapdragons, lilies, etc.

Exotic – excitingly or enticingly different or unusual. An informal term for tropical flowers and foliages: "exotics".

Extension – the act or process of increasing something in some way, e.g., an extension wire – lengthening a wire by taping another wire to it.

Facing (design technique) – the turning or directing of a flower head in a certain way in order to increase interest or movement in a design.

Faux finish – literally, "false" effects. A finish simulated with paint products to imitate another material such as marble.

Feathering (personal flowers) – dividing or separating a flower into small components, preparing and reassembling them to resemble a different version of the original. Also known as Frenching.

Fibonacci – a shortened version of Leonardo Pisana's nickname, Filius Bonacci. A mathematician of the 1200's, he clarified the logarithmic sequence, which bears his name: 1, 1, 2, 3, 5, 8, 13, etc.

Filler flower (flower form) – any branched or clustered flower; used to fill in between other blossoms.

Flat spray (sympathy) – a singular flat-backed spray of flowers, either tied or picked, which is displayed by the funeral director on a special rack or on the grave.

Floral adhesive (mechanics) – liquid or aerosol spray glue used to secure fresh flowers or mechanical aids.

Floral art – designing with flowers for the purpose of artistic effect rather than commercial endeavor.

Floral foam (mechanics) – a highly porous plastic compound used to support stems of flowers, foliage and accessories. There are two types: a) wettable, which absorbs water to hold fresh materials, b) dry, which will not absorb water, and is used to hold non-living materials. Floral foam is manufactured in various densities and is usually sold in the shape of a brick, although other specialty shapes and sizes are available.

Floral food (care and handling) – a chemical preparation to make flowers last longer.

Floral tape (mechanics) – a waxed crepe paper tape, which sticks to itself when stretched. Used to wrap floral wires, bind materials and assemble corsages and wedding bouquets. Also known as corsage tape or stem wrap.

Florescent light – tubular shaped bulbs with primarily cool ray light source.

Flower girl (wedding) – female child attendant of the bride.

Focal area/focal point (secondary principle) – area(s) of greatest visual impact or weight; center(s) of interest to which the eye is drawn most naturally.

Forcing (care and handling) – deliberately inducing tightly budded plant materials to come into flower by placing them in optimum conditions: light, humidity, warm temperature and floral food solution.

Form (element) – the actual configuration of an individual component of a design and/or the shape or configuration of the entire design.

Formalinear (design style) – an asymmetrically balanced design of European origin with few materials, usually placed in groups, that emphasizes forms and lines. Generous use of space accentuates individual flowers, leaves, stem angles, colors and textures. Radial stem placement is typical.

Form flower (flower form) – any flower whose shape is its most interesting characteristic; frequently used at the focal area or as an accent; has more impact with space around it.

Found object – an item not intended as art but exhibited by an artist, usually without being altered.

Framing (design technique) – Using branches, foliage or man-made materials to enclose, partially enclose, delineate or showcase the material within a design.

Free-form design (design style) – a style of creative design inspired by unconventional ideas, styles, and patterns, yet adhering to the elements and principles of design. Realistic interpretation: A design in which the materials used are not contrived. Nonrealistic interpretation: A design in which the materials used are striking and unusual with no illusion to reality.

Funeral (sympathy) – ceremony connected with burial or cremation of the dead.

Garland (wedding) – a chain of interwoven foliage or flowers.

Gauge (mechanics) – a standard measure of the thickness of wire. The higher the number, the thinner the wire.

Geometric design (design style) – a radial composition based on the fundamental forms of geometry, which should be composed of line, mass or line-mass concepts. Recognizable forms include vertical, diagonal and horizontal shapes, various circular shapes and triangular shapes, and Hogarth curves and crescents.

Glamellia (personal flowers) – a composite flower constructed of gladiola florets, resembling camellia blossoms and is often larger.

Glycerin – an organic emollient used for preserving foliage. When properly absorbed by stems, it keeps plant materials soft and pliable.

Golden Proportion – the ideal standard of perfect proportion, defined as a line cut in such a way that the ratio of the smaller section to the greater is the same as the greater is to the whole. The value of the ratio is 1.618 and provides the approximate ratio 3:5:8. Also known as golden mean. It is called phi. All the "goldens": ratio, rectangle, section and spiral have the same ratio and are considered to be standards of beauty.

Gradation/Sequencing (design technique) – the progression of placing flowers or foliage in an ordered sequence from largest to smallest or darkest to lightest, etc.

Groomsmen (wedding) – Groom's attendants.

Grouping (design technique) – placement of identical materials within a specific, limited area, with each material maintaining its individual identity.

Growth point – the actual point, or the interpretation of the point, from which a plant emerges from the ground. Also known as point of growth.

Hand-tying (design technique) – arranging the stems of flowers, foliage and accessories in the hand using a disciplined method of diagonals and spiraling around the center of the design where the hand grasps the stems (binding point). When the bouquet is completed, the stems are bound with waxed string, raffia or binding cord at the binding point, thus creating a hand-tied bouquet.

Hardening (care and handling) – the process of placing flowers, after they have been conditioned, into the refrigerator to become crisp and "hard".

Harmony (primary principle) – Compatibility. The aesthetic quality created through the pleasing interaction of a combination of components in a composition when there is a satisfying agreement of parts.

Headpiece (wedding) – ornamental and/or floral piece to be worn on the head.

Hodgepodge – an unorganized mixture of various, dissimilar items or elements.

Hog rings (mechanics) – "C" shaped copper rings, which are applied with special clamping pliers (hog ringer) as a fastening device.

Hot melt glue (mechanics) – solid glue that melts at a controlled high temperature; the heated glue is used to fasten materials in place. Used in glue guns and glue pans.

Hue (color) – the descriptive name of a color, any color.

Humidity/Relative Humidity (care and handling) – the amount of water vapor present in the air at a given temperature compared to the maximum amount the air could hold at that same temperature.

Hydrating solution (care and handling) – a commercial solution that quickens water uptake helping flowers recover from dry shipping or other water stress.

Hydration (care and handling) – the uptake of water.

Ikebana (Ikebana term) – the Japanese art of floral design, literally means "to arrange flowers." Ikebana designs feature three main line placements called shin, soe, and tai (heaven, man and earth). In traditional Ikebana, flowers and plant materials are used as they would appear in nature, with respect to seasons, growth habits and color harmonies.

Ikenobo (design style) – the oldest school of floral design, established about 1470AD, in Japan. Ikenobo lineage dates back to 621 AD, to a Buddhist priest, Ono-no-Imoko, who is thought to have originated the concept of floral offerings at Buddhist altars.

Incandescent light – round, spot or flood bulbs with primarily warm ray light source.

Individuality – the expression of a designer's personality, which is immediately recognizable, in style and sensitivity toward materials, making a design personal.

Interpretive design (design style) – the organization of design elements to suggest a given theme, idea, occasion, mood or atmosphere; a variation from the authentic; an adaptation of a pure style or form.

Kenzan (Ikebana term) – a metal or steel pad filled with needle-sharp steel pins upon which stems are impaled; see pin point holder.

Kubari (Ikebana term) – a method of supporting stems by wedging natural straight or forked twigs into the neck of a vase. While the concept originates in Ikebana, many current adaptations are both useful and aesthetically pleasing.

Lacing (design technique) – a method of crossing and interlocking stems to form a framework for holding the flowers, themselves, in place in a vase. Successive stem additions result in a mechanically sound vase design that is deliverable.

Language of Flowers – the codified meaning ascribed to certain flowers, herbs and other plant materials during the Victorian times.

Layering (design technique) – covering a surface with foliage or other materials horizontally placed, by overlapping the individual units leaving little or no space in between them.

Leafwork (design technique) – The process of creating a decorative surface by applying foliage (small sprigs or individual leaves) in an overlapping manner to give textural and visual interest to the outside of an object.

Lei (personal flowers) – a garland of flowers or foliage strung, bound or woven together to be worn about the neck or shoulders; of Polynesian origin.

Line (element) – the visual path that directs the eye movement through a design.

Line design – a flower arrangement in which lines are emphasized over form and mass.

Line flower (flower form) – a spike or spike-like inflorescence with an elongated stem.

Line Mass design – linear-based designs in which additional materials add volume and strengthen the existing lines. A design in which both line and mass are important, but neither dominate the design.

Man-made – any object or material born of man's ingenuity as opposed to nature.

Mass design – a classification of floral designs utilizing a large quantity of materials in comparison to the size of the container, with little or no use of negative space.

Mass flower (flower form) – a single round head at the end of a stem; frequently used to add volume to a design.

Massaging (design technique) – the bending or curving of a flower stem by applying gentle pressure and warmth with the thumbs, fingers and hands. Working with materials at room temperature facilitates this process.

Mechanics – devices that help to secure materials and create stability in a design; normally concealed, but may be exposed for artistic effect.

Memorial Service (sympathy) – the name of a funeral service when the body of the deceased is not present.

Military Service (sympathy) – a funeral service that follows the prescribed protocol of the particular branch of the service to which the deceased belonged. Flowers are never placed on the casket when it is draped with a flag.

Millefleur – from the French meaning "1000 flowers", this design utilizes many varieties and many individual blossoms of similar sizes primarily in circular shapes.

Minimalism – the use of few materials; any style or method that is spare or simple.

Mirroring (design technique) – Placing two identical materials in a composition such that one appears to reflect the other. Mirroring may be accomplished with the technique of facing.

Monochromatic (color) – a color harmony featuring different values (tints, tones, shades) of one hue.

Monofilament (mechanics) – strong, transparent polyethylene thread available in various weights; fishing line.

Moribana (Ikebana term) – an Ikebana style originated in the late 19th century by the Ohara School, that is arranged in a low flat bowl or suiban to accommodate short stemmed material. Plant materials are usually held in place in a kenzan.

Nageire (Ikebana term) – an Ikebana style which is arranged in tall vases or baskets with plant materials often resting against the lip of the container. Plant materials are usually held in place by a kubari.

Natural/Naturalistic – relating to or determined by nature.

Neutral colors (color) – see Achromatic.

Nosegay (personal flowers) – a hand-held cluster of flowers designed as a small bouquet; often used in weddings. Dating from the 14th century, this clutch of flowers and foliage was originally used to mask unpleasant odors.

Ohara School (Ikebana term) – one of the major Ikebana schools in Japan, founded by Unchin Ohara near the end of the 19th century. The Ohara school used many new varieties of flowers and brought floral design to the average person.

Opposition (secondary principle) – total contrast that brings about tension in a design.

Originality – quality of being inventive; the product of ones thought and imagination; may apply to choice of materials or manner of usage.

Pall (sympathy) – a decorative piece of fabric, often displaying religious symbols, that is placed over a casket; flowers may be attached.

Parallel design (design style) – a concept of design in which the individual stems or groups of stems are placed in the same direction and are always the same distance apart from end to end.

Parallel system (design style) – a collection of parallel units combined (or that function together) into a larger and more complex composition.

Parallelism – a design theory in which all stem placements are parallel to each other.

Pattern (element) – a repeated combination of line, form, color, texture and/or space as a single component; e.g., coleus leaf, snowflake, spider web, etc; the silhouette or outline of an arrangement, or flower, as observed against its background, including solids and spaces.

Pavé (design technique) – a term borrowed from jewelry making, which refers to setting stones so close together that no metal shows. In floral design it is usually a basing technique using parallel or surface contoured insertions, which creates a uniform area with little or no variation of depth.

Perpendicular – situated at right angles to the plane of the horizon (or any plane).

Personal flowers – flowers designed to be worn or carried.

Petalling (design technique) – the covering of a surface with petals using floral adhesive.

Phi – see Golden Proportion.

Photosynthesis (care and handling) – the production of carbohydrates (sugars/food) from carbon dioxide and water in the presence of chlorophyll, using the energy from light and releasing oxygen.

Pick machine (mechanics) – a mechanical device that attaches steel picks to the ends of stems for easier insertion.

Pigment – a substance, which provides color to dyes, paints and plants, etc.; e.g., chlorophyll, the naturally occurring green pigment of leaves.

pH (care and handling) – the measure of acidity or alkalinity of a solution. 7.0 is neutral with higher numbers indicating alkalinity and low numbers indicating acidity.

Pillar candle – a candle of various lengths and widths. The diameter of the candle remains constant from end to end. Resembles a column or pillar in architecture.

Pin cup holder (mechanics) – a shallow waterproof vessel, generally made of metal and relatively heavy for its size, with a kenzan or pin holder affixed inside.

Pinholder (mechanics) – see Kenzan.

Point of growth/origin – see Growth point.

Polychromatic (color) – a combination of many colors, multicolored.

Potpourri – a mixture of dried flower petals and other materials, which are infused with fragrant oils and spices.

Pre-treatment (care and handling) – special treatments used prior to floral food in the care and handling process.

Primary colors (color) – Red, yellow and blue. The three colors from which all others can be made.

Principles of Design (principles) – fundamental guidelines to aesthetic design that govern the organization of the elements and materials in accordance with the laws of nature. Principles are divided into two groups: primary and secondary.

Processional (wedding) – the bridal party proceeding into the wedding ceremony, usually accompanied by special music.

Proportion (primary principle) – the comparative relationship in quantity, size and degree of emphasis between components within a composition. It is the relationship of one portion to another portion or a portion to the whole.

Pruning (design technique) – this technique reveals a stronger line or a more interesting shape by selectively removing branches, foliage, florets or petals to create a desirable negative space and produce materials that appear more sculptural.

Rabbi (wedding) – spiritual leader of a Jewish congregation.

Radiating Lines – a group of lines that extend outward from a central point; a type of stem placement.

Ratio – the relation in number, quantity, or degree between things.

Realistic – faithful portrayal of reality.

Receding colors (color) – colors primarily composed of the primary parent color, blue; green, blue green, blue, blue violet, violet. Also known as cool colors.

Receiving line (wedding) – the wedding party lines up to greet (receive) the guests, usually forming at the reception, but occasionally at the site of the ceremony. It is a time for the guests to meet the bride and groom and their parents.

Recessional (wedding) – the bridal party proceeding out of the wedding ceremony following its conclusion. Usually accompanied by special music.

Reflexing (design technique) – rolling or folding back the petals of a flower to achieve a more open and impressive look.

Repetition (secondary principle) – the repeating of like elements within a composition.

Respiration (care and handling) – the conversion of carbohydrates made during photosynthesis into energy used by the plant to carry on its life processes.

Rhythm (primary principle) – visual movement through the design, usually achieved by means of repetition or gradation. As in music, this principle gives a composition its feeling and flow.

Rikka (Ikebana term) – an Ikebana design style originating in the Ikenobo School; means standing arrangement and is typified by large elaborate and complex designs that tell a story.

Ring bearer (wedding) – designated male (usually) child who carries the rings on a pillow, and as a member of the wedding party, precedes the bride and groom into the ceremony.

Scale (secondary principle) – the relative ratio of size; the relationship of a composition to its surroundings.

Scalene triangle – an asymmetrical triangle in which all three sides are unequal in length.

Scepter (wedding) – an ornamental staff decorated with flowers and carried by a member of the wedding party.

Scrim (wedding) – a theater industry term for a thin gauze-like curtain that is used for special draping and/or lighting effects.

Secondary colors (color) – orange, green and violet; produced by mixing two primary colors together.

Sectioning (design technique) – confining like materials to specific areas within the composition. Also known as zoning.

Sequencing (design technique) – see Gradation.

Set piece (sympathy) – a floral tribute made in the shape of a symbolic design, such as a Bible, broken wheel, cross, gates ajar, heart, pillow, star, vacant chair, etc. The foundation is usually made of plastic foam and covered with flowers and foliage.

Sewing (design technique) – fastening materials together by piercing them with needle and thread or wire. This technique is most often used in the construction of casket blankets, leis, table runners or wall hangings.

Shade (color) – any hue to which black has been added.

Shadowing (design technique) – creating a three-dimensional appearance by the close placement of one identical material directly behind another, either lower or higher. This results in the appearance of a shadow or echo of the original.

Sheltering (design technique) – placing one or more materials over or around another, lightly enclosing the materials within, to create an impression of protection.

Shin (Ikebana term) – the main or strongest placement, usually upright, in a typical Ikebana design, corresponds to "heaven" or "spiritual truth". Often determines the character of the arrangement.

Size (element) – the dimensions of line, form and space.

Skeleton/Skeletal pattern – simple framework of a design, usually established by the first few stem placements. Applies particularly to geometric designs.

Soe (Ikebana term) – the second or intermediate placement, usually in a supporting attitude toward the main grouping (shin). Traditionally considered symbolic of man, situated between heaven and earth.

Sogetsu (Ikebana term) – the most contemporary school of Ikebana founded in 1926 by Sofu Teshigahara. Focuses on bringing out the individuality of the flower and the feelings of the designer. One of the most progressive schools, influenced greatly by the headmaster's passion for modern art.

Space (element) – the area in, around and between components of a design.

Spiraling (design technique) – a clear line movement circling around a central point in a flat curve that is constantly increasing or decreasing in size.

Split complementary (color) – a color harmony that features three colors, one hue plus two colors adjacent to its complement.

Stacking (design technique) – placing pieces of the same material in similar sizes on top of, or against one another, without space between each component, in an orderly (usually vertical) fashion.

Stem placement – A method of positioning stems into a composition. There are four categories: radial, parallel, abstract and integrated.

Style – distinctive or characteristic mode of presentation; characteristic manner of works of an individual, artist, school of thought, region or historical period.

Suitability – the state of being appropriate to or required by the circumstances.

Symbolism – representation of meanings; e.g., a red rose representing love.

Symmetrical balance (primary principle) – a state of equilibrium wherein the opposite sides of an arrangement are mirror images of each other in terms of line, form, space, color, texture pattern and size. Also known as formal balance.

Sympathy tribute (sympathy) – a floral design given as a token of love, honor, respect or gratitude for the deceased.

Tai (Ikebana term) – the third and lower placement in a classical Ikebana arrangement, usually of the shortest material, meaning earth, body or material substance.

Taste – a liking for or the enjoyment of something because of the pleasure it gives; the practice of discerning and enjoying whatever constitutes excellence; personal preference.

Tension (secondary principle) – the dynamic aesthetic quality created by the masterful use of the principle of contrast. To achieve tension is to skillfully convey the beauty of opposition, accomplished by the implication of opposing forces of energy.

Terracing (design technique) – placing like materials in stair-step fashion, creating spaced horizontal levels. This is a way to create depth in the concept of basing.

Tertiary (color) – third generation of colors created by mixing any primary color with an adjacent secondary color.

Tetrad (color) – a color harmony that uses any four colors that are equally spaced on the color wheel.

Texture (element) – the surface quality of materials as perceived by sight or touch; e. g., smooth, rough, prickly, velvety etc.

Theme – the concept around which a floral design, party or special event or is planned; all parts are unified to speak the same message through visual feeling and style.

Tint (color) – any color to which white has been added. Also known as pastel.

Tokonoma (Ikebana term) – a recessed alcove in a Japanese room; a place of honor. This niche is used to display precious objects including flower arrangements.

Tone (color) – any color to which gray has been added, does not become darker or lighter, but looses some of its brilliance.

Tradition/Traditional – a pattern of thought, action, belief, custom or style passed on from generation to generation.

Transition (secondary principle) – the easy visual movement that comes from gradual degrees of change in line, form, color space, texture, pattern and size.

Transpiration (care and handling) – the loss of water, usually in gaseous form, from plants through small openings in the leaves called stomata. Temperature and humidity directly affect the rate of transpiration.

Triad (color) – a color harmony composed of any three colors that are equally spaced on the color wheel; e. g., red, blue and yellow.

Tufting (design technique) – the placement of tufts, radial elongated clusters of short elongated materials tied together at a binding point, into a design, often at the base, to create interest and variation in the surface area.

Tussie Mussie (wedding) – a small round mixed bouquet of fragrant flowers and foliage that was popular in the Victorian period. Also known as tussy mussy and tuzzy muzzy.

Tying (design technique) – securing or fastening materials together by encircling them with cord, string, etc. See Binding.

Uniformity – similarity in characteristics; e.g., line, form, color, stage of maturity, etc.

Unity (primary principle) – oneness of purpose, thought, style and spirit; the organization of components into a harmonious whole, resulting in a cohesive relationship of all parts.

Ushers (wedding) – men selected to assist in seating the bride and groom's families and guests at the wedding ceremony.

Value (color) – the lightness or darkness of a hue achieved by the addition of white, black or gray.

Variation (secondary principle) – basic similarity but with minor differences.

Vegetative design (design style) – a naturalistic design style in which plant materials are placed as they would grow in nature, with emphasis placed on climatic, seasonal, geographical and topographical compatibility.

Veiling (design technique) – layering light materials such as bear grass, springeri, plumosa, metallic threads, etc. over more solid forms creating a light, almost transparent screen. This is often used in the waterfall design.

Void – empty space.

Volumetric design (design style) – a three-dimensional composition consisting of a clearly defined geometric form, which is wholly or partially filled or covered with plant or other materials. The addition of accessories must not violate the integrity of the form.

Votive cup (wedding) – small, typically glass container intended to hold a short candle that will burn for approximately ten hours. These glass cups were originally used for various church rituals, but have become popular for decorating at weddings and parties. They are made with flat bases and with pegs to fit into candelabrum.

Warm colors (color) – see Advancing Colors.

Water stress (care and handling) – the condition of lacking turgidity or being in need of hydration. Cut flowers that have been dry-shipped over long distances frequently show water stress.

Weaving (design technique) – interlacing materials to create a new dimensional texture or pattern.

Wedding consultant (wedding) – independent individual employed by the bride to assist in advising, planning, researching, reserving, scheduling and coordinating the many details of a wedding.

Wedding coordinator (wedding) – an on-site associate of the venue (church, hotel,etc.) who facilitates the part of the wedding and/or reception that takes place on their property.

William Hogarth – an artist (engraver) living in London, 1697-1764, who wrote an essay on beauty. He scrawled an "S" curve in the margin and labeled it "the line of beauty". Almost two centuries later the "S" curve design became popular and is now known as the Hogarth Curve.

Wrapping (design technique) – covering the length of a single stem, bundle of stems, dowel rod or cylinder, etc., by encircling it with decorative materials such as ribbon, raffia, or cording.

Zoning (design technique) – see Sectioning.

The History of Floral Art

ORIENTAL	B.C.	A.D.
Chinese (Buddha)	500	Today
Japanese (Ikebana)		586 – Today
OCCIDENTAL		
Egyptian	2800 – 28	
Grecian (Classical)	600 – 146	
Roman	28	325
Byzantine		325 – 600
Middle Ages		476 – 1450
Gothic		1200 – 1425
Persian		1300 – 1700
Renaissance		1400 – 1600
Flemish (Holland)		1550 – 1700
Baroque (Italy)		1600 – 1700
Early American (Colonial America)		1620 – 1780
Georgian (England – William Hogarth)		1714 – 1760
Rococo (France)		1715 – 1744
Classical Revival (Many Countries)		1762 – 1830
Federal (America)		1789 – 1801
Directoire (France)		1795 – 1799
Empire (France)		1804 – 1815
Regency (England)		1811 – 1830
Biedermier (Germany)		1820 – 1830
Romantic (Victorian – England, US)		1830 – 1890
Art Nouveau (Europe, US)		1880 – 1925
American – American Garden Club		1914 – Today
Art Deco (France, US)		1925 – 1930
Modern/Modernistic (US)		1930 – 1960
Beyond The Modern Movement (US)		
Geometric Design		1952 – Today
Free Form – Interpretive Design		1960 – Today
Abstract Design		1976 – Today

Flowers and Plants with Toxic Parts

Scientific Name	Common Name	Poisonous Part
Aconitum spp.	Monkshood	all parts
Alstroemeria spp.	Peruvian Lily	stems & leaves
Amaryllis spp.	Amaryllis	bulbs
Caladium spp.	Caladium	all parts
Celastrus scandens	Bittersweet	seeds
Consolida ajacis	Larkspur	seeds, young plants
Convallaria majalis	Lily of the Valley	all parts
Dieffenbachia spp.	Dumbcane	all parts
Digitalis purpurea	Foxglove	all parts
Gloriosa spp.	Gloriosa lily	all parts
Hedera helix	English Ivy	leaves & berries
Hyacinthus spp.	Hyacinth	bulbs
Hydrangea spp.	Hydrangea	leaves & buds
Lathyrus spp.	Sweet Pea	seeds
Narcissus spp.	Daffodil	bulbs
Ornithogalum spp.	Star of Bethlehem	all parts
Philodendron spp.	Philodendron	stems & leaves
Phoradendron spp.	Mistletoe	berries
Pittosprum spp.	Pittosporum	stem, leaves, berries
Rhododendron	Azalea	leaves & flowers

Flowers that are Edible

Scientific Name	Common Name	Flavor
Calendula officinalis *	Calendula	spicy, tangy, and peppery
Centaurea cynaus *	Bachelor's Button	spicy–sweet
Dendranthema spp. *	Chrysanthemum	strong pungent
Gardenia jasminoides	Gardenia	sweet light flavor
Gladiolus spp. *	Gladiola	similar to lettuce
Helianthus annus *	Sunflower	slightly bitter
Monarda spp.	Bee Balm	use in place of bergamot
Rosa rugosa **	Rugosa Rose	slightly sweet
Tropaeolum majus	Nasturtium	peppery–sweet
Viola wittrockiana	Pansy	wintergreen

* use only the petals
** remove white base of petals

Part 9

Index

ISBN 1-58544-171-6
90000
9 781585 441716